All Things
Bright & Beautiful

DESIGN IN BRITAIN
1830 to Today

All Things Bright & Beautiful

DESIGN IN BRITAIN
1830 to today

by FIONA MacCARTHY

GEORGE ALLEN & UNWIN LTD
LONDON

First published in 1972

ISBN 0 04 745002 9

Printed in Great Britain
in 11 pt. Baskerville type by
BAS Printers Limited, Wallop, Hampshire

This book has been designed by Walter Bloor DFA(Lond)

CONTENTS

I

The Cole Group 1830-1860

HENRY Cole, an early Victorian civil servant of adequate talent and exceptional zeal, decided to design a teaset. This decision turned out to be a great deal more important than it sounds. It grew into a movement for reform, a great campaign for improved design in industry, which even now goes on.

Cole had a motto: 'Whatsoever thy hand findeth to do, do it with all thy might'. And since his hand was forever occupied with projects for improvements of a limitless variety—from re-organizing the Public Record Office, introducing Penny Postage and reforming Patent Laws to unifying railway gauges and constructing Grimsby docks—Cole was a busy and influential man. He was really a professional reformer. But, when young, he found time to take a course in water-colour painting under David Cox; his sketches were shown at the Royal Academy; and, as a result, he was always sympathetic, through his other enterprises, to the cause of art. In 1839, he commissioned William Wyon, a painter, to design the Penny Black; and in 1845, he asked Horsley to produce an illustration for a Christmas card. The Christmas card itself was a Henry Cole invention; and so, for that matter, was the adhesive stamp. His excursions into the reform of children's books, resulting in *Felix Summerly's Home Treasury*, gave him more chances to commission illustrations: Redgrave and Townsend and Mulready were employed. It is not at all surprising, with this artistic background and his contacts with the influential painters of the time, that Henry Cole decided to extend his reforms directly to design.

The Society of Arts was offering prizes for a tea service and for beer jugs designed for common use. Henry Cole decided to compete, and as usual, he put his whole heart and soul into his job. He went to the British Museum and consulted Greek earthenware 'for authority for handles'. He went to Stoke-on-Trent and spent three days at Minton's superintending the throwing, turning, modelling and moulding. He set out to show that 'elegant forms may be made not to cost more than inelegant ones'. His teaset, submitted under his Summerly pseudonym, won a silver medal. It was also a best-seller for Minton's. It gave Henry Cole the idea that 'an alliance between fine art and manufacture would promote public taste'.

Cole's scheme, of course, was easier in theory than in practice. Fine art and manufacture were extremely far apart. The level of design in industry was then appalling, for a number of reasons. Among them was the fact that the industrial revolution had destroyed the old craft traditions of honesty and quality; as factories replaced small individual workshops, products became shoddier and also more pretentious. As stamping replaced chasing, as moulding replaced cutting, as transfer printing took over from hand-painting, as weaving became mechanized, there was no concurrent advance in design: though mechanical weaving was.

welcomed (and quite rightly) as one of the splendid offerings made by genius at the shrine of utility, this was not to say that the end product was inspired. On the whole, machine products merely imitated earlier designs for production by hand. Standards were chaotic. An ally of Cole's looked around him sadly in 1847 and commented on the confusion of the scene. He said 'There is no general agreement in principles of tastes. Every one elects his own style of art . . . Some few take refuge in a liking for "pure Greek", and are rigidly "classical", others find safety in the "antique", others believe only in "Pugin", others lean upon imitations of modern Germans and some extol the Renaissance. We all agree only in being imitators.'

Cole and his friends were not the first to realize the shamingly low level of design for mass-production. As early as 1832, Sir Robert Peel (who made his own fortune with the spinning jenny) had blamed falling exports on incompetent designs: he told the House of Commons that although British products were technically excellent, pictorial designs were 'unfortunately not equally successful'. The fact of the matter was they did not sell. The remedy, according to Sir Robert Peel, was simple: build the National Gallery to instil a sense of design in the manufacturer and to elevate the public taste. He urged the Government to grant £30,000 to finance an art collection. Lord Ashley supported the motion with the comment that artists and mechanics and the industrious classes in general would thereby be enabled to spend their leisure hours in an atmosphere of beauty 'instead of resorting to alehouses, as at present'. Mr Hume, perhaps more pertinently, contrasted the efficiency of the school at Lyons, which trained specialist designers for the textile trade, with the fact that in the whole of Coventry 'only one man was at all proficient in forming designs for silks'.

In 1835, eleven years before Henry Cole's conscientious teaset won its prize, Mr Ewart's Select Committee had been formed 'to inquire into the best means of extending a knowledge of the arts and principles of design among the people (especially the manufacturing population) of the country'. It was mainly concerned with the inferiority of English products compared with French, and the extent to which industry in England depended on plagiarized foreign designs; it also considered the comparative states of art education in England and abroad. For almost a year, the Committee collected the opinions of artists, industrialists and spectators, including James Nasmyth, inventor of the steam hammer (who insisted incidentally on 'the entire reconcileability of elegance of form with bare utility'). The views of the experts were collected together into a depressing 350-page report which concluded that 'from the highest branches of poetical design down to the lowest connexion between design and manufactures, the Arts have received little encouragement in this country'. The wit-

nesses stressed 'the want of instruction in design among our industrious population'. In a panic, a Normal School of Design
was set up by the Board of Trade in London straight away, and
by 1846, when Cole began campaigning, eleven outer Branch
Schools received Government support.

In spite of this activity—committees, national galleries, a dozen
far-flung schools intent on training in design—nothing much had
happened to convince the manufacturers that industry in Britain
had any need of art. This was Cole's first object: a practical
alliance between the fine artist and the manufacturer. In 1847, he
announced the formation of 'Summerly's Art Manufactures'. His
principal idea was to revive 'the good old practice of connecting
the best Art with familiar objects in daily use'. He was evidently
thinking of the time, about a century before, when George
Adams, the King's architect, designed pottery for Josiah Wedgwood, and John Flaxman, the sculptor, and other British artists
were employed from time to time by the potteries in Staffordshire.
With great enthusiasm, Cole rounded up a number of well-known
painters and sculptors, Dyce and Herbert, John Bell, Richard
Redgrave, Sir Richard Westmacott, and other academicians, to
co-operate with the 'most eminent British manufacturers' to
produce such things as vases, decanter stoppers, christening mugs,
mustard pots, bread platters; bread knives with handles in the
shape of Indian corn; a hall stand for hats, cloaks and umbrellas,
with a looking-glass; a lamp; a letter-box and brush-box and an
inkstand all combined.

In practice Henry Cole was not a revolutionary: the works of
Felix Summerly were hardly epoch-making; to a very large
extent, they were true products of their time with their craze
for ingenuity, their urge to tell a story. Cole is less important as a
visual innovator than as the first great propagandist for design.
Long before Frank Pick and Gordon Russell, far in front of any
government-supported Council of Industrial Design, Cole was
infiltrating his artists into industry and trying very fervently to
raise the public taste.

Summerly's Art Manufactures were apparently commercially
successful. Although the project ended in 1850, when Cole became preoccupied with plans for the Great Exhibition, his col-
laborators in this practical attempt to promote design in industry
stayed round him many years. The Cole group, which grew increasingly substantial, carried on the movement for reform in
other ways, constantly aiming to provide 'the enjoyment of taste
to the enormous and now all-powerful bourgeois class'. They
themselves belonged to it. They were the establishment: pedagogic
painters and sculptors and art critics, worldly artists, earnest
clubmen. The Etching Club, for instance, with its friendly monthly
meetings, was a Cole group social centre and recruiting gound as
well.

This was the essential Cole group: John Bell, sculptor and designer for Summerly; William Dyce, painter and friend of the Nazarenes, for five years head of the School of Design; George Wallis, artist and pupil of Dyce, principal of schools at Manchester and Birmingham; John Callcott Horsley, a painter specializing in domestic and countryside scenes, designer of Cole's first Christmas card and teacher at the School of Design; Richard Redgrave, painter, Summerly designer and, once again, a teacher at the School of Design; Gottfried Semper, German architect, writer and educationalist, who first came to England for the Great Exhibition; Owen Jones, Welsh architect, lecturer and theorist; Matthew Digby Wyatt, writer and designer, Secretary to the Exhibition executive. This active and articulate and more or less creative body of reformers was later to include Ralph Nicholson Wornum, critic and journalist, whose outbursts against Cole were pacified completely by the diplomatic offer of a job as Cole's librarian. After taking office, his views were well in line.

Cole's group was very worthy, level-headed and efficient; moderate in outlook and methodical in practice. Reform of design entailed a sequence of committees, a series of reports and pressures on the Government. But curiously close to these well-disciplined endeavours loomed the unconventional figure of Augustus Welby Northmore Pugin, architect, Gothic revivalist, author, pamphleteer, the man who wore a sailor's suit to travel on commissions, the man who received visitors flamboyant in his breeches, with silk stockings and a velvet cloak and candlestick held high. Before he died of madness (after three wives and innumerable children) at the age of 40, Pugin had established his own art workshops, anticipating Morris and all the Arts and Crafts. He had also propounded theories which quite obviously basically influenced Henry Cole and friends: in *True Principles of Pointed or Christian Architecture*, published in 1841, he maintains that 'all beautiful forms in architecture are based on the soundest principles of utility'. And although his ideals were more extreme than Cole's, springing from his passionate Catholic conviction that mediaeval Gothic was the godliest of styles, the two were in basic agreement on the point that 'the great test of architectural beauty is the fitness of the design to the purpose for which it is intended'. So much so that Pugin, who was not a born committee man, sat on the judging panel to select exhibits from the 1851 display for Cole's new Museum of Ornamental Art.

The rational side of Pugin, his 'soundest principles', his emphasis on fitness for purpose and good sense, are evident in all the Cole group writings of the period. They dominate Cole's *Journal of Design and Manufactures*. For Cole, like many subsequent reformers, had decided that to publicize his movement he must have a magazine. The first volume was issued in March 1849. There were 'Forty-Four Fabric Patterns inserted and upwards of two hundred engravings'. There were contributions from Dyce and Owen Jones, Matthew Digby Wyatt and John Bell and a paper from the German Gottfried Semper, all battering away at design in British industry. Wrote the critics of 1849: 'The more we see of this subject the more satisfied we become that every one concerned with it—the public, manufacturers, designers, art workmen, and ourselves—have all very much indeed to learn.' (One has only to turn to critics writing in 1949, the year in which *Design* magazine was first produced, to see that this view of things survived almost unaltered, in spite of all attempts at reformation of design.)

The Journal, like Henry Cole himself, was multi-purpose. It was published ostensibly for British manufacturers: in fact it purported, at one time, to be their spokesman. It was, simultaneously, Henry Cole's weapon in a running battle with the Schools of Design and with the *Art Union Journal*; it publicized (and even sometimes criticized) Summerly's Art. It had the general function of disseminating principles of ornament, of laying down the law that decoration should consist of appropriate motifs drawn from nature, strictly related to the object's use. In general, it advertised the stylized, flat patterns which in the view of Cole—and Pugin long before him—had more moral validity than freer natural styles. Criticism of new products, always frank and often rude, help throughout the *Journal* to put Cole's ideas across. A trowel with amorini decoration is detested: 'we think it ought to be unmistakeably a trowel'.

The first of the Journals was dedicated to Prince Albert, President of the Society of Arts: 'In respectful acknowledgement of the uniform and successful endeavours of His Royal Highness to aid the progress of the arts and manufactures of His adopted country.' This grateful dedication was more than surface politeness. Henry Cole and Prince Albert by then worked hand in glove. The Cole group's basic catch-phrase, 'art applied to industry', was said to have originated with the Prince. For Prince Albert was deeply interested in design, both in theory and in practice. His theories derived from the virtuous criteria of his fellow-countrymen, the Nazarenes, with their near-religious sense of vocation and their emphasis on honest, earnest craftsmanship, of which the work of Semper is a perfect, dull example. The practice of Prince Albert—who designed a small variety of trophies and adornments, a royal billiard table and the Balmoral tartan (grey, black, lavender and red)—was not perhaps distinguished, but endearingly wholehearted. The details of all palace decorations much concerned him; in 1845, for instance, he was busy with samples of new wallpapers to smarten Osborne House.

He and Henry Cole had a great amount in common: a moral sense of beauty, an obsession for detail. Their first meeting was propitious. The Prince was searching out old furniture from Carlton House, which was said to have been stored in Carlton Terrace. Prince Albert duly found it in the former Riding School, along with George IV's collection of armour. He then discovered Cole, working in an outpost of the Public Record Office, a model of efficiency with neat and tidy storage and exemplary methods of classification, and even a small hand-press used for printing ticket-dockets. Such care and ingenuity could not pass unadmired. Cole's reputation was, later, boosted further when Prince Albert went to lay the cornerstone at Grimsby docks. The Prince was entertained en route by train with a collection of relevant books and maps and charts and drawings, arranged in his carriage by the ever-thoughtful Cole. There was even a Dürer print on the wall. The Prince was reported to be 'very much pleased'.

The Prince had a natural interest in promoting art in industry. From 1843, as President of the Society of Arts, he stressed the great need to encourage 'more efficiently the application of the Fine Arts to our manufactures' in order 'to wed high art with mechanical skill'. He encouraged the Society to organize a series of selective industrial design exhibitions, with medals for outstanding examples of the marriage of art and technique. It was one of these medals, in 1846, which Cole's 'Felix Summerly' teaset had won.

Between them, Prince Albert and bemedalled Henry Cole tried hard to resurrect the Society of Arts which had been founded in 1754 'for the encouragement of arts, manufactures and commerce', but which from the day of its foundation had proved fairly ineffective: it was almost moribund. The Prince and Cole agreed that strictly-chosen exhibitions of industrial design would raise the public taste and prove to manufacturers how art might be applied. The scheme was quite successful: attendance figures rose from 20,000 in 1847 to 100,000 in 1849. But Cole came under fire for the preponderance of Summerly Art Manufactures in the displays at the Society of Arts. Cole's autocratic methods were apparently resented; inevitably, maybe, he was known as 'Old King Cole'.

These small exhibitions gave way to an immense one: the Great Exhibition of 1851. Who was the progenitor, Prince Albert or King Cole? Both were so involved in it that this is not quite clear. But Cole is on record as proposing to Prince Albert, in January 1848, a series of national industrial design exhibitions; Prince Albert sounded out some members of the cabinet and though, at this juncture, they were unenthusiastic, Cole's original suggestion no doubt paved the way for the Great Exhibition. There were long negotiations. Cole and Digby Wyatt went to canvass manufacturers and Cole, a little recklessly, hinted that Prince Albert was behind the exhibition scheme; this got him into trouble. Cole and Digby Wyatt also went to Paris to report on the French industrial exhibition of 1849. The London exhibition, to Prince Albert's greater glory, had by then become more or less a certainty.

Cole was on the planning committee, and was later granted leave of absence from the Public Record Office to serve on the Exhibition executive. He and his friends from the Art Manufactures and the *Journal of Design* were fully occupied with the Great Exhibition, making plans and making comments. They were jubilant. The *Journal of Design* rejoiced at the impending improvement in the standards of industrial products. Matthew Digby Wyatt expected Paxton's building to exercise a powerful influence on national tastes. All in all, a very splendid day of judgement was foreseen: in the words of a Cole spokesman, 'Since the period of the Reformation we believe the prospects of Design have never been so good as at the present time in England.' Prince Albert's prophecies were still more optimistic: praising 'the great principle of division of labour' and 'the stimulus of competition and capital', he came to a crescendo, 'So man is approaching a more complete fulfilment of that great and sacred mission he has to perform in this world.'

After this, the Exhibition was a fearful anti-climax. Queen Victoria liked it; but Queen Victoria would. Her comment that '*Such* efforts have been made, and our people have shown *such* taste in their manufactures' cut very little ice with Cole and his stern council of industrial design. The Queen 'felt so grateful to the great God', but the critics hit out at the tasteless manufacturers, condemning all objects offending against the principle of appropriate ornament. There were thousands: from blatant absurdities like the notorious Town Mansion House for bees to humbler iniquities like carpets filled with holes, wallpapers showing landscape in perspective, slabs of glass made to imitate marble, pieces of metal textured as chain-mail, creations in grass and dyed flowers and chocolate, beautiless contraptions of extreme complexity, in general—according to an irate spectator— 'startling novelty or meretricious decoration leading, in most cases, to an extreme redundancy of ornament'. Past styles, in all directions, underwent most gross revivals; Owen Jones, irritated and astounded, deprecated 'the vain and foolish attempt to make the art which faithfully represents the wants, the faculties and the feelings of one people, represent those of another people under totally different conditions'.

Owen Jones found the Great Exhibition most dispiriting: it proved that we were far behind our European neighbours; it showed that we were plunged in 'chaos and disorder in art'; it revealed the manufacturers' incredible stupidity: 'We are amazed at the shortsightedness of the manufacturers, who do not see how much it would be in their interest to begin by having a real and proper design from the hands of an artist.' Shortsighted manufacturers: this charge was to be levelled again and again by reformers of design. The artistic vicious circle which Jones described so forcefully recurs, of course, in every subsequent design campaign: 'No improvement can take place in the art of the present generation until all classes, artists, manufacturers, and the public are better educated in art, and the existence of general principles is more generally recognized.' Jones' plans for education involved the installation of an art museum in every town and a drawing-school in every village. Education by example was a basic Cole group creed.

For they speak with one voice, Cole and Jones, Semper and Wyatt, self-confident and reasonable, intelligent and crisp. Redgrave's *Supplementary Report on Design in the Great Exhibition* is typically sensible. His comments on the constant lack of fitness lead quite neatly into a Cole group lesson on design: for china and glass 'the purest forms should be sought, allied to the greatest convenience and capaciousness; and the requisite means of lifting, holding, supporting—of filling, emptying and cleansing, should engage the attention of the designer, before the subject of their ornamentation is at all entered upon'. He argues for the technical education of the designer, insisting that schools should contain workshops 'where the specialities of design may be fully explained'. He also recommends the employment of designers on an executive level in the firm. This long before the Bauhaus, a century ahead of the drive for Design Management: surprisingly advanced.

In fact the aesthetic criteria of the Cole group were those of the *Architectural Review* circa 1930. The objects which they tolerated are the products with no claim to beauty whatsoever: the functional machinery, the humble cooking stove, the invalid chair with its unpretentious structure. Gottfried Semper commented that, in the Exhibition, only 'objects in which the seriousness of their use does not allow for anything unnecessary, e.g. coaches, weapons, musical instruments and the like, sometimes showed a higher degree of soundness in decoration and in the methods by which the value of functionally defined forms is enhanced'. Wyatt, in the *Journal of Design*, wrote most ecstatically on the wonders of the Menai and the Conway iron bridges.

When the Exhibition ended, the Cole group was constructive. They had obviously decided to salvage what they could and to channel the £186,000 profit from the Exhibition towards 'the promotion of science and art and their applications in productive industry', trying to ensure that the 6 million people who contentedly thronged the Crystal Palace could be made to change their tastes. On Prince Albert's advice, and no doubt with Cole's approval, the Commissioners bought 87 acres at South Kensington for building an educational complex of museums and colleges. Wyatt finally judged the Exhibition an 'extraordinary stimulant', which could awaken all their energies: 'men's minds', he announced 'are now earnestly directed to the subject of restoring to symmetry all that had fallen into disorder.'

Henry Cole, who was of course the most symmetrical of men, was busily spending £5,000 on the most instructive exhibits he could salvage from the Crystal Palace for his own Museum of Manufactures. Agreeing with Semper that 'Public monuments and collections are the true teachers of a free people', a committee consisting of Cole, Herbert, Redgrave, Owen Jones and Pugin selected Elkington electrotypes, china from Minton and Sevres, oriental arms and armour, Belgian gold and silver, and other striking objects, including—perhaps from politeness—a few of Pugin's chalices. To this well-intentioned collection were added all the samples which had been kept in lamentable disarray at the Schools of Design, and objects which were bought from the 1844 Exhibition in Paris. Cole sifted them all through and set up his Museum of Manufactures in Marlborough House.

It was mainly for the benefit of students; but the public keenly attended the museum exhibitions. Prince Albert liked the scheme and gave Henry Cole permission to search the Palace cupboards for examples of Sevres china. The British manufacturers were less enthusiastic when Cole set up a Chamber of Horrors in design, naming the producers. Charles Dickens, to whom Cole was anathema, makes use of the Museum for the scene in *Household Words* in which Mr Crumpet of Clump Lodge in Brixton returns home discontented with his own design for living and is terribly haunted 'by horrible shapes'. Needless to say, such was the outcry that Cole's pedantic horrors were very soon dispersed. The Museum, renamed more grandly the Museum of Ornamental Art, later moved to South Kensington and later still became the Victoria and Albert. It is more of a monument, in fact, to Henry Cole.

Alongside the Museum, Cole was now in charge of the School of Design. He had been eyeing it for years. For Cole could not resist the call for reformation, and the School of Design had been an out-and-out fiasco. Already, two government committees had examined the failure of the institution, concluding wanly that 'there has been an immensity of time consumed in disputations on modes of instruction and management, that might have been far more beneficially devoted to the practical business of the School'. Already Henry Cole, requested to write an official report on improvements for the school, had untiringly produced not one report but three, recording the growing dissatisfaction of manufacturers. Cole sympathized, of course, with the industrialists' view.

The trouble was that no one, in the main school or the Branch schools, knew how to set about a training for design. They could not decide whether students should be given a broad training in art, including life drawing, or whether the course should be commercial and technical, with industrial machinery instead of human figures. The argument for nose-to-the-grindstone design training was forcefully expressed by Gabriel Tinto who claimed that

'The moment the artisan student is taught to be an artist instead of a draughtsman, his mind becomes unsettled and aspirations arise in his bosom calculated to lead him out of the sure and solid path of commerce into the thorny and devious tract which leads to Fine Art.'

When, in Manchester, a nude female model had a fit in a corridor, life drawing was banned for fourteen years.

Characteristically, Cole was well set on the sure and solid path of commerce. He believed that students should be trained to be of immediate use to industry: none of this high art, but a practical course in geometry and ornamental copying. 'This is the beginning of the end,' said the *Art Journal* at the news of his appointment. But Cole was quite impervious to rudeness. He was, luckily for him, utterly self-confident. Installed as Superintendent of the Department of Practical Art, with Richard Redgrave as Art-Superintendent in charge of the London School, he sat back and pronounced, with benign smugness,

'We cannot hope to escape from mistakes, but we trust that vigilance, firmness, prudence and conciliation, will reduce the number and afford a fair trial in this new attempt to afford practical art instruction.'

Systematically, Cole set off on a tour of Europe: Berlin, Dresden and Vienna. Systematically, he aimed to reorganize entirely national art training, to strengthen the school in London in its role as provider of designers for industry and teachers for the board schools, to establish a network of practical, and self-supporting, art schools in the provinces. He emphasized the need for national drawing classes, for he believed that 'the improvement of manufactures is altogether dependent upon the public sense of the necessity of it, and the public ability to judge between what is good and bad in art'. By 1864, at the time of another Select Committee, Cole's achievements were impressive: 90 art schools with 16,000 students; art teachers teaching 70,000 schoolchildren. On paper, Cole was excellent at making systems work.

But in practice his success was limited. His products, the Summerly Art Manufactures, made no lasting impact. His promotional activities got him almost nowhere: by 1874, a series of industrial design exhibitions had to be curtailed for lack of support. What is more, his friends and pupils, in terms of actual products, made little contribution to the progress of design. George Moore maintained: 'The schools were primarily intended as schools of design where the sons and the daughters of the people would be taught how to design wallpapers.' The attack is very waspish, but pretty nearly true.

The only designer of Cole's generation to work with manufacturers consistently and practically was Alfred Stevens, a sculptor outside Cole's group, with reactionary Italianate-academic views. The only designer of successive generations to work industrially with any genius was Dresser: Christopher Dresser, Doctor of Botany and lecturer on principles of ornamentation, on whom (so they said) Owen Jones' mantle seemed to have fallen. But he did not let it swamp him. He travelled to Japan, and returned to pursue a career of greater enterprise, working three-dimensionally in pottery and glass and metalware, and opening a shop in New Bond Street. At Dresser's Art Furniture Alliance the attendants were 'robed in many aesthetic costumes of the period in demure art colours'. This 'added a certain air to the place': an air which, one suspects, Cole could not tolerate.

For this was 1880 or so. By then, John Ruskin had spent a quarter-century attacking Henry Cole. Ruskin's swarthy Christianity, his love of natural nature and his overall idealism cried out against Cole's pompous and bleak commercial outlook, the Cole group's flat, prim patterns, Cole's systematic training for designers at South Kensington. 'Try first to manufacture a Raphael,' thundered Ruskin, 'then let Raphael direct your manufacture.' And in fellowship with Ruskin, and quite opposed to Cole, a new reforming movement, both gentler and more rugged, more romantic, more humanitarian, had begun. Cole's tight neat attempt to promote 'an alliance between fine art and manufacture' was swept away completely by the larger proposition, more practical and also a good deal more fantastic, that 'the beginning of art is in getting our country clean and our people beautiful'.

1
Henry Cole
Teapot made by Summerly's Art
Manufactures, 1846.

2
Christopher Dresser
Silver-mounted decanter and glasses,
made by Hukin & Heath, 1881–2.

1

2

3

4

5

6

3
Edward William Godwin
Ebonized oak side table made by
William Watt, about 1867.

4
Henry Cole
Teaset made by Summerly's Art
Manufactures, 1846.

5
Edward William Godwin
Ebonized oak chair made by
William Watt, about 1875.

6
William Burges
Painted cabinet, 1858.

7

8

7
Christopher Dresser
Silver-plated teapot made by
James Dixon, about 1880.

8
Bruce J. Talbert
'Hatton' silk damask made by
Warner, about 1880.

9
Christopher Dresser
'Clutha' glass vases made by
James Couper, about 1880.

10
Owen Jones
'Athens' silk damask made by
Warner, about 1870.

9

11

11
Richard Redgrave
Water decanter made by Summerly's
Art Manufactures, 1847

12
William Burges (?)
Painted bookcase, about 1860.

13
Edward William Godwin
Ebonized oak table made by
William Watt, 1867.

14
Edward William Godwin
Ebonized wood sideboard made by
William Watt, 1867.

13

14

15

16

17

15
Owen Jones
Silk tissue made by Warner, 1870–80.

16
Owen Jones
Silk tissue made by Warner, about 1870.

17
Alfred Stevens
Door-knocker, about 1865.

18
Bruce J. Talbert
'Kingfisher' silk damask made by Warner, about 1880.

18

2

The Arts and Crafts 1860-1915

WILLIAM Holman Hunt, long before he painted 'Little Nell and her Grandfather', 'The Light of the World' or 'Isabella and the Pot of Basil', had down-to-earth experience of industrial design. He had worked as a juvenile pattern designer, from the age of fourteen, in Richard Cobden's London office, producing commercial designs for cotton prints. This monotonous apprenticeship influenced his attitude for ever; it gave him a passion for reform. He explained: 'My past experience in pattern designing and my criticisms upon the base and vulgar forms and incoherent forms in contemporary furniture, to which I drew Rossetti's attention on his first visit to me, encouraged visions of reform in these particulars, and we speculated on improvement in all household objects, furniture, fabrics and other interior decorations.'

Holman Hunt could find no furniture to buy, so he designed some. He started work, it seems, in about 1855. When he showed his 'small group of household joys' to his brother Pre-Raphaelites, 'the contagion spread', and soon they were designing and painting, sometimes making, new artistic furniture for themselves and friends. For instance: Ford Madox Brown designed a chair inspired by the Egyptians and a series of countrified ladder-backs, rush-seated and stained green; Burne-Jones painted a piano with a 'chant d'amour', surmounting a picture of female musicians and death; Rossetti painted stories from Dante, and Sir Galahad, on a high-back settle for the rooms in Red Lion Square which Burne-Jones and Morris had taken over from him in 1856. At this stage their design work was all quite dilettante, a high-flown kind of hobby, done in camaraderie. A letter from Rossetti, on the move to Red Lion Square, stresses the high spirits: 'Morris is rather doing the magnificent there and is having some intensely mediaeval furniture made—tables and chairs like incubi and succubi. He and I have painted the back of a chair with figures and inscriptions in gules and vert and azure, and we are all three going to cover a cabinet with pictures.' He describes the large round table, 'as firm, and as heavy, as a rock'.

One may ask what this impulsive, very individual feeling for reforming household objects has to do with the improvement of design for British industry. The answer is, directly, very little. Unlike Cole, who from the first was concerned with British trade and the economic consequences of inept design, the Pre-Raphaelites and Morris and the Arts and Crafts designers on the whole were rather ignorant of commerce. Some were even hostile to it. Most of them cared more for the quality of life, for a 'standard of goodness', than for national trade figures. In one sense, their reforms were much less practical than Cole's. In another sense, of course, their reforms were ten times more so. It does seem fairly obvious that without William Morris and Lethaby and Gimson and others of their kind, setting a tradition of designers in small workshops, establishing a cult of straightforwardness and soundness, truth to materials, attention to detail, that British industrial design, as we now know it, could never have developed as it has. There is a direct link from the British Arts and Crafts men, through the Design and Industries Association (which was in fact an offshoot of the Arts and Crafts Societies), right on to the Council of Industrial Design.

In the Arts and Crafts movement, Morris is the central figure. It is almost true to say that he was the originator. Once Morris was married and had moved from Red Lion Square to his new Red House at Bexley Heath in Kent, the idea came to him of beginning 'a manufactory of all things necessary for the decoration of a house'. Philip Webb, his friend and architect, had already designed stained-glass windows for churches; and so, wrote Burne-Jones, 'the idea grew of putting our experiences together for the service of the public'. In 1861, Morris, Marshall, Faulkner & Co. brought out its first prospectus, stressing the need for 'artists of reputation' to devote their time to decorative art. The early results were on view the next year, at the 1862 International Exhibition; the Morris firm showed, among other things, a sofa by Rossetti, an iron bedstead, sideboard and washstand by Webb, a collection of tiles painted by Rossetti, Burne-Jones, Webb and Morris, a pair of copper candlesticks too heavy to carry (according to Rossetti) and a substantial range of furniture designed in the mediaeval idiom, 'of solid construction and joiner made'.

Morris, Marshall, Faulkner, Fine Art Workmen, were publicly protesting against the prevailing style of decoration: the ponderous and complex, bogus Second Empire fashion. Walter Crane, a Morris ally, maintained in retrospect that this practical protest 'represented in the main a revival of the mediaeval spirit (though not the letter) in design; a return to simplicity, to sincerity, to good materials and sound workmanship; to rich and suggestive surface decoration, and simple constructive forms'. It meant the simple black-framed old English Buckinghamshire elbow-chair instead of wavy-backed and curly-legged stuffed seating, French-polished and often unreliably constructed; it meant bordered Eastern rugs and fringed Axminster carpets on plain or stained boards or India matting instead of 'the stuffy planned carpets'. It recommended slender black wood or light brass curtain rods; plain white or green paint for interior woodwork; canopied settles, plain oaken boards and trestles and blue-and-white Nankin, Delft or Gres de Flandres to brighten the dresser. From Morris' workshops in Queen Square developed a sophisticated cult of everyday simplicity, intended to offset *objets d'art* of lustrous splendour, and unique palatial pieces of ornately-painted furniture. This became a powerful fashion among the cultured people. 'Soon,' says Crane, 'no home with any claim to decorative charm was felt to be complete without its vine and fig tree so to speak—from Queen Square.' Though Walter Crane was biased, this was partly true.

But there was more to Morris, of course, than vines and fig leaves, more than a new rarified rich style of decoration. For Morris had already, at Oxford with Burne-Jones, embarked upon a 'holy crusade against the age', the crusade against the tyranny of factory production which John Ruskin, the grand-master craftsman, had begun. As an undergraduate, Morris had been highly influenced by Ruskin and, in particular, by Ruskin's *Stones of Venice*, published 1851–53; the chapter on 'The Nature of Gothic,' Morris said, would 'be considered as one of the very few necessary and inevitable utterances of the century.' When he and his friends first read it, 'it seemed to point out a new road on which the world should travel': away from competitive capitalistic commerce to groups of men and maids working happily together, away from massive factories to individual workshops, from mechanized banalities to skilful craft and truth. Away from Academic convention in the arts to warmth and sincerity and Gothic spontaneity. Respect and affection for materials was essential to Ruskin's reformation, and to Morris's as well. Ruskin wrote, in *Stones of Venice*,

'The workman has not done his duty, and is not working on safe principles, unless he so far honours the materials in which he is working as to set himself to bring out their beauty, and to recommend and exalt, as far as he can, their peculiar qualities.'

Taking his doctrines to their logical conclusion—that designers should master practical techniques—Ruskin, in charge of the Oxford Museum, insisted on building a column himself. It had to be rebuilt by a professional bricklayer: Ruskin's experiment had not been a success. Morris, as technician, was a good deal more efficient. He was no doubt encouraged by the architect George Edmund Street whose office he joined briefly, first in Oxford, then in London, in the Pre-Raphaelite days at Red Lion Square. Street, a full-blown Gothicist, believing that an architect should also be conversant with the crafts, learned realistic ironwork, joinery and building; for one of his first houses, he even made the staircase. His ideal of the multi-skilled architect, and his practical energy in carrying it out, clearly affected Philip Webb and Morris who met in Street's office, and there made friends for ever. It was partly due to Street that Morris would be found with his arms dyed blue up to the elbows, in his vats; that before he began printing, he made a sheet of paper himself, out of fine white linen rags. Probably Street influenced his endless curiosity. Morris was always needing to do more. In a letter to Wardle of Leek, the printers of many of his chintzes, he admits this restlessness:

'I mean that I can never be contented with getting anything short of the best, and that I should always go on trying to improve our goods in all ways, and should consider anything that was only tolerable as a ladder to mount up to the next stage—that is, in fact, my life.'

A disciple, C. R. Ashbee, attributed the Arts and Crafts movement to the earnestness of the Pre-Raphaelite painters, the prophetic enthusiasm of Ruskin and the titanic energy of Morris. What he did not add, though it was in fact important, was that Morris' titanic energy was tempered by considerable realism. He could compromise. On the whole, his own designs were not produced by merry parties of men and maids showing pleasure in their work; nor were they available for all the world to buy them. Morris' productions were never for the poor. Failing an ideal society, he seemed able to make friends with, and take work from, the people he opposed, the advocates of commerce; designing the Green Dining Room for Henry Cole's Museum, acting as examiner in Henry Cole's new art school, and making the most of the South Kensington exhibits, which profoundly influenced the course of his design. Perhaps this was his strength. He was not a lone reformer, shouting out against the world; he was in the thick of it, with Burne-Jones on his left, romantic, insubstantial, and on his right the sane and solid, kindly Philip Webb.

This was a period of incredible activity in the decorative arts (as the friends of Morris termed them). It was a two-fold movement, with a lot of overlapping: the tendencies, on one hand, were the airy and symbolic, with Burne-Jones and Japonaiserie and Liberty and Beardsley; the urge was, on the other, for the soundly-made and practical. This trend was very well exemplified by Philip Webb. It was the Philip Webb school, the less fanciful designers, more anxious to avoid than to create an exhibition, who had profoundest influence on subsequent developments and indirectly much improved design in British industry.

'I never begin to be satisfied until my work looks common-place', said Philip Webb, developing Ruskin's rule of sound construction and honest work into a plea for a certain anonymity of style in household design. Philip Webb and William Morris, Norman Shaw and John D. Sedding, all at one time in Street's office, spread the principle of 'comely and workmanlike' building, the concept of pleasant modest living: in short, the decent home. Their concern took them backwards to form the Society for Protecting Ancient Buildings, and forward to advocate the garden city. According to a member, the 'Anti-Scrape' Society founded to protect the ancient, became 'a school of rational builders and modern building'. William Morris was the Secretary. Charles Eastlake's influential *Hints on Household Tastes*, published in 1868, encouraged a simple, clean and forthright style of living, with furniture in sturdy rustic style, hand-made by honest carpenters. For the next forty years these ideas, with variations, were carried through in practice by Mackmurdo, Frank Brangwyn, C. F. A. Voysey; by Ashbee, Baillie Scott, Wickham Jarvis, Walter Cave, Edgar Wood, and Lethaby and Gimson and the Barnsleys; and, almost more important, by a manufacturer and seller of furniture for bedrooms, Ambrose Heal.

In 1882, the Century Guild was founded by Arthur Heygate Mackmurdo, pupil of and traveller with Ruskin, devotee of Italy, a worldly and flamboyant personality, unlike the rather dogged English Arts and Crafts mainstream. He was half-way to being an 1880s aesthete. But his workshop and his Guild were, of course, pure Arts and Crafts. Like Morris's workshop and Pugin's still earlier, the Century Guild was established to design and produce household objects of a kind which were unobtainable elsewhere; it intended to restore building, decorations, glass-painting, pottery, woodcarving and metal to their right place beside painting and sculpture: in other words, to make them no longer trades but arts. Helping Mackmurdo, from the first, were Herbert Horne and Selwyn Image, who had for a while run concurrent careers as a curate and designer. But by 1882, the Church had had enough, and Image was dismissed from St Anne's in Soho and turned his attentions to Mackmurdo's Guild full-time. Other members, and associates, included Clement Heaton, specialist in cloisonné enamel; George Heywood Sumner, master of 'sgraffito', with which he decorated many churches, and stained glass; and William de Morgan, the potter and perfecter of lustre techniques and Persian blue-green glazes, an enthusiast who worked on almost undeterred when a fire in the kiln in his cellar burned his house down, and a visionary who stated, 'One obvious use of lustreware is its application to domes and towers, and to all parts of buildings that catch the level rays of the sun.' The work of the Guild, Mackmurdo's in particular shows brilliance, a great originality, almost eccentricity, both in use of pattern and in structural design. It seems to reach maturity in the much serener, more fastidious work of C. F. A. Voysey, a younger designer, not officially a member of the Century Guild, but connected all along.

In 1888, the Guild of Handicraft was founded by C. R. Ashbee, a broadly-cultured architect with socialist ideals. The Guild had its origins in the Ruskin Class which Ashbee, in time off from his office, organized at Toynbee Hall for three poor pupils. This developed into the School of Handicraft and, from there, the Guild. The aim was to draw in young journeymen and train them in design for their specific industry: for cabinetmaking, iron and coppersmithing, lithography, draughtsmanship, printing, house-painting, sign-writing and patternmaking. Meanwhile, workshops, run by guildsmen, would produce and sell professional handicrafts and help support the school. The system of co-partnership of workmen was evolved to counteract 'the unintelligent ocean of competitive industry'; it challenged 'a vast output of rotten, useless, sweated, cheap industries, and a vast growth of nerveless, characterless, underfed cheap men and women'. It aimed to establish a standard of goodness: goodness in work and goodness in life. In 1892, the Guild occupied a large, handsome building, Essex House in Mile End Road. In 1902, at the height of its idealism, family by family, the Guild moved in a body to a kind of promised land in Chipping Campden, Gloucestershire, where 150 men, women and children settled in cottages, kept their own pigs and dug their own allotments, acted comedies in winter, held swimming sports in summer, played in the foreman of the woodshop's splendid band, chased, engraved, enamelled, constructed honest furniture, made silver and jewellery of lovely reticence.

In 1890, Kenton & Co., a furniture workshop in Theobald's Road, was set up by Macartney and Blomfield, Colonel Mallet (a friend of Macartney's who 'had taste and knew people'), Gimson and Sidney Barnsley and Lethaby. Each of them contributed £100. Inspired, so they said, by what they had seen in Morris's shop window, they set to work producing their own designs in their own workshops with materials they had bought themselves. They were friends, as well as rivals, of Morris and Webb; Philip Webb was our 'particular prophet', said Lethaby. The fairness and the squareness of Webb's buildings and his furniture influenced the Kenton designers, then and later. For Kenton, which was never a very serious business, ended very amicably after two years. They enjoyed themselves greatly, Lethaby explains, 'making many pieces of furniture, selling some at little over cost price—nothing being included for design or for time expended by the proprietors': they finally drew lots for the remaining furniture, and went their separate and influential ways. Gimson and the Barnsleys went to workshops in the Cotswolds, developing a simple finely-detailed country style. Lethaby, in London, as the leading design teacher, and later as the father-figure of the DIA, promoted the same qualities: the measured and the modest, the soundly-made, the gentlemanly and the sociable.

Where there is a movement for reform, there are committees: even the Arts and Crafts meant many meetings. The St. George's Art Society, a small discussion group formed by pupils and former pupils of Norman Shaw, enlarged its membership to make The Art Workers' Guild in 1884. Meanwhile, a group of decorative designers, caught in a hurricane one January Tuesday in Lewis F. Day's house, had formed another group for discussion, meeting in rotation at members' homes or studios. This group, The Fifteen, under Lewis F. Day, included John D. Sedding and Walter Crane, who describes its 'happy if obscure life' over several years until it was absorbed by the Art Workers' Guild and the Arts and Crafts Exhibition Society in 1888. Crane points out that the craftsmen members came from very different backgrounds and used very different methods; but each aimed at 'a renaissance of the decorative arts which should act through and towards more humanized conditions for the workmen and employers' and, in this concern for society, 'there were few if any among them who would not readily have acknowledged Morris as their master'.

William Morris, at first, took no part at all in the Arts and Crafts Exhibition schemes; although he was in favour of the idea in theory, he had very little faith in its practical success. Certainly, its origins had not been very hopeful. It had in fact begun as a revolt against the Royal Academy system of exhibiting paintings; an angry splinter-group of artists, with the idea of holding their own exhibition, had written to the papers and met the leading craftsmen to explore the possibilities of collaboration. This project soon proved useless: all the painters wanted was reform of the Academy hanging committee. The craftsmen, quite disgusted, left the artists in a body, and W. A. S. Benson, the metalwork designer, organized a provisional committee to make plans for an independent Arts and Crafts exhibition. The New Gallery, which was then in reality only a few months old, was engaged for October 1, 1888. Walter Crane's introduction to the catalogue reminded the public—snidely but forgiveably—that art should be recognized in the humblest objects and materials and felt to be as valuable as 'more highly-rewarded pictorial skill'. The exhibition was enormously successful, in spite of William Morris' misgivings and Rossetti's dismay when he heard of the proposals: fastidious Rossetti was pleasantly surprised.

The Arts and Crafts Exhibition Society made a great impression with its first six exhibitions, in 1888, 1889, 1890, 1893, 1896 and 1899. The opening of the 1896 Exhibition was clouded, of course, by William Morris' death; but, said his admirers, 'it was a splendid moment for a hero to die'. The exhibition showed work of extraordinary quality and individuality. Craftsmen were making a name for themselves: for furniture, Barnsley, Lethaby, Cave; for textiles, Walter Crane, Lewis Day and Arthur Silver; for metalwork, Benson and Rathbone; for silver and jewellery, Ashbee, Henry Wilson, Nelson Dawson; for bookbinding, Cobden-Sanderson; for printing, Emery Walker; for glass, J. H. Powell of Whitefriars; for musical instruments, Arnold Dolmetsch; for a variety of wall papers and carpets and furniture, a mantelpiece, a clock-case and a lamp-post, Charles Annesley Voysey. His constructions were considered 'at once the most restrained and the most novel in the Exhibition'. *The Studio* magazine wrote of Voysey: 'His vivid personality is one of the chief factors in modern design—one that cannot fail to have immense influence on the design of the coming century'. And, as it happened, *The Studio* was right.

In Arts and Crafts catalogues, and in *The Studio*, there is a strong sense of the spirit of the movement: its deeply-held convictions and its almost courtly tolerance, its spiritual sweetness and its hearty slaps-on-backs. 'I want us all to be friends,' said William

Morris 'all to be gentlemen, working for the common good, sharing duly the common stock of pleasure and refinement.' Perhaps it was not difficult. The most important craftsmen were gentlemen already: they had been to public schools and on to university. Most of them were naturally friendly and gregarious: they liked long country walks, and discussions by the fireside with a great stone jar of ale, and suppers out at Gatti's where the old Italian waiter, whom they always called Tricino, was perpetually smiling. A typical enterprise, high-principled and jolly, was *Beauty's Awakening*, an Art Workers' Guild Masque, presented at the Guildhall to the Lord Mayor and Aldermen. The craftsmen had worked hard: Walter Crane designed the Dragon, Lethaby the Throne, Nelson Dawson (metalworker) the Sword for Trueheart, A. S. Haynes the Dress for Bogus. R. Rathbone, the lightmaker, of course produced the Lamp. Selwyn Image, the ex-curate, intoned a formal prologue. The *mis-en-scene*, one hopes, was rather better than the verse.

'The fullness of communal life' was the whole purpose. It led Ashbee to sing catches with his guildsmen after supper; it caused Gimson, in his village, to direct the merrymaking, personally leading the 29th of May. These genial impulses were very much connected with the new enlightened Socialistic movement in the country: with the Fabians, Sidney Webb and Bernard Shaw and Granville Barker, Bishops Ingram and Gore, with their ideas for Church reform, the foundation of new schools like Abbotsholme and Bedales with an open-air philosophy and brother-loving motto 'Work of each for weal of all'. The Arts and Crafts were fighting for humanized conditions; Walter Crane describes 'the movement in art represented by William Morris and his colleagues as really part of a great movement of protest—a crusade against the purely commercial, industrial, and material tendencies of the day'. If this crusade appears a little ineffective, perhaps it was because the protestors were perfectionists. When Morris left the Socialist League to form the Hammersmith Socialist Society, Walter Crane designed the banner and Morris' daughter settled down to work it. This is not the attitude which wins the revolution.

What the Arts and Crafts achieved was less a total reformation than a bit of added prettiness, a fresh and simple style, a new appreciation of the objects round the house, and a sudden quite fanatical respect for craftsmen's handwork. Faithfully or more or less erratically following the guidance of Ashbee, Guilds of Handicraft rose up in Birmingham and Newlyn and places far afield: Bromsgrove, for instance, had its Guild of Metalworkers and Keswick its School of Industrial Art. The Guild up in Scotland moved guildsmen to Stirling, seeking (like Ashbee) the pure country life. The Guild down in Bristol opened a showroom for 30 craft members to sell their work collectively. Even in Manchester where, said *The Studio*, 'discouragements beset the pursuit of handicrafts', Walter Crane, after two years' propaganda, established a substantial Northern Art Workers' Guild.

The Royal School of Needlework, founded in 1872, commissioning designs from Morris, Burne-Jones, Crane, Selwyn Image and Alexander Fisher, stimulated stitching in the school and in the home. The Home Arts & Industries Association, founded in 1885 by Mrs Jebb, with Mackmurdo's backing, propagated the idea of everyman a craftsman, and a vision of fair women all with needles in their hands. The romance of cottage craftsmanship was to a large extent responsible for numerous small craft groups, some professional, some wholly unprofessional, which quickly came to life: The Leek Embroidery Society, directed by Mrs Thomas Wardle, which issued sewing patterns; the School of Art Woodcarving in Pelham Place in London; the Haslemere Peasant Industries, founded by Geoffrey Blount, a Wykehamist, in 1896; St. Edmundsbury Weavers from 1901 in Haslemere; the Women's Guild of Arts; and many dozens more. The range and the enthusiasm of these peripheral arts and crafts revivals can be gathered from displays by the Home Art & Industries Association which annually managed to fill the Albert Hall. Exhibits included, in 1894, the brass and copper repoussé work, perfected by the parishioners of Compton Greenfield, Bristol, 'under the able guidance' of the Rector. The next year, pride of place was given to arts and industries from the royal home at Sandringham: a log-stand wrought in iron by the Princess of Wales, a little heart-shaped table with polished poker-work which H.R.H. Duchess of York had executed.

On a more commercial level, art potteries were thriving: the Martin Brothers, Southall; Doulton's of Lambeth; Della Robbia at Birkenhead (directed by Harold Rathbone, a painter and pupil of Ford Madox Brown). Howson Taylor, Bernard Moore, Moorcroft and Pilkington's Lancastrian Pottery were all experimenting with artistic lustrous glazes. When Pilkington's exhibited in 1904 in London, showing new opalescent and crystalline effects, curdled, mottled, flocculent and clouded texture glazes, a critic reported with a tone of ecstasy:

'In a great room draped with white were vases, bowls, dishes and trays, resplendent in all the colour of the rainbow and glittering like precious stones.'

Beyond the shining lustres, home-made silver, palace poker-work, the fluttering enthusiasms of the arts and crafts, a solider, more lasting side-effect was now emerging: the reform of official teaching of design. In 1894, William Richard Lethaby ('Richards' to his friends, who were the basic Arts and Crafts men) became an adviser on art to the Technical Education Board of the London County Council. George Frampton, the sculptor, was appointed co-adviser, and when in 1896 the Central School was founded 'to encourage the industrial application of decorative art', Lethaby and Frampton were made joint principals. Frampton never put in an appearance. So Lethaby himself was in fact in full control, concentrating all his energies into propagating the level-headed 'doing is designing' school of thought. Sweeping aside the method of training pursued at South Kensington since Henry Cole was there—a method which reminded Lethaby of learning to swim in a thousand lessons without water—the Central School developed a practical curriculum of craft techniques and training in the right use of materials. 'Art, construction, architecture,' exclaimed Lethaby to Central School pupils 'they are all one. You must go upstairs and see how stained glass windows are made and books are bound and gilding done.' The staff he employed were highly-skilled craftsmen: for example, Douglas Cockerell for bookbinding, Catterson Smith for wallpaper and textiles. Even a reputable plumber was brought in. Lethaby himself taught leadwork, and encouraged Arts and Crafts perfectionism mixed with lack of pomp, kneeling on the carpet, unembarrassed, to admire the workmanship of a metal coat of arms. He needed to keep up morale; for at first the Central School was very badly housed in Morley Hall, a building abandoned by the YWCA. The roof in the conservatory leaked, on rainy days, so fearfully that students had to put umbrellas up to listen to Harley Ricardo's lectures on architecture. But they struggled through, and *The Studio* reported that the first exhibition of work by Central School students fully justified the expectations raised by the staff.

With Lethaby installed at the Central School, another very vocal Arts and Crafts protagonist was appointed to South Kensington. In 1898, much to his amazement, Walter Crane was offered the job of Principal of the Royal College of Art. Crane, who had already been Director of Design at the Manchester School of Art, accepted reluctantly. When he arrived, he found that 'The School was in rather a chaotic state. It had been chiefly run as a sort of mill in which to prepare art teachers and masters'. He much disliked the system of cut-and-dried certificates: to Crane's admittedly unacademic mind, the curriculum seemed terribly mechanical and lifeless. He seems to have tried quite hard to put it right, to make the methods flexible and to improve equipment. But he found, as others have found before and since, that 'One could not order a flower or a bit of drapery, or obtain any ordinary immediate studio requirement without a proper form duly signed and countersigned in the right red-tape department.' It was all too much for Crane. He got on badly with the staff; a fierce attack of 'flu 'left depressing effects'; the job, which had been offered on a part-time basis turned out to be full-time, and Walter Crane was longing to finish the scenes in the Masque he was writing for the Guildhall performance by the Art Workers' Guild. Besides, his own design practice was suffering. He resigned at the end of the year.

But the influence of Arts and Crafts philosophies on the training at the Royal College of Art was not to end with Walter Crane's resignation. In 1900, Lethaby himself became the First Professor of Design at the Royal College of Art, doubling the influence of his theories that 'Designing is not the abstract power exercised by a genius. It is simply the arranging how work shall be done.' Until 1911, Lethaby divided his time between the Central School and RCA; then he retired from the Central to concentrate on his South Kensington professorship. Beresford Pike, the Professor of Architecture, watched the progress of Design at closest quarters: he describes Lethaby 'disintegrating the creepers and parasites of form, weeds which had planted themselves at South Kensington and taken root . . . and supplanting them with the healthy seed of truth and directness of expression'.

It is very interesting, although not at all suprising, that the influence of Arts and Crafts ideas was strong in Europe long before it got to Kensington. The Arts and Crafts, as usual, were more honoured on the continent than they were in Britain, and better understood. Early in the 1880s, Crane points out that 'In Belgium particularly, the work of the newer School of English designers has awakened the greatest interest.' The Belgian, Van der Velde, exclaimed that 'it was spring' when the first of the Arts and Crafts arrived from England. By 1895, when Bing's shop L'Art Nouveau opened in Paris, England was acknowledged as the international harbinger: 'When English creations began to appear, a cry of delight sounded throughout Europe. Its echo can still be heard in every country.' For Art Nouveau in France, Jugendstil in Germany, Secessionstil in Austria, Stile Liberty in Italy and all the variations in Holland, Scandinavia and even Spain and Russia can to some extent be traced right back to Britain, back to Ruskin and to Morris, to their new intense perception, to their love of handicraft. At the end of the century, to Loos in Vienna, the centre of civilization was London.

Morris and Crane, Ashbee and Voysey, Baillie Scott and Mackintosh, the Glasgow architect, were the best-known, most-admired of the designers on the Continent. Their work was illustrated in the magazine *The Studio* which had a reverential foreign circulation; Peter Altenberg describes the arrival of a new issue in a cultivated household in Vienna as 'a kind of silently aesthetic celebration, after which the master of the house had scant hopes of the fulfilment of more profane desires'. The British designers were shown in the flesh in the small avant-garde continental exhibitions: La Libre Esthetique in Brussels, for instance, showed Morris and Ashbee and Voysey and Beardsley. They later exhibited in the larger international displays which multiplied and prospered at the turn of the century: Paris 1900, Glasgow 1901, Turin 1902. British designers even worked abroad. Mackintosh decorated a music room for Fritz Warndorfer in Vienna. Baillie Scott, with six other artists—the elite of the continental movement—was asked to design the Grand Duke of Hesse's Palace at Darmstadt, the centre of a whole community of artists in which every object in every house was to be designed, in every detail, by the owner. This enthusiastic project, so immaculate in principle, was attributed to the influence of 'The English art of furniture making, the theories of Morris, the actions of men like Ashbee and Baillie Scott, of the Belgian, H. van der Velde, the Japanizing tendency introduced by the house of L'Art Nouveau (S. Bing) of Paris': not forgetting the contribution of the Germans, who by then had developed ideas of their own.

The Germans sent Hermann Muthesius to England. From 1896 to 1903, Muthesius, an architect, was attached to the German embassy in London, for official research into English housing. Sir Robert Lorimer later described how Muthesius 'showed the greatest interest and keenness in the British Arts and Crafts Movement. He travelled all over the country, interviewed everyone, got the loan of designs and of photographs of work and every kind of information he could lay his hands on'. He reported back to Germany. In 1898, he gave first-hand impressions of Ashbee's Guild and School of Handicraft in the German magazine *Dekorative Kunst*, stressing Ashbee's preference for functional forms. In 1901, Muthesius published a book on English contemporary architecture; in 1904 and 1905, he brought out three illustrated volumes on modern English houses, emphasizing sanity and sound use of materials, the fundamental principles of English Arts and Crafts. Simultaneously, encouraged by Muthesius, large folios of drawings by Baillie Scott and Mackintosh were published in Germany. Already, the Germans' design appreciation, with determined application, was a step or two ahead. In 1901, *The Studio* had noted in German government circles and manufacturers 'a far-sighted alertness to the practical value of good design'; the German manufacturers seemed to be determined 'to wrest from British craftsmen and designers their initiative supremacy in the applied art campaign'.

Once Hermann Muthesius returned to the Fatherland, lecturing and publishing, the Germans worked still harder. Wrote Lorimer disgustedly (as if the Germans cheated) 'every help and encouragement was given to the teaching of design for technical purposes. The immediate result was that a great amount of "New Art" design was produced, worse than anything of the kind produced here. But—and this is the remarkable and interesting part—a few years before the war, the Germans had worked through this phase, and arrived at the production of simple straightforward designs'. It was in fact in 1905 in Dresden that the Deutsche Werkstätten exhibited Richard Riemerschmid's mass-production furniture, a style of furniture specifically developed 'from the spirit of the machine'. And it was 1907 when, urged on by Muthesius (then Superintendent of the Prussian Board of Trade for Schools of Arts and Crafts), German manufacturers, architects and artists and interested laymen formed the Deutscher Werkbund, which aimed at 'combining all efforts towards high quality in industrial work'.

Meanwhile, back in England, the Arts and Crafts proceeded straightforwardly and calmly. They went their own sweet way. The Arts and Crafts Exhibitions of 1903 and 1906 showed the usual fine selection of expensive hand-made furniture, a sound display of admirable craftsmanship in oak, an English walnut cabinet inlaid with pearl, a pulpit inlaid with ebony, a decorative carving in silver, gilt-bronze and gold, forming a Gothic overmantel, intended 'for a room in which armour is hung'. Walter Crane designed a mace; May Morris had embroidered 'a truly beautiful cushion'; Mr and Mrs Arthur Gaskin showed 'a dainty little group of hat-pins and lace-pins', some of them with precious stones at the head. *The Studio*, which felt that it had all been seen before, was moved in 1906 to complain: 'The arts and crafts in this exhibition, almost failing to contend for improvements in the practical necessities of domestic comfort, have taken very seriously the covers of the books we shall read, and jewellery that will be worn in the evening.'

The Arts and Crafts, one must remember, were never open-minded. They were insular. They kept to their safe and sound ideals of wholesomeness. They disliked the new and foreign; they distrusted the extremes. Early on, they had detested the room which Edward Godwin designed for Oscar Wilde; according to May Morris, it was 'needlessly spartan—there was a hair-shirt vigour about it, opposed to all geniality or prandial humours'. With much the same suspicion, designers from Glasgow—Mackintosh, McNair and the Macdonalds—were disparaged, underestimated and labelled 'Spooky School'. Art nouveau was called 'the squirm'. When 'the squirm' arrived in Britain, when exhibits from Paris 1900 were displayed at the Victoria and Albert, Lewis F. Day and Walter Crane were outraged and three most upright architects with Norman Shaw connections wrote a very cross and stuffy letter to *The Times*, maintaining that 'This work is neither right in principle nor does it evince a proper regard for the material employed.' The spirit of the letter, the Arts and Crafts resistance to what was regarded as excessive novelty, also caused the architects and craftsmen, when the time came, to turn a blind eye to the events in Germany.

This is not to say that the English Arts and Crafts men opposed design for industry in principle. In fact, most of them designed for machine production regularly: Morris, Crane, Mackmurdo, Lewis Day and Voysey; Benson and Silver exclusively so. But, one way or another, design for mass-production was not what

they believed in; it was nowhere near their heart. The Society
they formed in 1888 for promoting art in industry was never very
earnest. This National Association for the Advancement of Art
and its Application to Industry—'a somewhat large order', said
Crane—held congresses in Liverpool and Edinburgh consisting
in the main of purposeless chit-chat and civic entertainments.
The society was doomed from the first, from the moment at the
inaugural meeting when Edmund Gosse brought in statistics of
trade and the cotton industry—' "Things," as Oscar Wilde said,
who followed him, "which we do not want to hear about at all." '

19

20

19
Ambrose Heal
Unpolished oak cupboard, about
1905.

20
Ambrose Heal
Wardrobe in chestnut, 1900.

21
Ambrose Heal
Unpolished oak sideboard, 1906.

22
Ambrose Heal
Inlaid oak wardrobe designed for
the Paris Exhibition, 1900.

21

22

23

24

23
Ernest Gimson
Inlaid ebony cabinet, about 1910.

24
Sidney Barnsley
Oak dresser, about 1899.

25
Ernest Gimson
Daneway House, Sapperton,
interior, about 1910

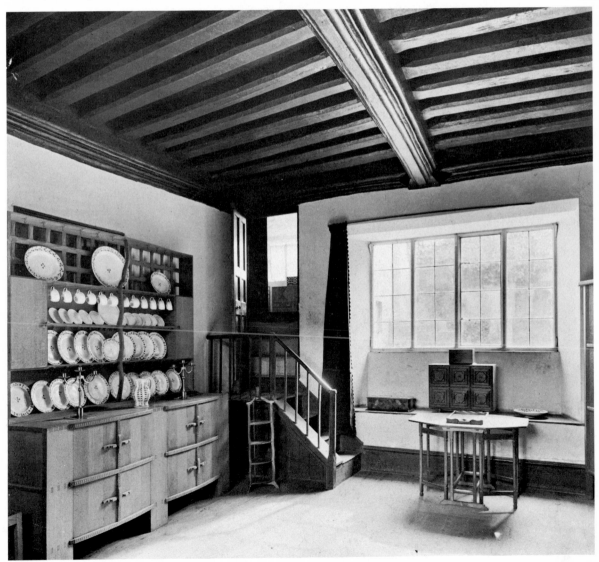

26

27

28

29

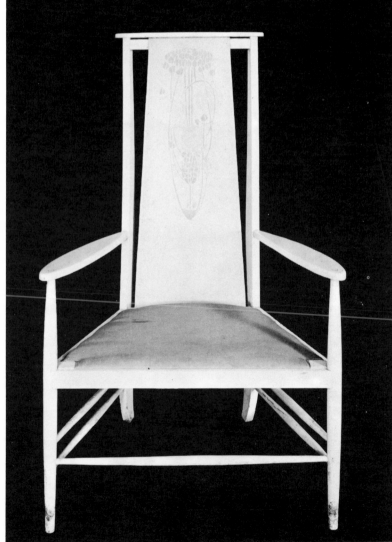

30

26
Ernest Gimson
Circular table, about 1905.

27
Ernest Gimson
Ladderback chair in ash, about 1888.

28
Ernest Gimson
Polished steel firedog, about 1908–10.

29
Charles Rennie Mackintosh
Silver-plated cutlery made for
Ingram Street Tea-Rooms, Glasgow,
1901.

30
Charles Rennie Mackintosh
White painted armchair, 1902.

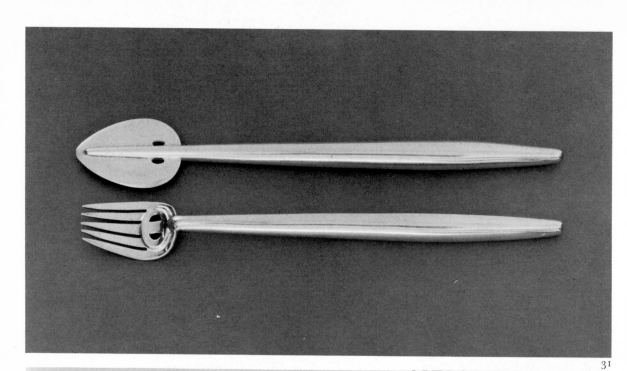

31

32

33

31
Charles Rennie Mackintosh
Silver-plated fish knife and fork,
about 1900.

32
Charles Rennie Mackintosh
Hill House, Helensburgh, bedroom
interior, 1902.

33
Charles Rennie Mackintosh
Chair in oak, about 1897.

34
Charles Rennie Mackintosh
Waitresses' chair, about 1907;
tea-room chair, about 1900;
tall tea-room chair, about 1901.

34

35

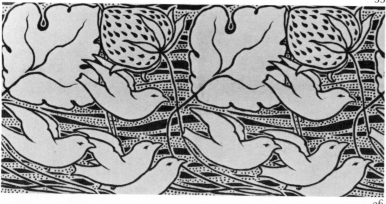

36

35
C. F. A. Voysey
'Purple Bird' silk tissue made by
A. Morton, 1897–8.

36
C. F. A. Voysey
Machine-printed cotton made by
Newman, Smith and Newman, 1897.

37
C. F. A. Voysey
Printed linen, 1900.

37

38

38
C. F. A. Voysey
Machine-turned brass teapot, about
1896.

39
C. F. A. Voysey
Oak writing desk made by
W. H. Tingey, 1896.

39

40
Philip Webb
Chimney-piece in Red House,
Bexley Heath, 1859.

41
Philip Webb and William Morris
Red House, Bexley Heath, interior,
1859.

42
R. Norman Shaw's office (?)
Oak chair with rush seat sold by
Morris & Co., about 1876.

43
William Morris
Sussex chair in ebonized beech made
by Morris & Co., about 1865.

44
Edward Burne-Jones
Painted wood upright piano made by
Priestly, about 1860.

40

41

42

43

44

45

46

45
William Morris
'Flower Pot' embroidered panel,
about 1880.

46
William Morris
'Cherwell' hand-block printed
velveteen, about 1885.

47
William Morris
'Brother Rabbit' hand-block printed
chintz, 1883.

48
William Morris
'Compton' wallpaper handprinted by
Jeffrey & Co. for Morris & Co.,
1896.

47

48

49

50

49
A. H. Mackmurdo
Oak writing desk, 1886.

50
A. H. Mackmurdo
Dining chair with fretwork back,
1881.

51
A. H. Mackmurdo
Printed cotton fabric made for
Century Guild, about 1882.

51

52

52
E. G. Punnett
Inlaid oak armchair made by
William Birch, 1901.

53
Liberty & Co.
'Thebes' stool in mahogany, 1884.

54

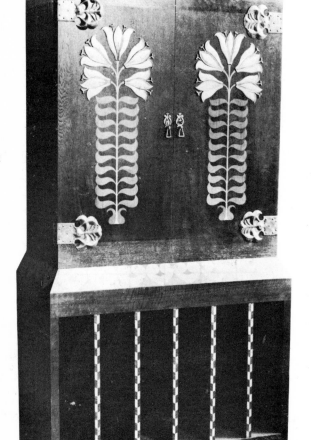

55

56

54
Philip Webb
Vases and glasses made by James
Powell, 1859.

55
M. H. Baillie Scott
Painted music cabinet made by
Guild of Handicraft for Palace of
Darmstadt, about 1898.

56
George Walton
Table glass made by James Powell,
1903.

57
M. H. Baillie Scott
Painted seat made by Guild of
Handicraft for Palace of Darmstadt,
about 1898.

57

58

59

58
C. R. Ashbee
Silver dish made by Guild of
Handicraft, 1900.

59
Della Robbia Pottery
Earthenware vase, late 19th Century.

60

60
C. R. Ashbee
Silver mustard pot and spoon, about
1900.

61
William de Morgan
'Peacock' dish, late 19th or early
20th Century.

61

62
W. A. S. Benson
Brass or copper lamp, about 1895.

63
W. R. Lethaby
Inlaid oak sideboard, about 1900.

64
M. H. Baillie Scott
Clock, about 1901.

65
Philip Webb
Oak table, about 1860.

62

63

64

65

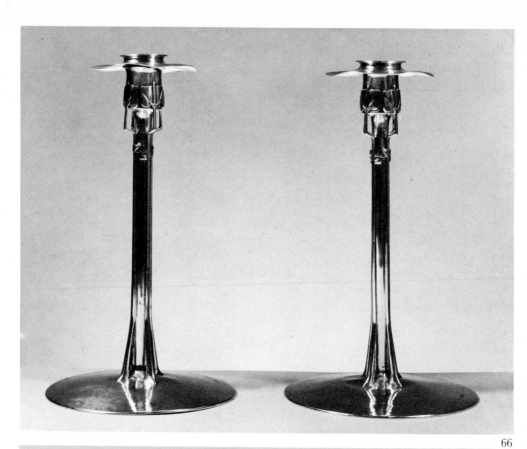

66

67

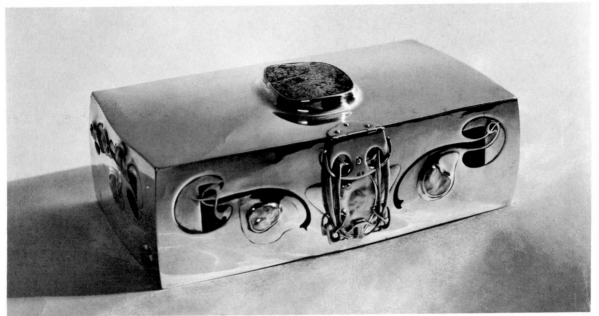

66
Arthur Silver
Silver candlesticks, 1906–7.

67
Arthur Dixon
Coffee jugs in copper-covered metal
made by Birmingham Guild of
Handicraft, about 1895.

68
Alexander Knox
Silver jewel box, about 1900.

69
Arthur Dixon (?)
Silver jug with ebony handle made
by Birmingham Guild of Handicraft,
1898–9.

70
W. A. S. Benson
Silver-plated coffee and tea set, made
between 1895 and 1910.

71
Lewis F. Day
'Strongstry' printed cotton made by
Turnbull & Stockdale, late 19th
Century.

72
W. A. S. Benson and Heywood Sumner
'The Charm of Orpheus' mahogany
and beechwood music cabinet, 1889.

73
Thomas Jeckyll
Wrought-iron sunflower, 1876.

74
F. Steiner & Co.
Roller-printed cotton, 1903.

72

73

74

3

The D.I.A.
1915-1928

ONE Sunday morning in 1914, late in the summer, two men sat talking, sanely and convivially, in a garden on Chiswick Mall. One was Harold Stabler, the silversmith: the other, the owner of the garden, was the artist Ernest Jackson. It could have been an Arts and Crafts discussion. As it happened, this was the beginning of the DIA.

The Design and Industries Association, which intended 'to instil a new spirit of design into British industry', was almost an extension, the phoenix from the ashes, of the English Arts and Crafts. By 1912, the Arts and Crafts triennial exhibition had become not only aesthetically timid but, at the same time, a financial disaster, and a group of younger craftsmen urged the elders to take action, suggesting that the Arts and Crafts should rent a shop in Bond Street. This suggestion was rejected. But the discontent continued: of the rebels, Harold Stabler was the busiest and noisiest.

The question had been raised repeatedly for decades: what future for the Arts and Crafts? What use to modern man? Nearly twenty years before, in 1895, *The Studio* had rather sacrilegiously commented that 'Mr Benson's lamps could be more influential on public taste than Mr Morris': meaning that the metalwork mass-produced by Benson was in a sense more valuable than the precious handwork, the tapestries, the bindings, the mosaic overmantels, which crowded exhibitions of the Arts and Crafts. Two years later, the campaign in *The Studio* was shriller: 'Is it,' they asked 'beyond the power of a body which numbers nearly every prominent architect, designer or craftsman to face the problem of beautiful yet economic furniture? Can they not institute a section devoted to designs with estimates of their cost attached? Is it unreasonable to suggest that they should offer diplomas of honour to those manufacturers who would submit cheap and comely furniture, well-decorated pottery for household use, dinner and tea services and the like, artistic but inexpensive table glass, low priced but satisfactory wall papers, cretonnes and carpets?'

Although this urgent challenge was never taken up—there were never any estimates of costs, still less diplomas for inexpensive tableware—there always were some members of the Arts and Crafts quite conscious of the need for a much broader-based improvement in design. In 1898, Ambrose Heal's first catalogue of Plain Oak Furniture appeared; in 1901, Lethaby, in Birmingham, urged sceptical industrialists to upgrade their design, insisting that 'A *quality* department in a *quality* business must bring reputation'—and usually profit. At this stage, much the strongest and most direct effect of Arts and Crafts on industry was obvious in printing: the private presses, Kelmscott, Doves, Pear Tree, Chiswick, Ashendene, and others, helped to transform standards in the printing trade in general. (Their influence on Germany, of course, was greater still). J. H. Mason's Imprint type, introduced in 1912 by the Monotype Corporation, was celebrated next year with the issue of the magazine *The Imprint*, in which Lethaby attributes the British renaissance in printing to Morris' and Walker's and Hornby's good example.

All this goes to show that within the Arts and Crafts there were people who could see a little further than their noses. Stabler and his colleagues objected to the fact that so much skill and energy was so much misdirected: everyday industrial products were appalling, while high-minded artist-craftsmen found it hard to sell their work. Stabler, Ambrose Heal and Cecil Brewer, Harry Peach, and other keen dissenters, made the journey to Cologne where the Werkbund Exhibition of 1914 showed what had been achieved by Muthesius' cajoling, by Government support for design, by the German campaign for public education 'by means of lectures, exhibitions, lantern slide displays, and other devices by which the attention of people of all classes could be arrested'. This had resulted in what then seemed to the British a modern spirit 'full of vitality and hope for the future', an absolute accept- ance of mechanization with its mass-production disciplines and anonymity. This spirit was summed up, in Cologne, by two ex- hibits, the model modern factory designed by Walter Gropius; the forward-looking glass house designed by Bruno Taut. The DIA forefathers travelled back with great excitement, exchanging notes and samples and proposals through the summer. Cologne 1914 had given them great visions: here, up to a point, lay Britain's future in design.

It was with these visions that Stabler and Jackson sat roughing out their campaign to begin the DIA, a British equivalent of the Deutscher Werkbund which had by then been active seven years. A provisional committee of seven was appointed. First meetings were held, not entirely inappropriately, close to William Morris' old workshop in Queen Square. The August declaration of war meant added urgency: for imports from Germany and Austria had ceased, and the Board of Trade, in order to drum up British substitutes, promoted exhibitions of 'enemy products' notable for cheapness and shoddiness, quite obviously untouched by the hand—or the machine—of Deutscher Werkbund.

The DIA, fast-acting in all the best traditions of Henry Cole's design group, wrote a memorandum to Sir Herbert Llewellyn Smith, Permanent Secretary to the Board of Trade, telling him the German exhibitions were one-sided: would he give the Werkbund a good showing? So he did. He lent several members of staff to the committee of the DIA, who had by then collected a small body of supporters, 'like-minded men and women'. They combed the shops of London, and ransacked their own homes, for well- designed German and Austrian products. Harry Peach, a stalwart member who always had his pockets and his rucksacks stuffed with samples, lent a number of exhibits, including a collection of finely-printed German books and pamphlets. The exhibits were amassed at Goldsmiths' Hall in London in March 1915. The exhibition acted, of course, as a recruiting ground for British DIA. A public meeting in the Great Eastern Hotel was followed, in May, by a more formal inaugural meeting in the Abercorn Rooms, with Lord Aberconway in the chair. At the first count, DIA members numbered 199. They were half of them, at least, Arts and Crafts men (the Images, the Anning-Bells, the Bensons) or architects inclined, in the way of Street or Ruskin, to believe in craftsmanship.

The executive committee met weekly, through the bombing and the anti-aircraft guns, far into the night, in Cecil Brewer's office in Queen Square. It was a period of strenuous activity and great good-fellowship. The shaping of the DIA, formation of branches in Edinburgh and Manchester (with more to follow), the drafting of the rules and agreement on a creed—consistent but 'not too inelastic'—all took time. Hamilton Temple Smith, the designer of furniture and member of this very first committee, later listed his eight colleagues. His comments in themselves, so stout-hearted and so tender, exactly show the spirit of the early DIA.

John Marshall, a Marshall and Snelgrove director, was 'a man of deep religious and artistic sensibility—a "spoiled priest" or perhaps a "spoiled artist". He it was who introduced (among other innovations) the bold pen-lettering for showcards, price tickets and advertisements, which soon ceased to be exclusive to Marshall's. But although he made his influence felt in the business world it was certainly not his spiritual home. When he volunteered for war I felt that he did so with a sense of escape; the news of his death in battle in September 1917 came as a bereavement but, somehow, hardly as a surprise'.

Cecil Brewer, the architect and cousin of Heal, 'combined an austere intellectual scepticism with a puckish sense of humour and a fastidious devotion to beauty. Already an ailing man when the DIA was first mooted, and while bearing his full share of work in a busy architectural practice, he yet found time to throw himself unstintingly into the task of forming and guiding the new Association. In so far as it can be said to have been built to any one man's design I would say it was his . . . by August 1918 he had worn himself out, leaving the DIA in his lasting debt'.

W. R. Lethaby, architect, designer, ex-Principal of the Central School, Professor of Design at the Royal College of Art, seemed 'the elder statesman—or, more aptly, perhaps the godfather of the DIA. He had been preaching the essence of its gospel for years, and had become an almost legendary figure during his own lifetime. He took little part in committee work, but his advice and pen were always at our service, and looking back, it seems to me that his philosophy of life was the touchstone by which we

78

continually tested the soundness of our own ideas'.

'Fred Burridge had succeeded Lethaby as Principal of the Central School of Arts and Crafts, and this fact threw into sharper emphasis the difference in their temperaments. Burridge was of the planning type, admirable at framing unambiguous rules, writing reports of meetings and drafting memoranda; and he had strong views about reforming the system of art education which were not shared by all his colleagues, least of all by Lethaby, who distrusted all systems, reformed or unreformed. But the DIA got the best that each man had to offer, and not the least of Burridge's contributions was a sort of Rabelaisian gusto.'

'Harold Stabler was not only a consummate artist and craftsman; he was also a man of wide vision and imaginative common sense. He came of Westmorland and yeoman stock and remained a countryman all his life; perhaps it was an inherited instinct for doing things in their right season that gave him his flair for producing the idea for a new activity at the psychological moment when it could be most effectively undertaken . . . it is only now that I find myself wondering, in retrospect, how many of our best ideas were *not* born in Stabler's fertile brain.'

'His friend Ernest Jackson was an artist first and last—observant, witty and detached: he brought a certain astringency into our discussions, which was invaluable in keeping enthusiasm within the bounds of what was practicable. How right he was! (and how I wished that he could sometimes have been wrong, bless him!).'

'If ever there was a man with fire in his belly that man was Harry Peach. His watchword was "quality work", and it governed all his varied activities. It was expressed in his "Dryad" products and in the numerous pamphlets he published upon handicrafts of all kinds. His first love had been printing, and I think it was never supplanted in his affections. He was an insatiable reader, and in spite of troublesome eyesight he seemed to find it possible to read every book on art and design, both English and foreign, as well as every magazine and pamphlet on those subjects. He travelled widely and kept himself abreast of all Continental developments in handicraft and industrial design. A sort of latter-day "Mr Valiant-for-Truth" he spent his life hitting out lustily and impersonally on all sides, and exchanging blow for blow without a trace of rancour. It might be said that Peach was the incarnation of the DIA militant, and certainly nobody influenced its course more strongly than he.'

And lastly there was Heal, shopkeeper par excellence, workshop-trained cabinet maker, the main link between the public and the artist-craftsmen, leading figure in improvements in design of furniture 'and of all that belongs to the furnishings of houses'. Ambrose Heal and his associates in Tottenham Court Road had made 'unswerving efforts to carry into everyday practice the DIA

principles of Right Design and Right Making'. Incidentally, the
DIA symbol was an Ambrose Heal design.

As Hamilton Temple Smith had pointed out, Lethaby's
philosophy of life was the touchstone for DIA ideas: Lethaby's
soundness and attention to detail, Lethaby's insistence that design
has no mystique. It is 'simply the arranging how work shall be
done'; it is 'just the appropriate shaping and finishing for the
thing required'; it is nothing but 'well doing what needs doing':
a work of art is 'first of all a well-made thing'. Lethaby's articles
in *Imprint*'s first issue expressed this in forthright culinary terms:
'Art is not a special sauce applied to ordinary cooking; it is the
cooking itself if it is good.' He chose his image nicely; it made its
proper impact; for DIA members were modest *bon viveurs*.

'The products of industrial design have their own excellence.'
wrote Lethaby for *Imprint*, in his essay *Art and Workmanship*; this
excellence is 'good in a secondary order, shapely, smooth, strong,
well-fitting, useful; in fact like a machine itself.' His view of industrial design as lesser craftsmanship—plain, without much
character, but none the worse for that—was not the German view:
there, machine-made products were whole-heartedly accepted,
judged on their own merits. But it summed up very fairly the
attitudes in Britain, the ideals of the DIA reformers, by and large.
These were moderate ideals: is it sound and is it sober? Is it
measured, is it modest; is it common sense? Are sideboards
appropriate to our belongings? Are drawers and cupboards of a
convenient size? Do washstands permit reasonable ablutions? In
short, has the product good reason-for-being? Stamp out seren-
dipity: 'For us,' cried the reformers, 'there is no content or peace
of mind till the community of plain honest folk may buy at
moderate prices commodities suited to their needs, and satisfying
their sense of beauty.' At DIA meetings, the members were incited
to clear the decks for action, for (mixing metaphors in the excitement of the moment) 'the tucket is sounding and somehow we
must go into action or strike our colours.'

The question remained: how? The DIA was friendless: the dyed-
in-the-wool craftsmen accused it of desertion; industry was
hostile, and the public mainly ignorant. How was it to propagate
the fairly novel theory of fitness for purpose in design for industry,
the 'essential prerequisite without which any design for an article
of common use was just silly'? How on earth was it to realize its
ideal of the DIA-indoctrinated business man in his pleasant office,
seeing to the proper housing of his workpeople in dignified
factories, pleasantly equipped canteens and recreation rooms?
For, as they remarked in 1916, the work on which the DIA reformers had embarked was ambitious and far-reaching: they took
in the total environment; they realized that few national industries
were outside their scope.

Practical as always, the DIA did not attempt to move heaven and earth immediately. It started fairly humbly, requesting loans or gifts of lantern slides 'illustrating good or (for contrast) bad design'. Members got together pamphlets, organized discussion meetings, lectured round the country, pushed and shoved and argued, brandishing the *DIA Journal* which in those days publicized 'fitness for purpose' with aplomb. Hoping that the public would eventually help the campaign by refusing to buy domestic articles which they could see to be ugly, the reformers set about exhibiting exemplary design. In 1915, the first DIA exhibition, 'Design and Workmanship in Printing', was held in the White-chapel Gallery, and later toured round Leicester, Leeds and Liverpool and Dublin, penetrating to South Africa. It showed great energy. The next year, in the Arts and Crafts Exhibition at Burlington House, the DIA—allocated one small room—showed pottery and textiles. Fabrics for West Africans, coloured very brightly to satisfy the natives, were acclaimed by *cognescenti*. On the other hand, the trade thought the exhibition dreadful: off-the-point and pretty tasteless. Who were these young crackpots to dictate to industry?

Stoke-on-Trent was in an uproar (an uproar which, in fact, lasted half-a-century and even now reverberates) because an outside body, and still worse a group from London, had dared to pass a verdict on the products of the potters. In Manchester, the textile manufacturers resisted the idea of selective exhibitions of design by totally ignoring the DIA's request for samples for display in the Manchester Art Gallery. The DIA had written to 60 textile firms, and only three replied. There was nothing for it, but for DIA contingents to travel round the factories to find their own ex-hibits. This was one of their great virtues: they were dogged and resilient. The trade would punch them viciously, and somehow they bounced back to carry on their programme: lecturing the Drapers Chamber of Trade on design and quality; encountering the potters on their own home ground in Stoke, a group 230 strong, to tell them that frankly, 'Expert craftsmanship does not go hand in hand with good design'. In 1919, the DIA intrepidly formed committees to persuade the manufacturers to produce articles in compliance with DIA aims. At the same time, a register of approved designs, 'efficiency-style' products, was brought into being. An earnest Exhibition of Household Things, designed of course 'primarily to serve their purpose', was held in 1920. Furniture and fittings, pottery and glass, hardware, brooms and brushes—the main preoccupations of the early DIA—were arrayed in eight neat rooms. A critique of every product, in the style of Henry Cole's *Journal of Design* of 1849, interspersed its praises with suggestions for improvement. Efficiency was everywhere apparent, and discretion.

'Art is indispensible in life, and therefore in education and work': this worthy pronouncement, so sweeping yet so moderate, sounds quite unmistakeably authentic DIA. In fact it occurs in a Ministry of Reconstruction pamphlet, *Art and Industry*. For once the war was over, there were signs that the campaign for improved design in industry was taken slightly seriously by the government and by industry itself. The Federation of British Industries formed its Industrial Art Committee in 1920: the Chairman was Charles Tennyson; the aim, which was well-meaning if vague, was 'to consider the question of industrial art in this country'. In effect, this at first meant attempting to bring the training at the Royal College of Art into line with industrial requirements. The deficiencies noted by the Commissioners in 1911—including lack of training in design for mass-production—which led them to contemplate the closure of the College, were nine or ten years later just as terrible, or worse.

Again in 1920, another institution for promotion of design, with Treasury support, began a new campaign, full of wishful thinking, to create a market for industrial designers. The British Institute of Industrial Art had, in fact, been in the air since 1914, when the Board of Trade and the Board of Education had combined to consider and approve the scheme. The war had postponed it. But in 1920 the Institute opened in a flurry of activity: a gallery in Knightsbridge was permanently occupied by Institute industrial art and handicrafts, while three temporary displays of modern products were held at the Victoria and Albert Museum. Clough Williams-Ellis, reviewing an Institute exhibition in *The Spectator*, pointed out how closely its standards and intentions resembled those of the DIA: 'Judging by the usual commercial products of British potteries, a missionary should certainly be sent into "Darkest Staffordshire" with the Institute's little exhibit of well designed and unpretentious chinaware.' The DIA approved of the Institute's Bureau of Information, under Major Longden; for a while they worked together, and perhaps, had all gone well, a national council for design might have emerged. But this is not what happened. With the slump, the public money granted to the Institute was soon withdrawn again, and although private subscriptions financed desultory activities, mainly exhibitions and design tours through the 'twenties, these were not in general a force to be reckoned with. The DIA was virtually on its own again.

It has to be remembered that the DIA was still very small, for all its energy, acutely short of money. Membership in 1916 was 292; it was only 602 by 1928. The mood of early meetings can be gathered from the General Discussion, reported in the *Journal* for 1918, on 'Memorandum to Ministry of Reconstruction and Proposed Memoranda to Government Departments on The State as Buyer.

'Mr Peach considered the Food posters particularly bad, but Mr Bayes defended the frieze of silhouettes at the recent War Exhibition at Burlington House as decorative and inspiring.'

'Mr Brewer said that though the things mentioned might be bad, the chief sins were to be found in the Government buildings; the Post Offices were glaring examples of inefficiency and discomfort.'

The chairman seems to have ended the discussion with the typical comment that the DIA must not be too drastic in its condemnation. For although the DIA connections with Morris and the Arts and Crafts were obvious, its methods were now closer to the Cole group: its discretion, its businesslike committees, its lucid memoranda. Instead of jars of ale, it drank tea in the Kardomah; instead of Gatti's suppers, it ate luncheon in the Kenilworth (2s 3d per person, gratuity included). A lot of the romance of the Arts and Crafts was over; the DIA had settled for a life of common sense, urging its designers to talk man-to-man to industry: in the interests of appeasement, never mention Art. Their founders, they insisted, 'were not dreamers in Jaeger sweaters, with blue eyes fixed on supra-mundane peaks'. Not at all: they were ordinary men with ordinary needs and ordinary talents, who practised what they preached.

Little by little, saner and saner, the DIA built up its membership and influence. It did its level best to break the vicious circle (bemoaned by Owen Jones and still as bad as ever) of maker-seller-buyer. The DIA could argue for reform from a position of relative authority; for now, for the first time, the reformers were themselves manufacturers and shopkeepers. They spoke with some experience, and were not shouted down. Manufacturers important in the movement in the 'twenties were Harry Peach, maker of Dryad cane and metalware; John Adams of Carter, Stabler, Adams, the Poole potters; in textiles, Frank Warner, James Morton of Morton Sundour and William Foxton of Foxton's; in printing, Harold Curwen of the Curwen Press and Francis Meynell, founder of the Nonesuch Press in 1923. (Meynell with Stanley Morison and Oliver Simon later formed the Double Crown Club, improving the standards of design in trade publishing, dining and discussing: a club within a club.) In furniture, Gordon Russell of Broadway—as the *DIA Journal* for 1927 commented—was 'carrying on, in both furniture and metalwork, the tradition of the greatest designer and maker of recent times, the late Ernest Gimson, whose modest retiring life in the Cotswolds made him neglected by his contemporaries, but whose influence has been felt on German and Austrian design and is beginning to be felt here'.

The most enterprising shopkeepers were Ambrose Heal in London and Crofton Gane in Bristol, a DIA convert of near-religious ardour. The most vital public servant, without doubt, was good Frank Pick, a DIA enthusiast of quite a different breed, a sober meticulous qualified solicitor who went into the railways and became a chief administrator, first of the London Underground

Railway and later the London Passenger Transport Board. Pick, from a conventionally cultured education, with a working knowledge of international art, before the DIA was born, commissioned Ernest Jackson and others to design him some posters for the Underground. He was one of the first 199 DIA members. As he advanced in status, he punctiliously turned the Underground (and later London Transport) into a travelling exhibition of design, commissioning new buildings, new posters right and left, new maps, a new typeface designed by Edward Johnstone for Underground publications and notices, a series of wall-tiles for stations from Stabler. In his range of influence, and his love for detail, Frank Pick was most important: his actions carried weight. Like Henry Cole before him, he was part of the establishment; he belonged to the Reform Club, he was known, he knew the ropes. His great respectability gave prestige, which was much needed, to the DIA campaign for improved standards of design. With support from Raymond Unwin (the town planner), Charles Tennyson (Deputy Director of the FBI), Sir Frank Warner (textile-magnate and Board of Trade Advisor, Vice-Chairman of the Empire Flax-Growing Commission), and Sir Lawrence Weaver (London Press Exchange director, an ebullient protagonist for DIA ideas), Frank Pick gave the DIA considerable substance. And, judging from events before and since, authority seems to be essential for progress in design.

The Cole Group had been statesmanlike and literate. The Arts and Crafts and Morris in particular were speechmakers and writers; the Glasgow School was not (which is probably one reason why Mackintosh and Walton were so badly underrated: they never had their say). The DIA was lucky that its speakers and its writers were professionally lucid, with amazing staying-power. The most vocal propagandists were Clough Williams-Ellis, the architect and author, who was in from the beginning; Noel Carrington, the publisher and editor of most of the DIA publications; John Gloag, fiery critic of design, who had been initiated at a DIA meeting in 1924 by designer Alfred Read, and who saw the light so strongly that he preached, just two years later: 'The "something safe to sell" spirit, as dangerously stupid and unconstructive as the red-hot air of communism, is the great enemy of industrial design.'

Efficiency-style had not quite superseded the missionary zeal, the old tub-thumping fervour. They somehow co-existed in the DIA in those days, when meetings, according to Carrington, were 'like a conventicle of some primitive sect'. The heathen manufacturer had still to be converted; the tucket was still sounding, the decks were still being cleared. The DIA was actively persuading its adherents to dedicate their lives to the cause of good design. Among them was John Waterer, designer of luggage, who after the first war adapted the slide-fastener (the 'zipper') from military to civilian use, and developed the whole concept of lightweight bags and cases, in new shapes and new colours. He was an enthusiast for art and woodwork and natural materials, and music was his heaven; he was also a technician, with practical knowledge of manufacturing. 'About this time,' he wrote, 'I became a member of the Design and Industries Association which I found to be imbued with the same spirit as myself. To my contacts with inspired, far-sighted manufacturers, shopkeepers and idealists, I owe much.'

At this stage, what exactly did the DIA approve of? What did the idealists, then and there, find tolerable? In the *Year Book* 1923–24, Edward Harland & Sons, of North Parade, Bradford, advertised 'Foxton fabrics, Poole pottery, Lygon stools, Dryad cane and metalwork, Rowley wood pictures. Simple furniture, soundly designed and well made of excellent materials'. They knew their readership. For this seems an accurate measure of average DIA taste in the twenties, which glorified plainness and stoutness and trueness, and loathed the pretentious, the lush and the sham. DIA idealists liked Heal's straightforward furniture, 'properly planned and thoroughly useful': his clean cottage cupboards, his bright painted chests, his comely elm dressers, his weathered oak tables. They liked Gordon Russell's sturdy Cotswold-craftsman products; they much admired the hand-block-printed fabrics of Miss Barron. Whitefriars glass and Blue Moorcroft Pottery and Cornish Ware were endlessly in favour, and Wedgwood's 'Honey Buff' underwent a Heal's revival, and was fervently promoted as setting 'standards of good taste'. By way of Crittalls' windows ('art and commerce come together'), Lanchester cars, the Rolls Royce, the Bristol plane, the largest accolade was given to the Underground which was—not surprisingly—'perhaps the outstanding example of Fitness for Purpose on a vast scale'.

DIA approval was virtuous and certain; it had the stamp of Stabler and his yeoman stock from Westmorland, and Peach, the cultured rambler in thick shoes with ruddy face. The DIA in practice was more countrified than mechanized; its standards were consistent and unadventurous. If DIA approval was wholesome and predictable, DIA distaste was equally hard-set. The DIA did not, on the whole, like coon music; 'barbarous patterns'; the ballet from Russia; the Omega workshop where, from 1913, Roger Fry, Duncan Grant and Vanessa Bell tried vaguely to make everyday products in a new and better way. In much the same spirit as the Arts and Crafts resistance to art nouveau, the 'Spooky School' and Continental Werkbunds, the DIA held out against exoticism, strangeness and mechanization carried to extremes. Developments at Weimar, where Gropius had founded the Bauhaus in 1919, made no impression; events in Scandinavia, the pottery and glass in Sweden, and Kaare Klint and his Copenhagen furniture, were noticed and admired but not assimilated; the Paris exhibition of 1925, with its international jazziness and cubism and fireworks, left the DIA quite cold. The DIA reformers were intent upon their target, their British clubman's vision of national improvement: looking straight ahead and preparing for the day 'when not 100 but 1000 members sit down to Dinner in a DIA hall with DIA service and furniture'.

The obvious result was that for about a decade the international modern movement did not come to Britain. In 1927, when the DIA assembled a country-craft display for the Leipzig exhibition, this was all too obvious. Even Harry Peach, who chose it, had a hard job to defend it:

'It is not very exciting as against what the modern schools abroad may offer, but it is something English, and like all English things, sane, good, with fine individual work which will hold its own against anything the others may produce.'

Minnie McLeish, who went to Leipzig, was much sharper: 'Broadly speaking, we do not understand this modern movement in design, and do not like it.'

For the moment, that was that. But here and there designers, Alfred Read for instance, were starting to push forward. Paul Nash designed some fabrics, and Marion Dorn some rugs; a painter, Francis Bacon, designed pseudo-Bauhaus furniture. In the Cotswolds, Gordon Russell, the follower of Gimson and hero of the craftsmen, began to change his tune. In Oxford Street, a Russian, Serge Chermayeff, was preparing the kind of exhibition which had not been seen before.

84

84
Gordon Russell
Circular table in Cuban mahogany,
1925.

85
Gordon Russell
Wardrobe in cherry, 1925.

85

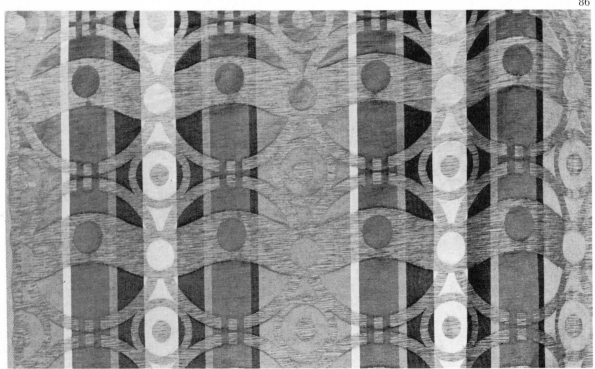

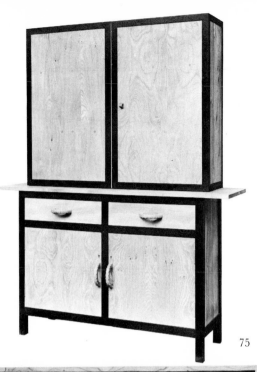

75 and 76
Ambrose Heal
Dresser in elm with black margins,
1914.

75

76

77

78

79

80

77
Ambrose Heal
Cottage furniture, 1918.

78
B. J. Fletcher (?)
Cane chair made by Dryad
Handicrafts, about 1920.

79
B. J. Fletcher (?)
Cane chair made by Dryad
Handicrafts, about 1920.

80
Gordon Russell
Cottage interior, 1928.

81
Gordon Russell
Cupboard in Cuban mahogany,
1925.

81

Gordon Russell
Chairs in English walnut, 1925.

Gordon Russell
Dressing table and mirror in English
oak, 1924.

88

89

86
Edward Bawden
Fireplace tiles made by Carter,
Stabler, Adams, about 1924.

87
Minnie McLeish
Jacquard woven cotton damask,
about 1925.

88
Claud Lovat Fraser
Printed fabric made by Foxton,
about 1920.

89
Gregory Brown
Printed fabric made by Foxton,
about 1920.

90
Minnie McLeish
Roller-printed cotton made by
Foxton, 1929.

90

91
Omar Ramsden and Alwyn Carr
Silver cup and cover, 1916.

92
Gordon Russell
Gilded metal fruit dish and biscuit
boxes, 1928.

93
Harold Stabler
Silver porringer and inkstand;
Wakely and Wheeler: Silver biscuit
bowl and cover; about 1925.

94
Harold Stabler
Silver tea set, 1928.

92

93

94

95

95
Truda Adams
Earthenware fruit plate made by
Carter, Stabler, Adams, 1923.

96
Ashstead Pottery
Breakfast set with oatmeal glaze,
about 1925.

97
William Moorcroft
Tea set with dark blue glaze,
1913–14.

98
John Adams
Early morning tea set made by
Carter, Stabler, Adams, about 1925.

96

97

98

4

The Architects 1928-1940

SERGIUS Ivan Chermayeff, a Harrovian, an impecunious Russian emigre of greatest glamour, who had trained in art in Paris, married quite improbably—though no doubt quite astutely—into Waring and Gillow, the traditional furnishers. The wedding was in 1928. That same December, Chermayeff had cleared space through Waring's Jacobean furniture to mount an exhibition of modern French and English decoration. The salesmen were astounded, and so no doubt were Waring and Gillow's clientele. But the *Architectural Review*, which was in those days the harbinger of Britain's modern movement, was ecstatic, exclaiming powerfully (if naively in the circumstances), 'it really is inspiring to find great decorating firms like Waring and Gillow, whose roots are firmly founded in tradition, proving their right to be counted amongst the important influences of the twentieth century, by boldly declaring their faith in a modern point of view'. Among the *cognoscenti*, there was general agreement that Mr Chermayeff had excelled himself.

What he had done was to decorate a bathroom in red and black with curtains of American cloth, and to furnish a modern English home without a sign of cosiness or hand-craft or the country-cottage dream. Serge Chermayeff—bringing chromium-plated metal-tubing furniture and unit storage systems and rough grey stippled walls—introduced the style the DIA had long resisted. The DIA most valiantly tried to change its mind. Still upholding sanity, but altering its concept of what constituted sanity and what in fact was madness, the *DIA Journal* praised Chermayeff's 'sane clear outlook unencumbered by ideas and traditions that no longer have any meaning for those who wish to live an honest twentieth-century existence'. With quite surprising eagerness, the DIA admitted—or commented, at least, that it could not be denied—that Serge Chermayeff's interpretation of up-to-date furniture differed very greatly from the attitudes and methods of those whose creed was the teaching of Gimson and Barnsley. In the *DIA Journal* John C. Rogers pleaded for a national conversion, an ultimate rejection of the Arts and Crafts philosophy, arguing

'. . . it only needs an effort on our part to lay aside insular prejudices, to admit that perhaps, after all, our progress is not what we imagined, and we shall acknowledge that here, in Oxford Street, is by far the best thing yet done in this country to re-establish the domestic crafts and to fire English designers with a new enthusiasm. In many ways, the right note is struck, and given the support it justly deserves, popular interest will increase, and in a few years good modern design will sweep the country.'

He was over-optimistic. The reform was not so sudden: good modern design has yet to sweep the country. And even with such prodding, the DIA moved slowly: the stalwart old regime to some extent went on. The LCC report, published 1930, on handicrafts in

elementary schools resounded with the DIA doctrine of Right-Living and Right-Making and the charitable down-to-earth ideas of Harry Peach. The DIA kept up its hopeful old activities: its little exhibitions in Bristol and in Birmingham; its lists of Sensible Presents for Christmas (from Gordon Russell's showroom, from the Workshops for the Blind); its advertisements for Jolly Rag Rugs (hearth size, 3 guineas) and the Legion Book printed by the Curwen Press; its earnestness and heartiness, its friendliness and cosiness, its frequent insularity, its members' tours abroad. The report in 1930 of the Stockholm expedition goes some way to showing the DIA unchanged, from Frank Pick's disappointment with Stockholm Town Hall—the brickwork, he found, was 'rough and ill-laid'—to a DIA lady's poem on returning, which for full-blown camaraderie is surely hard to beat:
'A's Association, our noble DIA,
B the Briny ocean, o'er which we sailed away,
C—commodious Cabin, a perfect little Ritz,
D the Dining-salon where our figures went to bits.'

And yet, despite the jollity, the DIA had obviously not been to Waring & Gillow's in vain. The feeling among architects, Chermayeff and the others, that design was not a 'Honey Buff' teapot or cane chair but concerned with life itself, with creating whole environments, made a certain difference to the DIA. This was the period of the Cautionary Guides to cities—St Albans, Oxford, Carlisle—for which DIA reporters, out on day-trips with their Leicas, brought back frightful evidence of national destructiveness. This was the era of the petrol station outcry, when the DIA published *The Village Pump: A Guide to Better Garages*, and even the *Daily Express* was moved to hold a competition for petrol pump design. The *DIA Year Book* 1929–30 was entirely given over to 'The Face of the Land'. The campaign had enlarged itself: the movement for reform was becoming more imaginative and more diffuse.

At last, though for the moment in superior circles only, in Hampstead, in the Arts Club, in the architectural schools, the British modern movement, with fervent sweeping statements and socialistic principles, was underway. Unlike the mid-Victorians—Cole and all his works—this movement did not stop at uniting art and industry. Improvements in industrial design, when they occurred, were only the by-products of the wider, more ambitious, architectural activity which aimed to rationalize man's whole environment, with hard-headed large-scale planning and logical use of the most modern industrial techniques. Far away from Ruskin and the cult of heart-felt building, remote from the DIA statement ten years earlier that standardization was the last thing it should father, the modern movement architects, standardizing avidly, with quips about the Arts and Crafts and simple-life rusticity, set about creating a reasonable Britain. To start with, they suggested that men must live in flats.

Young architects, trained at the Architectural Association or under Professor Charles Reilly at Liverpool, stood waiting for commissions. But such were the conditions in Britain then, in slump-time, that commissions rarely came. So instead of waiting idle, a few of these young architects filled up their days with design for household products, embarking on schemes so rash and so unprofitable that they would not otherwise have seen the light of day. For instance, Robert Goodden, in a very idle office behind Blackwell's bookshop in Oxford, decided to break the monotony and design and market some wallpaper, called 'Asterisk': a great *success d'estime*. Another jobless architect, Keith Murray, filled up time, inspired by the Swedish exhibition in London, designing modern glassware and later on some pottery: Stevens & Williams and Wedgwood took him on. Keith Murray, who was virtually the first freelance designer for industry since Dresser, delighted the converted with his smooth thick useful glassware in smoke violet and green, his sensitive cut crystal, his matt-green Wedgwood bookends and tobacco jars, his plain good modern silver for Mappin & Webb. Pearl Adam wrote an article of praise in *The Observer*; Herbert Read picked out some beer-mugs in matt-straw glaze, by Wedgwood, as 'better than anything else in modern ceramics'. But in spite of all the glory, one-man shows at the Medici and displays from Lady Colefax, Keith Murray designed mainly to earn money to survive. He recollected eating with enormous gratitude a 6d lunch at an ABC cafe: a roll and butter 2d, fish and chips 4d, and a glass of water which, of course, was free.

It was partly economics and partly architecture which prompted Gordon Russell to change his course from craft-made, finely-detailed furniture to plainer mass-production. His younger brother Richard returned from four years training at the Architectural Association with the fashionable concept of bare, functional design for mechanized production and the broader social view of the architect's involvement with the whole environment. He altered the outlook in the Cotswolds quite considerably. Gordon Russell, in his autobiography, acknowledges the definite effect of Dick's return to Broadway: 'it gave us a link with architects and taught us to think in terms of rooms rather than individual pieces'. This was the position at Gordon Russell Limited, in theory wholly modern, in practice half-and-half, when the Wall Street crash removed a good proportion of the market for elaborate craft-furniture and expensive good antiques which the Russells had been selling to prosperous Americans. *Faute de mieux*, yet not un-happily, the Russells concentrated on lower-price furniture for serial production and evolved some most remarkable designs for Murphy Radio. These cabinets, machine-made, economic, yet presentable, were models of British design for a decade.

For the British were in many ways becoming more receptive. At last, advanced designers had taken to machinery. At last, the many goings-on abroad were not so suspect. Substantial foreign influence was suddenly apparent: influence from Denmark, where from 1927 the architects and craftsmen worked together to produce immaculate furniture, elegant and sensible; influence from Finland, where round 1929 Alvar Aalto' designed furniture in laminated plywood (imported by Geoffrey Boumphrey of Finmar and by Findlater in Edinburgh, this soon became the rage at Fortnum & Mason, where the stools cost 7s.) Most of all, design in Sweden, its commonsense and modesty with bursts of great inventiveness in pottery and glass, affected Britain strongly when the Stockholm Exhibition and the London Exhibition of Swedish Art were on. The *Architectural Review* in 1930 gave over a whole issue to design in Sweden, and used Stockholm ammunition in its skirmishings with Harrods: if only Swedish standards were more evident in Knightsbridge, 'what a lovely shop Harrods would be'.

Temperamentally, the British and the Scandinavians were—and, by and large, still are—very much in tune: the history of design is one of constant interaction, backwards and forwards across the North Sea. But contact with the central modern movement in Europe, which was more extreme and tougher, was much harder to effect. In 1929, Jack Pritchard made a start by commissioning Le Corbusier to design—unlikely as it seems—an exhibition stand at the Building Trades Exhibition at Olympia for Venesta. Jack Pritchard, 'Plywood Pritchard', a young Venesta manager, an engineer-economist from Cambridge with great visions and a fair degree of impudence, worked hard to build up contacts with Gropius and the Bauhaus, the school which Gropius founded 'to exert a revitalizing influence on design' by providing 'a thorough practical, manual training in workshop activity engaged in production, coupled with'—most important—'a sound theoretical instruction in the laws of design'. In 1931, though Gropius had then left it, Jack Pritchard visited the Bauhaus in Dessau with Chermayeff and Wells Coates: the experience greatly moved him. Then Bauhaus work and attitudes quite soon infected England; wrote designer Clive Latimer, 'It was a revelation: here were logic and order, but also adventure'; progressive lighting companies soon turned out Bauhaus fittings; Gropius became a kind of household word. 'So great was our enthusiasm.' Robert Best, of Best & Lloyd and the DIA in Birmingham, wrote with admiration, 'that this name was even introduced into a DIA charade.' The DIA congenially acted out GROW PIOUS.

These were the elements which somehow came together in a good strong exhibition at Dorland Hall in London. It was 1933; the year that Wells Coates founded the MARS Group (for Modern Architectural Research); the year Berthold Lubetkin formed the

Tecton Group of architects and built the Highpoint Flats and rehoused the Zoo's gorillas. All this was important. For the Dorland Hall display was designed 'to give expression to a new type of civilization'. It was the result of a Board of Trade Committee on Art and Education under Lord Gorell: the 1932 report concluded (much as Peel had done a century before) that in order to raise national design standards, the citizen must be made design-conscious; he must be shown what constitutes a good design. The Report had strongly emphasized the need for exhibitions ('EXHIBITIONS mania', John Betjeman had called it) and Lord Gorell, the next year, wrote the foreword to the catalogue of the exhibition at Dorland Hall, which was privately sponsored and involved the DIA. With something of Prince Albert's paternal optimism and Gottfried Semper's theory that seeing is believing, Lord Gorell explained the exhibition was attempting to show the British public the best examples of the new industrial art.

What the public saw was a Minimum Flat, a Unit House, a large stone wall incised by Eric Gill with a joyful, frank and lustful scene of men and maidens, which the railway hotel in a northern seaside town had recently rejected, but which suited Dorland Hall. The mood there was permissive. The architect in charge, Oliver Hill, had given a free hand, in their individual sections, to Wells Coates, Serge Chermayeff and Raymond McGrath, and even the *Architectural Review* sounded a little overwhelmed by the results: both by the younger architects' talents and by the progress made by manufacturers, by Heal's and Gordon Russell, Carter Stabler Adams, Wedgwood, Dryad, Foxton and the Curwen Press which was showing wallpapers designed by Edward Bawden. The citizen, apparently, was pleasantly surprised. Bearing out the Gorell argument that selective exhibitions would improve the public powers of discrimination, a certain Mr Broadley (who afterwards wrote in to tell the DIA) went straight home to the suburbs to tour his local shops. He was quite surprised to find no Bawden papers there. 'I was saddened to discover,' he wrote glumly, 'that in hardly a single article displayed in any shop was there a trace of the Dorland House spirit.'

Remote as it might seem in the suburbs and the provinces, the British modern movement by then had spread just slightly. It had reached the Prince of Wales who himself designed a reading lamp for Easiwork, and rather in the manner of Prince Albert, maintained, 'There is always scope for new ideas, provided that the motto "Fitness for purpose" is born in mind, and no wildly exaggerated style is induced merely in order to cause a sensation.' This truly British sentiment was very often quoted. 'Design in Modern Life' had also reached the BBC which, in 1933, devoted programme after programme to the subject: Gordon Russell on 'The Living Room and Furniture', Francis Meynell on 'The Printed Word', A. B. Read on 'Light', Frank Pick on 'The

Street', Wells Coates on 'Dwellings', Elizabeth M. Denby on 'The Kitchen'. The list goes on and on. It went a bit too far for a listener in Southall who wrote to the *Radio Times*:

'I was relieved to find in your issue of the 23rd June that we had reached the last of the series of talks, "Design in Modern Life". We shall now be able to put the antimacassars back on the easy chairs and return our favourite vases to each end of the mantel-pieces, and enjoy them with clear conscience as before.'

Signed, Two Old Fogeys.

It was obvious in 1933 and 1934, in small ways and in great, that art and industry were approaching one another: if not with arms outstretched, at least with some politeness. Cadbury commissioned designs for chocolate boxes from nine quite famous painters, including Laura Knight. Harrods, maybe nettled by comparisons with Sweden, promoted new designs which Foley's China had commissioned from 27 artists. (Laura Knight was there again.) Jack Beddington, at Shell-Mex and BP, with all the zest of a mediaeval patron, paid artists to design a succession of Shell posters. A magazine called 'Shelf Appeal' was founded to publicize activity in packaging; featuring (for instance) the work of Reco Capey at Yardley's and Norbert Dutton at Metal Box, where a new Packaging Advisory Service was actually charging for the work of its designers. Designing was becoming a kind of a profession. In 1930, after plans and counter-plans, meetings in Chelsea studios, committees in The Cock Tavern in Fleet Street, the Society of Industrial Artists was founded to serve two purposes which, its manifesto insisted, were of particular importance at the time: 'It is hoped in the first place to establish the profession of the Designer on a sounder basis by forming a controlling authority to advance and protect the interests of all engaged in the production of Design for Industry, Publishing and Advertising. The second purpose is to assemble the resources of Design as a vital factor in British Industry and so to assist the advancement of British Trade, both at home and abroad.' Five years later, a number of designers had collected, with more sophistication than was usual in Britain, to form a design agency, Industrial Design Partnership. Both of these establishments, Society and Parnership, were coaxed into being by Milner Gray, a quintessential diplomat and capable designer, a clubman and a wit, a Cole group man reborn. One of his new partners was a much more unknown quantity, a Russian and an expert in display-work: Misha Black.

Round this time there was a sudden profusion of modernistic exhibitions: 'Modern Architecture' at the new RIBA, 'Modern Silverware' at Goldsmiths' Hall, 'Modern Living' at Whiteley's, another Dorland Hall which seems to have turned out a comparative fiasco. (Wells Coates, Serge Chermayeff, Ambrose Heal, Maxwell Fry, Jack Pritchard and other angry men wrote com-

plaining of frivolity and far too many fashionable 'amusing' ideas.)
Round this time, there was a sudden pile of books about design:
Geoffrey Holme's *Industrial Design and the Future*, John Gloag's
Design in Modern Life and *Industrial Art Explained*. Anthony Bertram, perhaps the most prolific design writer of the period, was
working on *Design in Daily Life*. Noel Carrington wrote books on
Design in the Home and *Design and a Changing Civilization*, and Herbert Read's *Art and Industry* was in its first edition. Milner Gray
later wrote respectfully of Read: 'he became the acknowledged
leader, mentor and guide of such young designers as myself. This
was in many ways the turning point for most of us in the clear
understanding of machine art, as we called it then'. Brian Grant,
at the time, was a great deal more impatient, with a tirade in the
Architectural Review:

'So much chatter and so very little apparent progress.
"Design and Industry", "Art and Industry", "Art in Industry",
"Industrial Art", "Commercial Art", "Design for Living",
"Architectural Design" AND SO ON.'

But as well as all the chatter, there were some true advances.
The DIA considered training for designers; the FBI thought hard
about industrial art management. In 1934, as a result of the Gorell
Report, a Council for Art and Industry was founded, with government support, to educate consumers in design appreciation, to
consider design training for industry and commerce, to encourage
good design 'especially in relation to manufacturers'. The Chairman of the Council was Frank Pick. Its first remarks were sober:
'a long time will be required to complete the task which the
Council has set itself'. And yet despite this caution, and despite
the fact that Government support was materially meagre, morale
was raised substantially. Pick's Council was official. As they felt
in 1850, things were happening at last.

It is not, in fact, far-fetched to compare the atmosphere in the
year which led up to the Great Exhibition to the general optimism
in 1934, the year before the Royal Society of Arts' exhibition
'British Art in Industry'. This was to be held at Burlington House,
whence the Arts and Crafts had been banished by fine artists.
This was intended to impress upon the British as well as the foreign
public the importance of beauty in the articles they purchased,
and to prove to manufacturers that British artists could supply
'original, attractive and technically suitable designs for the production of articles by mechanical means'. What more could people
ask? The exhibition sounded exactly what designers had been
waiting for for years. If the director John de la Valette, a small
and volatile Dutchman with a beard, raised a few small doubts,
or the selection committee of high Academicians (even Scott and
Lutyens) caused some slight anxiety, this was not admitted, or at
least it was not publicized. Everyone, serenely, was hoping for
the best.

Of course, 'British Art in Industry', just like the Great Exhibition, was a major disappointment to the British design purists. It was fanciful, extravagant, nothing to do with design for mass-production; it was totally unfunctional, completely inefficient, ladylike, directed towards Mayfair gracious living. Alas for Wells Coates and his Minimum Flat: the DIA, pride wounded, called it 'a grotesque failure'. With attacks more vitriolic than Owen Jones' or Redgrave's on the fateful Crystal Palace, the critics soon let fly. Herbert Read, with the excuse that the exhibition would do more harm than good unless it was demolished, went on to lash out at a bed by Betty Joel: 'It is made of beautiful Queensland walnut and maple twisted and contorted into a shape which I can only compare to a dislocated hip-bath.' Everywhere, the lack of form and functional efficiency very much distressed him; even Heal's, he said, had become 'modish and Mayfairish'; the elegant design in icing sugar by Mr Rex Whistler reduced him to silence; he was dreadfully unnerved. In the *New Statesman*, Raymond Mortimer insisted the exhibition was worse than none at all: 'the standards it sets are both costly and depraved'. Even Nikolaus Pevsner, a recent refugee who was treading rather carefully, not hurting people's feelings, admitted that the exhibition was embarrassing for anyone with foreign visitors in London: 'Yet,' he kindly commented, 'what such an exhibition might have been! It might have set up a milestone in the evolution of the Modern Movement in England.'

And, in a way, it did. For as the Crystal Palace had caused the Cole reformers to pause, take stock and start on a new constructive phase, this latest grotesque failure, which sent shudders down the spine of the British modern movement, was in the end quite useful. It stimulated action. For instance, J. M. Richards, then assistant editor of the *Architectural Review*, taken to task for his obstructionist attitude by Burlington House showmen and friends of de la Valette, wrote a long, important, thoughtful and of course defensive article, 'Towards a Rational Aesthetic'. This examined the character of modern industrial design, showing how it differed from handicraft design, arguing that it entails a changed vocabulary in conformity with a new unity of values. It insists upon simplicity and it emphasizes the impersonal. But standardization does not mean monotony: J. M. Richards was insistent on this point. He gave some illustrations of the rational aesthetic: a strong-room door showing 'the beauty of mechanical precision', laboratory glass, porcelain vessels by Doulton and Royal Worcester, an Imperial Airways monoplane, a Rolls Royce. He added a catalogue of everyday objects generally available: Anglepoise lamps, sports equipment from Fortnum & Mason, assorted baths and basins, kitchen cabinets and cookers, stoneware footwarmers, cane carpet-beaters, metal chairs and tools, 'everyday things in which a high standard of design has been unselfconsciously achieved'. Like Semper and Matthew Digby Wyatt, he had listed the ordinary products which do not strive for art.

What was most ironic was the way in which these everyday utilitarian objects became themselves a cult. Royal Doulton's Acid Jars were sold by Gordon Russell as objects of beauty to adorn the house, and Pevsner, in *Industrial Art in England*, published in 1937, states, 'At present they are amongst the best-sellers in most shops dealing in well-designed modern goods.' The same was true of Cornish Ware, which leads one to suspect that the peasant-life fixation was not so deeply buried. It was not wholly banished by the rational aesthetic, and in the post-war years it was to recur again.

Ironically, also, the drive for anonymity was largely the concern of a few dozen individuals who were quite outstanding, even manic, in their efforts. Shipowner Colin Anderson comes straight-away to mind. Though his family, the partners in the Orient Line, were hardly inartistic (Kenneth Anderson, a relative, had been the first Chairman of the DIA), their ideas on the design of the interiors of passenger ships seemed antiquated to him, in 1930. He made up his mind 'to meet the unexpressed need of the travelling public for surroundings that looked more in keeping with the practical achievements of modern engineer-constructors'. He was so persuasive, or so tiresomely insistent, that his elders handed the whole job on to him. Considering Wells Coates, Hill and Maufe and Serge Chermayeff, all of whom seemed then to him a little disconcerting, he chose as his designer Brian O'Rorke, a good outsider, a New Zealand architect with almost nothing to his name. Architect and client, who were then both twenty-eight, agreed extremely well; they were both of them determined to escape from damask patterns, floral sprigs and sprays, cut velvet, plush and chintz, and brass and bobbles and the vaguely Louis cutlery, traditional paraphernalia of ship decor. The 'Orion', delivered in 1935, and the 'Orcades', completed in 1937, set a startlingly new standard, both of overall design and of fixtures and fittings meticulously chosen. Colin Anderson wrote later:
'It would be hard to exaggerate the difficulties we met in persuading proud and successful industries that not a single object in their entire output was acceptable for a modern ship interior. We found ourselves having to discover designers capable of producing new designs for a wide range of products, from carpets to cutlery, the makers of which had no staff designers who understood what we were after.'
He employed, among others, E. McKnight Kauffer, Marion Dorn, Alastair Morton of Edinburgh Weavers; Brian O'Rorke designed the furniture and chairs, which were heavily tested by the Orient directors. Such courage and such competence, two Empire-building qualities diverted to the modern movement, stood it in good stead. The 'Orion' and 'Orcades'—like the BBC interiors of

1932 by McGrath, Coates and Chermayeff—altered the outlook of industry a little, just perceptibly broadening its mind.

Such as it was, the British modern movement in industrial design was wholly individual enterprise, involving a handful of impresarios, like Anderson and Pick (by then with London Transport); a few designers, a few manufacturers and, increasingly important, a few enlightened shopkeepers. The tinyness of movements for improvement was made obvious in Pevsner's *Industrial Art in England*, a survey carried out at Birmingham University, under Professor Sargent Florence. A conscientious plod round 149 manufacturers, 15 shops, 14 art schools, and 17 designers, artists and architects proved that things in general were extremely bad. 'When I say,' said Pevsner, 'that 90 per cent of British industrial art is devoid of any aesthetic merit I am not exaggerating . . . the aim of any campaign for better design can only be to reduce the percentage of objectionable goods, from 90 to 80 or perhaps 75 per cent.'

It might have been a losing battle. All the same, and in spite of Pevsner's words of warning, people thought it worth a try. Wherever there was progress, this progress could be traced back to just one person fighting the great tide, or as Gordon Russell put it, pushing a tank fanatically uphill. The designers pushing tanks were the Russells, Robert Goodden, Alfred Read, Keith Murray, Enid Marx, Marian Pepler (later Mrs R. D. Russell), Marion Dorn, Marianne Straub—in her 70 Welsh textile mills—Chermayeff, Coates, McGrath. As these were mainly architects, design for industry was a spare-time occupation in nine cases out of ten.

The manufacturers were, once again, the Russells; Jack Pritchard (Isokon); Gerald Summers (The Makers of Simple Furniture of Charlotte Street); Thomas Barlow of Barlow & Jones; Allan Walton Textiles; Sir James Morton of Edinburgh Weavers; the potter Susie Cooper; on the whole, Josiah Wedgwood; and three leading makers of light fittings, the Boissevains of Merchant Adventurers, Robert Best of Best & Lloyd and H. T. Young of Troughton & Young, who from the beginning was employing A. B. Read.

The shopkeepers included (from the old days) Ambrose Heal and more recently, his sons Anthony and Christopher, who joined the firm in 1934 and two years later was showing his designs, alongside Breuer, Fry, McGrath, Nicholson, O'Rorke and Jack Howe, in an exhibition entitled 'Seven Architects'. In Bristol, Crofton Gane, that very enterprising retailer, commissioned a pavilion for the Bristol Royal Show from Yorke and Marcel Breuer, late of the Bauhaus, by then practising in Britain. Gordon Russell's shop in Wigmore Street was, to all intents and purposes, an embryo Design Centre, and famous in its day. In Hitchin, Frank Austin and, in London, Ian Henderson and Alister Maynard were selling hand-made furniture of their own design. Peter Jones had an exclusive range of modern craftsman's furniture designed and made by R. Gordon Stark. George Breeze at Lewis's and Victor Sawtell at Bowman's, Camden Town, ran furniture departments of a popular modernity and a very reasonable standard of design. It was Sawtell who promoted the first unit furniture developed in Britain by Alpe Brothers of Banbury.

In Grosvenor Street, Cecilia Dunbar (now Lady Sempill) opened an exclusive shop with Athole Hay, Royal College of Art registrar. He sent her his students, and she placed their designs for china, glass, textiles and even carpets with co-operative firms. Four-fifths of the stock at Dunbar-Hay was specially made; in those days even Wedgwood would take on special orders. Eric Ravilious, who was retained by Dunbar-Hay, decorated Wedgwood urns and mugs with great inventiveness. and also designed glass, a dining-table and some chairs which were bought by the Victoria and Albert Museum.

In Bromley, Geoffrey Dunn, with the same enthusiasm but less rarified ambitions, joined his father's firm at the age of 23 and spent £10, illicitly, on Susie Cooper pottery which he then displayed, among the reproduction furniture, on hessian-covered cubes. It was all sold in three weeks. The Bromley modern movement went from strength to strength: by 1938, the shop was almost wholly modern. In 1938, Geoffrey Dunn and Crofton Gane and Gordon Russell, with the fine old British mixture of high ideals and *bonhomie*, had formed the Good Furniture Group. This was an association of retailers which collectively commissioned designs, had them manufactured and stocked them simultaneously: the simple aim, wrote Dunn, was 'to get some nice furniture designed and made and sold by a few real believers'. The most successful project was a dining suite: good furniture from Gordon Russell Limited.

Pleasant and straightforward, civilized and sensible, a reasonably idealistic, gentlemanly clique: the Good Furniture Group was a very true reflection of the British modern movement by 1938. In fact, the modern movement had come and almost gone again; the rational aesthetic had not really made much headway. Industrial design was still quite homespun in its attitudes, not so very far from the British Arts and Crafts: tolerant and gentle, unpretentious and careful, in friendly and predictable agreement with Frank Pick that national design should be 'modest and not too grandiose in scale . . . not too logical in form . . . a reasonable compromise between beauty and utility, neither overstressing beauty till it degenerates into ornament, nor overstressing utility until it becomes bare and hard'.

This is why Great Britain could not really stand the Bauhaus. Gropius' arrival, sponsored by Jack Pritchard, escaping from the Nazis in 1934, brought the British face-to-face with what had been a far-off theory. And on the whole they realized that it was not for them. It was too unnerving; it was too uncompromising; Gropius' belief that crafts and industry were opposites and handicrafts' sole function was industrial research, that handicrafts belonged in the factory laboratory, was a good deal too dogmatic for the British DIA. And the British DIA, in its turn, unnerved Gropius with its slowness and its politeness and extreme naivety. In Birmingham a member asked to see the Bauhaus timetable, thinking that it might be applied to the teaching at the Birmingham College of Arts and Crafts. Gropius was horrified: 'It would not tell you much,' he replied with deepest scorn, 'it was the *atmosphere*.' The difference of opinion, and simple lack of work, drove Gropius out of England: in partnership with Fry, he had only been commissioned to design one house, one college, and a few small oddments, a fire for Best & Lloyd and an aluminium waste-bin. Like Breuer and Moholy-Nagy, Eric Mendelsohn, Serge Chermayeff and Naum Gabo, Walter Gropius left Britain for America. He had been appointed Harvard Professor of Architecture. People said how sad they were, and even how surprised. Herbert Read and other mourners wrote a letter to *The Times* in a rather aggrieved tone:

'Professor Gropius has been resident in this country for the last three years, and it was the confident hope of many people that we were to have the benefit of his outstanding talents for many years to come. In this we have been disappointed.'

However, they gave Gropius a Trocadero dinner (25s a head, including wine) and settled back quite equably into the old routine.

Almost as a send-off to Gropius, and a sign of relief that the old order was unchanged, the British created some Royal Designers for Industry. Excited by the 1935 Exhibition of 'British Art in Industry' at Burlington House, the Royal Society of Arts had decided to decorate designers who consistently produced work of a high aesthetic standard, and set them on a level with the Royal Academicians. In 1936, ten Designers for Industry were formally appointed, and in 1937 the Home Office decreed that these Designers should be Royal. They were an odd collection: poster artists and typographers, decorators, old-time craftsmen, Eric Gill who hated factories, Keith Murray, Harold Stabler, aged Voysey—although Voysey loathed the modern movement, which he found unchristian.

The Faculty of Royal Designers for Industry—which still goes on, enlarged and a bit more level-headed—includes a little section for Honorary Members, distinguished industrial designers from abroad. Through the years, these foreign appointments have shown neatly the current allegiances of design in Britain. In 1939, for instance, before Alvar Aalto or Gropius was honoured, Raymond Loewy (USA) was received into the Faculty. This was an event of some significance. For it meant the recognition of the 'stylists' of America, the large expansive prophets of commercial design, Bel Geddes and van Doren, Dorwin Teague and Henry Dreyfuss who, like Loewy, had been spending the past decade in league with the great advertising agencies, promoting the idea that design is businesslike. An RDI for Loewy meant acceptance of the fact that design in Britain, too, was increasingly commercial: in Loewy's British office (with J. Beresford-Evans, Douglas Scott and F. C. Ashford), in Richard Lonsdale-Hands' thrusting new Design Unit, and the group which Norbert Dutton, Ronald Armstrong and Ronald Ingles had founded very recently, all leaving Metal Box. This regime meant rejection, or at least ruthless dilution of the DIA virtues and the old crusading zeal. As Milner Gray, in a later speech, expressed it:

'From the cosy gatherings of the converted and the high ideals of the highbrows of the 1920s, industrial design had come down to earth.'

But it did not stay there long. With the war, a time of fantasy, the businesslike designers, architects and art directors were hurried into uniform and set to work to hide the defences of the country as soon as they were built. The *Architectural Review* gave fine descriptions of the work of Her Majesty's Camouflage Corps in disguising the ubiquitous hexagonal pillboxes as tea-kiosks, bus stops, petrol stations, fair booths and public lavatories, as haystacks, road-menders' huts and even wood-piles. Wartime, for designers, was a kind of golden age in which almost unlimited money and labour were forthcoming to pursue the wildest fancies, masterpieces of inventiveness, from ivy-clad ruins to gypsy caravans, from cosy thatched toll-houses to resplendent Gothic lodge-gates. All this was perfect practice for the Festival of Britain, and helps greatly to explain the light fantastic atmosphere.

99

100

99
Marcel Breuer
Long chair in laminated birch made
by Isokon, 1936.

100
Gerald Summers
Chair in laminated birch made by
the Makers of Simple Furniture,
Charlotte Street, about 1934.

101
Gordon Russell
'Weston' dining furniture in oak,
1929.

102
R. D. Russell
'Thirty-Four' unit bedroom
furniture in oak, made by Gordon
Russell Furniture, 1934.

101

102

103

104

105

106

103
Alpe Brothers
Dining group including waxed oak furniture sold at Dunn's of Bromley, 1935.

104
Geoffrey Dunn
Bookcase and desk, with other furniture sold at Dunn's of Bromley, 1934.

105
Wells Coates
Radio cabinet in bakelite made by Ecko, 1934.

106
R. D. Russell
Radio cabinet made by Murphy in light walnut with dark stained sides, 1937.

107
R. D. Russell
Sideboard in Bombay rosewood with elm lines made by Gordon Russell Furniture, 1935.

107

108

109

108
Serge Chermayeff
Stacking chair for Broadcasting House, 1932.

109
Serge Chermayeff
Interior of flat at 42 Upper Brook Street, W.1., 1935.

110
Serge Chermayeff
Stacking chair for Broadcasting House, 1932.

111
Raymond McGrath
Balcony doors to Studio BB, Broadcasting House, 1932.

112
Raymond McGrath
Studio BB, Broadcasting House, 1932.

110

111   112

113

114

113
Maxwell Fry and Jack Howe
Living room from Heal's
'7 Architects Exhibition', 1936.

114
Walter Gropius
Waste-paper basket in perforated
aluminium sold by Gordon Russell
Ltd., 1937.

115
Brian O'Rorke
First-class lounge on Orient liner
Orion, 1935.

116
Brian O'Rorke
First-class café on Orient liner
Orion, 1935.

STONE

ENGRAVED DRAWINGS BY ERIC GILL STONE BY JENKINS AND SON

JADE
ED BY THE
N GALLERY

117
Design and Industries Association
Entrance vestibule, Dorland Hall
Exhibition, 1933.

118
Design and Industries Association
Dining room furniture in Portland
stone, Dorland Hall Exhibition,
1933.

119
London Transport
Bus shelter, 1939.

120
London Transport
Leicester Square Underground
Booking Hall, 1935.

121
London Transport
Staircase on LT-type bus, 1931.

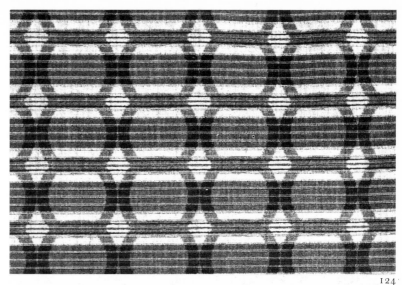

124

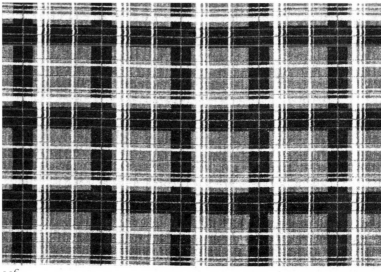

125

122
London Transport
Trolleybus, 1939.

123
London Transport
Tube train interior, 1938.

124, 125 and 126
Marion Dorn
Upholstery fabrics for London
Transport, 1939.

126

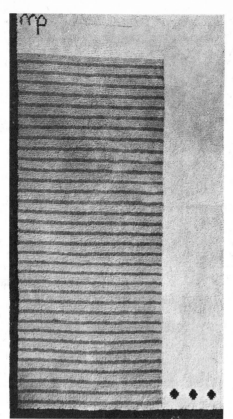

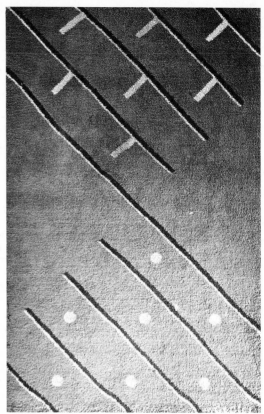

127

128

129

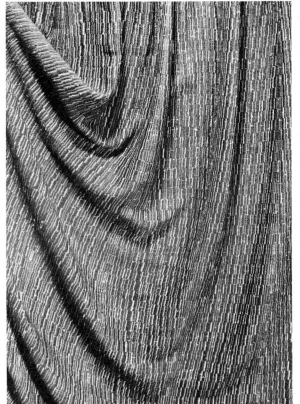

130

131

127
Marian Pepler
'Wood Ash' tufted rug, about 1933.

128
Marian Pepler
'45' tufted rug, about 1933.

129
Paul Nash
'Fugue' screen-printed linen, 1936.

130
Marianne Straub
Furnishing fabric, cotton and fibro,
made by Helios, 1939.

131
Duncan Grant
Hand-printed artificial silk made by
Allan Walton, 1932.

132
Duncan Grant
Screen-printed cotton satin made by
Allan Walton, 1938.

132

133

133
Keith Murray
Decanter and glasses made by
Stevens & Williams, about 1935.

134
Keith Murray
Earthenware beer mugs and jug
made by Wedgwood, 1935.

135
Keith Murray
Cocktail set and silver bowl made by
Mappin and Webb, 1935.

136
Keith Murray
Cocktail cups, matt white
earthenware with platinum bands,
made by Wedgwood, 1935.

137

138

139

137
Eric Ravilious
'Boat Race' bowl in earthenware
with transfer prints, made by
Wedgwood, 1938.

138
Susie Cooper
'Beechwood' hand-painted plate and
tea cup, 1937.

139
Joseph Bourne
Fireproof earthenware casseroles,
about 1935.

140

140
Eric Ravilious
'Garden Implements' mugs and jug
made by Wedgwood, late 1930s.

141
Milner Gray (three top designs) *and
Graham Sutherland*
Decoration for bone china for Foley
China, E. Brain & Co., 1935.

142

143

144

142
R. Y. Goodden
Small pressed glass bowl made by
Chance Brothers, 1934.

143
R. Y. Goodden
Pressed glass powder bowl made by
Chance Brothers, 1935.

144
Graham Sutherland
Decorated glassware made by
Stuart Crystal, 1935.

145
Milner Gray
Silver porringer and spoon for
D. & J. Wellby, 1946.

146
Milner Gray
Bottle and label for a ginger barley
wine for Clark's Creamed Barley,
1937.

147
Milner Gray
Stoneware wine jar and label made
for Mid-Sussex Canning and
Preserving Co., 1935.

145

146   147

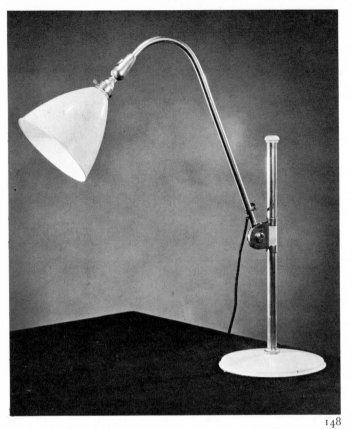

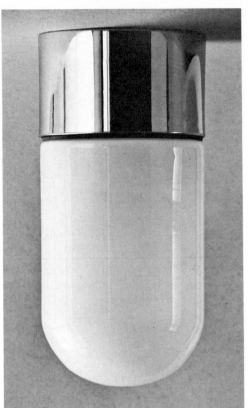

148

149

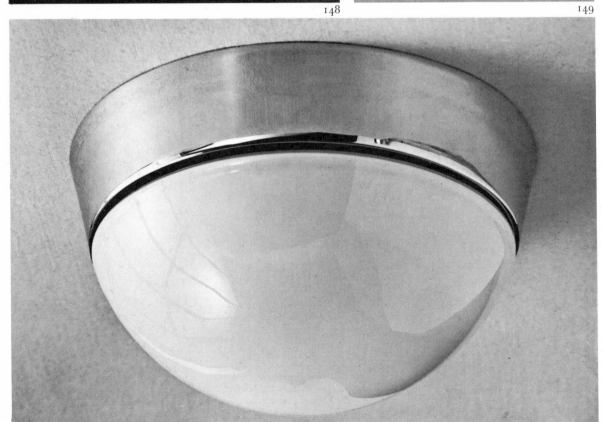

150

148
Best and Lloyd
'Bestlite' reading lamp, 1930.

149
A. B. Read
'Ultralux' light fitting made by
Troughton and Young, about 1930.

150
A. B. Read
'Ultralux' light fitting made by
Troughton and Young, about 1930.

151
E. S. Corner
Escor 7-seater car, late 1930s.

152
John Waterer
'Vogue' lightweight luggage in
cowhide made by S. Clarke, about
1937.

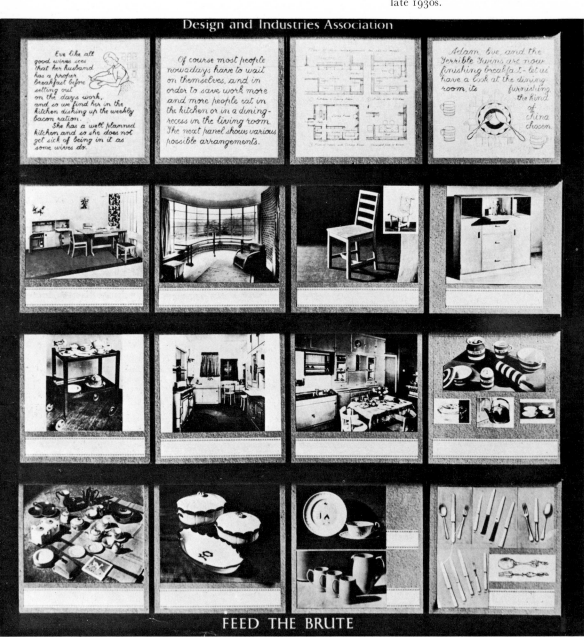

153

5
The Council of Industrial Design 1940-1951

IT was 1942 when Gordon Russell's country war-work, stone-carving, looking after bees and keeping pigs, was for ever interrupted: Hugh Dalton wrote requesting him to sit on a Utility furniture committee. Although he did not realize it, this sudden translation from the Cotswolds to an office at the Board of Trade would have long repercussions, both for him and for the progress of industrial design. Under Gordon Russell a new reform began, related to the earlier attempts, yet very different in its scope, organization and its government support. Government furniture was more or less a godsend. 'I felt,' wrote Gordon Russell, 'that to raise the whole standard of furniture for the mass of the people was not a bad war-job . . . Wartime conditions had given us a unique opportunity of making an advance.'

There had been an ultimatum: from November 1942 the only furniture to be manufactured in Britain was Utility. Hundreds of small firms throughout the country, with all kinds of methods of production, would then make a single range of furniture under the control of a central small committee. Dalton had selected this committee with finesse. Counteracting Russell there was Lebus, mass-producer; balancing John Gloag and Elizabeth Denby there was Mrs Wimborne and the Reverend Jenkinson, the voice of the consumer and presumably the church; there was trade and there was public, there were housing men and retailers, a beautiful cross-section of the national state of taste. Gordon Russell travelled up to London for the first of the meetings; with the deadline in November, it was by then July.

The President of the Board of Trade, Hugh Dalton, came in to his committee with some rules and regulations: Utility furniture must be soundly made of the best possible materials; it must be pleasant in design; and it must also be produced extremely quickly, to prevent a national famine. He departed very briskly, leaving the committee with a long list of materials, everything they needed, from plywood and blockboard to steel and paint and textiles, which were either unobtainable or else extremely scarce. He also left them puzzling over what he meant by pleasant: in common usage, 'pleasant' furniture was Jacobean. But—first round to Gordon Russell—as he wrote, 'the basic rightness of contemporary design won the day'. There was not enough timber for bulbous legs or labour for even the most rudimentary carving. Mr Clinch and Mr Cutler, stout designers from High Wycombe, evolved for new Utility a modern Gimson style, which the *Architectural Review* attacked as retrograde (too true to the DIA, too fit and far too honest), and the trade on the whole condemned as too advanced. Gordon Russell was contented to see shots from both directions: 'it looked', he recollected 'as if we were about right. I am never for forcing the pace, a limited advance and then consolidation is a sound principle, both in war and peace'. This calm, most British, attitude was usefully disarming in peacetime at the

Council of Industrial Design.

Meanwhile, Gordon Russell wrote a report—as Cole would have done—to his chairman, Charles Tennyson, whose work for the FBI Committee on design and the wartime Central Institute had proved him sympathetic. Gordon Russell suggested a programme of research into furniture design, for wartime use and for the future; he recommended a panel of not more than six designers with a knowledgeable chairman, probably an architect, who would be given a seat on the Utility Furniture Committee to speak for the designers. To Gordon Russell's suprise, the President asked him to take on the Chairman's job himself and set about appointing the members of the Panel. This, in fact, was none too easy for the best of the designers were abroad or inaccessible. Eden Minns, who had agreed to join, was without warning called up into the Navy and sent out to the Pacific; Dick Russell was in Admiralty camouflage and rapidly transported off to India and Burma; Ian Henderson, who thought the Foreign Office might have loaned him, found the scheme impracticable. But Jacques Groag, a Czech refugee, an architect and former pupil and assistant of Adolf Loos, was a most imaginative, vociferous addition to the Panel, counteracting the prosaic, though most worthy, Clinch and Cutler. Utility Furniture was ready to progress.

Installed at the Board of Trade, without a desk and carpet (for no one knew their status), working in a room furnished mainly with their own discarded prototypes, regarded with tender solicitude by permanent officials, even pointed out by the most venerable members as proof of what the country will resort to in a war, Gordon Russell and his Furniture Design Panel embarked on a programme of design research in two directions: into temporary furniture to cope with devastation if the bombing should intensify; and into long-term planning for furniture for peacetime, when supplies of plywood, blockboard, cellulose and steel would be once again at hand. With a doggedness that should have made a scene for Evelyn Waugh, the Design Panel investigated consumer needs, talking to the Board of Trade, talking to the Housing Centre, finding out how people live and how they use their furniture. Gordon Russell went to Toynbee Hall to meet the Peckham residents. One of them kept nothing but her knitting in a sideboard. Another complained fiercely that a piece of bombed-out glass had gone through the end of her Utility Furniture: 'You can't call that a piece of furniture,' she said. A black-eyed, hawk-nosed woman got up and asked the Panel whether Utility furniture would stand up to it. Stand up to what? She beat around the bush, then admitted that the furniture in question was the bed.

There were worries. Plain Utility shapes were sometimes decorated, under the counter, with the most appalling carving. The Committee, trying to meet the public need for a bit of wartime gaiety, discussed the possibility of a patterned range, taking up their problem with the sculptor Henry Moore whose interest in abstract patterns was well known. But Moore, though very willing, had nothing to contribute. Utility furniture remained plain solid modern, with a clodhopping character, until the war was ending, and the mass-production woodworking firms employed on aircraft could return to furniture. The Panel then developed a range of smaller, lighter, more sophisticated and more graceful furniture. To a chorus of approval from even the *Architectural Review*, the latest Utility range was unveiled on VE Day at a CEMA exhibition in the National Gallery: 'Some pieces such as a mahogany sideboard and some easy chairs are very attractive indeed.'

Gordon Russell's war-work had substantial influence, after an initial frenzied contrary reaction to Utility design, on the general run of furniture: within another fifteen years, plain Gimson-style was fashion. Gordon Russell set the scene for the general reformation of design in post-war Britain soberly, humanely, subtly, with a good use of committees, with a constant view to 'solid, not spectacular, progress'. From now on, and for many years, this was the general aim of the leaders of the movement. Designers emerged, like Gordon Russell, from their war-work with a new determination and realistic aims. Besides the Camouflagers, who were legion, there were others: Jack Howe, for example, had been drawing office manager for Royal Ordnance factories; Douglas Scott and Richard Huws had worked with aircraft firms; Jack Proctor had been trained in basic engineering, at the government's expense; Robert Cantor had learned about industrial design from working on radar instruments; and Ronald Dickens, at the request of the Fire Service Chief, and using the Hendon District Surveyor's office, had designed a blast-proof control shelter and received the personal thanks of Herbert Morrison. Kenneth Holmes, the Art School Principal at Leicester, was responsible for refurnishing the City General Hospital, organizing city-wide voluntary labour for the making of splints and urgent hospital equipment; plaster bandaging for Leicester and its environs was made, and sent out by the boxful, from the College of Art.

None of this was wartime wasted. In the Ministry of Information, Exhibitions Division, Milner Gray and Misha Black and Kenneth Bayes together made good use of their time. In the intervals of planning patriotic exhibitions, they evolved a new design group the size and scope of which had not been known in Britain, or this side of the Atlantic. As early as 1942, the aims and organization of Design Research Unit had been formulated by Milner Gray: in general,
'The purpose of the formation of a group such as is envisaged is to make available immediately a design service equipped to advise on all problems of design and to form a nucleus group which through contacts established during the war period with

specialist designers and experts in all appropriate fields, would be in a position at the end of the war to expand to undertake the wider services which may then be demanded of it.

'The final aim is to present a service so complete that it could undertake any design case which might confront the State, Municipal Authorities, Industry or Commerce.

'The scope of such a service would be so wide, within its sphere, that any description may seem to imply a limitation. But it is perhaps useful to remind ourselves of some of the fields of operation open to such an organization. All productions of industry necessary to the home life of the community and to the public services come properly within the purview of such a group. Every garment which we wear, every utensil that we use, every notice that we read, every service in transport and in our daily round of which we make use. Design for the banks, breweries, petrol, shipping and co-operative companies: design for Government printing, publicity and exhibitions: design for office, shop and warehouse: design for the lamp standard, the fire alarm, the letter-box, street name plates, traffic signs and traffic control box: design for the packing of products: design for kitchen, household and hotel equipment. Everything that is made is first designed.'

Although it seems impossible, an even vaster scheme for design was then afoot within the Board of Trade, involving Laurence Watkinson and Alan Hoskin, involving Francis Meynell (temporary adviser on Civilian Needs), involving Thomas Barlow (Director-General of Civilian Clothing) and, from time to time, involving Gordon Russell, at work among his prototypes along the corridor. The idea was a Council. Not a Council like Frank Pick's understaffed and undersubsidized and rather unconvincing, but a Central Design Council big enough and strong enough to raise the design standards in industry at large, with the ultimate purpose of improving British exports. The details were decided long before the war had ended. In 1943 Cecil Weir's Sub-Committee on Industrial Design and Art in Industry (set up by the Post-War Export Trade Committee of the Department of Overseas Trade) reported that since there *is* such a thing as recognizably good design, and since there *is not* a fundamental conflict between 'giving the public what it wants' and good design, then a Central Design Council, not directly responsible to a government department, should start work. In 1944, the Meynell-Hoskin Report (submitted to the Presidents of the Boards of Trade and Education) discussed ways and means of making art training more practical and useful for the 'post-war push', and recommended that the Central Design Council should be a grant-aided body, financed on the Board of Trade vote. This should all be discussed with the Ministry of Reconstruction, they said: and it was. And just as the FBI Industrial Art Committee was completing its own 'Proposals for a Central

Design Council and Industrial Design Centre', the Coalition
Government had moved ahead.

'Has the President of the Board of Trade,' asked John Dugdale in
Parliament on 19 December 1944, 'taken steps to encourage good
design in British industry?'

'Yes sir,' said Dr Hugh Dalton. 'I have appointed a Council of
Industrial Design to promote by all practicable means the
improvement of design in the products of British industry.'

With that assurance, the Government went on to consider
British Engines (Spare Parts) and Discharged Service Men
(Badge): the Prime Minister maintaining that no man's patriotism
could be challenged because he wore civilian clothes.

One has to remember the emotions of the period, the surging
hopefulness, the urge for great renewal, the feeling that the man
and the woman in the street deserved a better life, deserved improved design. All this comes pounding through the speech which
Dr Hugh Dalton made to his new Council in 1944:

'We must, therefore, make a sustained effort to improve design,
and to bring industry to recognize the importance of this task.
You have to arouse the interest of ordinary men and women . . .
If you succeed in your task, in a few years' time every side of our
daily life will be better for your work. Every kitchen will be an
easier place to work in; every home a pleasanter place to live in.
Men and women in millions will be in your debt, though they
may not know it; and not in Britain alone but all over the world.
. . . Industry itself will have much cause to thank you. Our export
trade, and our volume of business at home, will both be the greater
if our goods are planned and made, with skill and imagination,
to meet the user's real need, to give pleasure in the using.'

Listening, and taking note were the two dozen first members of
the Council, including Francis Meynell, Ernest Goodale, Charles
Tennyson, Josiah Wedgwood, Allan Walton, Gordon Russell (all
old aesthetic warriors). The Chairman was Sir Thomas Barlow.
The Director was S. C. Leslie, who came to the CoID from the
Home Office, where he was Principal Assistant Secretary. Though
hardly a DIA tub-thumper in his outlook, he was not inartistic.
He soon learned about design.

The Government had changed, as governments will change—
often spelling doom to small grant-aided bodies. But the Council of
Industrial Design, which was the offshoot of a coalition government, was blessedly immune, and in 1945, the election of Labour
brought an extra supporter for reformers of design. It brought
Sir Stafford Cripps, an eager weekend-carpenter, to replace Dr
Hugh Dalton at the Board of Trade. This was good for the Council
of Industrial Design, for Cripps (and Cripps' wife) had still more
heart in it than Dalton. Within twenty-four hours of his appointment, he was over at the CoID offices in Petty France telling the
Director to stage an exhibition: never mind about the money,

there would be a special grant.

With an extra £234,757; with much talk of turning swords into ploughshares and producing 'goods as suitable for peace time as were the weapons the country produced for the war', 'Britain Can Make It', a great exhibition—great for post-wartime—was rapidly planned. There had already been two excellent post-war design displays: the CEMA Exhibition 'Design in the Home' (by Milner Gray) and the substantial Exhibition of Wallpapers (displayed on Eric Brown and Stefan Buzas). But this new exhibition was to be much more ambitious. 'Britain Can Make It' was planned for 90,000 square feet of the Victoria and Albert Museum, which at the time was empty (it was also without windows: a minor difficulty which Cripps soon overcame by diverting London's next two months' entire supply of glass). It was meant 'to intensify the interest of manufacturers and distributors in industrial design, and their awareness of the desirability of rapid progress; to arouse greater interest in design in the minds of the general public, as consumers; and to stage a prestige advertisement, before the world, for British industry, industrial design and standards of display'. Cripps saw it as the first blossoming of British industry after the devastating effects of war.

This was all very well. But what was there to show? The *Architectural Review* was very nervous, suggesting that Cripps was rather overdoing things, pointing out:
'It is he who conceived the idea of the exhibition and insists on its early date. Council and manufacturers will have a tough job, with no materials yet to make new things, and no skilled labour, with plenty of designers still in the forces, with an understandable dislike to show the old 1938 things again, and an equally understandable dislike to show new designs not yet in production. What will be exhibited then? Prototypes, models, products available for export only? One feels unable even to guess, and yet one ardently wishes this test show the greatest possible international success.'

And a great success it was. Although most of the exhibits were in fact still unobtainable, although the exhibition was renamed by the public 'Britain Can't Have It', Cripps' wildest schemes were justified. It pleased a lot of people in many different ways. It was ideal for the *Architectural Review*, showing British products deprived of frills and furbelows by wartime stress and shortages, as close as they had ever been to rational aesthetics. (This was rationality perforce: it did not last.) 'Britain Can Make It' pleased the King and Queen, who made a special journey from Balmoral for the opening. It very much pleased *Punch*, which joked about the imitation farmer's bedroom designed by David Medd with a Kenneth Rowntree picture of a tractor on the wall. Most of all, and in great numbers, the Exhibition pleased the people: a million and a half formed patient queues (which they were used to) down the road as far as the Brompton Oratory, and wandered round the Exhibition with amazement, a third of a mile of it, almost in a dream.

They wandered through the Foyer designed by Basil Spence (assistant to James Gardner, Exhibition Designer). They moved into a section called 'From War to Peace' which showed 'side by side with their warlike origins' some 20 domestic articles evolved from the new processes, new materials and new techniques developed during the war: a new type of saucepan was shown beside the exhaust stub of a wrecked Spitfire, inflatable reclining chairs lined up with dummy weapons, and in case the swords-to-ploughshares theme escaped the public, the products were exhibited against a dim background of bomb-shattered London, picked out by shafts of light. On and on to the Textiles, Metal, Rubber, Glass and Timber, Plastics and Paper; to the Shop Window Street, with its hosiery display and its fanciful Glove Tree:

'On entering this section the visitor obtains his plastic coins at the QUIZ BANK on the left of a large entrance platform, paved with rubber, from which he surveys the brightly-lit displays set under a dark blue sky, charged with a faint afterglow of sunset . . . Each visitor is presented with 10 coins for QUIZ BOXES placed in various parts of the hall. Each box contains 3 photographs of comparable articles, and 3 coin slots. The visitor can thus register a "vote" for the design he favours.'

On, via Quiz Boxes, to 'Things in Their Home Setting' (commentary John Betjeman): The Working Class Utility Kitchen, the Middle Class Kitchen with Dining Recess, the Suburban Living Room for a hard-up curate (a keen naturalist and great reader) and his wife (who collects modern pottery) and his three children (who do homework in this room). On to the Dress Fabrics, displayed from winged horses in flight and from the arms of 'tree-women'. On to the Tea Lounge, a gypsy encampment in which 'the service counter takes the form of a caravan'. On to Women's Dress, beneath a vast white nylon canopy, and then to 'Things for Children', a child's bedroom 'out of the window of which a girl looks on to a garden animated by fairies, elves, frogs and suchlike creatures of a child's imagination, all attired in the newest children's wear'. Not for nothing was James Gardner Chief Development Officer for Army Camouflage during the war: in 'Britain Can Make It' he camouflaged austerity. He made a post-war fantasy. The public was convinced.

The public was also, very gently, introduced to the idea of industrial design. Designers' work was credited throughout the exhibition; at the end, beyond the Rest Lounge (designed by Robert Goodden), Misha Black told the public 'What Industrial Design Means', using simple examples to explain the way an industrial designer works and the way in which different materials and processes influence design: 'This theme is vividly illustrated in a section called "The Birth of an Eggcup". "Who designs the eggcup? Not the machine, which cannot think. The hen is partly responsible; she lays the egg to which all bowls to all eggcups must conform."' But the hero of the piece was the industrial designer. This was something which the public had, bit by bit, to learn.

'Design At Work', a follow-up, a smaller exhibition of products by Royal Designers for Industry, was held in 1948. It was jointly sponsored by the Royal Society of Arts and CoID. It had two quite important results, one very positive: Prince Philip came to it, encouraged by the painter who was working on his portrait, and from then on was a vigorous promoter of design. The other was more negative: the exhibition showed that designers for industry had very far to go. The exhibition was not bad, but it was thin. A handful of designers had done a few nice jobs. But the national limitations, cleverly glossed over at 'Britain Can Make It', were all too obvious now.

The position was this: there were not enough designers trained specifically for industrial design. The nucleus of staff designers in the country—in the Potteries for instance, in the carpet industry, in textiles and in silver—were obviously unlikely to raise standards on their own, both by reason of their skimpy, narrow-minded education and by reason of their fairly menial status in the trade. But how should they be supplemented? The National Register of Industrial Art Designers (founded in 1936 and resurrected as the Record of Designers by the CoID) showed on investigation that professional standards of practice left much to be desired. The Society of Industrial Artists' publication *Designers in Britain*, with examples of their work, proved all too plainly that in 1947 competent designers were in fact in short supply; though the spirit of the enterprise was businesslike and workmanlike, the same old names came round with disconcerting frequency. Though the influx of designers from abroad before the war and through it (Jacques Groag, for instance, George Fejer, Stefan Buzas, Margaret Leischner, Tibor Reich, Marianne Straub, Natasha Kroll, Hans Schleger, Willi de Majo, Lewis Woudhuysen and F. H. K. Henrion) enlivened the profession, there were virtually no national sources of supply for designers in the future. Although it was agreed the days for amateurs were over—an opinion reinforced by John Gloag's *Missing Technician*, published in 1944— and although by then it seemed obvious to the experts an architect's training was not ideal for design, it was difficult to know what to do about designers. Where could they be found, and how should they be taught?

For many, many years, back to Cole and even earlier, the British had been conscious of the lack of proper training for artists for industry (as they liked to call them). The Schools of Design, set up with best intentions, provided quite impractical art

training, for a century. All through the 1930s the complaints
accumulated: from the FBI, the DIA, Gorell and Pick, the Nugent
Committee on Industrial Art Education, the Hambledon Committee on Industrial Art Education in London. They all said
much the same. The system was no good: it did not produce
designers of any use to industry, immediate or potential. The
system must be changed. There were new laments in wartime;
complaints from Meynell-Hoskin and the interdepartmental
Committee on art training; a positive cry of despair from Herbert
Read in the *Architectural Review*: 'The present educational system
being not aesthetic, only a minority who have managed by luck
or illness to escape its deadening influences show any natural
desire to become artists or designers.' This was very true.

The most violent abuse, through the years, had been hurled at
the Royal College of Art. It was useless: a waste of public money
and a national disgrace. So said the innumerable committees
of enquiry set up to consider its maladministration from the 1830s
onwards; so, more or less, said Hambledon in 1936; so said Meynell-Hoskin; and so said Herbert Read. They all urged the College
to return to its original function: the training of *industrial* designers.
In 1946, the report *The Visual Arts*, sponsored by the Dartington
Hall Trustees, still spoke extremely gloomily of amateurishness,
unsuitable premises, inadequate equipment, hindering development at every turn:

'Throughout its chequered history it has never been adequately
supported by the Ministry of Education . . . the College has yet
to fulfil adequately its original purpose of training designers for
industry.'

All these inadequacies at the RCA were more obvious because of
the developments at other art schools: courses in design for machine
production had begun, before the war, at Leicester and the Central,
and immediately afterwards in Glasgow, although these courses
at that date were still in embryo.

The state of education naturally worried the Council of
Industrial Design. For how could it promote design in British
industry when British designers were so few and far between? A
Training Committee was appointed very quickly, and by 1946
their verdict was prepared. Robin Darwin, the Council's Education Officer, acted as Secretary and wrote the report. This report,
though never published, was a most impressive document; with
logic and proper common sense, it deprecated the traditional division in British education between the arts and sciences, the art
schools and the technical schools, and schools of commerce and
the universities. It argued the need for much broader and more
realistic training for designers than there ever was before. The
functions of the Royal College of Art were deeply considered, and
Robin Darwin commented that 'Much would, of course, depend
upon the Principal, and the initial appointment would be a factor

148

of pivotal importance for the ultimate development of the school.'

And who was the new Principal? Who but Robin Darwin, author of the Council's large, profound report. The appointment, he said later, took him rather by surprise: he was by then Professor of Fine Art at Durham University. Gordon Russell, up in Newcastle for one of the CoID 'Design Weeks', came to dinner and they talked about the Principal's appointment, which was to be made the next Tuesday. Very casually, Darwin took a piece of paper and wrote down five conditions on which the new Principal ought to insist: these included a complete change of staff, five-year appointments (renewable) as well as the entire reorganization of the academic courses. Casually, Russell must have put the piece of paper in his pocket and gone off. For on Tuesday, the appointment day, arriving at his club in London for lunch, Robin Darwin found a summons to a meeting with John Maud; and when he reached the meeting and discovered 17 or 18 people sitting round a table, all thoroughly conversant with his views and five conditions for appointment, it was then obvious that the game was up.

On January 1, 1948, as Darwin recollected in *The Dodo and the Phoenix*, a day of dreadful wetness and coldness, the new Principal arrived at his new College, not exactly afraid of being eaten (like Lethaby) but slightly apprehensive. It was all extremely grim. The entrance hall, by any account a depressing place, was painted the deadliest and most institutional grey that the Ministry of Works could devise. There was nobody about, except two aged stewards playing shove ha'penny on the second floor. On his desk he found an oblong green official attendance book: the elder of the aged stewards said that in it Darwin must record the times of his arrivals and departures. The Principal quite crossly threw it in the bin, from which it was retrieved by the same steward who, instructed by the Ministry of Education, himself took note of Darwin's entrances and exits until finally the Principal, in utter desperation, was forced to tear the awful green oblong book in half.

Conditions in the College were amazing. The buildings had in 1911 been thoroughly condemned as 'unworthy of a national establishment'; in 1948 the College was still kept in a series of shacks scattered round South Kensington, without a lecture theatre, and almost without studios. A ramshackle tin drill hall, a Boer War relic, still served as the students' all-purpose common room. The drawing desks were stamped 1870; the looms for students of weaving were even more historic; the printed textiles students were reduced to using Morrison shelters for tables; and worse, there was only one sewing-machine to be shared between all unfortunate students of Dress. Conditions were so frightful that William Rothenstein, Principal in 1920, had decided, rather

than embark on an ever-losing battle, to concentrate on painting
and forget about design.

The staff was just as primitive. Jowett, Darwin's predecessor,
asked him to tea to meet them in a body. According to Darwin,
some had never met before and many of them did not know their
colleagues' names at all. The Council of the College had no set
terms of reference, and seemed to be discouragingly blank about
finances. The pupils, up to then, had all been pre-selected not by
the professors, but by the outside visitor. All this must be changed.
As luck would have it, Robin Darwin was related to John Maud—
later Lord Redcliffe-Maud, and at that time in a powerful position at the Ministry of Education—and began negotiations for
reforms with great determination and a fair degree of confidence.

Maxwell Hyslop, a Ministry official, who just then was con-
valescing from a rather serious illness, had been given what were
classed as light Ministerial duties: responsibility for three so-
called gentle subjects: Women, Agriculture and the RCA. He
cannot have found Darwin an aid to convalescence, for the regime
now demanded for the College was quite new. Darwin wanted
(and received) full academic freedom, with the right for the
College to choose its own students, devise its own teaching methods,
frame its own examinations, grant its own awards; in addition,
the right for teaching members to select their own colleagues
without outside interference; in addition, the sharing of financial
responsibility (consistent with the use of public funds) between
the Council and Principal and staff. The Principal himself should
decide broad lines of policy in conjunction with the Council and
should provide general and if possible equal inspiration to departments in his care. Beyond this his job was mainly 'to support
his staff and act as a guardian and a watchdog of their freedom'.

One of Darwin's innovations was this dependence on, and great
faith in, his staff: he said, 'Herein must lie the real power and
vitality—and if the power is not real, the vitality will not spark.'
A bit like Cole in theory, but more pertinent in practice, he
appointed as Professors active practising designers. He equipped
the design schools for actual production: again like Henry Cole,
who had had a scheme for students making government furnishings, and like Cole's friend William Dyce who, attempting to be
practical, had brought in a loom and a Jacquard machine.
But where Cole's and Dyce's training schemes, so admirable in
principle, collapsed or were diluted, Darwin pushed his through.
And in point of fact the Cole group was never in the minds of
reformers of the College in 1948. In those days it was the Bauhaus,
with its emphasis on knowledge of materials in training for industrial design, and its well-established principle of working on
professional commissions in the classroom, which so excited
them.

In a way, the Bauhaus principles seemed to them ideal. But

these of course were tempered, as they always have been tempered, by a very British, civilized and gentlemanly attitude. It was Darwin's idea to send out from his college people with broad interests and deep sophistication, people whose minds were 'amused and well-tempered', literate, articulate and generally cultured. This traditional university ideal of a total education was well-expressed by Darwin, in superb romantic flight, in an address to the Royal Society of Arts. He explained that he had spent much of his childhood up in Cambridge. He continued:

'As I came back on a winter's evening from children's parties through the great court of Trinity or through King's, the windows of the Chapel would still be glowing from the candles lit for Evensong, with lights twinkling in the fellows' rooms upon all sides. The power that has kept them shining day in, day out, for six centuries and more, depends on the deep impulse which makes mature men come together in one place and associate with one another in learning and research, and in the common pursuit of ideas more important than themselves . . . This is the spirit which hallows all universities and gives them their timeless traditions, and I believe something of this spirit has begun to move within the Royal College of Art.'

And probably it had. Gordon Russell, with a comparable taste for the timeless traditions of the land, was certainly delighted by Darwin's appointment, and especially pleased that the announcement appeared in *The Times* on the day that Russell's own appointment as Director of the CoID became official, Clem Leslie having moved to a more straightforward job as Director of Information at the Treasury. The announcements in *The Times* were printed side-by-side, with a great sense of occasion: for this was the beginning of strong and, on the whole, affectionate ties between the CoID and the College. To start with, Gordon Russell's brother Dick was now Professor of Wood, Metal and Plastics (a temporary School which was later divided into Furniture Design, still under R. D. Russell, and design for Engineering). Robert Goodden, a great friend and ally of the Russells, was Professor of Silversmithing, Jewellery and Glass, and later the Vice-Principal. Gordon Russell recollected how, in times of trouble at the Council of Industrial Design, he could easily be comforted by the arrival of the regular pink list, beautifully illustrated and composed by Edward Ardizzone, of wines just purchased for the College Senior Common Room. Despite the fact that Gatti's, haunt of Morris and his confreres, had now been designated a club for H.M. forces, a little of the Arts and Crafts delight in proper living, good food and wine and fellowship, lingered nicely on.

Gordon Russell needed comforts: at the time when he took over at the CoID, the situation was not promising. As he said, he got the backwash from Utility furniture and from 'Britain Can Make It'. The trade—all the trades put together—disliked the

idea of outside selection, as of course they always had: their order
books were full, in the spate of post-war buying, and they argued
very crossly that what sold was well-designed. The retailers were
angry at aspersions being cast on their own ability to choose the
finest products. Designers were annoyed because they felt the
Council's standards were too lenient; the trade thought them
ridiculously high. There was trouble from the people who were
not Council-members, and insisted that they ought to be; and
there was yet more trouble from people on the Council who felt
that it should work at simple sales promotion, never mind about
design. The trade press fought the Council, and Russell was
alarmed in case the export trades united to denounce the Council's
work to the Board of Trade, maintaining that the Council was
jeopardizing exports by criticizing products which were bringing
income in. On top of this the Chairman, Thomas Barlow, wrote
resigning because of overwork.

'My army experience stood me in good stead,' wrote Gordon
Russell, reminiscing on this period when rebellion was rife and
there were traitors in the camp and the battle for improvement of
design was fierce and endless. He left his forces fighting, and went
off to Kew Gardens and drafted a plan for Council development,
a good efficient plan by means of which the Council managed in
the end to effect a kind of truce. In the Annual Report 1948–1949,
he explained how and why he had now regrouped his staff (which
for Britain Can Make It had worked in one big body) into two
divisions:

'Without an effective demand for better design there can be no
adequate supply of it and without examples of good design being
put before the public there can be no standard of comparison on
which to base the demand. The twin drive for better design must
therefore be pursued at the same time—the Industrial Division,
to encourage a supply of well-designed products from, and the
flow of trained talent to, industry, and the Information Division
to stimulate public demand for higher standards.'
Chief Industrial Officer was Mark Hartland Thomas; Chief
Information Officer was Paul Reilly, son of Sir Charles Reilly, the
pre-war Professor of Architecture at Liverpool University.

Convincing by showing, reforming by exhibiting, encouraging
industry to mend its ways; this was nothing new. It was just what
Henry Cole, Gottfried Semper and Prince Albert had been setting
out to do; and the DIA, and Pick's sadly ineffective Council. And
nothing much had altered; very little had improved. Gordon
Russell, undeterred, with the added great advantage of a grant
of £164,000 and a staff of 165, started off again to end the ever-
lasting circle of apathetic manufacturers and shopkeepers and
ignorant consumers. He was systematic. While industrial officers
went round the manufacturers, examining, entreating and jollying
along, the Information Division was travelling the country, en-

lightening the people, in a kind of caravan: taking its Design Fair, a mobile exhibition, to join in such civic displays as 'Sheffield on Its Mettle'; creating whole Design Weeks in Newcastle and Nottingham, Southampton, Bristol, Bradford and other hopeful towns, drawing in the civic dignitaries, retailers and housewives, Rotarians, Soroptomists and even children to special exhibitions, often in museums, to lectures and discussions. They laid on Housewives Forums to which women came demanding squarer saucepans, larger castors and higher three-piece suites. They indoctrinated sales staff with residential conferences, speeches on 'What We Mean by Good Design', and Brains Trusts. They distributed small booklets called 'Four Ways of Living' (dress designer, doctor, chain-store keeper, clerk). They brought out little leaflets saying to the public:

'Design is what makes a thing
      easy to make,
      easy to use,
      easy to look at.'

They sent around their newsheets and analyses of dishracks and pamphlets on 'How to Furnish Your Home', and in 1949 they started to publish large-scale propaganda, *Design* magazine—an act of such confidence, just then, that Francis Meynell, calling it megalomania, resigned.

Design began most tactfully. With just the same soft-pedalling as *Journal of Design* a century before, the first editorial announced that 'This journal begins publication with one purpose, and one purpose only: to help industry in its task of raising standards of design.' With this aim, the first issue included a feature entitled 'Neater Meter' (a before-and-after story), and an article by Gordon Russell asking patiently, for about the hundredth time, 'What is good design?' The answer—a product which is true to its materials, good in appearance and, above all, fit for use—shows how very close the Council's thinking was in those days to the basic pre-war doctrine of the DIA. But the illustrations emphasize a most important difference, something which the DIA had never really tackled. The Beetle plastics sugar dredger shown by Gordon Russell, the strainer and potato masher, proved that with a vengeance the Council was determined not to be too rarified. This was design within the people's ken.

One way and another, by roughly 1950, partly through the Council's efforts, partly independently, design in British industry was visibly improving. Besides the pre-war devotees there were some newer converts. Besides Gordon Russell, there was HK, Race and Hille and Morris of Glasgow. Besides Edinburgh Weavers, there was now Whitehead and Tibor. The pre-war Good Furniture Group had been revived, and a counterpart in Scotland, Scottish Furniture Manufacturers, by then had commissioned new designs. Alongside Heal's and Dunn's, there were many other shops showing sudden post-war interest in modern merchandise: Liberty's in London, Bainbridge's of Newcastle, Hopewells of Nottingham, David Morgan, Cardiff, Hammonds of Hull, Brown's of Newcastle, John Bowler of Brighton. Said *Design* magazine, very pleased, 'The list will grow, for the tide is turning.' It quite definitely was.

In 1946, the *Architectural Review* was grumbling that the daily press, which publicized authors, never mentioned industrial designers. By 1950, *Design* was saying:
'Note the increasing frequency of constructive references to design in the home; see how the women's pages examine the design of household goods; watch the rising demand by editors for hand-picked photographs from the Council of Industrial Design and consider that full page in the Daily Mirror given up to a serious review of *Designers in Britain* under the four-column headline: DESIGN HAS COME INTO YOUR LIFE.'

Surely this deserved a celebration. And in fact, a celebration was underway: an enormous celebration, a national merry-making, a heyday to be known as The Festival of Britain, a grand design bonanza, a sudden burst of glory for the CoID, DIA and even Arts and Crafts. For patriotic Lethaby had said long, long before:
'Nothing better could be thought of as likely to bring real interest back into our towns and villages as some form of Festival.'

154

154
Utility Furniture Committee
'Chiltern' oak sideboard, 1945.

155
Utility Furniture Committee
'Cotswold' living-room furniture,
1943.

156
Utility Furniture Committee
'Cotswold' dining table, 1943.

157
Utility Furniture Committee
Printed cotton furnishing fabric,
1943.

158
Utility Furniture Committee
'Cotswold' bedroom furniture, 1943.

156

157

158

159
British Army Camouflage Centre
Pneumatic chair developed from wartime techniques, and shown in 'War to Peace' section, Britain Can Make It Exhibition, 1946.

160
David Medd
Farmer's bedroom from Britain Can Make It Exhibition, 1946.

161
R. Y. Goodden
Sports Section from Britain Can Make It Exhibition, 1946.

159

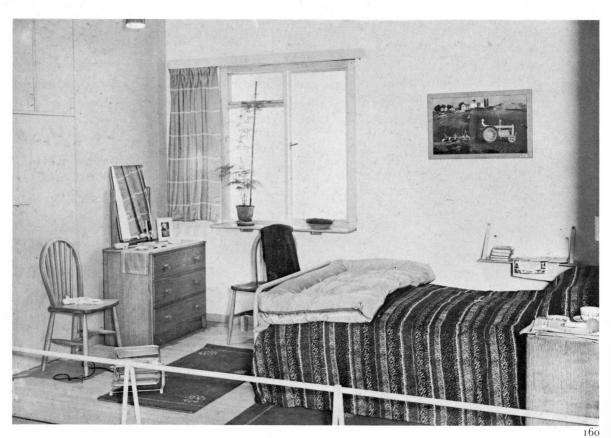

160

162

163

164

162
Howard Keith
'Cavalier' chair made by
H.K. Furniture, 1949.

163
Howard Keith
'Intruder' chair made by
H.K. Furniture, 1949.

164
Howard Keith
'Simplon' settee made by
H.K. Furniture, 1948

165
Basil Spence
'Allegro' chair made by H. Morris,
1949.

166
Geoffrey Dunn
Partition shelving and lamp for
Dunn's of Bromley, 1950.

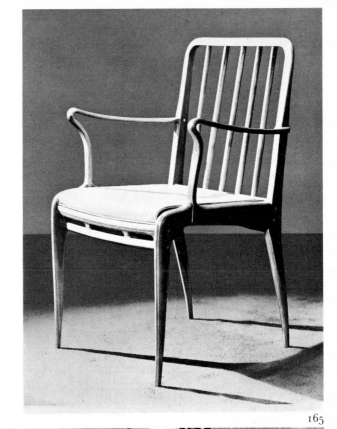

165

166

167

168

167
R. D. Russell
Console television receiver made by
Murphy, 1947.

168
Ernest Race
Chairs, table and sideboard made by
Race Furniture, between 1946 and
1950.

169
Lucian Ercolani
Windsor chair made by Ercol for
Britain Can Make It Exhibition,
1946.

170
Robin Day and Clive Latimer
Storage system, prizewinning design
in Low-Cost Furniture Competition,
Museum of Modern Art, New York,
1948.

169

171

172

173

174

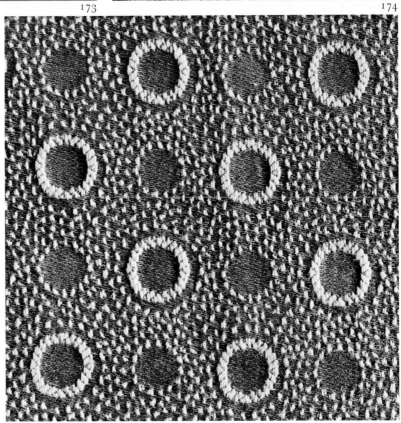

171
Marian Pepler
'Kelim' woven rug, 1948.

172
Marian Pepler
'Key' tufted rug, 1948.

173
Enid Marx
'Skelda' upholstery fabric, designed
for Utility Furniture Committee
1945.

174
Enid Marx
Woven fabric, designed for
Utility Furniture Committee 1946.

175
Enid Marx
'Ring' cotton tapestry, designed for
Utility Furniture Committee, 1945.

175

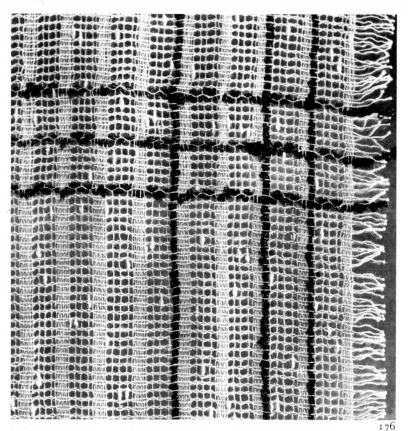

176

176
Margaret Leischner
Woven fabric, 1945–50.

177
Margaret Leischner
Woven fabric, 1945–50.

177

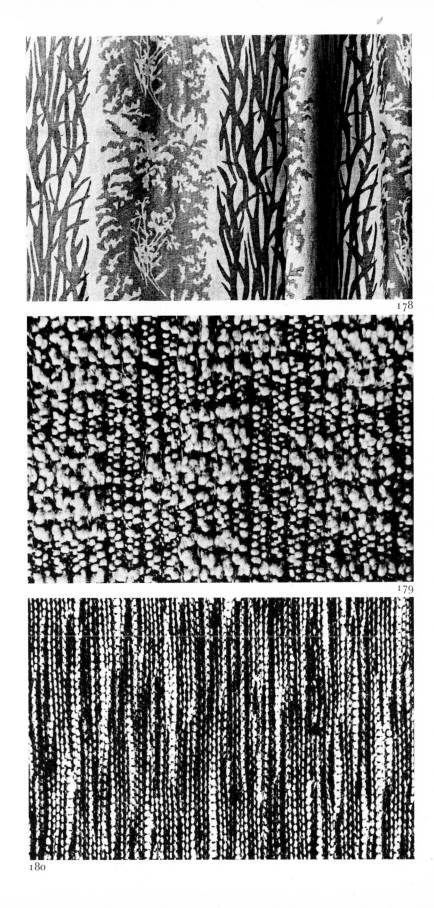

178

179

180

178
Sheila Pickersgill
Hand-printed linen, 1949.

179
Tibor Reich
Woven furnishing fabric, early
post-war.

180
Tibor Reich
Woven furnishing fabric, early
post-war.

181

181
Gaby Schreiber
Stacking cups in plastic, 1946.

182
Susie Cooper
'Spiral Fern' earthenware, 1940–41.

183
Susie Cooper
'Laurel Border' hand-painted
earthenware, 1935.

184
A. B. Read
'Versalite' table lamp made by
Troughton and Young, about 1945.

185
John Waterer
'Oxford' leather zipper bags made
by S. Clarke, about 1947.

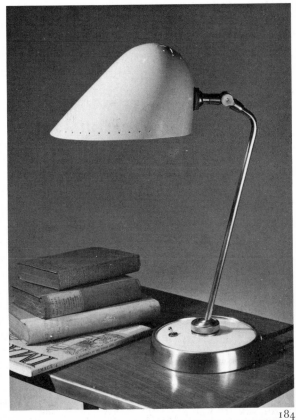

183

184

185

6

The Industrial Designers 1951-1960

HUDDLED in a cubby hole, a former footman's bedroom, in one of those imperious red houses behind Harrods, Hugh Casson and his Festival Design Group apprehensively sat hour after hour sipping Bisodol and wondering how ever they could make an exhibition on their badly-blitzed and desolate, depressing South Bank site.

The idea of the Festival was mooted some years earlier: incongruously enough, in the middle of the War, the Royal Society of Arts had proposed a 1951 exhibition to commemorate Prince Albert's glorious outburst a hundred years before. This private suggestion was reinforced more publicly in 1945 when John Gloag, voice of the DIA resurgent, wrote to *The Times*, and almost simultaneously Gerald Barry, then editor of the *News Chronicle*, published an Open Letter to Sir Stafford Cripps. What they both wanted was an international exhibition, and as it turned out, they hardly need have asked. For Cripps, an exhibition enthusiast who had built 'Britain Can Make It' almost singlehanded, was already making plans for a festival in Britain. He sent one of his urgent red-ink letters back to Barry, expressing his sympathy; within another fortnight, the Ramsden Committee was set up, which recommended 'a first category international exhibition,' held at the earliest practicable date, 'to demonstrate to the world the recovery of the United Kingdom from the effects of the war in the moral, cultural, spiritual and material fields'.

This was 1946. By the time it reached Hugh Casson, three years later, the Festival of Britain was not so grandiose. By then it was not international, just British; the country's economics, lack of housing, loss of factories, had cut down the plans to a more manageable size, reducing the theme from universal showmanship to national reassessment. The Festival would now be a national morale-booster, a time for fun and fantasy; after a decade of war, deprivation and darkness, it was to be a moment of remembrance of things past and incentive to things future. In this heady atmosphere, the organizers were directed to display 'the British contribution to civilization, past, present and future, in the arts, in science and technology, and in industrial design'. Stafford Cripps, the President of the Board of Trade, had handed on the Festival— which was no longer tradesmanlike—to the Lord President of the Council, Herbert Morrison. The Festival Council had been appointed. Under Gerald Barry, by then (what fitter person?) Director-General of all festivities, the Festival Executive Committee was at work; and under the Committee was the Presentation Panel, and then beneath the Panel was Hugh Casson's Design Unit, appointed to give shape to the patriotic concept, to bring the fun and fantasy alive beside the Thames.

'They enjoyed it,' said Hugh Casson on the BBC, talking to the Schools in 1951, 'they laughed a lot and from the very beginning they made up their minds that it shouldn't be pompous or boring.'

He and James Holland, James Gardner, Ralph Tubbs and Misha Black sat shivering in overcoats for hours, day after day, in the attic room in Knightsbridge with drawing boards on their knees and tracing paper piling up around them, determined that the Festival should be bright, gay and popular and totally inspiring on its awkward tiny site. No long palatial vistas, but small ones, interlocking; no ponderous pavilions, but buildings grouped informally: Hugh Casson described it, to the Schools and Olive Shapley (who was trilling with excitement), as a very large house with the roof taken off and the pavilions laid out like outdoor rooms.

Who was to design the various Pavilions and Restaurants and showpieces? Hugh Casson and his Unit needed men of genius, but as time was short, they could not afford men of temperament. They settled, very wisely, for themselves and many friends: Black and Holland on the Upstream Circuit, 'The Land'; James Gardner on the Downstream Circuit, 'The People'; Ralph Tubbs on the Dome of Discovery—provided that the Dome could in fact be fitted in. ('It seemed doubtful,' said Casson, 'because in a fit of exhibitionism we had decided it must be 365 feet across and we clung to that dimension with pathetic assurance.') The Lion and the Unicorn Pavilion was assigned to Robert Goodden and Dick Russell; Homes and Gardens to Katz & Vaughan; the Tele cinema to Wells Coates; the Shot Tower to Casson and Gardner. The teamwork was quite breathtaking for Britain—a country where up to then team spirit in design was non-existent—extending to the litter bins (Jack Howe) and chairs (by Race) and signposts (by Milner Gray and Robin Day). A hundred or more designers were employed. There was somebody responsible for every little detail, the ice-cream stalls and flower-pots, the sculpture and the murals, the knives and forks and pottery, the bird boxes and even the breed of ducks selected for the ornamental lake.

The Council of Industrial Design was much involved; the Council and the Festival seemed made for one another. The Council was the source of all the manufactured objects; the Festival the carrot (or the stick) for manufacturers, urging them to try a little harder with design. The original scheme had been for a pavilion, a separate pavilion, of industrial design, but Gordon Russell who argued—much like Morris—that design is all around us, resisted the idea of a Good Design Pavilion. Fearing clumsy WCs and basins in the public lavatories, unco-ordinated lettering, badly-chosen chairs and a general lack of function throughout the Festival, he suggested that his Council, far from being confined to one exemplary pavilion, should oversee the lot. The rule was made that nothing in industrial production should be included without CoID approval, thus eliminating free-for-all Halls of Textiles, Pavilions of Confectionery, Palaces of Gas: there were to be no Winston Churchills in Swiss roll, no effigies of royalty in edible fats; a paper manufacturers' proposal to exhibit a model of the South Bank in lavatory paper was regretfully declined. 'No stunts,' said Gordon Russell to his industrial officers before he sent them out to gather British products: 'They will be real goods to go into real shops and so be available for real people. This may not be an earth-shattering statement, but it is British common sense.'

Sensibly, the Council thought up and implemented the 1951 Stock List, a card-index of all the well-designed articles the officers could search out in a systematic survey of the industries, from locomotives to henhouses, from tableware to sailing boats, all organized so neatly in 70 categories that finally the Stock List was itself exhibited, renamed (more festively perhaps) 'Design Review'. Doggedly, the Council persuaded twenty-eight British manufacturers to work for eighteen months in the Festival Pattern Group, decorating products with patterns derived from crystal structure diagrams, taking advice from a scientist at Girton, triumphantly producing dress-prints based on haemoglobin, crystal-structure curtain fabrics, plastic sheets and ties, crystal-structure lighting fittings, dinner plates and wine-glasses, a crystal-structure foyer for the Science Exhibition. Sir Lawrence Bragg politely wrote to say how pleased he was. The *Architectural Review* was not so keen. It is certain that the project, mingling art and science and industry, would have been dear to the heart of Henry Cole.

Cole would have approved of the whole conduct of the Council at the Festival of Britain: its calmness and efficiency; the way (against all odds) it organized the loan of a large locomotive from Glasgow; the way in which it collected, stored and catalogued and finally returned 10,000 objects from 3,500 firms—an operation managed by Benoy, a retired major-general, whose experience with moving troops for the African invasion in World War II stood him in good stead. Best of all, the Council had succeeded in not ruffling, and not being ruffled by, industry too much. The standards of selection were deliberately moderate. Wrote Gordon Russell in The *Architectural Review* (which had complained, as usual, about the Council's leniency):
'Our aim was to find something worth showing from the greatest number of firms possible, otherwise we should run the risk of all the exhibits in certain trades coming from three or four firms, which could hardly be tolerated in an operation financed by public funds on this scale.'

Perhaps it was this moderation, the discovery that modern design was, after all, approachable; perhaps it was the fact that the Festival was billed as 'the people's show, not organized arbitrarily for them to enjoy, but put on largely by them, by us all, as an expression of a way of life in which we believe'; perhaps it was the intoxication of the time when Churchill, in medals, rode up the escalator in the Dome of Discovery and everybody cheered and danced in the open-air along the Fairway and set off in balloons for unknown destinations; perhaps it was the brilliance of Casson's small piazzas and pretty outdoor cafés and the cat-walk and the Skylon; perhaps it was the crystals which the purists so despised: whatever the reason, or accumulated reasons, modern design seemed suddenly all right. The public, which had for a century resisted all benevolent attempts to bring them good design—from Prince Albert's workmen's cottages of 1851, the 1905 Cheap Cottages at Letchworth, the display of 'Industrial Art for the Slender Purse' in 1929 at the Victoria and Albert, the DIA pre-war working-class showhouses, 'Homes for the People' in Manchester in wartime, Pick's well-intentioned survey of 'The Working-Class Home' (about which they cared nothing)—over-night came round. They went off in their thousands to the show-house at Lansbury furnished entirely, with CoID approval, for £143 4s 7d; where Bill, a dock-worker, his wife Mary (35) who had been in service and understood good housekeeping, their children, Jack, Jill, Jane and Baby Tom (4–5 months) lived happily with blue distemper walls and dark blue paper, starred and dotted, on the wall above the chimney, an extending dining table, an expanding coffee table, a reversible trolley convertible to card-table, 'Jack and Jill' easy chairs, a brass-stem standard lamp and russet wild-flower curtains (7s 11d a yard).

Gerald Barry had insisted that 1951 must be something more than a year of bigger and better exhibitions and more and merrier festivals; his idea that the Festival should be a sort of springboard for young architects and artists and designers had in fact come beautifully true. Neville Ward, for instance, wrote that 'Ward and Austin were (just) in practice, two of the three of us still in our twenties; so to be invited to take part in the South Bank project was wonderful. It was, in a time of few and small opportunities, a big thing.' The repercussions, both for design and for designers, are still not really over—nearly twenty years beyond. The Casson-Black contingent went from strength to strength; the Royal College of Art was greatly glorified by the contributions of its practising professors, and the students on the fringe of its absorbed the optimism and understood the discipline and teamwork of it all. The British began paying more attention to detail: to good letter-ing on captions and on signposts, to interior and exterior furniture, electrical fitments, litter-bins and landscaping, to texture and the colour of paving and to lighting, things which they had hardly bothered with before. Individual objects, which were first seen on the South Bank, ranging from Race bright steel-rod chairs to concrete flower bowls, were soon found far and wide. Barry, who saw everything, summed it up quite wisely: 'In this bold use of colour, in the marriage of architecture and sculpture, in scrupulous use of landscaping, in attention to elegance and finish in interior and exterior fittings, new standards and a new style were set up—the 'Festival Style'—which evidently caught the imagination of other designers and also created a public or commercial *demand*. It was copied all over the country—copied, and gradually debased. In due course the Festival style became a cliché. Probably this was inevitable.'

Making the most of Festivaliana, of course, was Gordon Russell with his Council lined behind him. This was their great moment, in the national excitement, in the year in which a public outcry had demolished a Tudor refreshment car thought up by British Railways, to consolidate for ever the movement for reform, to try once and for all to break down the vicious circle which for ages had prevented real progress in design. They kept 'Design Review', the Stock List from the Festival; by then they had accumulated rather more good-will from the manufacturers; contemporary case-histories prove time and time again, unlikely as it seems, that manufacturers whose products were rejected had afterwards come to the Council for advice. In the greatly improved climate of the fifties, a system—simple in outline, elaborate in operation—was developed, and soon became the envy of, and model for, reformers of design in other European countries. (It was not very long before Muthesius walked again.)

What happened, and still happens, was this, in briefest outline. The CoID might suggest to a British manufacturer that one (or maybe all) of his designs could be improved on. The manufacturer might then come back to the Council for the names of some designers with the relevant experience. A designer might be chosen to work with the manufacturer (on staff or freelance basis) to produce a new design, which might then be submitted to the Council for approval, which might then be accepted for 'Design Review', exhibited to retailers, shown to the public in the various design centres, ultimately—in the most ideal conditions—winning a Design Centre Award.

This may sound cut-and-dried, but the system evolved slowly. It took years for the Council to make its purpose known, and years to gain enough support for tangible achievement. Through the early fifties, the scale of operations (compared with that in 1962 or 1963) was small. In 1953, the Record of Designers had only 350 requests from manufacturers; and one must remember that the Haymarket Design Centre was not in fact opened until 1956, and Design Centre Awards did not in fact begin until 1957. But onwards from the Festival, the system was immeasurably strengthened by designers trained to be designers, from the RCA and other colleges of art. This was one large reason for the Council's rush of confidence; the training of designers at long last seemed secure. It was 1951 when the Des. RCA was first awarded to students completing the design course at the Royal College of Art (in addition to 9 months' experience in industry). In 1952, the students held an exhibition on Liberty's Fourth Floor and RCA designers' names, which later appeared almost ad nauseam, were for the first time listed in *Design* magazine: for instance, Ronald Carter, Eric Clements, Gerald Benney, David Mellor, Robert Jefferson; Frank Guille designed a cot for Prince Charles and Philip Popham made intricate medallions for decorating it. The next year, *Design* reported favourably on the students' exhibition in the Victoria and Albert Museum: this time Alan Irvine, with two chairs and a razor-case, and Geoffrey Baxter's glass designs emerged with honour, and Pat Albeck was reported to have sold a design of fruit in green and yellow on cambric to Horrockses. By 1953, the RCA reported that out of the 59 students who had left, 44 had posts in industry. By 1957, *Designers in Britain* (the SIA catalogue) showed Des. RCA products on every other page: Guille's designs for Kandya, Robert Welch's stainless steel for Wiggin, David Mellor's cutlery for Walker & Hall, Robert Heritage's furniture for Evans. Also in the issue was a certain Terence Conran (though he was at the Central School and not the RCA) with a picture of an unusually long sideboard produced by Conran Furniture, more or less home-made.

A new kind of designer was emerging: not architect, not artist and not exactly craftsman, British but not necessarily a gentleman, a well-trained and ambitious young self-made one-man show. The scale of operations in America, where offices were sometimes 50-strong, seemed most unsympathetic to students who were trained in knowledge of materials and personal experiment. The Scandinavian system of individual offices seemed rather more ideal, and many of the students, from the RCA especially, set up on their own as designers straightaway, with a faith, enthusiasm and love and care for detail which had not been seen in Britain since the days of Arts and Crafts. For instance: the RCA-trained furniture designers Ronald Carter and Robert Heritage; the textile designers Audrey Levy, Pat Albeck, Shirley Craven; the jeweller John Donald; the silversmith/industrial designers Gerald Benney, Robert Welch and David Mellor. Robert Welch, in Chipping Campden, opened his own workshop in Ashbee's old headquarters; in Sheffield, David Mellor set up his own office and metal-working shop. The difference, of course, was that whereas C. R. Ashbee and his craftsmen worked mostly on special commissions, Robert Welch and David Mellor, besides their one-off silver, used their workshops for production of industrial prototypes: alongside special silver for Churchill College, Cambridge, Robert Welch would be working on designs for stainless steel; as well as a cross for Southwell Minster, David Mellor would design a cast-iron heater or a lamp-post or a litter-bin. In Britain in the fifties a new realistic breed of designers was evolving a new realistic style: or, in point of fact, developing traditional

British virtues of common sense and wholesomeness, simplicity and reticence, designer's lack of pomp and craftsman's truth to his materials, into a good, decent, measured, modest, modern style.

Decency, just then, was meat and drink to the Council of Industrial Design, which in 1953 had made the sound announcement that

'Though rules of thumb and narrow definitions are neither feasible nor desirable, the general principle can be stated that the object of the Council's selections is to promote good design as comprising good materials and workmanship, fitness for purpose and pleasure in use.'

This was the principle of all its activities: its bulletins and lectures, its photographic library, its visual aids for schools, its travelling exhibitions. It was clearly to be seen in the illustrations chosen for the Annual Reports: the office dictaphone, the pickled beetroot label, the dress-shield display dispenser, all shown in 1953, along with the unit bedroom furniture designed by Frank Austin, 'as a result of the meeting between CoID staff and the firm's managing director'. Goodness and fitness and pleasure were all obvious in the CoID show-flats and show-houses round the country, and the CoID Ideal Home displays of decent living, with Ward & Austin pianos, and shelves by Robert Heritage, Stag wardrobes designed by John and Sylvia Reid, Kandya chairs, Reynolds Woodware sideboards and Conelamps, adjustable and washable and pleated, clean and neat in acetate, by Cooke-Yarborough and Homes.

A pleasant time it was, when standards seemed so certain, and good design meant comeliness and usefulness and sense, and the London Design Centre was opened by the Duke of Edinburgh who wished it the very best of luck. It had taken so long coming— back in 1931 Gorell and his committee had stressed the crying need for a central exhibition, and committees ever after had demanded and demanded a Pavilion of Design—that once the Centre opened in 1956, thanks to Walter Worboys, CoID Chairman, thanks to Gordon Russell's indefatigable spadework, and thanks to £27,000 from industry, it seemed a great occasion. DIA prayers seemed answered. Here at last in London was a showplace for design. What if Buckminster Fuller called it 'Bargain basement stuff; you're designing for today in the idiom of ten years ago'; and what if Charles Eames, visiting the Centre, found it 'very creepy'. Mr Gaitskell and his wife had said that they wished they had seen the Centre earlier, before they had altered their Hampstead home, and Marghanita Laski had felt that 'any woman who is at all interested in good design will feel an immense debt of gratitude to the CoID for starting the Centre'. The *Daily Telegraph* even predicted it might make us the best-furnished nation in the world.

So on with honest business: selection committees on Tuesdays and on Thursdays to assess the various products submitted to the Council. A group of outside specialists, designers, architects and retailers, backed up by Council members and CoID staff, sat in judgement on up to 200 products, regaled at 3 o'clock by a cup of Council tea, asking, in general, the old DIA questions on fitness for purpose and pleasure in use. Will it pour or cut or hold things? Is it man-size, child-size, ship-shape? Is it functional and proper? Is it fair and square and good, performing (when it needs to) reasonable ablutions? Provided that the judges, heirs of Ambrose Heal, were satisfied, the product could then (on payment of a fee) be shown in the Design Centre and (if the manufacturers wrote in for special labels) could be emblazoned 'Design Centre Approved'.

Ten years before, such a scheme would not have worked: British manufacturers would not have dreamed of paying for space in a selective exhibition of design. Though even now some grumbled and fumed about the Council and its ignorant committees and its high-falutin' principles, the fact that every day 2,000 people came to see the exhibition in the Haymarket bore weight. Bit by bit, by conferences, with a Scottish Design Centre (under Alister Maynard, the furniture designer and one-time ADC to the Governor of Bengal), with Design Centres attached to Building Centres in the provinces, the cause of good design was patiently argued and precisely illustrated. By tactful, careful conduct, by general efficiency, by constantly opposing the idea of long-haired art, the Council showed the manufacturers that there was nothing so extreme about its policy. The level of selection remained thoroughly Home Service, design for a large public, the aesthetic middlebrow.

What is interesting is that, in spite of all this tolerance, the Council was then, in a sense, quite narrow-minded. This, again, was a great strength: through the early and mid-fifties, Gordon Russell was almost exclusively intent on raising design standards in consumer industries. No dallying, at this stage, with design in engineering; no veering off to contemplate the face of the land, few thoughts about environment and mass-communications. For the moment, the main aim was better teacups, chairs and tables. 'Limited advance and consolidate', his motto, reached its point of glory with Design Centre Awards. In 1957, two RCA Professors (Goodden and Russell), Brian O'Rorke the architect, Milner Gray, Master of the Faculty of Royal Designers for Industry, and Mrs Astrid Sampe, picked out twelve outstandingly simple and practical objects: dinner and teaware, table glasses, wallpaper, cutlery, a curtain fabric, a carpet, plastic tableware, a lamp shade, a TV set, a convertible settee-bed, Pyrex casseroles and a convector open fire.

'Although,' wrote the judges, on a note of some surprise, 'none of the articles selected was chosen for its affinity with another, in the case of the table glass, dinner ware and cutlery it is interesting to see in the result how well the selected examples would combine as a place setting.' Interesting certainly; but surely not surprising. It was thoroughly predictable—might one say inevitable?—given the Council's emphasis on clean appearance, sound workmanship and suitability for purpose, that Design Centre Awards would tend to look alike. They were in a sense the Council's own great prizes. They pointed out, discreetly, what the Council had achieved.

For 1957 Awards and the prizes given on each successive year (with the bonus of the Duke of Edinburgh's Prize for Elegant Design) brought extraordinary glory to the partnerships beginning to build up between the freelance designer and his clients. Year after year, design awards were given (or seemed to be given) to Robin Day and Hille, the Reids and Rotaflex, Hulme Chadwick and Wilkinson Sword, Humphrey Spender and Edinburgh Weavers, Audrey Levy and Wall Paper Manufacturers, Edward Pond and Bernard Wardle, Robert Welch and Old Hall, Robert Heritage and Archie Shine, and David Mellor and Walker & Hall. Year after year—and this was no illusion—design awards became an accolade for Royal College of Art training. Robin Darwin wrote a letter to *Design* magazine in 1958 pointing out that 35 per cent of the 20 'Designs of the Year' was the work of designers who had studied at the RCA during the previous seven years. Besides—he added, to be fair—'two other winning designers belong to an earlier generation'.

Design was still in many ways an amiable clique. Identical professors seemed forever giving prizes to their own RCA students, identical designers were forever smiling thanks to the Duke of Edinburgh. The DIA still talked of 'spreading the gospel', and for that very purpose held house-parties at Ashridge, gentle country gatherings they called 'Design Weekends'. The fact was that the Council of Industrial Design had stolen the DIA's thunder; through the fifties, its activities were altogether cosy and low-key, with lunch meetings at Overseas House (sample topic: *Design Starvation in the Public Schools*); with musical evenings in the Geffrye Museum; with little exhibitions in Charing Cross Station, 'Register Your Choice' and later 'Make or Mar'. In the course of these meanderings, all leisurely and friendly, the only thing which seemed to rouse the DIA to fury was the fashionable, frivolous, dreadfully unreasonable, totally un-functional stiletto heel. In 1959, Lord Conesford, the President, clinging as if to a lifebelt to the principle that 'Fitness for purpose is the very essence of good design', launched an attack as furious as any of the thunderings of Gloag:

'A woman wearing such shoes does far more destruction to the floor of an aeroplane in which she travels than a wild rhinoceros, which can be transported without doing any damage at all.'

And yet, in spite of the family circle of DIA and RCA and CoID, in spite of the assumption that design was still the gospel to be spread to unbelievers, unseen by some old preachers there was by now a change. Hamilton Temple Smith, by then the oldest, had noticed it as early as 1951: 'The heathen,' he wrote, 'no longer stone us out of their cities: they are more likely to offer us a cocktail. And this frightens me.' Marghanita Laski had noticed it, and rather to the horror of the courteous DIA, stated in the *Year Book* 'The day of the design we have fought and struggled for these many years is already over. It is popular, accepted and boring.' In a way, she was right: from the Festival onwards design —or Design as it became—was all around. Design was on the railways: in 1956, British Railways Design Panel was hopefully established. (George Williams, the first Design Director, had been on the staff of the CoID.) Design had reached the Ministry of Works, where Harold Glover, the Controller of Supplies, persistently raised standards. The LCC Architects Department, in particular the Furniture Section directed by Frank Height, designed official furniture for LCC schools, colleges, offices and welfare homes, controlling all the colours for all LCC buildings. The Ministry of Transport offered what amounted to bribes for good design, subsidizing lighting on trunk roads on condition that local authorities selected lighting columns already approved by the CoID. Meanwhile Ernest Marples, the new Postmaster General, announced a design policy which, if it had matured, might have towered above the rest: he would modernize the Post Offices, posters, greetings telegrams; redesign the telephone kiosks and consider new telephones. Mr Marples himself would test all the mock-ups; he would listen to advice but he would not always take it.

This was the age in which Design became a factor in public image-building. Successive PMGs promised the public better-designed pillar-boxes; managing directors of forward-looking companies commissioned themselves symbols and new, dynamic letter-headings. Corporate identity programmes began flourishing on airlines, in laundries, in off-licences, in banks. The reformers' age-old plans for uniting art and commerce had at last materialized, not quite as they imagined. Design was advertising; Design was serious commerce; Design was the concern of Boards of Directors, a development acknowledged with characteristic pomp by the Royal Society of Arts which from 1954, the year of its Bicentenary, awarded (and awards) annual medals to people who 'in a manner other than as industrial designers have exerted an exceptional influence in promoting art and design in British industry'. The first four medals went to good artistic businessmen: 1954 Sir Colin Anderson, 1955 Sir Charles Tennyson, 1956 Sir Walter Worboys and 1957 Sir Ernest Goodale.

This was the era of management consultants: design consultants fitted neatly in beside them. This was the beginning of consumer-dom: Design of course, appealed strongly to readers of *'Which?'*. This was the age of 'Outrage' and the Anti-Ugly demonstrations when people shouted 'Hell' and beat drums and carried coffins to appalling modern buildings: Design (and William Morris' ghost) was here as well. Design was in the shops and Design was in the showrooms, the posters and advertisements. Design was on TV: 'Design Review' became a monthly woman's feature, introducing Moira Hallifax of Peter Jones, Sloane Square. Design was, most of all, on the bookstalls. A vast factor in promotion of Design were the magazines, from prestigious *Ambassador* (the export publication munificently managed by Hans and Elspeth Juda) to the mass-circulation monthlies and weeklies for the housewife by the fireside. Home editors were born.

In 1953, at Coronation time, *Ideal Home* made the rousing, very patriotic statement that 'The finest efforts of living designers, encouraged by everyone's desire for the best, will safeguard our heritage.' In fact this was a turning point. The work of living designers—up to then a specialist subject for *Design* magazine, the *Architectural Review* and esoteric foreign publications, like *Mobilia, Graphis, Domus*—was featured in more general, domestic magazines. In 1953, *Ideal Home* was running features on 'Silver in the Home', showing RCA silversmiths; 'At Home with the Days', showing Lucienne and Robin chatting in their studio; a genial and encouraging lecture by Paul Reilly called 'Don't be Afraid of Contemporary Design'.

'Our hearts and Heal's,' wrote Diana Pollock, who joined the magazine in 1956, 'obviously beat as one although we often have to present a different picture (like any other form of communication we have our potential and our limitations).' Mrs Pollock, first and most determined of Home Editors, concocted Ideal Home Commissioned Designs, a true project of the fifties—brave, consumer-minded, very sound yet mildly gay. She found gaps in the market 'created by the new social climate'; she found the young designers equipped to fill these gaps; she found the manufacturers to try out the ideas, with guaranteed publicity. She then arranged the meeting between the manufacturer and the designer, with the editor of *Ideal Home* in the chair. The results of this benevolence ranged from Mozart pianos to saucepan-lid racks, from multi-glide storage to heated trolleys, from matching p.v.c. curtaining and Con-tact to 'Plantagon', a decorative unit flower-pot. 'Form' seating system, designed by Robin Day, went on to win a Design Centre Award.

Home and *Homes and Gardens, House Beautiful* and *Housewife, Everywoman, Woman and Home* and *Woman's Journal*: within the next few years, the homely magazines enlarged and multiplied. In *Woman*, the most basic, Edith Blair (alias Norah Schlegel, another editor whose heart beat much like Heal's and a DIA subscriber) with extraordinary patience watered down *Design* for a mass-readership, using orange on the walls in 1957, in 1958 recommending lilac blue with coffee and cream and by 1961 suggesting dark brown paint with jewel colours in the furnishing. Meanwhile *House and Garden*, *Vogue*'s domestic counterpart, most superior and cleverest of housebound magazines, was promoting a whole range of *House and Garden* colours—forest green and cardinal red, middy blue, light gunmetal and other urbane shades—and Olive Sullivan, the Decoration Editor, was evolving, in her room sets, an influential style, fresh, clean and pseudo-countrified, elaborate and charming, combining fine new pieces with a nice accumulation of well-picked bric-a-brac.

As fervent propagandists for design the journalists were considerably fiercer than the CoID. On factory tours, immaculate small parties of lady journalists in smart imposing hats would tackle manufacturers, who generally seemed dumbfounded, and ask them why their standards of design were mediocre. Why cut that glass decanter when it looks much better plainer? Why paint that cup with roses when it looks so lovely white? Why not treat designers the way they do in Sweden? Why not be like Gustavsberg, Arabia or Orrefors? For this was the time when Scandinavia, to the journalists and other tasteful people, approximated heaven.

To encourage them, Paul Stemann at Finmar was importing Wegner chairs and Gense stainless steel, Arabia pottery and Kaare Klint paper lampshades which RCA designers seemed to buy in bulk. The Green Group (the Good Furnishing Group of retailers in a new and more Nordic incarnation) was importing substantial quantities of Scandinavian furniture. Little shops, craft-orientated, Scandinavian in tenor, with a comfortable love of well-made little things, now appeared in Britain: the first was Primavera, Henry Rothschild's shop in Sloane Street in 1945, and by the later fifties they were opening in dozens. In Sheffield, Interior Decorations; in Manchester, Malcolm Bishop; in Doncaster and Retford, York Tenn, Yorkshire design shops apparently directly inspired by Scandinavia, based on the Swedish design shop, Svensk Tenn. And everywhere you went, you were almost sure of finding a Svensk or Norsk or Dansk shop, full of stainless steel and teak.

This love of Scandinavia was at its most fastidious in the upper reaches of the RCA, in the Western Galleries, the long dank College workshops above the Aeronautical Museum. On top of Wilbur Wright and his experimental aeroplane, Professor R. D. Russell and David Pye were teaching their furniture students to respect the plain and simple, to understand construction, to care for natural wood, to appreciate the Swedish understatement of Carl Malmsten, to worship the finesse of the Danish school of Klint: Scandinavian designers who were, in their turn, indebted to the British eighteenth-century fine sturdy craftsman style.

Design had gone full circle; the British avant-garde was influenced by Denmark which was influenced by Britain. At the same time, more directly, the British craft tradition revived by Webb and Gimson in the later nineteenth century began to be appreciated. Morris and his friends, up to now the rather private preserve of *Architectural Review* readers and Pevsner, were revealed in all their beauty and virility and Britishness, their quaintness and their honesty, for all the world to see. For the Festival of Britain 'The Cotswold Tradition' was exhibited in Cheltenham by Oliver Hill, showing Ashbee and Gimson and the Barnsleys in their setting of patient Cotswold building and sheep-shearing and hay-making. The next year Peter Floud, Keeper of Circulation at the Victoria and Albert Museum, an addict of the period, put on an exhibition of 'Victorian and Edwardian Decorative Arts', showing Godwin, showing Dresser, showing central Arts and Crafts, and offshoots as far-flung as Peasant Industries in Haslemere. An era which had seemed almost wholly unimportant, of negligible interest if not an outright joke, seemed suddenly quite vital. Voysey was a hero; and people began noticing Charles Rennie Mackintosh.

In 1959, Gordon Russell, a designer with the Cotswold tradition very much at heart, a philosopher in tune with Gimson and with Ashbee, the British modern movement in a way personified, retired from the Council of Industrial Design. By then he had been knighted and the Queen, as she had tapped him gently on the shoulder with the sword, had kindly murmured a few words on the success of the CoID, and—wrote Sir Gordon—'I felt gratified that her reaction, as usual, would be that of a great many of her subjects.' In 1959, the Council was awarded the Gran Premio Internazionale la Rinascente Compasso d'Oro, recognition from Milan 'as the oldest and most efficient government organization for the development and popularization of good design'. Calling himself the Council's scheduled ancient monument, feasted and presented with an English oak staircase by the CoID members, and a tankard from the Arts Club, and an old cut-glass decanter from the Scottish Committee, Gordon Russell went his way, back to Kingcombe in the Cotswolds, and soon the entire character of British design changed.

186
Robert and Roger Nicholson
Dining recess from Homes and
Gardens Pavilion, Festival of
Britain, 1951.

187
Robert and Roger Nicholson
Sitting room for an old lady from
Homes and Gardens Pavilion, 1951.

188
Ernest Race
'Springbok' chairs made by Race
Furniture, on South Bank, 1951.

189
K. G. Browne
Unicorn restaurant sign, 1951.

190
Robert Sevant
Festival Pattern Group wallpaper
derived from crystal structure
diagram of insulin, made by
John Line, 1951.

188

189   190

191

192

191
Ernest Race
'Antelope' chair made by Race
Furniture, 1950.

192
Ernest Race
'Cormorant' deck chair made by
Race Furniture, on board the
Oriana, 1955.

193
Ernest Race
'Flamingo' chair made by Race
Furniture, 1956.

194
Howard Keith
'Eloquence' easy chair made by
H.K. Furniture, 1952.

195
Robin Day
'Hillestak' chair in moulded plywood
made by Hille, 1951.

196
Booth and Ledeboer
Mahogany sideboard with recessed
rosewood door fronts made by
Gordon Russell Furniture, 1951.

193

194

195

196

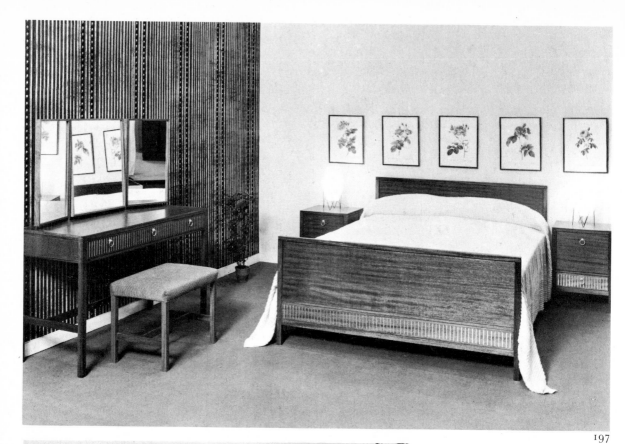

197

197
Ward and Austin
Bedroom furniture made by
Loughborough, 1955.

198
Ward and Austin
Bedroom furniture made by
Loughborough, 1957.

199
Robin Day
Convertible bed settee made by
Hille, 1957.

200
Robin Day
'Form' unit seating made by Hille,
1957.

201

202

203

201
Robert Heritage
Storage unit made by G. W. Evans,
1952.

202
Robin Day
Television receiver made by Pye,
1957.

203
Robert Heritage
'Hamilton' sideboard made by
Archie Shine, 1958.

204
John and Sylvia Reid
Dining-room furniture in teak made
by Stag, 1959.

205
George Fejer and Eric Pamphilon
'Manhattan' chairs and settee made
by Guy Rogers, 1958–9.

204

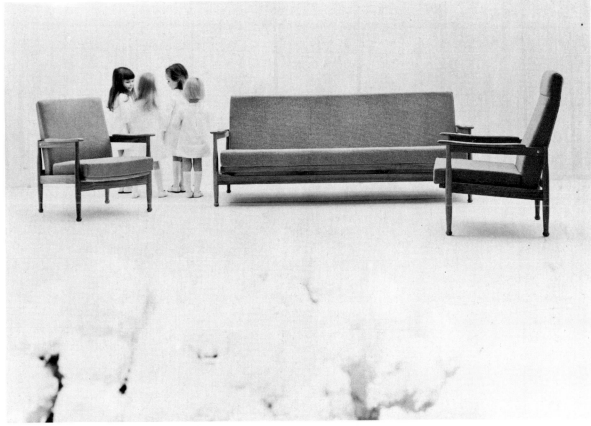

205

206

207

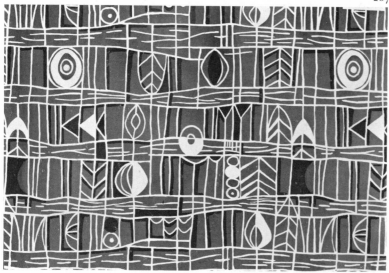

208

206
Marian Mahler
Printed fabric made by David
Whitehead, late 1940s.

207
Marian Mahler
Printed fabric made by David
Whitehead, late 1940s.

208
Jacqueline Groag
Printed fabric made by David
Whitehead, late 1940s.

209
Lucienne Day
'Calyx' printed cotton made by
Heal Fabrics, 1951.

210
Lucienne Day
'Fothergay' linen glass cloths made
by Thomas Somerset, 1960.

209

210

211

212

213

211
Humphrey Spender
'Inglewood' cotton/rayon furnishing fabric made by Edinburgh Weavers, 1959.

212
Tibor Reich
Furnishing fabric, mid-1950s.

213
Ronald Grierson
'Regatta' carpet made by Stockwell, 1953.

214
F. G. Hobden
'Vision Net' in cotton/terylene made by Clyde Manufacturing Co., 1958.

215
Audrey Tanner
'Mandala' Wilton carpet made by Carpet Manufacturing Co., 1959.

214

216

217

218

216
Susie Cooper
'Whispery Grass' china, 1956.

217
Edward Bawden
'Heartsease' muffin dish and teaset
made by Wedgwood for Orient Line,
1952.

218
Robert Stewart
Kitchen storage jars in earthenware,
1959.

219

220

221

219
R. Stennett-Willson
'Tower' table glass made by
Nazeing Glassworks for Wilmart,
1959.

220
*Milner Gray with Kenneth Lamble
and John Cochrane of Design Research
Unit*
Part of a range of Pyrex oven-to-
table glassware made by James
Jobling, 1955–65.

221
Noel London and Howard Upjohn
'Chef Royal' enamelled steel
saucepans made by Edward Curran,
1960.

222

223

224

222
Robert Welch
Stainless steel jugs made by Old Hall,
1958.

223
Robert Welch
Silver coffee urn made for Churchill
College, Cambridge, 1960.

224
David Mellor
'Pride' silver teaset made by
Walker and Hall, 1958.

225
Robert Welch
Stainless steel toast rack made by
Old Hall, 1955.

226
David Mellor
'Pride' silver cutlery made by
Walker and Hall, 1954.

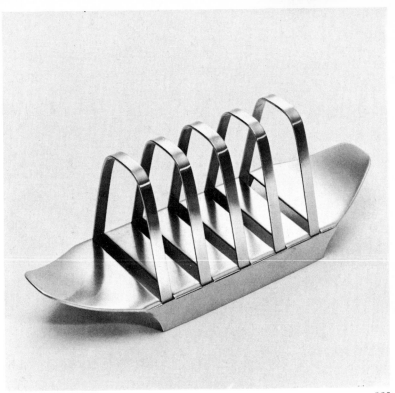

225

227
E. Cooke-Yarborough and Ronald Homes
Electric light fitting made by
Conelight, 1954.

228
D. W. Morphy
Electric iron made by Morphy-
Richards, 1952.

229
C. W. F. Longman
'Packaway' refrigerator made by
Prestcold Division of Pressed Steel,
1959.

230
Jack Howe
Electric wall clock made by Gent,
1956.

231
David Ogle
'Rayburn' convector fire made by
Allied Ironfounders, 1957.

227

228

229

230

232
R. David Carter
'Orbit' castor made by J. Gillott, 1961.

233
John Waterer
Coach hide case for typewriter made
by S. Clarke for British Olivetti, 1951.

234
Hulme Chadwick
Pruner made by Wilkinson Sword, 1956.

232

231

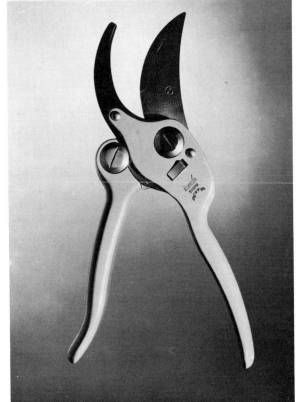

233   234

235

Christian Barman
Bus stop for London Transport, 1959.

236

Richard Stevens
Street lighting column made for
Atlas Lighting, 1959.

237

Neville Conder
Telephone kiosk designed for G.P.O.,
1958.

238

Douglas Scott
'Pay-on-Answer' telephone coin box
designed for G.P.O., 1955–7.

239

Jack Howe
Transport shelter in timber designed
for London Transport, 1954.

235   236

237

238

239

7
Union Jacks and the Computer 1960-1969

'The Princess Margaret, Countess of Snowdon and
The Earl of Snowdon this evening visited an
Exhibition of Perspex at the Royal College of Art.'

THIS was the announcement from Kensington Palace, published
in *The Times* Court Circular and showing how far the royal spirit
of patronage had moved from Prince Albert's workmen's cottages,
the Duchess of York's poker-work, Prince Edward's functional
reading lamp of 1933, and even the Duke of Edinburgh's Prize for
Elegant Design, first awarded in 1959. For in the 1960s, in Lord
Snowdon, a professional photographer and film-maker, designer
of an aluminium Aviary for London Zoo, reformers of design had
a most practical supporter—more convincing than Prince
Edward, more useful than Prince Albert—with an interest in
science and a wordly sense of fashion: two contrary directions in
which design was shifting. Lord Snowdon joined the Council of
Industrial Design.

When, in 1961, Lord Snowdon was installed in a CoID staff
office in the Piccadilly building, helping with the CoID's endeavours to promote 'by all practicable means' design in British
industry, the movement for reform in design was nothing new.
It was over a century since Henry Cole was trying to effect the
alliance of fine art and manufacture, and a hundred years exactly
since William Morris opened his art workshops, and was preaching
to his friends and fellow-craftsmen the importance of simplicity,
sincerity, good materials and sound workmanship. It was, by
then, more than forty years since the Design and Industries
Association was first sounding its tucket and striking its colours.
It was almost thirty years since Frank Pick's Council for Art and
Industry began its conscientious work. It was even (although at
the time it did not seem it), sixteen years since the formation of the
Council of Industrial Design. By this time, the Council employed
204 people; the Board of Trade Grant was £240,000. Government
support for the reformers was substantial. What exactly, at this
stage, could they be said to have achieved?

They had made a certain headway with the manufacturers.
The output of decent tea-cups, well-made tables and neat refrigerators was much higher than it used to be. They had also
made a certain headway with the retailer. The number of shops
stocking decent tea-cups, well-made tables, and Council-approved
products in general was greater. At the same time, the imagination
of the public—and this was most important and extremely interesting—had been seized, much more than ever, by ideas of
good design. Design for modern life: it became a kind of craving.
So much so, as we shall see, that the Council of Industrial Design,
which had encouraged it, was almost left behind.

The thing was that the ideals of the *cognoscenti*, the reverential
feeling for the nicely-designed object, largely through the efforts

of successions of reformers, had gradually reached a much, much wider public.

The cult of special objects for the house, precisely chosen for their individuality and beauty of design, goes back as far as Morris and art furniture workshops and the days when Morris wall-papers adorned most tasteful houses. The singling out of teapots, chairs and tables, books and cushions as positive examples of the designer's art was a Walter Crane obsession: art, he said, should be recognized in the very humblest objects. This intense discrimination, this emphasis upon the designer of the product— *Gimson* chairs, *De Morgan* pottery—essential to the character of the British Arts and Crafts, reached its heights, of course, in Glasgow, with Mackintosh and Walton and Miss Cranston's spotless tea-rooms, in which even the cutlery was specially designed. Wrote Mrs Jessie Newbery, wife of the Director of the Glasgow School of Art, herself a fine embroideress and cushion-cover maker:

'I believe that nothing is common or unclean; that the design and decoration of a pepper pot is as important, in its degree, as the conception of a cathedral.'

This was the principle sophisticated people (the DIA, the *Architectural Review*) hung on to through the century. They glorified the pepper pot. They carried on the cult of the nicely-chosen object; a pleasant household snobbery for people in the know. In the twenties and the thirties, they cultivated craftsmanship: an Edward Barnsley cupboard, a bowl by Bernard Leach. They also came to worship certain new industrial products: a beer mug by Keith Murray, an Edward Bawden tile. At the same time, and increasingly, they loved an *objet trouvé*, or an object which they found to be much better than it seemed: plain old things like porridge bowls were suddenly invested with an awesome sort of glamour. By 1945, pre-dating Terence Conran by almost twenty years, the *Architectural Review* went into raptures over white enamel ironware, red-rimmed and workmanlike; shiny black earthenware jugs (which 'look particularly well if used for milk') and burnt sienna-colour pint mugs 'discovered in a country iron-monger's store'.

By then the war had ended. The aesthetically painful time of taking what you got was shortly to be over. For even if utility furniture and pottery had been a lot more tolerable than anyone had thought, this did not compensate for lack of choice: and in reaction, the urge for great uniqueness was starting up again. This was one good reason for the magic of the Festival, when every designer in the country had his head. This was why the magazines, especially *House and Garden*, could entice their readers out to search for butchers' blocks in hornbeam, antique leeches' urns and other little curios, individual to the point of obscurity. This also explains well the success of the Council of Industrial Design in promoting the idea of special household products designed by special people. The cult of the designer expanded and expanded; by 1962 a discriminating couple would knowledgeably buy a Robin Day convertible, a David Mellor coffee pot, a Brian Asquith boiler, a Martyn Rowlands baby bath, some David Carter castors, a Lucienne Day glasscloth, a chair by Ernest Race, and a Duke's Prize cordless razor designed with utmost elegance by Kenneth Grange. 'Cuttings from *Design*,' wrote a man in Wendover to that magazine, 'are almost our Bible.' In a letter to *The Guardian*, a Wolverhampton reader, wanting advice on the rug to buy, explained:

'I have painted walls and woodwork white and covered the floor with Olive Sullivan's 'Bachelors Button' carpet in burnt orange chestnut. Upholstery is Donald Brothers' unbleached linen mullein cloth. Curtains are orange in a bright Sekers fabric and I am relying upon pictures, books, cushions and rug for bright contrasting accessories. I have found a winner in London Transport's poster 'Greenwich Observatory' which I think looks marvellous against the white walls.'

Such sense and information, such care and such enthusiasm: this was the design-conscious consumer of the sixties.

People knew about designers and design. For there they were in focus everlastingly at Heal's, on every floor, and in an exhibition held in 1960 and entitled 'Designers of the Future'. At the Cotton Board Design and Style Centre in Manchester, under Donald Tomlinson, young textile designers were picked out for publicity: for instance, Pat Albeck, Robert Dodd, Colleen and Gillian Farr with their delicately twining fashionable florals. At Goldsmiths' Hall in London, Graham Hughes the Art Director, was busily promoting the young jewellers and silversmiths: Andrew Grima and John Donald, Gerald Benney, David Mellor, Robert Welch, Keith Tyssen, Keith Redfern, Gerda Flockinger. Commercial firms were boosting their designers: Viners advertised the expertise of Benney, 'famous goldsmith designer'; Old Hall then went one better and described its stainless steel as 'noble metal shaped to perfection by Robert Welch who is recognized as a leading British designer'.

The immense design palaver (which, of course, infuriated basic engineer-designers, whose praises were unsung) happened at a time when youthfulness in general had taken hold of Britain in a rather startling way. The era of the pop group, the boutique and soon the mini-skirt; the heyday of Bazaar and Woolland's 21 Shop; concentration on the personal, the off-beat and the jolly: this sudden burst of fashion made 'design' more popular. Soon what had begun as a small and earnest movement was wilder and much noisier, extremely young and gay. Art nouveau and William Morris were brought back into favour by a larger populace than they had ever known: 'In Carnaby Street,' said the *Daily Express* in 1965, 'Gear have run out of £80 Chesterfields upholstered in William Morris fabrics'; 'William Morris ties the latest vogue', said the *Mail*; 'William Morris wallpapers for bathrooms', said the *Sun*. In *Industrial Design and the Community* Ken Baynes, with inordinate approval, commented on the way that ordinary people and the designer were moving towards one another: 'It is,' he found, 'a *rapprochement* based on a reawakening delight in gaiety, vulgarity, and humour.' To the fury and amazement of some of his profession, Michael Wolff made a statement in the *SIA Journal*: 'Basically it is true that the sort of designers in Britain who have really given people a bang in the past two years are Ken Adams, art director of the James Bond films; Frederick Starke, with his clothes for Cathy Gale; and Ray Cusick, with his Daleks. People like Mary Quant and John Stephen have had the same sort of impact on a more limited age-range. It is their zing, their zest, and their vigorous understanding of what design is all about which should be one of the main contributions of industrial designers to modern society. It'll be a great day when cutlery and furniture designs (to name but two) swing like the Supremes.'

Given the zing and zest, and the concurrent country cottage visions of the glossy magazines; given the great build-up for design and the designer, from William Morris onwards; given the long cult of special household joys, the artistic status symbols, Terence Conran and his Habitat had everything to gain. Habitat, a household shop, 'a shop for switched-on people', opened in South Kensington in 1964. It offered, quite blatantly, 'instant good taste': 'We hope we have taken the foot slogging out of shopping by assembling a wide selection of unusual and top quality goods under our roof. It has taken us a year to complete this pre-digested shopping programme and we are confident that many women will take to this new style of buying with enthusiasm.'

Here, on a plate, were all the things the design pundits had hunted for and gloated over all these many years: workmen's mugs and rustic cooking pots and sturdy peasant furniture, baskets, cheap pub glasses, butchers' aprons, wooden toys, an overall good humour and indomitable Britishness. The debt to Arts and Crafts was altogether obvious. But where Arts and Crafts were genuine (or almost), this was phoney: a brilliant and timely commercial pastiche.

'I am not,' wrote Terence Conran, 'interested in "pure" design, which designers sell to other designers, and architects to other architects. I am interested in selling good design to the masses.' The idea of pre-selection—the principle at Heal's and shops like Dunn's of Bromley—was now carried to extremes. Hand-picked by Terence Conran, Habitat was selling a whole fashionable, jovial, pseudo-rural way of life. And all around the country, in small shops called Trend or Scope, Shape or Gear or Spectrum (instead of Svensk and Dansk), pre-selected furnishings and odds and ends were sold with vast conviction and informal, personal service. At Design Design in Lancaster the owners concentrated on things which they themselves had either bought or admired in the past, or things handmade by friends. A firm called Goods & Chattels had a pre-selected stock of storage jars and bentwood, dried dyed flowers and cut-out guardsmen and suchlike for the shopkeepers too ignorant or lazy to pre-select themselves.

In the face of the supermarkets, individual shopkeepers, usually with very little capital, began. None were perhaps braver, more Christian, harder-working than the people who elected to sell proper children's toys: not the mass-produced monstrosities which quickly fell to bits, but strong good toys with play-value, substantial in design. Perhaps they did not know it, but they shared the purist outlook of the parents of John Ruskin, who expected him to play with just a wooden cart and bricks. They certainly acknowledged the influence of Abbatts, who opened shop in Wimpole Street in 1933, stocking stoutest trucks and jigsaws and the bricks which H. G. Wells designed when he wrote *Floor Games*: all toys of lasting worth. By 1967, there were probably a dozen shops with Abbatt's outlook—Galts, John Dobbie, John for Toys, The Owl and the Pussycat, the Boy and Girl Shop, Play and Learn and so on—addicts for sound workmanship, immaculate and bright.

Stressing the importance of design, with fervent feeling for children, life and beauty and the joy of natural wood, individual craftsmen or very small-scale factories produced conscientious toys for these conscientious shops: John Spence's little animals, hand-carved; John Gould's minute, neat, shiny lacquered tugs; Tim Green's honest village bricks; Susan Wynter's whirling roundabouts, and Annette Shelley's cats; Pinny Mice and Tubby Bears from Richmond terrace houses; Sydney Dogs and Lionel Lions and Dilly's Donkeys made in Essex, Pop-Up Rabbits and Black Sambos, Crannie Toys, and Brenda Toys, Coach House Toys, Old Cottage Toys and Ding-Dong hand-made rattles, Simple-Sew Rag Dolls and Make-Your-Own Glove Puppets. Small, wayward cottage industries were fashionably revived.

It was with the instinct that anything is possible Doc Hudson began candle-making, Nigel Quiney started decorating paper-bags and wrapping-paper, Ian Logan put the first of his bold swirling patterns on to plain tin trays. The sense that self-indulgence was now becoming saleable caused Natalie Gibson to embellish tiles with hearts. 'News' in *Design* in 1967 included perspex clocks, paper earrings, patterned pillowcases, and three very jokey cushions that matched up to form a woman. *Design* was less respectful; there was much more shoulder-shrugging. Students left their colleges quite confident and nonchalant. If British manufacturers resisted their ideas, then (like Grierson and like Harcourt) they would sell designs abroad. If British firms showed no enthusiasm for producing whatever they designed, they would market it themselves. This was the attitude that led to little firms like JRM and OMK and Osborne-Little wallpapers, Impetus and Genesis and all the new purveyors of paper chairs and blow-up, knock-down, stack-flat coloured furniture; the dozens of small jewellers; the individual clockmakers.

What is interesting is the way in which a number of these individual enterprises reached a wider market: the way in which Clendenning's experimental furniture was taken up by Race; the way in which the toys designed and made painstakingly by Kristin Baybars and her friends were later mass-produced. What is interesting too is the way designer-craftsmen—designers and/or craftsmen—were so interchangeable. Apart from the few dedicated potters or craft silversmiths, the students leaving college had developed a new attitude: designers were beginning to be far less interested in the means than the results. They cared most for the effect. If industry could make it, and would, then they were happy. If industry would not, then they sat down to it themselves.

All this was quite a change: a rather disconcerting change for the Council of Industrial Design which, through the sixties, had been steaming on respectably, with Centre and with Index, with Awards and Conferences. With Lord Snowdon to the fore (he had given up his job, but worked for the Council as Honorary Adviser) the CoID was still plodding round the industries explaining the virtues of a modern design policy. It had won a famous victory, with questions in the House, over the design of the new Cunard liner, demolishing for ever the tendency in industry to leave design decisions to the Chairman's wife. Its labours had been praised and its achievements had been listed in a House of Lords debate in 1964, in which Viscount Chandos memorably said, 'I never feel comfortable sitting in a chair with the Pytchley hounds in full cry,' and Lord Drumalbyn, Minister of State at the Board of Trade pronounced 'At least we can take comfort from the fact that the task of encouraging design is in good hands', and Baroness Eliot of Harewood said most poignantly, 'I well remember the work of the late Sir Ambrose Heal.'

For that was just the trouble: at this point, the Council seemed much closer to the world of Ambrose Heal than Terence Conran. It looked out of touch with OMK and JRM and swinging London; its zing and zest was minimal; it seemed almost out of date. The dilemma was perceptively explained by Paul Reilly who succeeded Sir Gordon Russell as Director of the CoID, in a leader for the *Architectural Review* in 1967, 'The Challenge of Pop'. Ten years earlier, he said, it had all been so much easier: selectors, armed with yardsticks of Deutscher Werkbund origin, with standards of functional efficiency and fitness for purpose, truth to materials, economy of means, had easily picked out sound design from meretricious; there was then a 'concensus of informed professional opinion in favour of direct, simple, unostentatious, almost neutral solutions'. So much so that the Council, without quite intending it, had seemed to establish its own sober, neutral style.

'London,' wrote Paul Reilly, 'was not yet actually swinging, but she was on the move and rediscovering the excitements of *fin de siecle* colours and patterns. At this point the Design Centre, which until then had spearheaded the campaign against feeble imitations in favour of modern common sense, came into real danger of being hoist with its own petard.' In other words, the Council, so upright and so sensible, was looking rather dowdy, not to say irrelevant. In an SIA Oration, Stephen Spender had cruelly summed up a situation which was to become increasingly obvious through the early 1960s, when the standards of design which the Council propagated were appearing too inflexible, too boring, too austere. He complained of the simple furniture, the unobtrusive yet tasteful hangings, clean-limbed flat irons, innocuous cups and saucers, limpid glass, governessy electric clocks, glacial refrigerators, flat-chested cupboards, disinfected panels of linoleum, all suggesting the young married couple wearing plastic overalls and washing up together after a wholesome and simple meal of foods which are a harmony of oatmeal and pastel shades, at the end of a day in separate offices equipped with electric typewriters. Was this what the DIA ideals had come to? And, if so, what did the Council plan to do?

'Writing in retrospect,' continued Paul Reilly, 'it is easy to give a false impression of deliberate policy decisions being taken by subtle, pliable men sitting round a Council table and recognizing the danger signals and trimming their sails accordingly.' This, he assured readers, was not at all what happened. But one way or another, policy was altered: 'We are shifting, perhaps,' he explained, 'from attachment to permanent universal values to acceptance that a design may be valid at a given time for a given purpose to a given group of people in a given set of circumstances, but that outside those limits it may not be valid at all; and conversely there may be contemporaneous but quite dissimilar solutions that can still be equally defensible for different groups— mini-skirt for the teenager, something less divulging for the matron; painted paper furniture for the young, teak or rosewood for the ageing—and all equally of their times and all equally susceptible to evaluation by a selection committee. All this means is that a product must be good of its kind for the set of circumstances for which it has been designed.'

That attitude was, of course, a very different thing from the other older theories of absolute correctness: the precise, dogmatic principles of Henry Cole; the Arts and Crafts' great love for solid, lasting values; the DIA insistence on interminable worth; Gordon Russell's gentle urge for 'making rich the daily round'. But Paul Reilly was of course a very different kind of person, educated as more of an international modernist than British country craftsman, more cerebral than practical, astute more than romantic, ambitiously benevolent, an opportunist rather than a steady slow advancer, articulate and sociable, quick and diplomatic. His background in the British modern movement of the thirties, with its optimistic principles of taking the broad view, no doubt encouraged Paul Reilly to develop a workable and tolerant philosophy as Director of the Council of Industrial Design: a theory that stretched from paper chairs to great machine tools, from Union Jack dishcloths to, say, cranes or AC motors. From 1960, when he became Director, Paul Reilly seized all possible chances to enlarge.

So it was that the Council of Industrial Design, not content with promoting decent teacups, well-made tables, and neat refrigerators, moved on to bigger things as well: to machine tools and computers, to heavy engineering. It seemed clear that the British engineers' exceptional talent, a century before, for producing a design which was technically and aesthetically admirable, somehow, somewhere, through the years, had gone astray. Since Brunel and Stephenson, Fowler and Baker (with his statement that 'honesty is the guiding light of the designer'), engineers appeared to have lost their sensitivity. It was the old, old story; the Feilden Committee put it bluntly in the report on engineering design submitted in 1963 to the Department of Scientific and Industrial Research, 'British machines are being compared with foreign machines whose designers had understood better the refinements of design and the requirements of the user.'

This was the problem which W. H. Mayall, the new officer for Capital Goods at the Council, had to think about. An inaugural conference in Birmingham convinced him that it was necessary to strengthen the concept of industrial design in engineering and in particular to define its relationship with engineering design. In other words, no one—not design engineers, not industrial designers—knew quite what they were aiming at. Bill Mayall formulated a basic design doctrine, which he carried around like a banner from then on. This doctrine was, briefly, that the design objective contains within it two related aims: the achievement of a functional purpose and the marrying of this purpose to human needs and desires. The former is primarily the engineering design objective, the latter the industrial design objective. Good design is the symbiosis of the two.

This particular movement for reform was the most solemn, the slowest, hardest going and the loneliest of all. Far from the gregarious Arts and Crafts and DIA, remote from the Design Centre Awards and other jollities connected with consumer goods, Bill Mayall, very deadpan, conducted a solitary campaign for design. His strategy was to give lectures and write articles for the engineering press and so awaken interest, then cultivate the people who seemed hopeful and persuade them to take on a professional industrial designer to work with the firm's design engineers. Odd pockets of improvement in different industries affected the converted firm's competitors: for instance, one microscope maker modernized his products and soon the other microscope makers followed suit; a machine-tool manufacturer worked with a designer, and gradually other manufacturers came asking the Record of Designers for a list of possibilities. The five or six companies employing an industrial designer in 1958, through soundly-reasoned argument and sensible persistence, had ten years later multiplied to 200 or more.

As it was in the thirties, it is interesting still, beyond the official propaganda and persuasion, to find in every firm making progress in design, one person pushing hard. Individuals still counted. Rupert Kay at AEI, since 1933, had fought for and achieved, in the end, his own design centre, a fully-equipped model shop, a professional design staff, a series of inter-departmental design conferences: this was, in its day, a considerable victory. J. H. Hilton at Mather & Platt, with consistent encouragement from William Mather, then Director of the General Machinery Division, built up an industrial design unit, establishing a new company design philosophy based on three fundamental notions of SIMPLICITY, STANDARDIZATION and MODERN CONFIGURATION. British design, with emphasis on ergonomics, cybernetics and scientific concepts quite unknown to Henry Cole (though he would soon have learned them), had become a different thing.

Now, more than ever, the industrial designer steered clear of frills and fripperies, avoided the word 'art'. The SIA renamed itself, as hastily as possible, Society of Industrial Artists and Designers, and serious Colleges of Art (and sometimes Craft) were transformed into Colleges of Art and Design. They were businessmen, not artists, Douglas Scott and F. C. Ashford, Alan Kirkbride, Wilkes & Ashmore and avuncular Jack Howe who, insisting that industrial design is a serious activity and designers are sincere and capable individuals, most sanely explained in a *Financial Times* article, the industrial designer's role as a member of a whole industrial team:

'In the field of engineering design there are very few activities which can be performed single-handed, but must of necessity be the result of team work. The design team may be composed of several people, each making his particular contribution in the field in which he is an expert. The industrial designer's contribution is made principally from the point of view of the user, but he must also study the appropriateness of materials and methods of manufacture and combine the results into the final form of the product. All this of course is done in close and constant touch with the other members of the team.

'The engineer's approach is from a different angle because he is concerned primarily with those aspects of design which must be considered in order to meet a given technical specification. He must be concerned with performance, economics, manufacture and cost. The other members of the team also approach the problem from their particular specialist viewpoint and thus it is that we have the same problem approached from different angles but meeting in the middle.

'Teamwork demands a sympathetic human relationship and understanding between every member. The solitary artist or craftsman can go away and work happily on his own without having to worry about other people but in industry this is impossible. A degree of interdependence is called for which can produce jealousies and misunderstandings; prejudice and traditional attitudes must often be broken down before the design process begins to run smoothly. A designer or engineer is involved not only with technicalities but with other people who are also highly trained essential members of the design team—the economist, technician, salesman and manager. Sometimes this involvement can lead to an unsatisfactory tug-of-war of opposing and misunderstood attitudes, or it can add up to a total clearly defined brief and working pattern which is the prerequisite to good design.'

For this was an age of designing by committee: a commercial committee or a government committee, a British Rail or London Transport Design Panel, a committee set up by the Ministry of Public Building and Works to commission design for British embassies, committees convened by the Ministry of Transport to consider new road signs and design new traffic signals. Standard Telephones & Cables appointed Richard Stevens as Industrial Design Manager; Michael Farr set up as management consultant in design; the Royal Society of Arts gave out more medals to encourage 'consistently distinguished design policies'. Industrial design manuals, reports and regulations, directories of house styles, official memoranda on corporate identity, proposals and amendments and paper-work, piled up. And with them the offices of the design consultants, led by Design Research Unit, expanded: as Milner Gray had stated back in 1955 'In my view, a design consultant's services can be best employed through a design committee . . . is it not part of the industrial designer's responsibility to accustom himself to the techniques of inter-departmental administration? I believe it is.'

This was the period of large all-purpose offices, the advent of the general consultant designer: designer of products and packaging and graphics, house styles, exhibitions, offices and shops, space planner and environmental architect, market researcher almost ad infinitum. 'We can,' maintained Hulme Chadwick, 'do almost anything; the scope is unlimited.' Others said the same: Gaby Schreiber, Lewis Woudhuysen, F. H. K. Henrion, Willi de

Majo, Ogle Design, Richard Lonsdale-Hands, Tandy Holford Mills (employing 45), Allied Industrial Designers (employing 51, with offices in Brussels, Oslo and Stockholm, with clients in the Netherlands and Germany and Switzerland, with design teams operating in French, German, Swedish, English). Eric Marshall, an American-style cut-and-thrust designer, as far from William Morris as the British have yet gone, summed up his philosophy: 'The company believes that industrial product design, by definition, is engineering orientated design and that industrial graphic design is market orientated. Aesthetics alone are of no value.'

Large-scale designers, through the sixties, had been holding large-scale conferences on huge and complex subjects, like 'The Frontiers of Perception'. Professor Misha Black, a monumental speaker, has addressed the world's designers at ICSID and UNESCO. Designers have been mingling with psychologists, ergonomists, statisticians, sociologists and anthropologists, founding Design Research Societies, Ergonomics Research Societies and so on; holding symposiums on the computer; discussing the designer in industrialized building; embarking with vast earnestness, and systematic method, on programmes of research which might well last them for ten years.

The great project of the sixties, which went on year in year out, was research into design of a hospital bed. This was carried out by Bruce Archer's Research Unit, attached to the School of Industrial Design (Engineering) at the Royal College of Art. It involved a worldwide search of literature: 100,000 documents, a mammoth filing system. It meant postal enquiries and face-to-face interviews, evolving a performance specification with 85 statements of user requirements: for instance to accommodate 19 British males out of 20 in comfort a bed must provide a lying space 86 inches (218 cm) long. The Research Unit built its own prototypes, identifying 41 critical factors and 85 problem areas. Every step in the design development was recorded, even the false trails, and these provided material for subsequent design methods studies. The Unit submitted the prototype for inspection and test by selected doctors, nurses and Ministry of Health technical officers, and built a ward-setting in the RCA workshop for preliminary assessment. A final year Textile student designed curtaining and a bedcover to realistic specification; two engineering students designed and built a combined table-locker unit; another made a unit for lighting, communications and services; meanwhile the Department of Industrial Glass supplied the ash tray and non-spill flower vases. A number of simple user tests were performed in semi-realistic conditions in the ward. Next, the Ministry of Health undertook to pay for the construction of a number of beds to this design, and organize and carry out trials in hospitals, with attendant pathologists, anaesthetists, radiologists, physiotherapists and work study staff. Next, a team of nursing tutors and staff nurses examined the prototype in practice, and recorded their comment on standard forms. Next, twenty beds were installed in a 'characteristic hospital' near London for field trials: the ward was observed continuously from 6 in the morning to 10 o'clock at night; every activity involving every bed was recorded on specially devised forms; each patient and each nurse was then subjected to attitude survey interviews by social scientists; there was then a measured study of the energy expended by nurses using old and new bed designs and a methods study on efficiency. The trial was designed to yield information on 60,000 activities, 4,500 samplings and about 270 attitude surveys: in all, about 1,700,000 pieces of information. The forms were designed so that the results could be directly transcribed onto punched tape for computer analysis, answering—or partly answering—the final questions:

1. Does the bed fulfil the specification?
2. Does the specification correctly describe the user's needs?
3. Is the ward-patient-nurse system created by the use of the new specification markedly better or worse than existing systems?

An SIA member wrote to *The Designer* asking if this was not an extremely cumbersome and expensive way of tackling a problem which could be solved as easily by more intuitive methods. And probably it was. But this was not the point: the hospital bed project was building up a body of knowledge, and advancing the status of design. That was the mood, scientific, sociological, infinitely patient, of Bruce Archer and his team, and the other research units, with commercial backing, at Manchester and Hornsey and other intellectual colleges of art. For all this sudden emphasis on systematic method, this insistence on rationalizing design processes, was a bid for intellectual respectability: something which designers before now had done without. In the sixties, the whole set-up for the training of designers had become much more ambitious, broader-based, more literate. The Diploma in Art and Design, an equivalent of a university degree, was introduced in 40 colleges in England and Wales. Five of them also offered post-diploma studies. Half of these big colleges by now had been absorbed into centrally-administered, large polytechnic schemes. Besides, with trumpets blowing and specially-embroidered ceremonial robes, the Royal College of Art had now been granted university status, and gave master's degrees to its students of design.

With the news that the Council of Industrial Design was likely very soon to be incorporated in a National Design Council, a larger, richer, and more influential body, covering the whole range of industry, from light to heavy and from craft-based to highly-technical, a new phase for reform of design appeared to be beginning. An age of anonymity for the designer. An age of teamwork and systematic method and industrial design manuals.

A time for talk of total-activity-patterns and the designer's contribution to the expanding technological universe.

How William Morris and Voysey would have hated it. How hard Harry Peach would have tried to understand it. But how very satisfactory, neat, tidy and rewarding, Henry Cole would have found it, after all.

POSTSCRIPT

1971, and one has a distinct feeling that design—or anyway 'design'—has had its heyday. The glorious visions of a nicely designed Britain now seems a little faded. The old reformers have died, or been subdued.

It has suddenly become extremely obvious to designers that the notion of a close, harmonious, idealistic collaboration between designer, manufacturer and shopkeeper—the theory so dear to the hearts of the reformers, from the Council of Industrial Design and D.I.A. right back as far as Cole and his forays into industry—is just a bit too hopeful. One finds these days, when talking to designers leaving college, that this is not the thing they really aim for any more.

The future, as far as one can see it at the moment, seems to be less with official propaganda and high-minded little groups of design enthusiasts, more with designers themselves getting out and doing things. Young designers seem less inclined to work within a ready-made system of industrial consultancy. They more often want to make their individual contribution, and within the next few years the numbers of designer-manufacturers, designer-distributors and designer-shopkeepers is bound to multiply.

Hopes for all things bright and beautiful have dwindled. But other ideas and attitudes have overtaken them and, realistically, the future of design in Britain now lies with the British designers themselves.

240

241

242

240
Stefan Buzas and Alan Irvine
Entrance to Standard Bank,
Northumberland Avenue, London,
1966.

241
Stefan Buzas and Alan Irvine
Interior, Standard Bank, 1966.

242
Clive Bacon
Linking/stacking chairs in beech
made by Design Furnishing
Contracts, 1963.

243
Ronald Carter
'Brompton' chair made by Dancer
and Hearne, 1963.

244
Robin Day
Polypropylene stacking chair made
by Hille, 1961.

245
Conran Design Group
Kitchen furniture, 1966.

246
Ernest Race
'Sheppey' easy chair and settees
made by Race, 1961–2.

247
Nigel Walters
'International' kitchen units made by
F. Wrighton, 1968.

244

245

246

247

248
Robert Heritage
'Queen Elizabeth II' restaurant
chairs made by Race, 1967.

249
Martin Grierson and Keith Townend
Pre-formed plywood units made by
Kandya, installed in laboratory at
Imperial College, London, 1961.

250
Nicholas Frewing
'Flexible' chair made by Race, 1966.

251
Ronald Carter
Storage units for Consort, 1965.

248

249

250

251

252

253

254

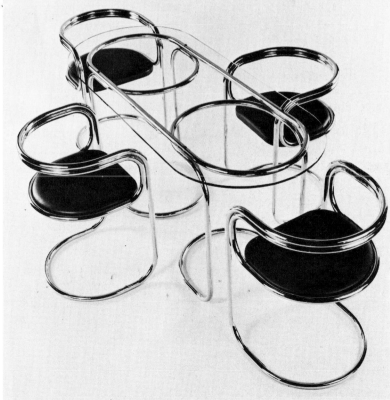

252
OMK Design
Chair in chrome-plated tubular
steel and leather, 1966.

253
Polycell Design Group
Nursery furniture in corrugated
fibreboard, 1967.

254 and 255
R. V. Exton and P. K. Wigglesworth
Tubular steel dining table and chairs
made by Plush Kicker, 1968.

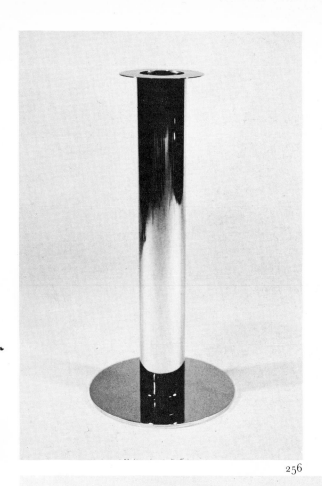

256

256
Zeev Aram and Associates
Floor-standing ashtray for
Simpson's, London, 1967.

257
Zeev Aram and Associates
Executive desks system, 1965.

258
Zeev Aram and Associates
Floor mirror for Simpson's, 1967.

259 and 260
Zeev Aram and Associates
Interior, Trend Department,
Simpson's, 1967.

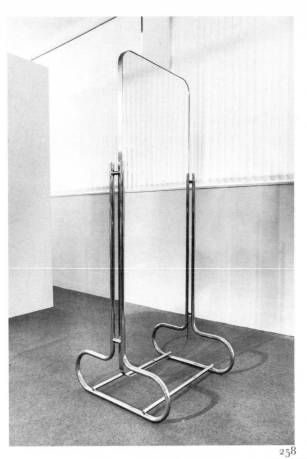

258

259

260

261

262

263

261
Frederick Scott
Seating in polyurethane foam made
by Hille, 1968.

262
Max Clendenning
Dining furniture in pre-formed
plywood made by Race, 1966–7.

263
Robin Day
'Disque' knock-down table made by
Hille, 1967.

264
Peter Murdoch
'Hexagon' seating in polyurethane
foam made by Hille, 1968.

265
Howard Carter
'Sunflower' printed cotton made by
Heal Fabrics, 1962.

266
Gillian Farr
'Ambergate' satin union fabric made
by Bernard Wardle, 1964.

267
Shirley Craven
Printed cotton satin made by Hull
Traders, 1963.

268

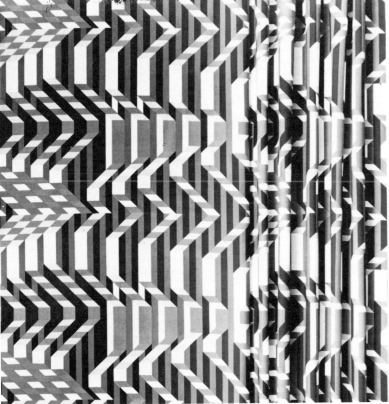

268
Shirley Craven
'Five' printed linen and cotton made
by Hull Traders, 1966.

269
Haydon Williams
'Extension' printed cotton made by
Heal Fabrics, 1967.

269

270

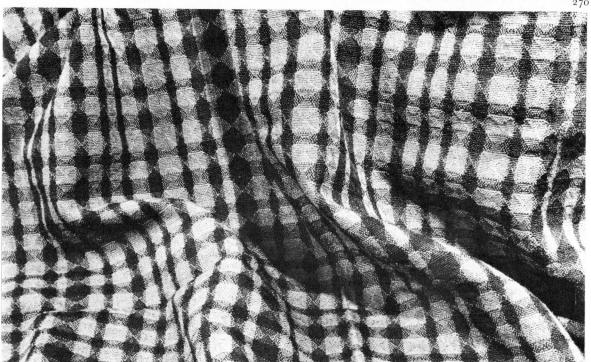

271

270
Cathryn Netherwood
'Concentric' satin cotton made by
Heal Fabrics, 1968.

271
Tamesa Fabrics
'Allegro' two-tone weave for
upholstery, 1963.

272
Tamesa Fabrics
'Visor' striped textured cotton, 1967.

273
William Robertson and Peter Simpson
'Glendale' woven linen/rayon/cotton
made by Donald Brothers, 1963.

272

273

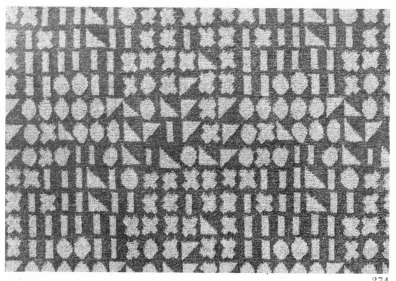

274

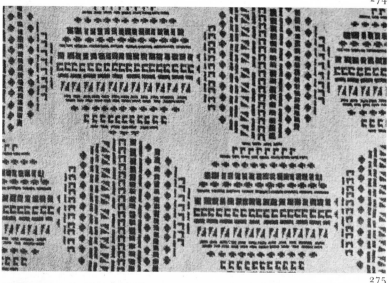

275

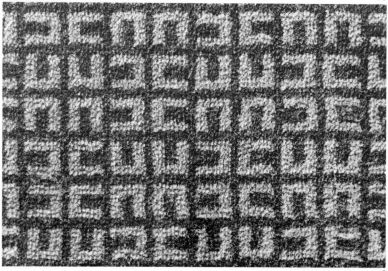

274
Lucienne Day
'Signum' carpet made by
I. & C. Steele, 1965.

275
Lucienne Day
'Big Circle' carpet made by
I. & C. Steele, 1965.

276
Mary Yonge
'Magnetic' carpet made by
I. & C. Steele, 1965.

276

277

277
Catherine Beevers
'Katrina' carpet made by Andrew
Gaskell, 1965.

278
Catherine Beevers
'Scene Collection' wallpaper made
by Crown, 1967.

278

279

280

281

282

283

279
Robert Welch
Cast-iron table heater and casseroles, 1965.

280
Tarquin Cole and John Minshaw of Ceramic Consultants
Stoneware casseroles made by Govancroft, 1964.

281
Frank Thrower
'Victoria' wine suite made by Dartington Glass, 1964.

282
David Queensberry and Jessie Tait
Tableware made by Midwinter, 1965.

283
Robert Welch
Cast-iron candlesticks, 1962.

284
David Mellor
'Embassy' silver teapot designed and
made for Ministry of Public Building
and Works, 1962.

285
Robert Welch
'Alveston' stainless steel teapot made
by Old Hall, 1963.

286
David Mellor
Polystyrene cutlery made by Cross
Paperware, 1970.

287
Robert Welch
Condiment set in stainless steel and
plastic made by Old Hall, 1963.

288
David Mellor
Tea and coffee pots in stainless steel
and plastic made by J. R. Bramah,
1969.

284

286

287

288

289

290

291

292

293

289
Robert Welch
'Merlin' electric alarm clock made by
Westclox, 1962.

290
D. M. R. Brunton
'Corinthian' electric fire made by
Belling, 1963.

291
Kenneth Grange
'Vecta' Brownie camera made by
Kodak, 1962.

292
Kenneth Grange
'Courier' electric shaver made by
Milward, 1961.

293
Robert Heritage
'Quartet Major' light fittings made
by Rotaflex, 1964.

294
Norman Stevenson
Bells and bell pushes made by
Friedland, 1963.

295
Kenneth Grange
'Classic' electric iron made by
Morphy-Richards, 1966.

296
Hulme Chadwick
Garden shears made by Wilkinson
Sword, 1963.

297
Joy and Malcolm Wilcox
Cut-out doll sheet made by Sari
Fabrics, 1964.

298
Martyn Rowlands
Telephone made by Standard
Telephones and Cables, 1963–4.

299
John Gould
Toy train made by Nicoltoys, 1962.

295

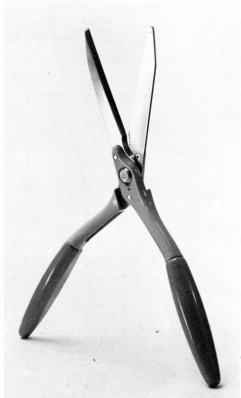

296

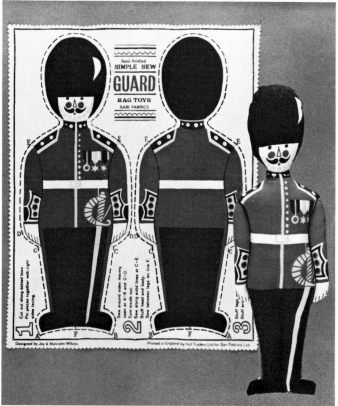

297

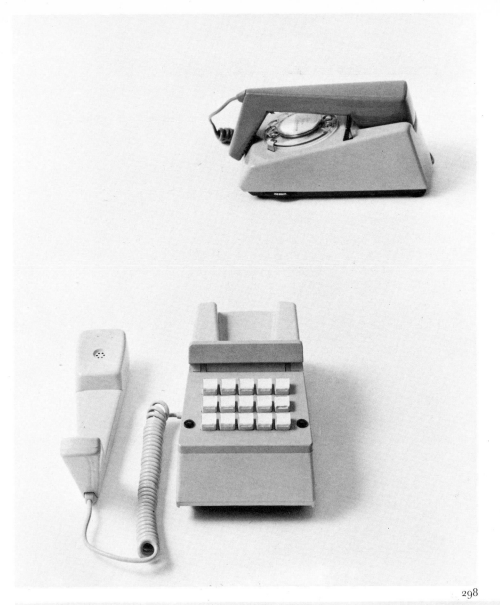

298

299

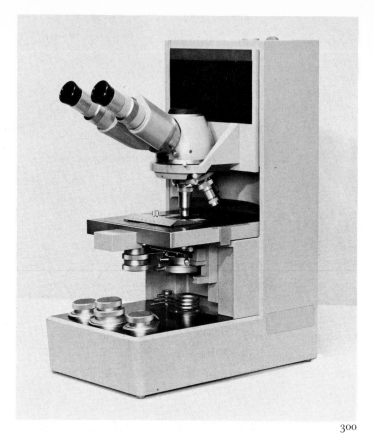

300
Noel London and Howard Upjohn
'Patholux' microscope for Vickers
Instruments, 1964.

301
Noel London and Howard Upjohn
'1901' system for '1900' computer
series, made by International
Computers, 1965.

300

301

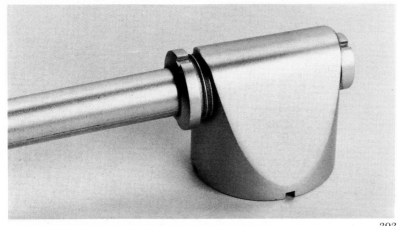

302
R. David Carter
Gas fitting from Gas-Flo system
developed by Wales Gas Board, 1967.

303
David Mellor
Gear-measuring machine for
J. Goulder, 1965.

302

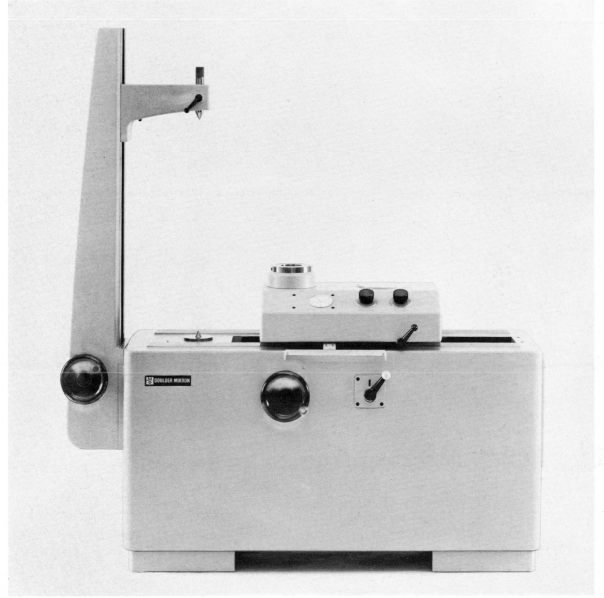

303

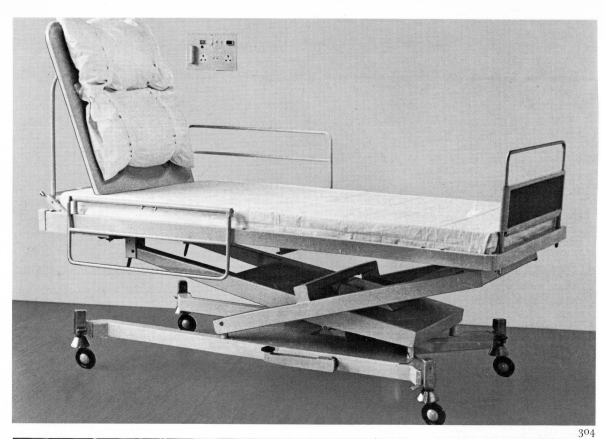

304

305

307

306

304
Royal College of Art, School of Industrial Design (Engineering) Research Unit (Director, Dr L. Bruce Archer)
Prototype hospital bed, developed 1963–7.

305
Mather and Platt Industrial Design Department with Electrical Engineering Designers
Flameproof motors, 1966.

306
David Mellor
Traffic signal system designed with Ministry of Transport, 1969.

307
Jock Kinneir
Directional traffic sign system designed for Highway Authorities, 1963.

308

309

310

308
Alex Moulton
Moulton Major bicycle, 1963.

309
Alec Issigonis
Mini Minor made by British Motor
Corporation, 1959. De luxe version,
1967.

310
Douglas Scott Associates
Hy-Mac 580B Excavator made by
Rhymney Engineering, 1964.

311
*Misha Black and James Williams of
Design Research Unit*
Beagle B206 made by Beagle
Aircraft, 1961.

312
*Misha Black and J. Beresford-Evans of
Design Research Unit*
25 kv. 3,200 h.p. AC/electric
locomotive designed for British
Railways, 1956.

311

312

Chronological Table

1836   Mr Ewart's Select Committee reported to the Government on 'the best means of extending a knowledge of the arts and the principles of design among the people (especially the manufacturing population) of the country'.

1837   Normal School of Design established at Somerset House (later to develop into Royal College of Art).

1841   *True Principles of Pointed or Christian Architecture* by Augustus Welby Northmore Pugin published.

1844   Society for the Encouragement of Arts, Manufactures and Commerce held first Exhibition of the Products of National Industry.

1846   Felix Summerly (alias Henry Cole) won silver medal for design for tea-set in Society of Arts Competition.
Society of Arts began to give annual prizes to students of design in art schools.

1847   Summerly's Art Manufactures founded.
Society of Arts granted Royal Charter.

1849   *Journal of Design and Manufactures* first published.
Seven Lamps of Architecture by John Ruskin published.

1851   Great Exhibition held in Hyde Park.

1851–3   *Stones of Venice* by John Ruskin published.

1852   Ornamental Art Collection opened at Marlborough House (later to form basis for Victoria and Albert Museum).

1856   Department of Practical Art created (later to become Department of Science and Art) at South Kensington under Henry Cole.
Grammar of Ornament by Owen Jones published.

1857   *Report on the Present State of Design as Applied to Manufactures* by Richard Redgrave published.

1861   Morris, Marshall and Faulkner, Fine Art Workmen, issued first prospectus.

1862   International Exhibition held in South Kensington.

1868   *Hints on Household Taste* by Charles Eastlake published.

1875   Arthur Lasenby Liberty opened shop in Regent Street, specializing in Oriental merchandise.

1877   Society for Protecting Ancient Buildings (Anti-Scrape) formed.

1880   Art Furniture Alliance opened by Christopher Dresser in Bond Street.

1881   George Edmund Street died.

1882   Century Guild formed by Arthur H. Mackmurdo.
Sir Henry Cole died.

1884   Art Workers' Guild founded.
Home Art and Industries Association formed.

1888   Arts and Crafts Exhibition Society founded, holding successful exhibitions in 1888, 1889, 1890, 1893 and 1896.
National Association for Advancement of Art and its Application to Industry founded.
C. R. Ashbee formed Guild and School of Handicraft.

1890   Kenton & Co., furniture workshops, opened by Lethaby, Gimson and Sidney Barnsley.
William Morris founded Kelmscott Press.

1893   *The Studio* first published.

1895   Bing's shop, L'Art Nouveau, opened in Paris, selling a large number of Arts and Crafts from England.

1896   Society of Designers established 'To advance the arts of design and the status of designers; and for friendly intercourse' (but little appears to have been heard of it again).
Central School opened 'to encourage the industrial application of decorative art' and Lethaby appointed joint Principal.
Hermann Muthesius attached to German Embassy in London for research into British architecture and crafts.
William Morris died.

1897–99   Glasgow School of Art, first phase, built to design by Charles Rennie Mackintosh.

1898   Heal's first catalogue of Plain Oak Furniture produced.
Northern Art Workers' Guild held first exhibition.
Walter Crane appointed Principal of the Royal College of Art but resigned the same year.

1899   Grand Duke of Hesse's artistic colony at Darmstadt established with designs for the Palace by Baillie Scott and Mackintosh.

1900   Paris Exhibition: British designers represented (Heal's winning two silver medals).
Ernest Gimson and the Barnsley brothers settled in the Cotswolds.
Lethaby became first Professor at the Royal College of Art (retiring as Principal of the Central School in 1911).

1901   Glasgow International Exhibition.
Die Englische Baukunst der Gegenwart by Hermann Muthesius published in Germany.

1902   Turin International Exhibition.

Ashbee's Guild of Handicraft moved to Chipping Campden, Gloucestershire.

1904 Christopher Dresser died.

1904–5 *Das Englische Haus*, 3 illustrated volumes by Hermann Muthesius, published in Germany.

1905 Exhibition of Cheap Cottages at Letchworth, sponsored by *The Spectator*.

1910 Lewis Day died.

1911 Report of the Departmental Committee on the Royal College of Art recommended closure of the College.

1914 Harold Stabler, Ambrose Heal, Harry Peach and others visited the Werkbund Exhibition in Cologne and returned convinced of the importance of designing for machine production.

1915 Government-sponsored wartime exhibition of German industrial design held at Goldsmiths Hall.
Design and Industries Association founded with 199 members.
DIA held first exhibition 'Design and Workmanship in Printing' at Whitechapel Gallery.
Walter Crane died.

1916 DIA exhibited at Arts and Crafts Exhibition at Burlington House.

1918 Cecil Brewer died.

1919 *Art and Industry* pamphlet issued by Ministry of Reconstruction.

1920 British Institute of Industrial Art founded and gallery opened in Knightsbridge but official grant withdrawn the next year.
Federation of British Industry formed Industrial Art Committee, with Charles Tennyson as Chairman, 'to consider the question of industrial art in this country'.
DIA 'Exhibition of Household Things' held at Whitechapel Gallery.
Ernest Gimson died.

1923 Exhibition of 'Industrial Art Today'.
Francis Meynell founded Nonesuch Press.

1924 Designers' Register and Employment Bureau opened by Industrial Art Committee of FBI.
Royal Society of Arts, encouraged by Sir Frank Warner, began series of annual competitions for design open to all British subjects.
W. A. S. Benson died.

1925 Paris Exhibition.
Sidney Barnsley died.

1927 DIA exhibited at Leipzig Fair.

1928 Chermayeff exhibition held at Waring & Gillow.
Gordon Russell exhibited furniture at Powell's London showroom.
Charles Rennie Mackintosh died.

1929 'Industrial Art for the Slender Purse', British Institute of Industrial Art exhibition, held at Victoria and Albert Museum.

Gordon Russell opened shop in Wigmore Street.

Jack Pritchard commissioned stand from Le Corbusier for Venesta at Building Trades Exhibition.

The Face of the Land, DIA Year Book, published.

1930   Society of Industrial Artists founded.

Memorandum on State-aided Art Education published by Industrial Art Committee of FBI, recommending that regional colleges should be established and the Royal College of Art reorganized.

Report on Handicrafts in Elementary Schools published by LCC.

Report on Design in the Cotton Industry published by H.M. Inspectors.

1931   Board of Trade appointed Committee on Art and Industry, under Lord Gorell.

Exhibition of Swedish Art held in London.

William Richard Lethaby died.

1932   Association of Artists in Commerce founded (but never came to much).

Raymond McGrath, Wells Coates and Serge Chermayeff designed interiors for new BBC building.

Report on Art and Education, in particular industrial art exhibitions, published by Gorell committee.

1933   Dorland Hall exhibition held, in collaboration with DIA.

DIA exhibitions of model houses held in Manchester and Welwyn.

BBC held series of talks, 'Design in Modern Life'.

Paul and Marjorie Abbatt opened toyshop in Wimpole Street.

Ghastly Good Taste, by John Betjeman, published.

1934   Council for Art and Industry set up by Board of Trade, with Frank Pick as Chairman, to encourage good design, 'especially in relation to manufacturers'.

Pick Council held small exhibition of Silverware at Victoria and Albert Museum.

Second, less successful, Dorland Hall exhibition held.

DIA exhibition held in Birmingham.

'Exhibition of Modern Living' held at Whiteley's.

Walter Gropius arrived in England, and left again two years later.

Art and Industry by Herbert Read published.

Memorandum on Art Education, with particular reference to the Royal College of Art, sent by the DIA to the Board of Education.

1935   'British Art in Industry' exhibition held at Burlington House.

Pick Council held pottery exhibition at Victoria and Albert Museum.

Orion, architect Brian O'Rorke, launched by Orient Line.

Industrial Design Partnership founded by Milner Gray, Misha Black and others.

Report on Industrial Art submitted by Nugent Committee to Minister of Education.

Memorandum on industrial art training for management and staff of firms (full-time and part-time) and for foremen, travellers and salesmen, published by Industrial Art Committee of FBI.

Report on Education for the Consumer, particularly training in design in elementary and secondary schools, published by Pick Council.

Harold Stabler died.

1936 First 10 Designers for Industry appointed by Royal Society of Arts (from 1937, *Royal* Designers for Industry): Douglas Cockerell, Eric Gill, James Hogan, J. H. Mason, H. G. Murphy, Keith Murray, Tom Purvis, George Sheringham, Harold Stabler, Fred Taylor, C. F. A. Voysey.

National Register of Industrial Art Designers formed by Board of Trade on recommendation of Pick Council.

Committee on Advanced Education in London, under Viscount Hambledon, appointed by Board of Education.

Pick Council held exhibition of domestic metalwork.

'Exhibition of Everyday Things' at Royal Institute of British Architects.

'Seven Architects' Exhibition at Heal's.

Dunbar Hay furnishing shop opened in Albemarle Street.

Crofton Gane commissioned pavilion for Royal Show, Bristol, from Marcel Breuer and F. R. S. Yorke.

Report on The Working-Class Home: its Furnishing and Equipment by Mrs C. G. Tomrley, published by Pick Council.

Harry Peach died.

1937 Paris Exhibition included British Pavilion by Pick Council.

Working-Class Home exhibition, based on Pick Council report, held at Building Centre.

BBC Talks on Design by Anthony Bertram held with concurrent travelling exhibitions by DIA.

Industrial Art in England by Nickolaus Pevsner published.

Report on Design and the Designer in Industry published by Pick Council.

Report on Advanced Art Education in London published by Hambledon Committee recommending that 'a new orientation should be given to the Royal College'.

Proposal for an Industrial Art Centre completed by Pick Council but never published.

1938 Glasgow Exhibition.

Royal Designers for Industry appointed: Reco Capey, E. Gordon Craig, Milner Gray, Percy Metcalfe, Ethel Mairet.

Royal Society of Arts Industrial Bursaries Competition began.

Good Furnishing Group formed by Geoffrey Dunn, Crofton Gane, Gordon Russell and others.

1939 Central Institute of Art and Design formed ard artists'
a d designers' interests i
R Designers for Ind ed Irving, Sir

Ambrose Heal, Brian O'Rorke.

1940   Cotton Board Fashion Design & Style Centre opened in Manchester.
Royal Designers for Industry appointed: Susie Cooper, E. W. Grieve, A. B. Read, Gordon Russell, Percy Delf Smith, Allan Walton, Anna Zinkeisen.

1941   Royal Designer for Industry appointed: Duncan Grant.
C. F. A. Voysey died.
Frank Pick died.

1942   Utility Furniture Committee and subsequently Design Panel, Chairman Gordon Russell, set up by Board of Trade.
DIA, with Army Bureau of Current Affairs, began to send mobile design exhibitions round army camps, art galleries and schools.
Arthur H. Mackmurdo died.
C. R. Ashbee died.

1943   Report on 'Industrial Design and Art in Industry' completed, but not published, by sub-committee under Cecil Weir (set up by Post-War Export Trade Committee of Department of Overseas Trade), recommending the establishment of a Central Design Council.
Design Research Unit set up by Marcus Brumwell, Misha Black, Milner Gray and others, with Herbert Read as first manager.
Royal Designers for Industry appointed: Charles Holden, Barnes Wallis.

1944   Report on Art Training by Meynell-Hoskin Committee, submitted to Board of Trade and Education, supported the idea of a Central Design Council, recommending that it should be a grant-aided body.
Proposals for a Central Design Council and Industrial Design Centre published by Industrial Art Committee of FBI.
Council of Industrial Design (with separate Scottish Committee) formed 'to promote by all practicable means the improvement of design in the products of British industry': first Chairman was Sir Thomas Barlow; first Director, S. C. Leslie.
Rayon Industry Design Centre established.
The Missing Technician in Industrial Production by John Gloag published.
Royal Designers for Industry appointed: Wells Coates, Sir Geoffrey de Havilland, Enid Marx, Charles Nicholson, R. D. Russell.

1945   'Design for the Home' exhibition, designed by Milner Gray, held by Council for the Encouragement of Music and the Arts.
'Historical and British Wallpapers' exhibition, designed by Eric Brown and Stefan Buzas, held at National Gallery.
CoID Record of Designers developed from National Register of Industrial Art Designers.
Primavera opened by Henry Rothschild in Sloane Street.
Royal Designer for Industry appointed: Francis Meynell.

1946   'Britain Can Make It' exhibition held by CoID at Victoria and Albert Museum, designer James Gardner.

Design and Research Centre for the Gold, Silver and Jewellery Industries established.

National Diploma in Design introduced in art schools, with emphasis on specialization.

Report on the Training of the Industrial Designer completed by CoID but never published.

Report *The Visual Arts* sponsored by Dartington Hall trustees, published in collaboration with PEP.

1947   Gordon Russell succeeded S. C. Leslie as Director of the Council of Industrial Design; Dr Ralph Edwards succeeded Sir Thomas Barlow as Chairman.

'Enterprise Scotland' exhibition held by CoID in Edinburgh.

Royal Designers for Industry appointed: James Gardner, Robert Goodden, Ashley Havinden.

1948   Robin Darwin appointed Principal of Royal College of Art.

'Design at Work' exhibition of products by Royal Designers for Industry sponsored by RSA and CoID.

Robin Day and Clive Latimer won prize in International Low-cost Furniture Competition, Museum of Modern Art, New York.

Central Institute for Art and Design disbanded.

Royal Designer for Industry appointed: Christian Barman.

1949   CoID exhibited abroad for first time, in 'International Exhibition of Industrial Design' in Amsterdam.

BBC series of programmes, 'Looking At Things', for schoolchildren began.

Royal Designers for Industry appointed: Edward Bawden, Barnett Freedman, Roger Furse, Eric Ottaway.

1950   Royal Designers for Industry appointed: Edward Molyneux, Sir James McNeill, Alastair Morton.

1951   Festival of Britain: South Bank Exhibition Design Group, Hugh Casson, James Holland, James Gardner, Ralph Tubbs, Misha Black.

'Living Traditions of Scotland' exhibition held in Edinburgh.

Exhibition of Industrial Power held in Glasgow.

Des.RCA first given to students awarded design diplomas at Royal College of Art.

Royal Designers for Industry appointed: Hugh Casson, J. Laurent Giles.

1952   Exhibition of Victorian and Edwardian Decorative Arts at Victoria and Albert Museum.

CoID Street Furniture design competition.

Time-Life building in Bond Street completed, with interiors co-ordinated by Hugh Casson and Misha Black.

1953   Walter J. Worboys succeeded Dr Ralph Edwards as Chairman of the CoID.

'Register Your Choice' DIA exhibition, at Charing Cross.

Royal Designers for Industry appointed: John Waterer, Ernest Race.

1954   Government approved establishment of The Design Centre for British Industries.

First Royal Society of Arts Bicentenary Medal, for people who 'in a manner other than as industrial designers have exerted an exceptional influence in promoting art and design in British industry', awarded to Sir Colin Anderson.

Royal Designer for Industry appointed: William Lyons.

1955   *Design in British Industry* by Michael Farr published.

Royal Designer for Industry appointed: Uffa Fox.

RSA Bicentenary Medal awarded to Sir Charles Tennyson.

1956   Design Centre, Haymarket, opened by Duke of Edinburgh.

'Management of Design' conference organized by CoID.

British Railways Design Panel set up; George Williams Director of Design.

Royal Designer for Industry appointed: Reynolds Stone.

RSA Bicentenary Medal awarded to Sir Walter Worboys.

SIA Design Medal awarded to Milner Gray.

Gordon Russell knighted.

Design magazine began to include regular reviews of engineering products.

1957   Scottish Design Centre opened by Scottish Committee of CoID.

'Make or Mar', DIA exhibition, held at Charing Cross.

Report on Art Examinations submitted to Minister of Education by Freeman Committee on Art Examinations, recommending greater administrative freedom for individual colleges.

Royal Designer for Industry appointed: Misha Black.

RSA Bicentenary Medal awarded to Sir Ernest Goodale.

SIA Design Medal awarded to Jan van Krimpen.

First Design Centre Awards selected by Milner Gray, Professor R. Y. Goodden, Brian O'Rorke, Professor R. D. Russell, Astrid Sampe:

> Pyrex ovenware—designers, John D. Cochrane in conjunction with Milner Gray and Kenneth Lamble of Design Research Unit; maker, James A. Jobling.
>
> Convertible bed settee—designer, Robin Day; maker, Hille.
>
> Rotaflex lampshade—designers, John and Sylvia Reid; maker, Rotaflex.
>
> Rayburn convector fire—designer, David Ogle; maker, Allied Ironfounders.
>
> Television set—designer, Robin Day; maker, Pye.
>
> Midwinter Melmex plastics ware—designers, A. H. Woodfull and John Vale; maker, Streetly, for W. R. Midwinter.
>
> Impasto wallpaper—designer, Audrey Levy; maker, The Wall Paper Manufacturers.
>
> Strawberry Hill tableware—designers, Victor Skellern and

Millicent Taplin; maker, Wedgwood.

Pride cutlery and flatware—designer, David Mellor; maker, Walker & Hall.

Connoisseur wine glasses—designer, S. Fogelberg; maker, Thomas Webb.

Flamingo furnishing cotton—designer, Tibor Reich; maker, Tibor.

Imperial Axminster carpet—designer, Lucienne Day; maker, Tomkinsons.

1958   'The Design Centre Comes to Newcastle' exhibition: first in series of promotions in provincial stores.

'Industrial Design and the Engineering Industries' conference organized by the CoID in Birmingham.

Wells Coates died.

RSA Bicentenary Medal awarded to John Gloag.

SIA Design Medal awarded to Robin Day.

Design Centre Awards selected by Sir Walter Worboys, Noel Carrington, Geoffrey Dunn, Wyndham Goodden, Jack Howe:

Carlton lavatory basin—designers, staff; maker, Shanks.

Satina pendant lighting fitting—designer, Nigel Chapman; maker, Hailwood and Ackroyd Ltd for AEI.

Hiflo bibcock tap—designers, staff; maker, Barking Brassware.

Knifecut pruner—designers, staff with Hulme Chadwick; maker, Wilkinson Sword.

Occasional chair—designer, J. N. Stafford; maker, Stafford Furniture.

Tallent paraffin oil convector heater—designers, staff; maker, Tallent Engineering.

Prestwick range of suitcases—designer, K. H. Paterson; maker, S. E. Norris.

Phantom Rose handscreen printed wallpaper—designer, Audrey Levy; maker, The Wall Paper Manufacturers.

Old Hall stainless steel toast rack—designer, Robert Welch; maker, Old Hall.

Conference tableware—designers, Tom Arnold (shape), Pat Albeck (pattern); maker, Ridgway.

Hamilton sideboard—designer, Robert Heritage; maker, Archie Shine.

Adam woven textile—designer, Keith Vaughan; maker, Edinburgh Weavers.

Vision Net lace curtaining—designer, F. G. Hobden and staff; maker, Clyde Manufacturing.

Royal Gobelin Axminster body carpet—designers, Neville and Mary Ward; maker, Tomkinsons.

Queensberry enamelled cast iron ovenware—designer, David Queensberry; maker, Enamelled Iron & Steel Products.

Artkurl Wilton broadloom carpets—designers, staff; maker, William C. Gray.

Riviera tablecloths and napkins—designer, Arthur Ingham; maker, James Finlay.

Gold Seal baby bath—designer, Martyn O. Rowlands; maker, Ekco Plastics.

Minster printed textile—designer, Humphrey Spender; maker, Edinburgh Weavers.

Vistavu slide viewer—designers, Harold R. Stapleton assisted by Howard Upjohn; maker, Rank Precision Industries.

1959   National Advisory Council on Art Education, under Sir William Coldstream, formed.

CoID awarded Gran Premio Internazionale la Rinascente Compasso d'Oro in Milan.

Design Centre labelling scheme began.

Oriana launched by Orient Line.

Sir Gordon Russell retired as Director of CoID.

Sir Ambrose Heal died.

Royal Designers for Industry appointed: Robin Day, Abram Games, F. H. K. Henrion, Hans Schleger, Berthold Wolpe.

RSA Bicentenary Medal awarded to Frank Mercer.

SIA Design Medal awarded to Tapio Wirkkala.

Duke of Edinburgh's first Prize for Elegant Design awarded by Lady Casson, Sir Basil Spence, John Summerson and Audrey Withers to C. W. F. Longman, designer (in association with Edward G. Wilkes) of Packaway refrigerator made by Prestcold Division of Pressed Steel Company.

Design Centre Awards selected by Sir Colin Anderson, Geoffrey Dunn, F. H. K. Henrion, Jack Howe and Monica Pidgeon:

Swoe garden tool–designers, staff, with Hulme Chadwick; maker, Wilkinson Sword.

Ilford K1 professional tripod—designer, Walter Kennedy; maker, Ilford.

Ellipse series lighting fittings—designer, Paul Boissevain; maker, The Merchant Adventurers.

Pride EPNS teaset—designer, David Mellor; maker, Walker & Hall.

Aristocrat socket chisels—designer, staff; maker, Ward & Payne.

Planit system: ceramic glazed tiles—designer, Derek Hodgkinson; maker, H. & R. Johnson.

Flamingo easy chair—designer, Ernest Race; maker, Race Furniture.

Fluorescent kitchen light—designers, John and Sylvia Reid; maker, Atlas.

Lever handle—designer, Roger Peach; maker, Dryad Metal.

Mandala Wilton body carpet—designer, Audrey Tanner; maker, Carpet Manufacturing.

Queen-heater solid fuel room heater—designer, David Mellor; maker, Grahamston Iron Co.

Malindi printed furnishing fabric—designer, Gwenfred Jarvis; maker, Liberty.

Piazza plastics coated fabric—designer, Edward Pond; maker, Bernard Wardle.

Inglewood woven furnishing fabric—designer, Humphrey Spender, maker, Edinburgh Weavers.

Circular dining table—designer, Hassan El-Hayani; maker, Design Furniture for the New Furniture Design Group.

1960 Paul Reilly succeeded Sir Gordon Russell as Director of CoID; Sir Duncan Oppenheim succeeded Sir Walter Worboys as Chairman.

'Designers of the Future' exhibition held at Heal's.

Competition for better litter bins sponsored by CoID.

First Report on Art Education by Coldstream Committee submitted to Minister of Education, recommending new courses of a higher standard to replace the National Diploma in Design.

Industrial Design (Engineering) Research Unit set up at Royal College of Art, under Bruce Archer.

Royal Designers for Industry appointed: Stanley Morison, Basil Spence.

RSA Bicentenary medal awarded to J. Cleveland Belle.

Duke's Price for Elegant Design awarded by Lady Casson, Robin Darwin, Gaby Schreiber and Basil Spence to Neal French and David White for Spode Apollo tableware made by W. T. Copeland.

Design Centre Awards selected by Professor Misha Black, J. Beresford-Evans, F. H. K. Henrion and Jo Pattrick:

Street lighting columns and lanterns—designer, Richard Stevens; maker, Abacus.

Irish linen glass towels—designer, Lucienne Day; maker, Thomas Somerset.

Chelsea lighting fittings—designers, Richard Stevens and P. Rodd; maker, Atlas Lighting.

Le Bosquet printed cotton satin—designer, Shirley Craven; maker, Hull Traders.

Brownie camera—designers, staff with Kenneth Grange; maker, Kodak.

Low voltage display fitting—designer, Richard Stevens; maker, Atlas Lighting.

Queensberry Ware nursery china—designers, David Queensberry (shape), Bernard Blatch (pattern); maker, Crown Staffordshire.

Pannus wallpaper—designer, Humphrey Spender; maker, The Wall Paper Manufacturers.

Lemington glass vases—designer, R. Stennett-Willson; maker, Osram.

Fiesta melamine plates—designer, Ronald E. Brookes; maker, Brookes and Adams.

Vynide coated fabric—designers, staff; maker, ICI.

Formation Furniture office desk units—designers, Yorke, Rosenberg and Mardall; maker, Bath Cabinet Makers.

Ely Stripe woven furnishing—designers, staff; maker, Donald Brothers.

Anniversary Ware oval casseroles—designers, John and Sylvia Reid; maker, Izons.

Judge stainless steel stewpans—designers, Misha Black and Ronald Armstrong of DRU; maker, Ernest Stevens.

Denison Vision Net drip-dry furnishing lace—designer, F. G. Hobden; maker, Clyde.

Royal Gobelin Axminster carpet—designer, Graham Tutton; maker, Tomkinsons.

1961   National Council for Diplomas in Art and Design, under Sir John Summerson, set up on Coldstream Council's recommendation as an independent self-governing body to administer the award of diplomas.

Antony Armstrong-Jones (later the Earl of Snowdon) joined staff of CoID.

'Design Policy for Corporate Buying', international design congress organized in London by CoID.

Modern Jewellery Exhibition held at Goldsmiths' Hall.

CoID Street Furniture exhibition installed on South Bank.

Royal Designers for Industry appointed: Stefan Buzas, Jack Howe.

RSA Bicentenary medal awarded to Audrey Withers.

SIA Design Medal awarded to Abram Gaines.

Duke's Prize for Elegant Design awarded by Sir Kenneth Clark, Robin Darwin, Jane Drew and Gaby Schreiber to Eric Marshall for Rio transistor radio made by Ultra.

Design Centre Awards selected by Whitney W. Straight, Neville Condor, Jo Pattrick, J. M. Richards, and Gary Schreiber:

Kodaslide 40 slide projector—designers, staff with Kenneth Grange; maker, Kodak.

Cormorant folding outdoor chair—designer, Ernest Race; maker, Race Furniture.

Table mirror—designer, Colin Beales; maker, Peter Cuddon.

Towel rail—designer and maker, Peter Cuddon.

Town Number One litter bin—designers, Derek Goad and John Ricks; maker, G. A. Harvey.

Adjustable spotlights—designers, John and Sylvia Reid; maker, Rotaflex.

Monte Carlo carving set—designer, G. G. Bellamy; maker, George Wostenholm.

Chef Royal saucepans—designers, Berkeley Associates; maker, Curran.

Orbit furniture castors—designers, staff with R. David Carter; maker, Joseph Gillott.

Redfyre Centramatic 35 oil fired boiler—designers, staff with Brian Asquith; maker, Redfyre.

Form unit furniture—designer, Robin Day; maker, Hille.

Paragon chemical closet—designer, Martyn Rowlands; maker, Racasan.

1962 First conference on systematic design methods held at Imperial College, London.

Second report of Coldstream Council, on vocational courses in Colleges and Schools of Art, published.

Royal Designers for Industry appointed: Lucienne Day, David Mellor.

RSA Bicentenary medal awarded to Robin Darwin.

SIA Design Medal awarded to Pier Luigi Lervi

Duke's Prize for Elegant Design awarded by Sir Kenneth Clark, Sir Trenchard Cox, Lucienne Day and Jane Drew to Nicholas Sekers for furnishing fabrics made by West Cumberland Silk Mills.

Design Centre Awards selected by Martin Moss, Stefan Buzas, Elsbeth Juda, David Queensberry, Brian Shackel and Nigel Walters:

BR heavy duty settee—designer, Robin Day; maker, Hille.

Stainless steel dishes—designer, Robert Welch; maker, Old Hall.

Pick-up arm—designers, A. Robertson-Aikman and W. J. Watkinson; maker, SME.

Hoe and rake—designer, Brian Asquith; maker, Spear and Jackson.

Dimex ceramic tiles—designer, Michael Caddy; maker, Wade.

Trifoliate wallpaper—designer, Cliff Holden; maker, The Wall Paper Manufacturers.

Sunflower printed cotton—designer, Howard Carter; maker, Heal Fabrics.

Symbol cutlery and flatware—designer, David Mellor; maker, Walker & Hall.

Vacco de luxe vacuum flask—designer, L. Leslie-Smith; maker, Vacco.

Cawdor woven linen fabric—designers, staff and Peter M. Simpson; maker, Donald Brothers.

1963 Report on Engineering Design produced by committee appointed by Department of Scientific and Industrial Research, Chairman G. B. R. Feilden, to consider the present standing of mechanical engineering design.

London Transport Design Panel formed.

Systematic method for designers by L. Bruce Archer published.

Royal Designers for Industry appointed: Tom Eckersley, Robert Heritage.

RSA Bicentenary Medal awarded to Paul Reilly.

SIA Design Medal awarded to Ernest Race.

Duke's Prize for Elegant Design awarded by Sir Trenchard Cox, Lucienne Day, The Viscountess Eccles and David Hicks to Kenneth Grange for the Milward Courier Cordless electric shaver made by Henry Milward.

Design Centre Awards selected by O. B. Miller, Elgin Anderson, Trevor Dannatt, Natasha Kroll, David Mellor and Eirlys Roberts.

Pay-on-answer coin box—designers (engineering), Associated Automation with GPO, (case) Douglas Scott; maker, Associated Automation.

Harrington screen-printed cotton—designer, Humphrey Spender; maker, Cepea.

Heritage range of wall storage units—designer, Robert Heritage; maker, Archie Shine.

Trays and sectional hors d'oeuvre dishes (in grey translucent plastics)—designer, Noel Lefebvre; maker, Xlon.

Linking/stacking chair—designer, Clive Bacon; maker, Design Furnishing Contracts.

Lightweight slide storage box—designer, Albert Cragg; maker, Boots.

Cruachan screen printed cotton—designer, Peter McCulloch; maker, Hull Traders.

Corinthian inset fire unit—designer, David Brunton; maker, Belling.

Sheppey settees and chair—designer, Ernest Race; maker, Race.

Sola wash basin—designer, E. Stanley Ellis; maker, Twyfords.

Oregon dining chair—designer, Robert Heritage; maker, Archie Shine.

1964   House of Lords debate on industrial design: Lord Peddie rose to draw attention to the Annual Report of the CoID and 'to stress the importance of encouraging original design as a factor in the stimulation of exports and the improvement of home standards'.

First report of Summerson Council for Diplomas in Art and Design published.

Third report of Coldstream Council, on Post-Diploma Studies in Art and Design, published.

Terence Conran opened first Habitat household shop in Fulham Road.

Hornsey Mobile Caravan, designed by staff/student team under Clive Latimer, won Grand Prix at Milan Triennale.

Ernest Race died.

Royal Designers for Industry appointed: Hardy Amies, Alan Irvine, Alec Issigonis.

RSA Bicentenary Medal awarded to Anthony Heal.

SIA Design Medal awarded to Edward Bawden.

First Royal Society of Arts Presidential Awards for Design

Management made to Heal's, Conran, Hille, London Transport, Gilbey, Jaeger.

Duke's Prize for Elegant Design awarded by The Viscountess Eccles, Lucienne Day, Sir Trenchard Cox and David Hicks to David Queensberry for cut crystal glassware made by Webb Corbett.

Design Centre Awards selected by A. E. Everett Jones, Audrey Levy, Neville Ward, Katharine Whitehorn and George Williams:

> Friedland 972 bell kit—designers, staff with Norman Stevenson; makers, V. & E. Friedland.
>
> Moulton bicycle—designer, Alex Moulton; maker, Moulton Bicycles.
>
> Brompton chair—designer, Ronald Carter; maker, Dancer & Hearne.
>
> Nubian laminate—designer, Helen Dalby; maker, Formica.
>
> Glendale woven fabric—designers, William Robertson and Peter Simpson; maker, Donald Bros.
>
> Memory master clock—designer, staff and Robert Heritage; maker, English Clock Systems.
>
> Brownie Vecta camera—designer, Kodak in consultation with Kenneth Grange; maker, Kodak.
>
> Palladio Lamina wallpaper—designer, Deryck Healey; maker, The Wall Paper Manufacturers.
>
> Insulated tumbler—designer, H. D. F. Creighton; maker, Insulex.
>
> Garden shears—designers, staff and Hulme Chadwick; maker, Wilkinson Sword.
>
> Printed fabrics, Shape Sixty-three and Division—designer, Shirley Craven; maker, Hull Traders.
>
> Merlin electric clock—designers, staff and Robert Welch; maker, Westclox.

1965 Society of Industrial Artists renamed Society of Industrial Artists and Designers.

Report on Industrial and Engineering Design produced by working party of Federation of British Industries under G. B. R. Feilden.

Royal Designers for Industry appointed: Herbert Spencer, Robert Welch.

RSA Bicentenary Medal awarded to Hans Juda.

SIA Design Medal awarded to Misha Black.

Duke's Prize for Elegant Design awarded by The Viscountess Eccles, David Hicks, Ernestine Carter and Milner Gray to Peter Dickinson for auditorium seating by Race.

Design Centre Awards selected by Anthony Heal, Helen Challen, Shirley Conran, Robert Gutmann, Richard Stevens:

> 'Meridian One' Sanitary Suite—designers, Knud Holscher and Alan Tye with Alan H. Adams; maker, Adamsez.
>
> 'Arrowslim' fluorescent light fittings—designers, Peter Rodd

and John Barnes; maker, Atlas.

'Gaylec' convector heater—designer, Bernard Burns; maker, Carnscot.

Cotton Satin 'Legend' 0700—designer, Alan Reynolds; maker, Edinburgh Weavers.

Yard Arm Pick-up Stick—designer, D. A. Morton; maker, Mabar.

'Embassy' Sterling Silver—designer and maker, David Mellor.

'Alveston' cutlery—designer, Robert Welch; maker, Old Hall.

Hille Wall Storage System—designers, Alan Turville and John Lewak; maker, Hille.

Rag Dolls—designers, Joy and Malcolm Wilcox; maker, Sari.

Plastics Handled Saw—designer, Brian Asquith; maker, Spear & Jackson.

Thornton Pic Slide Rules—designer, Norman Stevenson with staff; maker, Thornton.

'Kistna' furnishing fabric—designer, Sir Nicholas Sekers; maker, West Cumberland Silk Mills.

Hille Polypropylene Stacking Chair—designer, Robin Day; maker, Hille.

Ceiling Roses and Switches—designer, London & Upjohn; maker, GEC.

Hospital Wall Light—designer, Roger Brockbank; maker, Atlas.

Students' Striped Bedspreads—designers, H. W. Rothschild and Primavera Design Group; maker, Primavera.

1966   Plans first announced for combined London headquarters of Institute of Contemporary Arts, The Society of Industrial Artists, the Institute of Landscape Architects and the Designers and Art Directors' Association in Nash House Terrace, London.

Diplomas in Art and Design, equivalent to a first degree, first awarded to students completing courses at Colleges of Art.

Report 'A Plan for Polytechnics and Other Colleges', published by Department of Education and Science, proposing that many of the largest British Art Schools should be incorporated in local Polytechnics.

Engineering Design Centre established at Loughborough University.

Leverhulme Trust gave first travelling scholarships in industrial design.

George Williams, Director of Design, British Railways, died.

Royal Designer for Industry appointed: Natasha Kroll.

RSA Bicentenary medal awarded to Graham Hughes.

SIAD Design Medal awarded to Mary Quant.

Duke's Prize for Elegant Design awarded by Ernestine Carter, Mary Ward, Sir Colin Anderson and Milner Gray to Andrew Grima for jewellery.

Design Centre Awards selected by Sir Duncan Oppenheim, The

Hon. G. C. H. Chubb, Elsbeth Juda, Leslie Julius, Michael Laird, Leonard Manasseh:

'Automatic 1501' washing machine—designer, staff with Industrial Design Unit; maker, AEI–Hotpoint.

'Modric' architectural ironmongery—designers, Knud Holscher and Alan Tye; maker, G. & S. Allgood.

Desk Lamp 'Cantilever 41555'—designer, Gerald Abramovitz; maker, Best and Lloyd.

Hamilton stoneware—designers, Tarquin Cole and John Minshaw; maker, Govancroft.

Thrift Cutlery—designer, David Mellor; commissioned by Ministry of Public Building and Works.

1108 and 1111 Radios—designer, Robin Day with Douglas Jones; maker, Pye.

Flexible Chair—designer, Nicholas Frewing; maker, Race.

Quartet Major Lighting—designer, Robert Heritage; maker, Rotaflex.

Credaplan Individual Quick-Discs hotplates—designer, staff; maker, Simplex Electric.

STC Deltaphone and Deltaline Telephones—designer, Martyn Rowlands; maker, Standard Telephones and Cables.

Barbican hand rinse basin—designer, Chamberlin, Powell and Bon with staff; maker, Twyfords.

1967   Royal College of Art given University status (as a result of Robbins report on Higher Education, 1963).

Design Centre Awards renamed Council of Industrial Design Awards and scope broadened to include engineering design.

Crofton Gane died.

RSA Bicentenary Medal awarded to Harold Glover.

SIAD Design Medal awarded to Charles Eames.

RSA Presidential Awards for Design Management made to BTR Industries, Sainsbury, Clydesdale Bank, A. G. Thornton.

Duke's Prize for Elegant Design awarded by Sir Colin Anderson, Ernestine Carter, Milner Gray and Mary Ward to R. David Carter for 'Gas-Flo' system of points and fittings developed by Wales Gas Board.

CoID Design Awards—Consumer Goods Section—selected by Jasper Grinling, Brian Asquith, Rosamind Julius, Alan Irvine, Fiona MacCarthy:

'Iced Diamond' Refrigerators by Hotpoint

Ilfoprint Processors by Ilford

'PU Work Station' Office Furniture by Interiors International

Graphic System for Directional Road Signs commissioned by Ministry of Transport

'International' Range of Electric Convector Radiators by Morphy-Richards

'Tempest' Yacht by Richardson Boats and Plastics.

CoID Design Awards—Capital Goods Section—selected by W. L.

Mather, Professor Misha Black, H. G. Conway, Professor W. F. Floyd, C. H. Flurscheim, H. R. Heap, Jack Howe, D. B. Welbourn:

    Mascot 1600 Centre Lathe by Colchester Lathe Company
    Co-ordinate Inspection Machine by Ferranti
    Thompson-Watts Map Plotter by Hilger & Watts
    1900 Series Computer by International Computers and Tabulators
    Power Rammer by Pegson
    Gas Cylinder by Reynolds Tube Company
    Hy-Mac Excavator by Rhymney Engineering for Peter Hamilton Equipment.

1968   Working party set up by Institute of Mechanical Engineers, at the request of the Council of Engineering Institutions, submitted report to Ministry of Technology advocating a single design council to promote design across the whole span of British industry.

Joint Coldstream/Summerson Committee of Inquiry into structure of art and design education prompted by student disturbances at Horney, Guildford and other colleges of art.

Stedjelich Museum, Amsterdam, held international exhibition of industrial design: Britain represented by Robin Day, Kenneth Grange, David Mellor and Robert Welch.

Paul Reilly knighted.

RSA Bicentenary medal awarded to Marcus Brumwell.

SIAD Design Medal awarded to Thomas Maldonado.

Duke's Prize for Elegant Design awarded by Sir Colin Anderson, The Marchioness of Anglesey, Robert Heritage and Mary Ward to David H. Powell for 'Nova' plastics tableware by Ecko.

CoID Awards—Consumer Goods—selected by Peter Tennant, Kathleen Darby, Althea McNeish, Geoffrey Salmon, Alan Tye:

    'Clamcleat' rope cleats by Clamcleats
    Furnishing fabrics 'Chevron', 'Complex' and 'Extension' by Heal Fabrics
    Kompas 1 table by Hille
    Furnishing fabrics 'Simple Solar' and 'Five' by Hull Traders
    'Trilateral' poster display unit by London and Provincial Poster Group
    'Trimline' light by Merchant Adventurers
    'Those Things' children's furniture by Perspective Designs
    'Reigate' rocking chair by William Plunkett
    'Coulsdon' coffee table by William Plunkett
    'Silverspan' flourescent light fittings by Rotaflex
    'Sealmaster' door and window seals by Sealmaster
    'International' kitchen units by Wrighton.

CoID Awards—Capitals Goods—selected by A. R. Miller, F. C. Ashford, J. Atherton, Professor D. H. Chaddock, H. R. Heap, C. C. Mitchell, Professor W. T. Singleton, E. G. M. Wilkes:

'Hainsworth' worm gear reducer by J. H. Fenner
Flameproof motors by Mather and Platt
Colour television camera Mark VII by Marconi
'Sentinel' diesel hydraulic shunting locomotive by Rolls-Royce
'Crimpspin' CS12-600 false twist crimping machine by Ernest Scragg
'DD2' dockside crane by Stothert and Pitt.

1969   Proposals pressed forward for National Design Council, incorporating Council of Industrial Design, to cover engineering design as well as industrial design.

International Council for Societies of Industrial Design (ICSID) held conference in London.

SIA and DIA (with Institute of Contemporary Arts, Institute of Landscape Architects and Designers and Art Directors' Association) moved into headquarters in Nash House Terrace.

QE2 launched by Cunard, joint design co-ordinators James Gardner and Dennis Lennon.

Walter Gropius died.

Royal Designers for Industry appointed: Kenneth Grange, Mary Quant, Margaret Leischner, Ian Proctor.

RSA Bicentenary Medal awarded to Sir Duncan Oppenheim.

SIAD Design Medal awarded to Willy de Majo.

Duke's Prize for Elegant Design awarded by the Marchioness of Anglesey, Robin Day, Robert Heritage and Mary Quant to Jack Howe for cash dispenser MD2 by Chubb.

CoID Design Awards—Consumer Goods—selected by F. E. Shrosbree, Inette Austin-Smith, Gontran Goulden, Martin Grierson, Gilian Packard:

> Audio equipment by The Acoustical Manufacturing Company,
> 'Superjet' 4448 reading light by Concord Lighting
> 'Ease-e-load' trolleys by Deavin-Irvine
> Bollard light by Frederick Thomas
> Furnishing fabrics 'Polychrome', 'Concentric' and 'Mitre' by Heal Fabrics
> 'Vinyl' wall coverings 'Gemini', 'Solitaire' and 'Tempo' by ICI
> 'Kangol Reflex' car safety belt by Kangol
> Upholstery fabrics 'Spruce', 'Larch', 'Rowan' and 'Aspen' made by Margo
> 'Big Screen' exhibition and display units by Marler Haley,
> 'QE2' chair by Race
> 'Roanrail 2' curtain track by Roanoid
> 'Mercury 33' automatic deadlock by Yale.

CoID Design Awards—Capital Goods—selected by Matthew Wylie, Professor D. H. Chaddock, Dr R. Conrad, Ewen M'Ewen, Frank Height, B. G. L. Jackman, Noel London, C. C. Mitchell:

> Ceramic collar insulator by British Insulated Callenders & Cables
> 'Monobox' overhead travelling crane by J. H. Carruthers

'Kaldo' steel furnace made by Ashmore, Benson, Pease
'K Major' diesel engine by Mirrlees National
'Vision Comparascope' by Vision Engineering
Knitting machine by Wildt Mellor Bromley.

1970   Joint Coldstream/Summerson Committee of Inquiry into structure of art and design education recommended replacement of vocational courses by new design technician's course.

Government decision 'not to proceed to set up the new Design Council in present circumstances' interpreted by optimists as a postponement, not a cancellation.

Association for Design Education formed to promote design in general education.

Experimental G.C.E. 'A' Level design syllabus introduced in Leicestershire schools.

Institute for Consumer Ergonomics jointly sponsored by Consumers Association and Loughborough University of Technology.

100 millionth Design Centre label produced for display on product selected for Design Index.

Exhibition of Modern Chairs at Whitechapel Gallery.

Royal Designers for Industry appointed: David Gentleman, G. Allan Hutt.

R.S.A. Bicentenary Medal awarded to T. C. H. Worthington.

Duke's Prize for Elegant Design awarded by the Marchioness of Anglesey, Mary Quant, Robert Heritage and Robin Day to Patrick Rylands for Trendon Toys.

CoID Design Awards—Consumer Goods—selected by Terence Conran, Alex Gordon, John Vaughan, Juliet Glynn Smith, Kenneth Grange:

> 'Opella 500' bath tap by I.M.I. Developments
> 'Star' mobile radiophone by Standard Telephones and Cables
> 'Apollo' lamp by J. R. M. Design
> Knockdown storage unit by Kewlox
> Disposable plastic cutlery by Ecko
> Dining table and chair by Plush Kicker
> 'Savannah' heating unit by Redfyre
> 'Hedway' sign by Syncronol
> 'Muraweave' jute wallcoverings by Boyle
> Range of hand-printed wallpapers by Osborne & Little
> 'Hebridean' upholstery fabrics by Donald Brothers
> 'Spiral' and 'Automation' furnishing fabrics by Heal Fabrics
> 'Hexagon' Brussels carpets by John Crossley.

CoID Design Awards—Capital Goods—selected by G. B. R. Feilden, Frank Height, Sir Arnold Lindley, Richard Stevens, S. H. Grylls, Dr. R. Conrad:

> 'Boss Mark III' range of forklift trucks by Lancer Boss
> Weighing machine TP30 by L. Oertling
> 'Autotest' system by Marconi Instruments
> 'Dualform Model 4E' press by Press & Shear Machinery Co.

The McArthur microscope made for Dr. John McArthur
'Wee Chieftain Mark 3' boiler by John Thompson Cochran
Additions to '1900' range of computers by International Computers
Container transporter crane by Stothert & Pitt.

1971 Arne Jacobsen died.
Royal Designers for Industry appointed: Gerald Benney, Ronald Carter, Jocelyn Herbert, Richard Levin, Neville Ward.
Duke's Prize for Elegant Design awarded by Robin Day, Peter Shepheard, Mary Quant and Lady Windlesham to Derek Power for atomic physics teaching apparatus by Teltron.
CoID Design Awards—Consumer Goods—selected by Leslie Julius, Joanne Brogden, Peter Glynn Smith, Derek Phillips and Norman Stevenson:
  'Impregnable' padlocks by Ingersoll
  'Avenger 16' power boat by Avenger Boat Co.
  'Mariner' battery-powered clock by Taylor Instruments
  'Globoots' children's boots by Globoot Footwear
  Preview screen by Boots
  Photographic darkroom equipment by Paterson Products
  Pedestrian bridge by Butterly Engineering
  'Powerflood' floodlamp by Concord Lighting.
CoID Design Awards—Capital Goods—selected by Dr. Alexander Moulton, David Carter, D. Downs, S. H. Grylls, Professor Brian Shackel, Richard Stevens, D. T. N. Williamson:
  Automatic draughting system by Ferranti
  Grinding machine by Churchill
  'Spate' pump by William R. Selwood
  Tensile testing instrument by Instron
  Unican spectrophotometers by Pye Unican
  'M41 Photoplan' research microscope by Vickers.

Book List

This reference list consists primarily of books about industrial design in Britain. Books about developments abroad are included only in so far as they are relevant to what was (or what was not) happening in Britain at the time.

ABBATT, L. (ed) — *The Stanley Book of Designs for Making Your Own Furniture*, 1966.

ADBURGHAM, Alison — *Shops and Shopping*, 1964.

AMAYA, Mario — *Art Nouveau*, 1966.

AMES, Winslow — *Prince Albert and Victorian Tastes*, 1967

ARCHER, L. Bruce — *Systematic method for designers*, 1965.

ARCHER, Michael — 'Pre-Raphaelite Painted Furniture', *Country Life*, 1 April 1965.

ARNOT, R. Page — *William Morris, the Man and the Myth*, 1964.

ASHBEE, C. R. — *A Few Chapters on Workshop Reconstruction and Citizenship*, 1894; *An Endeavour towards the Teaching of John Ruskin and William Morris*, 1901; *Craftsmanship in Competitive Industry*, 1908.

ASHFORD, F. C. — *Designing for Industry—Some Aspects of the Product Designer's Work*, 1955.

ASLIN, Elizabeth — *The Aesthetic Movement*, 1969

BANHAM, Rayner — *Theory and Design in the First Machine Age*, 1960.

BATTERSBY, Martin — *The Decorative Twenties*, 1970.

BAYNES, Ken — *Industrial Design and the Community*, 1967; (ed) *Attitudes in Design Education*, 1969.

'Bauhaus, 50 years', Catalogue of Exhibition at Royal Academy, 1968.

BEARD, Geoffrey — *Modern Glass*, 1968.

BELL, Quentin — *The Schools of Design*, 1963.

BEMROSE, Geoffrey — *19th-Century English Pottery and Porcelain*, 1952.

BERESFORD-EVANS, J. — *Form in Engineering Design*, 1954.

BERTRAM, Anthony — *Design in Daily Life*, 1938.

BIRKS, Tony — *The Art of the Modern Potter*, 1967.

BLACK, Professor Misha — Cantor Lectures on Training of Industrial Designers for the Engineering Industries, *RSA Journal*, 1965.

BLAKE, John and Avril — *The Practical Idealists, a History of Design Research Unit*, 1969.

BOE, Alf — *From Gothic Revival to Functional Form*, 1954.

BRIGGS, Asa (ed) — *William Morris, Selected Writings and Designs*, 1962.

'British Art in Industry', illustrated catalogue of exhibition at Burlington House, 1935.

'Britain Can Make It', illustrated catalogue of CoID exhibition, Victoria and Albert Museum, 1946.

CAPLAN, David and Stewart G. — *British Trademarks and Symbols*, 1966.

CARRINGTON, Noel — *Design in the Home*, 1933; *Design and a Changing Civilization*, 1935; *The Shape of Things*, 1939; *Design in Civilization*, 1947; *Design and Decoration in the Home*, 1952.

CARRINGTON, Noel and HARRIS, Muriel (eds) — *British Achievement in Design*, 1946.

CASSON, Michael — *Pottery in Britain Today*, 1967.

CHAPMAN, Nigel — *Heating*, 1967.

CLARK, Sir Kenneth — *The Gothic Revival*, 1928.

COLE, Sir Henry — *Fifty Years of Public Work*, 1884.

CRANE, Walter — *The Claims of Decorative Art*, 1892; *An Artist's Reminiscences*, 1907; *William Morris to Whistler, Papers on Arts and Crafts and the Commonwealth*, 1911.

DAY, Lewis — *Everyday Art: Short Essays on the Arts Not-Fine*, 1882; *Nature and Ornament*, 1929.

Design Centre Book I, published by Council of Industrial Design, 1961.

Design Centre Book II, published by Council of Industrial Design, 1962.

Designers in Britain, illustrated review of SIA members' work, 1947, 1949, 1951, 1954, 1957, 1964.

DOREN, Harold Van — *Industrial Design (A Practical Guide)*, 1940

DOWLING, H. G. — *A Survey of British Industrial Arts,* 1935.

EASTLAKE, Charles L. — *Hints on Household Tastes in Furniture*, 1868.

EDWARDS, Ralph and RAMSEY, L. G. G. (eds) — *Early Victorian (1830–1860) Connoisseur Period Guide*, 1958.

FARR, Michael — *Design in British Industry—A Mid-Century Survey*, 1955; *Design Management*, 1966.

'Festival of Britain', Illustrated catalogue, 1951. Souvenir booklet 'Design in the Festival', 1951. Souvenir book of Crystal Design (The Festival Pattern Group), 1951.

'Festival of Britain, The Story of', official report, 1951.

'Festival of Britain, Three Cantor Lectures on', by Sir Gerald Barry to RSA, reprinted in *Journal 4880*, August 22, 1952.

FLOUD, Peter — BBC talks on William Morris, reprinted in *The Listener*, October 7 and 14, 1954.

FRANKLIN, Colin — *The Private Presses*, 1969.

FRAYN, Michael — Account of 'The Festival of Britain' in *The Age of Austerity*, ed. Michael Sissons and Philip French, 1963.

GIBBS-SMITH, C. H.   *The Great Exhibition of 1851*, 1950.

GILL, Eric   *Autobiography*, 1945.

GILLIATT, Mary   *English Style*, 1967.

GLOAG, John   *Design in Modern Life*, 1934; *Industrial Art Explained*, 1934; *The Missing Technician in Industrial Production*, 1944; *English Tradition in Design*, 1947; *Good Design means Good Business*, 1947; *Self-training for Industrial Designers*, 1947; *Victorian Taste*, 1962; *The Englishman's Chairs*, 1964.

Goldsmiths, Worshipful Company of   *Modern Silver*, 1954; *Modern Silver, Review of Gold and Silver*, 1959; *Modern British Silver, Illustrated Review*, 1963; *Modern British Jewellery, Illustrated Review*, 1963.

GOSLETT, Dorothy   *Professional Practice for Designers*, 1961.

GOULDEN, Gontran   *Bathrooms*, 1966.

Great Exhibition 1851. Illustrated Catalogue of, 1851.

Great Exhibition 1851, Reports by the Juries, 1852.

GROPIUS, Walter   'Bauhaus': Paper given to DIA, reprinted *RIBA Journal*, May 19, 1934; *New Architecture and the Bauhaus*, 1935; *Design and Industry*, 1950.

HENDERSON, Philip   *William Morris, his Life, Work and Friends*, 1967.

HENRION, F. H. K. and PARKIN, Alan   *Design Co-ordination and Corporate Image*, 1967.

HILLIER, Bevis   *Art Deco*, 1968.

HIRSCHFELD-MACK, L.   *The Bauhaus*, 1963.

HOLME, Geoffrey   *Industrial Design and the Future*, 1934.

HOUGH, Graham   *The Last Romantics*, 1949.

HOWARTH, Thomas   *Charles Rennie Mackintosh and the Modern Movement*, 1952.

HUGHES, Graham   *Modern Jewellery, 1890–1963*, 1963. *Modern Silver, 1880–1967*, 1967.

HUGHES-STANTON, Corin   *Transport Design*, 1968.

International Exhibition of 1862, illustrated booklet of exhibits issued in conjunction with 'London 1862' exhibition at Victoria and Albert Museum, 1962

JAFFE, H. L. C.   *De Stijl*, 1956.

JARVIS, A.   *Things We See—Indoors and Out*, 1946.

JOEL, David   *The Adventure of British Furniture*, 1953.

JOEL, David   *The British Furniture Revolution, 1851 to the Present Day*, 1970.

JONES, Prof. J. Christopher   *Design Methods*, 1970.

JONES, Owen   *Grammar of Ornament*, 1856.

KLEIN, Bernat   *Eye for Colour*, 1965.

LARKIN, Brian   *Metalwork Designs of Today*, 1969.

LAVER, James   *The Liberty Story*, 1959.

LEACH, Bernard   *A Potter's Work*, 1967.

LETHABY, W. R.   *Philip Webb and his Work*, 1935. *Form in Civilization, Papers on Art and Labour*, 1957.

LETHABY, W. R. and others   *Ernest Gimson, his Life and Work*, 1924.

LOEWY, Raymond   *Never Leave Well Enough Alone*, 1951.

LOUDON, John C.   *Encyclopedia of Cottage, Farm and Villa Architecture and Furniture*, 1833.

MACKAIL, J. W.   *Life of William Morris*, 1899.
'Mackintosh, Charles Rennie: Furniture', illustrated catalogue of Glasgow School of Art Collection, 1968.
'Mackintosh, Charles Rennie: Ironwork and Metalwork', Illustrated catalogue of Glasgow School of Art Collection, 1968.
'Mackintosh, Charles Rennie: Architecture, Design, Painting', catalogue to Centenary Exhibition at Royal Scottish Museum and Victoria and Albert Museum, 1968.

MACLEOD, Robert   *Charles Rennie Mackintosh*, 1968.

MADSEN, S. T.   *The Sources of Art Nouveau*, 1952.

MARTIN, J. L. and
SPEIGHT, S.   *The Flat Book*, 1939.

MAYALL, W. H.   *Industrial Design for Engineers*, 1967; *Machines and Perception in Industrial Design*, 1968.

MEADE, Dorothy   *Bedrooms*, 1967.

MIDDLETON, Michael   *Group Practice in Design*, 1967.

MOODY, Ella   *Modern Furniture*, 1966.

MORRIS, May   *William Morris, Artist, Writer, Socialist*, 1936.

MORRIS, William   *Collected Works*, 1910–15.
Morris, William, Illustrated Booklet of Designs, Victoria and Albert Museum, 1958.
'Morris & Company 1861–1940', Catalogue of Commemorative Exhibition, Arts Council, 1961.
'Morris, William, The Work Of', Catalogue of Exhibition at The Times Bookshop, by William Morris Society, 1962.

NAYLOR, Gillian   *The Bauhaus*, 1968.

PEVSNER, Nikolaus   *Pioneers of the Modern Movement*, 1936, revised version, *Pioneers of Modern Design*, published Penguin, 1960; *An Enquiry into Industrial Art in England*, 1937; *Academies of Art*, 1940; *High Victorian Design*, 1951; *The Englishness of English Art*, expanded version of Reith Lectures broadcast in 1955, 1956; *The Sources of Modern Architecture and Design*, 1968; *Studies in Art, Architecture and Design*, 1968.

PHILLIPS, Derek   *Lighting*, 1966.

PILDITCH, James and
SCOTT, Douglas   *The Business of Product Design*, 1965.

PRIZEMAN, John   *Kitchens*, 1966.

PUGIN, A. W. N.   *Gothic Furniture*, 1835; *Contrasts*, 1836; *The True Principles of Pointed or Christian Architecture*, 1841.

PYE, David   *Nature of Design*, 1964.

RAYNER, Claire   *For Children*, 1967.

READ, Sir Herbert   *Art and Industry*, 1934.

READ, Sir Herbert (intr.)   *Practice of Design*, 1946.

REDGRAVE, Richard   *Report on the Present State of Design as Applied to Manufactures*, 1857.

ROGERS, J. C.   *Modern English Furniture*, 1930.

ROLT, L. T. C.   *Victorian Engineering*, 1970.

ROTHENSTEIN, Sir William   A Plea for a Wider Use of Artists and Craftsmen, lecture to Sheffield Technical School, 1916.

RUSKIN, John   *Seven Lamps of Architecture*, 1849; *Stones of Venice*, 1851–3.

RUSSELL, Sir Gordon   *Furniture* ('Things we See' Series), 1953; *Looking at Furniture*, 1964; *Designer's Trade*, 1968.

SALMON, Geoffrey   *Storage*, 1967.

SCHEIDIG, Walther   *Crafts of the Weimar Bauhaus*, 1967.

SCHMUTZLER, Robert   *Art Nouveau*, 1964.

SEDDING, John   *Art and Handicraft*, 1893.

SEIZ, P. and
CONSTANTINE, M.   *Art Nouveau—Art and Design at the Turn of the Century*, 1959.

SHARP, Peter   *Sound and Vision*, 1967.

SKELTON, Robin (ed)   *Herbert Read, a memorial symposium*, 1970.

SPEAIGHT, Robert   *The Life of Eric Gill*, 1966.

STENNETT-WILSON, R.   *The Beauty of Modern Glass*, 1958.

STEWART, Cecil   *Art in Adversity, A Short History of the Regional College of Art*, Manchester, 1953.

TEAGUE, Walter Dorwin   *Design This Day: The Technique of Order in the Machine Age*, 1940.

THOMPSON, Paul   *The Work of William Morris*, 1967.

VALLANCE, Aymer   *William Morris, His Art, Writings and Public Life*, 1909.

'Victorian and Edwardian Decorative Art', catalogue to Victoria and Albert Museum Exhibition, 1952.

'Victorian Furniture', illustrated booklet by Victoria and Albert Museum, 1962.

'The Visual Arts' report, sponsored by trustees of Dartington Hall, published by Political & Economic Planning and Oxford University Press, 1946.

WARD, Mary and Neville   *Living Rooms*, 1967.

WATKINSON, Ray   *William Morris as Designer*, 1967.

WINGLER, Hans M.   *The Bauhams*, 1969.

WYATT, M. D.   Report on the Furniture at the Paris Exhibition of 1855, 1856. Industrial Arts of the Nineteenth Century, at the Great Exhibition, 1851, 1851–3.

YOUNG, Dennis and Barbara   *Furniture in Britain Today*, 1964.

PERIODICALS

Architectural Review, 1897– .

Ark, Journal of Royal College of Art.

Art and Design, Monthly bulletin of Central Institute of Art and Design, 1942–48.

Commercial Art and Industry, later *Art and Industry*, 1926–58.

Council of Industrial Design Annual Reports, 1944– .

Design, published by Council of Industrial Design, 1949– .

Design and Industries Journals, News Sheets and Year Books, 1918– .

Design in Industry, published by DIA, 1932; replaced by *Design for Today*, published in association with DIA, 1933; later replaced by *Trend in Design of Everyday Things*, 1936.

House and Garden.

Ideal Home.

Journal of Design and Manufactures, 1849–52.

Royal Society of Arts Proceedings.

Society of Industrial Artists, newsheets and journals, later *The Designer.*

The Studio, later *Studio International*, 1893– .

Acknowledgements

In preparing this book I have had a great deal of valuable assistance, including special facilities for visits, from manufacturers, retailers, schools of art and various public bodies and societies.

I should like to thank the following:

Paul and Marjorie Abbatt; Aram; Armitage Ware;

Beithcraft Furniture; Birmingham College of Art and Design; Bowman's; Briglin Pottery; Brinton's; Bristol Guild of Applied Art; British Motor Corporation; British Rail;

Caithness Glass; Camberwell School of Arts and Crafts; Carpet Manufacturing Co; Carpet Trades; Central School of Art and Design; Colston; Confederation of British Industry; Conran; Council of Industrial Design; Crafts Centre;

Dartington Glass; Design and Industries Association; Design Furnishing Contracts; Design Workshop; Donald Brothers; Dryad; Dunn's of Bromley; Charles Early;

Edinburgh College of Art; Edinburgh Weavers; Ercol;

Firth Carpets;

Glasgow School of Art; Goodearl; Govancroft; T. G. Green;

Heal's; High Wycombe College of Art and Technology; H. K. Furniture; Hoover; Hopewell's; Hornsey College of Art; Hygena; H. & R. Johnson;

Kingston College of Art; Kosset;

Leeds College of Art; Leicester College of Art; Liverpool College of Art; L. M. Furniture; London Transport;

Hugh MacKay; A. H. MacIntosh; Malkin; Manchester College of Art and Design; Merchant Adventurers; Metamec; Minty; Moorcroft; Morris of Glasgow; Moulton; Myers;

Nairn Linoleum; National Council for Diplomas in Art and Design;

Old Hall; O. M. K. Furniture;
Peerless Built-in Furniture; Perspective Designs; Pilkington Tiles; Poole Pottery; Pye;
Race; Ravensbourne College of Art and Design; Remploy; Reynolds Woodware; Richards Tiles; Guy Rogers; Royal Society of Arts; Royal Worcester; Rural Industries Bureau; Gordon Russell;
Sanderson; Sekers; Sheffield College of Art; Archie Shine; Slumberland; Smith's Clocks; Society of Industrial Artists and Designers; Stag; Stockwell; Stoddard; Stourbridge College of Art;
Tamesa; Tibor;
Victoria and Albert Museum; Viners;
Walker and Hall; Bernard Wardle; Webb Corbett; Wedgwood; Westclox; David Whitehead; Wolverhampton College of Art; Worshipful Company of Goldsmiths; Wrighton; Wylie & Lochhead.

I should like to thank the following people, all of whom I have either talked to or written to, and who have given me helpful information and ideas for this book:

Pat Albeck; Geoffrey Alpe; Sir Colin Anderson; Zeev Aram; Dr L. Bruce Archer; Tom Arnold; Brian Asquith; Frank Austin; H. Jefferson Barnes; John Barnes; Edward Barnsley; Edward Bawden; Gerald Benney; J. Beresford-Evans; Robert Best; Professor Misha Black; John Blake; Ronald Brookes; Paul Burall; Shirley Bury; Stefan Buzas;
Dugald Cameron; Robert Cantor; Noel Carrington; R. David Carter; Ronald Carter; Sir Hugh Casson; Hulme Chadwick; Tarquin Cole; Neville Conder; E. Cooke-Yarborough; James Cousins; Shirley Craven; Robin Cruikshank;
Helen Dalby; Sir Robin Darwin; Tarby Davenport; Robin Day; Ronald Dickens; Peter Dingley; Robert Dodd; John Donald; Geoffrey Dunn;
Brian Edwards;
Ronald Facius; Colleen Farr; Gillian Farr; Michael Farr; George Fejer; J. Findlater;
James Gardner; Alec Gardner-Medwin; John Gloag; Harold Glover; Professor Robert Goodden; Kenneth Grange; John Grant; Milner Gray; Roy Gray; Martin Grierson; Andrew Grima; Frank Guille;
Geoffrey Harcourt; Claude Hart; Colin Haxby; Christopher Heal; Adrian Heath; Frank Height; F. H. K. Henrion; Robert Heritage; Peter Heyward; Oliver Hill; the late Oliver Hill; Jack Hilton; Kenneth Holmes; Felix Holtom; Ronald Homes; Jack Howe; Kenneth Howes; Miriam Howitt; Derek Hudson; Corin Hughes-Stanton; Richard Huws;
Peter Inchbald; Ronald Ingles; Alan Irvine;

Dan Johnston; J. W. Noel Jordan; Elspeth Juda; Rosamind Julius;
Tom Karen; R. M. Kay; Bernat Klein; Peter Kneebone;
Clive Latimer; Howell Leadbeater; the late Margaret Leischner; S. C. Leslie; Richard Levin; Audrey Levy; Ian Logan; Noel London; W. M. de Majo; Eric Marshall; Enid Marx; Alister Maynard; Peter McCulloch; Raymond McGrath; Professor Andrew McLaren Young; David Medd; John Mellor; Peter Metcalfe; Sir Francis Meynell; Sir Bernard Miller; John Moon; Martin Moss, Keith Murray;
Neville Neal; Evelyn New; S. H. Nichols; James Noel-White; the late Harry Norris;
Eric Pamphilon; Geoffrey Peach; James Pilditch; William Plunkett; Diana Pollock; Edward Pond; T. E. Preston; Jack Pritchard; Jack Proctor; Patrick Purcell; David Pye;
The Marquis of Queensberry;
A. B. Read; Tibor Reich; Sir Paul Reilly; Martyn Rowlands; Sir Gordon Russell; R. D. Russell;
Norah Schlegel; Gaby Schreiber; Douglas Scott; Cecilia Lady Sempill; Herbert Simon; George Sneed; The Earl of Snowdon; Humphrey Spender; Jack Stafford; R. Stennett-Wilson; Richard Stevens; Norman Stevenson; Robert Stewart; Frank Stockwell; Marianne Straub;
John Tandy; Mirjana Teofanovic; Donald Tomlinson; Cycill Tomrley; Michael Tree; Alan Tye; Keith Tyssen;
Howard Upjohn;
Peter Wall; Nigel Walters; C. Leslie Ward; Neville Ward; John Waterer; John Webb; Robert Welch; David White; E. G. M. Wilkes.

I should also like to thank Mrs and the late Mr Colin Mellor, Mrs G. W. Parsisson and Mrs Sandra Pascoe who have assisted in many different ways.

Sources of Illustrations in Text

27 Ernest Gimson chair, *Victoria and Albert Museum.*
28 Ernest Gimson firedog, *Leicester Museum.*
29 Charles Rennie Mackintosh cutlery, *T. and R. Annan, Glasgow.*
30 Charles Rennie Mackintosh chair, *Photograph, Keith Gibson; Paul Hamlyn.*
31 Charles Rennie Mackintosh fish knife and fork, *Museum of Modern Art, New York.*
32 Charles Rennie Mackintosh interior, Hill House, *Photograph, Keith Gibson; Paul Hamlyn.*
33 Charles Rennie Mackintosh chair, *Victoria and Albert Museum.*
34 Charles Rennie Mackintosh chairs, *Photograph, Keith Gibson; Paul Hamlyn.*
35 C. F. A. Voysey fabric, *Victoria and Albert Museum.*
36 C. F. A. Voysey fabric, *Victoria and Albert Museum.*
37 C. F. A. Voysey fabric, *Victoria and Albert Museum.*
38 C. F. A. Voysey teapot, *Victoria and Albert Museum.*
39 C. F. A. Voysey writing desk, *Victoria and Albert Museum.*
40 Philip Webb chimney-piece, *National Monuments Record.*
41 Philip Webb and William Morris interior, Red House, *Country Life.*
42 R. Norman Shaw (?) chair, *Victoria and Albert Museum.*
43 William Morris chair, *Victoria and Albert Museum.*
44 Edward Burne-Jones piano, *Victoria and Albert Museum.*
45 William Morris embroidered panel, *Victoria and Albert Museum.*
46 William Morris fabric, *Victoria and Albert Museum.*
47 William Morris fabric, *Victoria and Albert Museum.*
48 William Morris wallpaper, *Victoria and Albert Museum.*
49 A. H. Mackmurdo writing desk, *William Morris Gallery, Walthamstow.*
50 A. H. Mackmurdo chair, *William Morris Gallery, Walthamstow.*
51 A. H. Mackmurdo fabric, *Victoria and Albert Museum.*
52 E. G. Punnett chair, *Victoria and Albert Museum.*
53 Liberty and Co. stool, *Victoria and Albert Museum.*
54 Philip Webb glass, *Victoria and Albert Museum.*
55 M. H. Baillie Scott cabinet, *Victoria and Albert Museum.*
56 George Walton glass, *Victoria and Albert Museum.*
57 M. H. Baillie Scott seat, *Victoria and Albert Museum.*
58 C. R. Ashbee silver dish, *Victoria and Albert Museum.*
59 Della Robbia pottery vase, *Victoria and Albert Museum.*
60 C. R. Ashbee mustard pot, *Kunstgewerbemuseum, Zurich.*
61 William de Morgan dish, *Victoria and Albert Museum.*
62 W. A. S. Benson lamp, *Victoria and Albert Museum.*
63 W. R. Lethaby sideboard, *Victoria and Albert Museum.*
64 M. H. Baillie Scott clock, *Victoria and Albert Museum.*
65 Philip Webb table, *Victoria and Albert Museum.*
66 Arthur Silver candlesticks, *Victoria and Albert Museum.*
67 Arthur Dixon coffee jugs, *Victoria and Albert Museum.*
68 Archibald Knox jewel box, *Museum of Modern Art, New York.*

110 Serge Chermayeff chair, *B.B.C.*

111 Raymond McGrath interior, *Raymond McGrath.*

112 Raymond McGrath interior, *Raymond McGrath.*

113 Maxwell Fry and Jack Howe interior, *Heal and Son.*

114 Walter Gropius waste-paper basket, *Gordon Russell.*

115 Brian O'Rorke interior, *P. & O.*

116 Brian O'Rorke interior, *P. & O.*

117 Dorland Hall exhibition entrance, *Architectural Review.*

118 Dorland Hall exhibition dining room, *Architectural Review.*

119 London Transport bus shelter, *London Transport Board.*

120 London Transport Underground booking hall, *London Transport Board.*

121 London Transport LT-type bus, *London Transport Board.*

122 London Transport trolleybus, *London Transport Board.*

123 London Transport Underground coach, *London Transport Board.*

124 Marion Dorn fabric, *London Transport Board.*

125 Marion Dorn fabric, *London Transport Board.*

126 Marion Dorn fabric, *London Transport Board.*

127 Marian Pepler rug, *R. D. Russell.*

128 Marian Pepler rug, *R. D. Russell.*

129 Paul Nash fabric, *Victoria and Albert Museum.*

130 Marianne Straub fabric, *Straub.*

131 Duncan Grant fabric, *Design and Industries Association.*

132 Duncan Grant fabric, *Victoria and Albert Museum.*

133 Keith Murray glass, *Victoria and Albert Museum.*

134 Keith Murray beer mugs, *Murray.*

135 Keith Murray cocktail set, *Murray.*

136 Keith Murray cocktail cups, *Murray.*

137 Eric Ravilious bowl, *Victoria and Albert Museum.*

138 Susie Cooper china, *Wedgwood.*

139 Joseph Bourne casseroles, *Victoria and Albert Museum.*

140 Eric Ravilious mugs, *Wedgwood.*

141 Milner Gray and Graham Sutherland china, *Design Research Unit.*

142 R. Y. Goodden glass bowl, *Goodden.*

143 R. Y. Goodden powder bowl, *Goodden.*

144 Graham Sutherland glassware, *Design Research Unit.*

145 Milner Gray silver bowl, *Design Research Unit.*

146 Milner Gray Ginger Jack bottle, *Design Research Unit.*

147 Milner Gray wine bottle, *Design Research Unit.*

148 Best and Lloyd 'Bestlite', *Best and Lloyd.*

149 A. B. Read light fitting, *Read.*

150 A. B. Read light fitting, *Read.*

151 E. S. Corner car, *Galt.*

152 John Waterer luggage, *Waterer.*

153 'Feed the Brute', *Design and Industries Association.*

196 Booth and Ledeboer sideboard, *Gordon Russell.*

197 Ward and Austin bedroom furniture, *Photograph, Millar and Harris; Ward and Austin.*

198 Ward and Austin bedroom furniture, *Photograph, Dennis Hooker; Ward and Austin.*

199 Robin Day bed settee, *Photograph,.Mann; Day.*

200 Robin Day seating, *Photograph, Mann; Day.*

201 Robert Heritage storage unit, *Heritage.*

202 Robin Day television, *Council of Industrial Design.*

203 Robert Heritage sideboard, *Council of Industrial Design.*

204 John and Sylvia Reid dining furniture, *Photograph, Pilkington Studios; Stag Cabinet Co.*

205 George Fejer and Eric Pamphilon furniture, *Gee Advertising.*

206 Marian Mahler fabric, *David Whitehead.*

207 Marian Mahler fabric, *David Whitehead.*

208 Jacqueline Groag fabric, *David Whitehead.*

209 Lucienne Day fabric, *Day.*

210 Lucienne Day linen, *Council of Industrial Design.*

211 Humphrey Spender fabric, *Council of Industrial Design.*

212 Tibor Reich fabric, *Tibor.*

213 Ronald Grierson carpet, *Photograph, George Miles; Stockwell.*

214 F. G. Hobden fabric, *Council of Industrial Design.*

215 Audrey Tanner carpet, *Foote, Cone and Belding.*

216 Susie Cooper pottery, *Wedgwood.*

217 Edward Bawden muffin dish, *Victoria and Albert Museum.*

218 Robert Stewart storage jars, *Council of Industrial Design.*

219 R. Stennett-Willson glass, *Council of Industrial Design.*

220 Milner Gray, Kenneth Lamble and John Cochrane glassware, *Photograph, John Maltby; Design Research Unit.*

221 Noel London and Howard Upjohn saucepans; *Council of Industrial Design.*

222 Robert Welch jugs, *Photograph, Dennis Hooker; Welch.*

223 Robert Welch silver, *Welch.*

224 David Mellor teaset, *Council of Industrial Design.*

225 Robert Welch toast rack, *Photograph, Dennis Hooker; Welch.*

226 David Mellor cutlery, *Photograph, Dennis Hooker; Mellor.*

227 E. Cooke-Yarborough and Ronald Homes light fitting, *Conelight.*

228 D. W. Morphy iron, *Morphy-Richards.*

229 G. W. F. Longman refrigerator, *Council of Industrial Design.*

230 Jacke Howe clock, *Howe.*

231 David Ogle fire, *Council of Industrial Design.*

232 R. David Carter castors, *Carter.*

233 John Waterer leather bag, *Photograph, Briggs; Waterer.*

234 Hulme Chadwick pruner, *Council of Industrial Design.*

235 London Transport bus stop, *London Transport.*

236 Richard Stevens lighting column, *Photograph, John Maltby; Stevens.*

237 Neville Conder telephone kiosk, *Council of Industrial Design.*

274 Lucienne Day carpet, *I. & C. Steele.*

275 Lucienne Day carpet, *I. & C. Steele.*

276 Mary Yonge carpet, *I. & C. Steele.*

277 Catherine Beevers carpet, *Andrew Gaskell.*

278 Catherine Beevers wallpaper, *The Wall Paper Manufacturers.*

279 Robert Welch cast-iron, *Welch.*

280 Tarquin Cole and John Minshaw casseroles, *Photograph, Jane Gate; Ceramic Consultants.*

281 Frank Thrower glass, *Dartington Glass.*

282 David Queensberry and Jessie Tait tableware, *Council of Industrial Design.*

283 Robert Welch candlesticks, *Welch.*

284 David Mellor teapot, *Council of Industrial Design.*

285 Robert Welch teapot, *Welch.*

286 David Mellor cutlery, *Photograph, Banks Turner; Mellor.*

287 Robert Welch condiment set, *Welch.*

288 David Mellor tea and coffee pots, *Photograph, Dennis Hooker; Mellor.*

289 Robert Welch clock, *Council of Industrial Design.*

290 D. M. R. Brunton fire, *Council of Industrial Design.*

291 Kenneth Grange camera, *Council of Industrial Design.*

292 Kenneth Grange shaver, *Council of Industrial Design.*

293 Robert Heritage light fittings, *Council of Industrial Design.*

294 Norman Stevenson bells, *Council of Industrial Design.*

295 Kenneth Grange iron, *Grange.*

296 Hulme Chadwick garden shears, *Council of Industrial Design.*

297 Joy and Malcolm Wilcox cut-out doll, *Council of Industrial Design.*

298 Martyn Rowlands telephone, *Council of Industrial Design.*

299 John Gould train, *Paul and Marjorie Abbatt.*

300 Noel London and Howard Upjohn microscope, *London and Upjohn.*

301 Noel London and Howard Upjohn computer installation, *Photograph, Peter Waugh; London and Upjohn.*

302 R. David Carter gas fitting, *Carter.*

303 David Mellor gear-measuring machine, *Council of Industrial Design.*

304 R.C.A. Research Unit hospital bed, *Royal College of Art.*

305 Mather and Platt flameproof motors, *Council of Industrial Design.*

306 David Mellor traffic signals, *Photograph, Dennis Hooker; Mellor.*

307 Jock Kinneir traffic sign, *Council of Industrial Design.*

308 Alex Moulton bicycle, *Moulton Bicycles.*

309 Alec Issigonis car, *British Motor Corporation.*

310 Douglas Scott Associates excavator, *Council of Industrial Design.*

311 Misha Black and James Williams aircraft, *Photograph, Cyril Peckham; Design Research Unit.*

312 Misha Black and J. Beresford-Evans electric locomotives, *Photograph, Sam Lambert; Design Research Unit.*

SOURCES OF ILLUSTRATIONS
USED AT CHAPTER OPENINGS

Chapter One   Great Exhibition closing ceremony, October 1851.
Victoria and Albert Museum.

Chapter Two   Philip Clisset chair bodger, portrait by Maxwell Balfour, 1898.
City Museum, Hereford.

Chapter Three   Harry H. Peach (1874–1936).
Geoffrey Peach

Chapter Four   London Transport bus stop signs, Knightsbridge, 1936.
London Transport.

Chapter Five   'Britain Can Make It'
queues outside Victoria and Albert Museum, 1946.
Hulton Press.

Chapter Six   The Duke of Edinburgh with his Prize for Elegant Design 1959, the Prestcold 'Packaway' refrigerator.
Judges: left to right, Sir John Summerson, Sir Basil Spence, Audrey Withers, Lady Casson.
Council of Industrial Design.

Chapter Seven   Some of the 370 delegates to the International Design Congress, London 1966.
Council of Industrial Design.

Index

320

QUEEN ♥

The most Illustrious ANNA Sophia of Hannover Born 1630.

KNAVE

F. King

E. Bava.

Knaves are Fools

The Pillar Set up at Hogsted by Mr Stepne in Memory of ye Famous Victory Obtaind by the Duke of Marlborough.

I ♥

Arye bright Chariot of the quickning Sun Dos over noisome Clouds and Vapours rise So mighty ANNE on Victory dos ride And tramples down ye Popes & Tyrants Pride

VII ♣

The Reverse of ye Medal Struck at Utrecht upon ye Victory obtain'd at Ramelies.

X ♣

Prince Eugene of Savoy born October 18. 1663.

KING ♦

Victor Amadeus D. of Savoy born Octobr 18. 1663

QUEEN ♠

At first dishonest when I Turkeys fed Little I thought t'enjoy a Monarks bed but now ye dotard Glutted wth a baudy Reign I may to Turkey keeping go again.

V ♥

The States & Clergy of Brabant present ye D. of Marlborough with a Tun of wine called the wine of Honour.

**COMHAIRLE CHONTAE ÁTHA CLIATH THEAS
SOUTH DUBLIN COUNTY LIBRARIES**

**SOUTH DUBLIN BOOKSTORE
*TO RENEW ANY ITEM TEL: 459 7834***

Items should be returned on or before the last date below. Fines,
as displayed in the Library, will be charged on overdue items.

of Marlborough.

CORRELLI BARNETT

MARLBOROUGH

EYRE METHUEN
LONDON

First published in the United Kingdom in 1974
by Eyre Methuen Limited, 11 New Fetter Lane,
London, EC4P 4EE

This book was designed and produced by
George Rainbird Limited, Marble Arch House,
44 Edgware Road, London W2

Picture research: Joy Law
Design: Margaret Thomas
Maps: Tom Stalker-Miller
Index: Irene Clephane

© Correlli Barnett 1974

The text was set and printed and the book bound by
Jarrold & Sons Limited, Norwich, Norfolk
Colour plates and jacket originated and printed by
Westerham Press Limited, Westerham, Kent

ISBN 0 413 29540 0

Printed in England

Other books by Correlli Barnett:
The Desert Generals, 1960
The Swordbearers, 1963
Britain and Her Army, 1970
The Collapse of British Power, 1972

END PAPERS *Facsimiles of playing cards published in 1707
depicting Marlborough's victories*

REVERSE OF FRONTISPIECE *The Habsburg two-headed
eagle adopted by Marlborough as part of his coat of arms.
Painting on one of the overdoors in the Saloon at Blenheim Palace
by Louis Laguerre*

FRONTISPIECE *'. . . the lips were firm and sensuous; the skin
muscles around the mouth and chin taut with leashed energy . . .'
John Churchill: this is said to be the portrait before which, in his
old age, Marlborough murmured, 'This was once a man.' Painting
by Sir Godfrey Kneller*

FOR RUTH, MY WIFE,
WHO DOES SO MUCH

War is the province of uncertainty.
KARL VON CLAUSEWITZ

. . . uncertainty is the worst of all conditions,
for death itself is easier than the fear of it. . . .
JOHN CHURCHILL, FIRST DUKE OF MARLBOROUGH

CONTENTS

AUTHOR'S ACKNOWLEDGMENTS

In the first place, I wish to express my gratitude to the Earl Spencer for his kindness and hospitality; and in particular for granting me access to the Muniment Room at Althorp, and for showing me the Althorp Silver and the Marlborough family portraits.

I am most grateful to His Grace the Duke of Marlborough for his kindness in giving me permission to carry out research in the Blenheim Papers at Blenheim; to Mr P. F. D. Duffie, Administrator at Blenheim Palace and to Mr W. L. Murdock and his staff in the Blenheim Estate Office.

I wish to express my particular gratitude to Professor J. R. Jones, of the University of East Anglia, who was kind enough to read and comment on the entire typescript, and save me thereby from many errors and omissions.

I would like to express my appreciation of the courtesy and helpfulness of the staffs of the Central Library, the Ministry of Defence; the Royal United Services Institute Library; the National Army Museum; the National Portrait Gallery; the London Library; the British Museum Reading Room and Manuscripts Room; the University of East Anglia Library; the Norwich City Library; the Public Record Office; and the Archives de la Ministère des Affaires Etrangères, Paris.

I am indebted to Mrs Joy Law for her resourcefulness in finding the illustrations, together with Miss Georgina Dowse; to Mr John Hadfield for his helpful and ever-courteous advice; to Mr Paul Brown for his kindly but acute criticisms; to Mr Jeremy Whitaker and Mr Derrick Witty for their skilful photography. My thanks are also due to Mr Tom Stalker-Miller who turned my rough sketches into exemplary maps.

To Mrs Iris Portal (Iris Butler) I must express my appreciation of the many stimulating conversations I have enjoyed with her on the subject of this book.

And finally I would like to thank my wife for reading and criticizing the narrative; for her patience in typing the first draft from a manuscript which might have baffled a trained cryptographer; and for once again tolerating my prolonged mental absence 'in the field'.

AUTHOR'S NOTE

Dates Owing to the English delay in adopting the Reformed Calendar of Gregory XIII, English dates (known as Old Style) were ten days behind Continental European dates (New Style) in the seventeenth century, and eleven days behind in the eighteenth century. It was also the official English custom to begin the New Year on Lady Day, 25 March; so that, for example, 24 March 1705, was followed by 25 March 1706. In the present book, however, all dates have been rendered as New Style, except where specifically stated otherwise; and new years commence on 1 January.

Spelling of Placenames The author has sought to avoid a merely pedantic consistency. In principle he has followed modern spellings (i.e. Douai instead of Douay; Nijmegen instead of Nimwegen), unless a contemporary spelling has become hallowed by usage (i.e. Blenheim instead of Blindheim; Oudenarde instead of Audenarde or Oudenaarde). Where French versions of German placenames were current in Marlborough's time (as in the case of Trèves for Trier; Aix-la-Chapelle for Aachen), this version has been used, with the modern name in parentheses.

General Spelling Here again the author has wished to avoid pedantry. Contemporary letters and documents have been rendered in the spelling of the particular source whence they are quoted. In the case of original documents and certain printed collections, the spelling is therefore that of Marlborough's own day; in the case of standard reference works, such as Coxe's *Life*, and Murray's edition of the *Dispatches*, where the authors or editors have modernized the spelling, this modernized spelling has been followed.

AUTHOR'S FOREWORD

John Churchill, First Duke of Marlborough, has been little better served by some of his admirers than by his detractors. They have made of him an exemplary hero in the Victorian mould; a leader of flawless performance and yet at the same time remote and impersonal. The man himself has been buried, like a pharaoh in a pyramid, beneath a massive heap of military, political and diplomatic detail.

As a consequence Marlborough has become eclipsed in the national memory by Wellington, whose pungent outward personality is a gift to his biographers. Yet of the two men, John Churchill, Duke of Marlborough, is in many ways the richer and more interesting character – sensitive, emotional, highly strung even, pulled by complex motives, impulses and anxieties. Marlborough is, moreover, a tragic figure, whose gradual descent from greatness to dismissal is deeply moving.

The purpose of this book therefore is not to offer a 'definitive' scholarly study, omitting no fact or document, but to present Marlborough as a living, feeling man; a man enduring such strains and grappling with such a weight and variety of responsibility as have befallen no other English soldier in history.

C.B.

CHAPTER ONE

THE PARTING BY
THE WATER'S SIDE

For days he had been held in the Kentish port of Margate by contrary winds, but now the wind had veered westerly at last, and the ship was waiting for him to embark. Amid a throng of officers Her Majesty's Captain-General and Ambassador-Extraordinary to the Dutch Republic, John Churchill, Earl of Marlborough, took leave of his wife Sarah. Their marriage had already known many such enforced farewells; nor was it a novelty to them that such private moments as this, charged with feeling, should take place under numerous watchful eyes. John and Sarah Marlborough had been accustomed to living in public since they each of them came to court long ago in the reign of the late King Charles II. They were so close in love and understanding that they could be alone together even in a crowd.

Yet this parting was special. Three weeks earlier, on 4 May 1702, Garter King of Arms, escorted by heralds, had ridden out from St James's Palace in a blaze of tabards to Charing Cross and the City of London, and there proclaimed amid shrilling trumpets and unthinking cheers the Queen's declaration of war on Louis XIV of France. Marlborough was now on his way to the Netherlands to shoulder the responsibility of leading a ramshackle coalition of European states against the French absolute monarchy, the super-power of the time.

He was fifty-two; six years older than Wellington and Napoleon when their active service came jointly to an end at Waterloo. By the standards of Marlborough's own era, indeed, a man at the age of fifty-two was thought to be ripening towards his retirement and old age.

Nevertheless, he still looked remarkably young, 'with a clear red and white complexion which could put the fair sex to shame',[1] in the words of a Dutch contemporary. Although the flesh was thickening a little along the line of the jaw he still remained almost impossibly handsome, his features uniting strength and grace like a classical hero in a painting come to life in a periwig instead of a laurel wreath. Under a broad, high forehead and darkly curving eyebrows his eyes were large and luminously blue; and in their calm gaze there was imagination as well as high authority. Beneath the straight nose, the lips were firm and sensuous; the skin muscles round the mouth and chin taut with leashed energy. Marlborough was of middle height, 'with as fine a figure as you could see'.[2] That he was usually rather carelessly dressed only added to the easy charm which was one of the most formidable components of his personality.

Marlborough's '. . . features uniting strength and grace . . .'
Painting by John Riley (1646–1691)

Sarah Marlborough '... a masterful glance ...' Oil sketch c. 1690–5 by Sir Godfrey Kneller (1646–1723)

OPPOSITE *Europe at the time of the War of the Spanish Succession*

Of all the men that I ever knew in my life, [Lord Chesterfield was to recall] (and I knew him extremely well), the late Duke of Marlborough possessed the Graces in the highest degree, not to say engrossed them. . . . His figure was beautiful, but his manner was irresistible, by either man or woman.[3]

Had it not been for his commanding presence the man who was bidding a reluctant farewell to his wife on the Kentish seashore that spring day might have been a beau stepped out of a play by Congreve: a Mirabel of a general. And back in the late 1660s and 1670s Marlborough, as Jack Churchill, a hard-up young officer in the Duke of York's household, had been just such a sparkish rake. He had fought at least two duels and been wounded in both. The most notorious of his love affairs had brought him to bed with Charles II's own mistress, the luscious and animated Barbara Villiers, Lady Castlemaine and later Duchess of Cleveland. They became lovers in 1671, when he was twenty and she was twenty-nine. Their mutual entertainment had lasted for three years; and Barbara's last child, a daughter born in 1672, was almost certainly his. An untimely visit by the King to Barbara's chamber had inspired Churchill to an early display of presence of mind and physical courage in a crisis. Although her chamber was on the first floor he escaped discovery by jumping from the window into the courtyard.

In 1702, however, all that remained of dashing Jack Churchill of the First Guards were the slim good looks, the virility and the charm. The rake in him had died in 1675, when he first set eyes on fifteen-year-old Sarah Jennings, one of the Duchess of York's maids of honour, and for the first and last time in his life he fell in love. Now that she was forty-two, and thickened by many pregnancies, he was still completely absorbed by her, to the covert amusement of a polite world in which marital fidelity was not exactly fashionable. In middle age Sarah had become majestic in her beauty, with straw-blonde hair springing thickly from a fine forehead, brilliant colouring and a masterful glance; some felt rather too masterful. An admirer attempted to convey her fascination to a friend of his:

> Did you know her but half as well as I have the happiness to do, she would make you think of her as one said of the sea, that it infinitely surprised him the first time he saw it, but that the last sight of it made always as wonderful an impression as if he had never observed it before. She hath a most acute and elevated understanding, equally partaking of the solid as well as the shining faculty, a mind so richly furnished with all those amiable talents of prudence, justice, generosity, constancy and love of her native country that she ought to have been born in the golden age![4]

Now she had jolted down by coach to the little harbour of Margate to see 'my dear Lord Marl' off to the wars. They would not see each other again until the beginning of next winter, when he returned after the year's campaign; if indeed he did return, for in the eighteenth century generals faced the same dangers as their private soldiers.

They parted, and he was alone in his cabin as the ship made sail towards the Nether-lands. Ahead of him lay a host of intricate problems, a colossal burden of responsibility, incalculable risks and perils. But his mind was not on all that awaited him at his landfall,

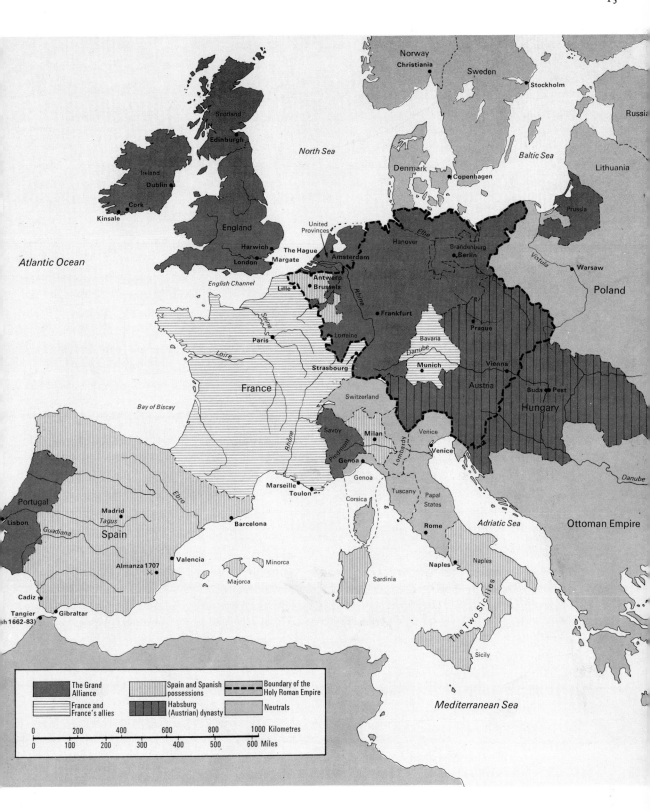

Norway
Christiania
Sweden
Stockholm
North Sea
Baltic Sea
Russia
Denmark
Lithuania
Copenhagen
Scotland
Edinburgh
Prussia
Ireland
Dublin
England
United Provinces
Hanover
Brandenburg
Berlin
Warsaw
Cork
Harwich
The Hague
Amsterdam
Elbe
Vistula
Kinsale
London
Margate
Antwerp
Brussels
Rhine
Poland
Atlantic Ocean
English Channel
Lille
Frankfurt
Prague
Seine
Lorraine
Bavaria
Vienna
Paris
Strasbourg
Danube
Munich
Loire
Switzerland
Austria
Buda
Pest
France
Rhone
Savoy
Milan
Venice
Hungary
Bay of Biscay
Piedmont
Genoa
Lombardy
Venice
Genoa
Tuscany
Marseille
Toulon
Corsica
Papal States
Danube
Ebro
Barcelona
Rome
Adriatic Sea
Ottoman Empire
Portugal
Madrid
Tagus
Lisbon
Guadiana
Spain
Valencia
Minorca
Naples
Almanza 1707
Majorca
Sardinia
Naples
Cadiz
Sicily
Tangier
(h 1662-83)
Gibraltar
The Two Sicilies

Mediterranean Sea

	The Grand Alliance		Spain and Spanish possessions		Boundary of the Holy Roman Empire
	France and France's allies		Habsburg (Austrian) dynasty		Neutrals

0 200 400 600 800 1000 Kilometres
0 100 200 300 400 500 600 Miles

but on Sarah. He yielded to an overriding need to reach out to her again, even if only in a letter:

It is impossible to express, with what a heavy heart I parted with you when I was by the water's side. I could have given my life to come back, though I knew my own weakness so much that I durst not, for I know I should have exposed myself to the company. I did for a great while, with a perspective glass, look upon the cliffs, in hopes I might have had one sight of you. We are now out of sight of Margate, and I have neither soul nor spirits, but I do at this time suffer so much that nothing but being with you can recompense it. . . . I pray

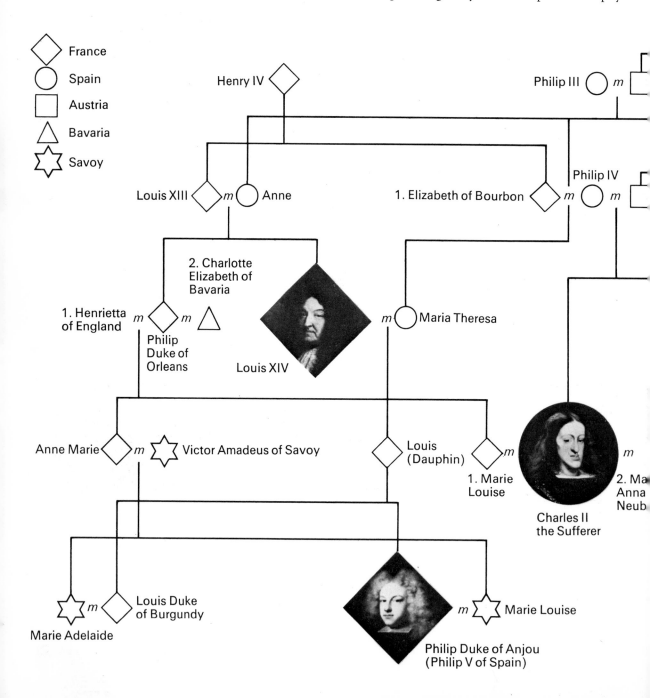

France

Spain

Austria

Bavaria

Savoy

Henry IV

Philip III ○ m

Louis XIII ◇ m ○ Anne

1. Elizabeth of Bourbon ◇ m ○ m

Philip IV

2. Charlotte Elizabeth of Bavaria

1. Henrietta of England   m ◇ m △

Philip Duke of Orleans

Louis XIV

m ○ Maria Theresa

Anne Marie ◇ m ☆ Victor Amadeus of Savoy

Louis (Dauphin) ◇ m

1. Marie Louise

Charles II the Sufferer

m

2. Ma Anna Neub

☆ m ◇ Louis Duke of Burgundy

Marie Adelaide

Philip Duke of Anjou (Philip V of Spain)

m ☆ Marie Louise

to God to make you and yours happy: and if I could contribute anything to it with the utmost hazard of my life, I should be glad to do it.[5]

The war Marlborough had now to fight had been sought by none of the combatants, not even Louis XIV. For the last European conflict, which only ended in 1697, had left France exhausted by the prolonged leakage of blood and treasure. Nevertheless the powers were dragged into this fresh struggle by the chains of unlucky circumstance. At the root of the quarrel lay the question of the succession to the Spanish throne. Spain,

The interrelationship of the claimants to the Spanish throne: Louis XIV of France, painting by Hyacinthe Rigaud (1659–1743); Philip Duke of Anjou (Philip V of Spain), painting by Hyacinthe Rigaud; Charles II of Spain 'Carlos the Sufferer', painting c. 1685 by J. Carreno de Miranda (1614–1685); Emperor Joseph I, engraving by J. J. Thurneyser (1668–1730); Emperor Leopold I, engraving. Archduke Charles, Emperor Charles VI ('Charles III' of Spain), engraving; Maximilian II Emanuel, engraving by C. Vermeulen (1644–c. 1708) after J. Vivien (1657–1735)

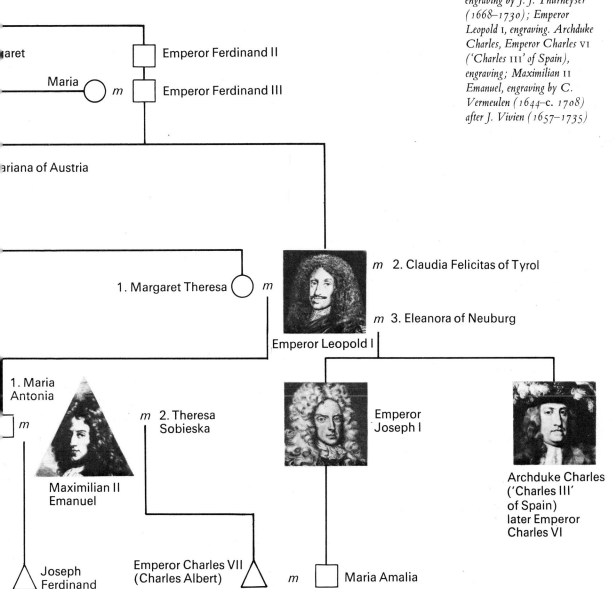

although in decline, still possessed the greatest empire in the world: the Spanish Nether-lands (roughly modern Belgium and Luxembourg); more than half Italy; Mexico and most of Central and South America; the Philippines; the Canaries; and part of the West Indies. In 1698 it appeared all too likely that the Habsburg King of Spain, Charles II, a deformed and diseased semi-imbecile aptly nicknamed 'the Sufferer', was about to die. Since Charles was childless, who was to inherit his vast possessions?

It was a question which vitally affected the balance of power in Europe, especially since Louis XIV's son, the Dauphin, heir to the French throne, had as good a claim as any, his mother being the daughter of Philip IV of Spain and half-sister to Charles the Sufferer. Even if one of the Dauphin's sons rather than the Dauphin himself succeeded to the Spanish throne, Louis XIV would effectively control a combined Empire so vast as to render him autocrat of Europe and much of the known world. France would become mistress of the world's trade. And there was the distant but real danger that one day France and Spain might be permanently united under a single crown.

France's neighbours saw more immediate dangers too. The Spanish Netherlands, which at present served as a buffer state, a barrier, between the Dutch people and French military power, would fall under Louis XIV's control. Such a possibility was little less alarming to England, for it was already her traditional policy to prevent the Low Countries from passing under the influence of a hostile great power. And English and Dutch merchants alike were alarmed that France might win a monopoly of the lucrative trade with the Spanish overseas empire.

The Habsburg Emperor Leopold in Vienna was equally opposed to a French prince succeeding to the throne of Spain. He had no wish to face the rivalry of a Franco-Spanish super-power at a time when he enjoyed his full portion of trouble with rebellious Hungarian subjects and the still formidable Turkish Empire on his eastern borders. There was also his own dynastic greed. For his, the Austrian, branch of the Habsburg family could put forward two convincing claimants for Charles the Sufferer's throne. This each-way bet, for a winner and a place, consisted of the Emperor Leopold himself, a grandson of Philip III of Spain, and husband (in his first marriage) of a daughter of Philip IV; and the Emperor's grandson from that first marriage, Prince Joseph Ferdinand of Bavaria. Of the two Habsburg runners, Prince Joseph was the more likely, since other European powers would dislike the idea of a Habsburg Empire from the Danube to Cape Horn under the Emperor Leopold hardly less than a union of Spain with France.

Such, in all its intricacy, was the problem. William III of England (who was also Stadtholder of the Dutch Republic) and Louis XIV made manful and sincere efforts to solve it by an agreed compromise. For Louis realized that to make good the Dauphin's claim to the whole Spanish Empire would demand victory in a general war, and for the moment he had had enough of general wars. William's and Louis's first attempt, the Partition Treaty of 1698, came to nothing a year later because of the ill-timed death of their agreed candidate for the Spanish throne, Prince Joseph of Bavaria. With admirable pertinacity they set to it again, and, in 1700, concluded the Second Partition Treaty. The Emperor Leopold's second son, the Archduke Charles, was to succeed Charles the Sufferer as King of Spain, and to have the Spanish Netherlands and the Spanish Empire beyond Europe. The Dauphin was to receive, by way of a consolation prize, Naples, Sardinia and Lorraine.

It was an admirably workmanlike solution. Unfortunately Europe's destiny was to be decided not in a gilded conference chamber but in a Spanish deathbed. Charles the Sufferer and the advisers who clustered round him, the Spanish people even, were resolute that their empire should not be carved up in this summary fashion for the convenience of others. Just before he finally managed to die, in November 1700, Charles signed a will bequeathing his throne and his entire empire to Philip, Duke of Anjou, a grandson of Louis XIV.

Charles's will offered a temptation to Louis which his character was ill-equipped to resist, even though to accept the will meant breaking the Second Partition Treaty, and risking a European war. Louis was aware, however, that his potentially most dangerous opponents, the English and Dutch, were at the moment in a profoundly unwarlike mood, their minds on profits rather than power. He therefore decided to accept the will. So at first did the English and the Dutch. War was still far from inevitable.

But Louis had now recovered from his uncharacteristic fit of moderation and compromise. In February 1701 he asserted his grandson's right to succeed to the French throne. Even though Philip of Anjou, as the Dauphin's younger son, was second in line of succession, this raised again the bogey of a future union between France and Spain.

Louis XIV of France accepting Charles II's will leaving the Spanish throne to his grandson, Philip of Anjou. Engraving

Furthermore Louis ordered his armies forward into the Spanish Netherlands, surprising and taking prisoner the garrisons in the barrier fortresses the Dutch occupied in that country under the previous peace treaty. By this sudden pounce Louis had wiped out all the gains won by William III in years of patient campaigning. Moreover, in the captive Dutch garrisons he now held hostages to compel the Dutch government to recognize 'Philip v' as King of Spain; unless such recognition was forthcoming, Louis would not allow them to go home. However, this return to Louis's earlier style of brigand diplomacy served brusquely to awaken English and Dutch opinion. On 8 June 1701 Parliament had authorized William III to seek allies. On 28 June the King, who had already appointed Marlborough Captain-General of the English troops gathering in the Netherlands, made him Ambassador-Extraordinary as well. For it was to Marlborough that he now entrusted the crucially important task of negotiating a treaty of alliance with the Dutch and the Habsburg Empire.

The bargaining had lasted from July to September 1701, under the constant threat that the French armies in the Spanish Netherlands might open hostilities by invading the territory of the Dutch Republic. In northern Italy French and Habsburg armies were already marching and fighting, as Louis XIV sought to lay hands on the territories bequeathed to his grandson by Charles the Sufferer. His marshals were, however, beaten back by Prince Eugène of Savoy, the Habsburg monarchy's most accomplished soldier. The roar and rattle of the conflict in Italy echoed in the minds of the diplomats at The Hague, as they pursued their grave and ceremonious discussions.

The negotiating of the grand alliance displayed the public Marlborough. In Lord Chesterfield's words:

> He was always cool, and nobody ever observed the least variation in his countenance; he could refuse more easily than others could grant; and those who went away from him the most dissatisfied as to the substance of their business, were yet charmed with him, and, in some degree, comforted by his manner.[6]

Yet the affable charm was only the deceptive cover for formidable diplomatic talents: an understanding of the links between home politics, foreign policy and strategy; the gift to read men's minds while concealing his own; patience; a superb sense of timing.

During the negotiations Marlborough's constant purpose was to thwart French efforts to divide the prospective allies by alluring offers, and so prevent an alliance being created at all. In this attempt the French met their first defeat at Marlborough's hands, for on 7 September the Grand Alliance between England, the United Provinces (as the Dutch Republic was officially titled), and the Habsburg Empire was concluded in a splendid ceremony at The Hague. Marlborough signed for England, watched by Sarah who had crossed the sea to share his triumph. The Treaty was like a precise business contract; it stipulated the war aims of the alliance, and the forces each ally was to contribute to the struggle. The political objectives were realistically moderate. Louis XIV's grandson was to be allowed to retain the Spanish throne, along with the Spanish Indies, given only the proviso that France should formally agree that the crowns

*... luscious and animated ...'
Barbara Villiers, Lady Castle-
maine and later Duchess of
Cleveland (1641–1709). She
was simultaneously the mistress
of both Charles II and the young
John Churchill. Painting by Sir
Peter Lely (1618–1680)*

Mrs IENYNS WIFE TO
IOHN DVKE OF MARLBORO

of France and Spain should never be united. Milan, Naples and Sicily, together with the Spanish Netherlands, were to pass from Spanish sovereignty to the Habsburg (or Austrian) Emperor. Moreover, the Spanish Netherlands, even when they had more safely become the Austrian Netherlands, were to be organized and maintained 'as a fence and rampart, commonly called a barrier, separating and keeping off France from the United Provinces'.

After some keen bargaining, the total of each ally's military contribution had been agreed at 100,000 men for the Dutch, 82,000 for the Habsburg Empire, and 40,000 for the English (who were also to maintain an equal number of men in their fleet). It had been one of Marlborough's shrewdest strokes in his conduct of the negotiations to insist to the English government at home that Parliament rather than the King alone by his prerogative should agree to the English total. This ensured that war, when it came, would be Parliament's war and not just the King's.

Marlborough's success had entirely vindicated William III's confidence. However, William III had had a deeper motive in appointing him to this crucial role. The King's own health, never robust, was giving way after thirty years of diplomacy and war. He recognized that he was unlikely to live to lead this new coalition to victory. Yet he knew that at his death the alliance would almost certainly disintegrate. His dour lifetime of effort would come to nothing, and Louis XIV would at last enjoy the hegemony of Europe. So, with far-sighted realism, William looked for a man to succeed him as lynchpin of the alliance, a man whom he could install in good time at his side, ready to take over smoothly and at once. Yet William himself was King of England and Stadtholder (executive head of state and warlord) of the Dutch Republic; a brilliant diplomatist, an experienced and competent general, if far from brilliant; a great European figure. To replace him, no mere soldier, however able, would do; no mere statesman, however wise and practised. It called for a man of outstanding capacity and range, equally at home in the cabinet room and the camp; it called for immense personal ascendancy. William chose Marlborough.

It was not so obvious and inevitable a choice as it was later to seem in the brilliant retrospect of victory. Nor had relations between William III and Marlborough always been so close and cordial as in 1700–1. Only eight years earlier William had summarily dismissed Marlborough from the court and from all his offices of state; the dénouement of a mutual ill-feeling, ever sharper, and all too public.

Yet their relationship had begun promisingly enough. During the Glorious Revolution in 1688, Marlborough had done much to help William of Orange to the crown of England. The defection of Lieutenant-General Lord Churchill (as he then was) from James II's army at Salisbury and his night ride over to William's camp had shattered James's nerve and demoralized his troops. Instead of advancing to a perhaps victorious battle against the far smaller force which had landed with William at Torbay, James had only retreated to London, dispersed his army and ignominiously fled the country.

'My Soull, I love you so trully well . . .' Sarah Jennings at the age of fifteen. This painting attributed to Simon Verelst (1664–1710) hung in Sarah's dressing room at Holywell House.

Moreover, it was Churchill and his wife Sarah who, by virtue of their intimate friendship with Princess Anne and their influence over her, had arranged for her to make a timely escape from London and join her father's enemies.

Churchill's role in the destruction of James II had been the more significant because he was one of the most trusted members of James's personal entourage. But faced with James's unbending purpose to turn England into an absolute Roman Catholic monarchy, on the model of Louis XIV's France, Churchill, who was a staunch Anglican, found that the cause of religion was worth a technical act of betrayal.

In the aftermath of the Revolution Churchill rendered William another service, and one of immense value: he persuaded Princess Anne to waive her right to succeed when Queen Mary should die, so that William could continue to reign for his own lifetime.

Churchill, as the son of a poor and obscure West Country gentleman, was a self-made man in the social context of his own era. He was possessed of all the self-made man's appetite for wealth and status. Having rendered the new king great services, he looked forward to great rewards – the Garter, the Master-Generalship of the Ordnance with its fat perquisites. Rewards to his satisfaction had not materialized. He was made Earl of Marlborough at the Coronation. He was confirmed in his rank of lieutenant-general; he was put in charge of the reconstruction of the army; and that was all. He had not regarded it as enough. Nor had he been the only prominent Englishman to become disgruntled. For the important field commands, the best government posts, the richest pickings, the places in the new King's intimate circle, had almost all gone to William's Dutch associates. While William dined, Marlborough and other English peers had to stand behind his chair in respectful attendance, never to be invited to sit and eat with the Dutchmen at his table.

Nor had Marlborough concealed his bitter disappointment behind his customary bland discretion. Instead he had made himself the rallying point for the general court resentment of the Dutch favourites. He informed a company at Lord Wharton's that whereas in the previous reign, when King James was filling the army with Irishmen, the only question was, 'Do you speak English?', now all that happened was that the word 'Dutchmen' had been exchanged for 'Irishmen'. He also publicly referred to William's favourite minister, Bentinck, as 'a wooden fellow'. He even taxed the King himself about his neglect of Englishmen, to that bleak man's evident annoyance.

The breach between them had been compounded by a quarrel of sisterly virulence between Princess Anne and Queen Mary. In January 1692 the Queen had ordered Anne to dismiss Sarah Marlborough from her household. Anne, in stubborn loyalty to her dearest friend, refused. Next morning, two hours after Marlborough in his capacity as Gentleman of the Bedchamber had handed William his shirt, he in turn was handed by the Earl of Nottingham a letter from William dismissing him not only from all his offices but also from the court.

For the King, on his part, had come to magnify the discontented Marlborough into a positive danger to his new throne; the potential leader of a palace revolution.

'. . . cold-headed ability to subordinate personal feelings to state policy . . .' William III of England. Painting by Godfried Schalcken (1643–1706). 'As the piece was to be by candlelight he [Schalcken] gave his majesty the candle to hold till the tallow ran down upon his fingers. As if to justify this ill-breeding he drew his own picture in the same situation.' (Vertue)

In May of that year Marlborough had even found himself in the Tower of London, whose dank stones had seen so many great personages die under the headsman's axe, or rot slowly away down months of failing hope. Princess Anne was being only too accurate when she wrote sympathetically to Sarah that 'methinks it is a dismal thing to have one's friends sent to that place . . .'.[7] This was the nadir of Marlborough's career. In fact, together with other notables, he had been a victim of a Jacobite plot. A letter had been planted (appropriately enough in a bishop's flowerpot) bearing their forged signatures in order to incriminate them in treasonable relations with the court of the exiled James II at St-Germain. Six anxious weeks had passed before the plotters and their forgery were exposed, and Marlborough set at liberty. The whole episode had been a bleak reminder, if he needed a reminder, of how insecure was the world in which he was making his career: divided in its loyalties and devoid of trust, tormented by suspicion, shadowed by treason and plot.

It was not until Queen Mary's death in 1695 had effectively put an end to her implacable quarrel with her sister and with her sister's friends the Marlboroughs that Marlborough and the King had become gradually reconciled, and his career set in motion again.

Nevertheless, for William in 1701 to select Marlborough as his successor as leader of the coalition against France was a mark of his cold-headed ability to subordinate personal feelings to state policy. But why Marlborough and not one of his favourite Dutchmen? Marlborough's experience of war and high command could not compare with theirs, even if William had been kind enough to say after his capture of Cork and Kinsale in 1690, 'No officer living who has seen so little service as my Lord Marlborough, is so fit for great commands.'[8] As this remark implies, William, with a lifetime of judging men, had perceived Marlborough's potential powers of leadership. But there were two other factors which governed his choice, both decisive. In the first place England was the key to victory. But the English, who had so grudgingly accepted William's own leadership, who entertained so plain a dislike of Dutchmen in high places, would never follow a Dutch general or statesman. It must be an Englishman. And secondly, that Englishman could only be the man who enjoyed Princess Anne's total confidence; whose wife was her beloved friend; the man who, once Anne became Queen, would in any case be the most powerful figure in the country. In 1701, as in 1688–92, the Marlboroughs' intimacy with Anne was their strongest asset.

On 20 February, while William was riding near Hampton Court, his favourite horse had stumbled over a molehill and thrown him. Although he suffered nothing worse than a broken collarbone, this was enough in his low state of health to open the gate to secondary infections. Within three weeks he was dead.

Just as he had foreseen, his death occasioned instant disarray both in England and among the allies. Just as he had arranged, Marlborough stepped neatly into his place, and the disarray was shortlived. As Count Wratislaw, the Habsburg Emperor's ambassador, reported:

ZIIN MAJESTEIT VERWELLEKOMT OP HET BINNENHOF.

RECEPTION DE SA MAJESTÉ DANS LA COUR.

William III at the Binnenhof, The Hague, on a state visit in 1691. Engraving by Romeyn de Hooghe (1645–1708)

The greatest consolation in this confusion is that Marlborough is fully informed of the whole position and by reason of his credit with the Queen can do everything.[9]

Wratislaw's confidence was shared by the Dutch agent in London:

There is a general conviction of Marlborough being a very clever man whose character is honest, simple and conciliatory, and whose whole interest is in making things go well.[10]

As soon as possible Marlborough had paid a short visit to The Hague, where William's death had caused more serious dislocation. To the States-General (or legislative assembly) of the Dutch Republic, meeting in the gaunt, banner-hung brick of the Hall of Knights in the medieval Binnenhof, he personally presented an address from the Queen:

... She will not only exactly and faithfully observe and execute the treaties and alliances made between the Kings her predecessors and your High and Mighty Lordships but ... is likewise ready to renew and confirm them. ... Her Majesty is likewise disposed to enter into such other stricter alliances and engagements, which shall most conduce to the interests of both nations, the preservation of the liberty of Europe, and reducing within just bounds the exorbitant power of France. ... In the meantime Her Majesty is ready from this moment and without delay to concur with your High and Mighty Lordships and the other allies to this end, with all her forces as well by seas as by land. ...

Then he added:

And Her Majesty to show her zeal the more has been pleased to authorize me to concert ... the necessary operations.[11]

Henceforward England and England's general would lead the grand alliance: a complete reversal from the reign of William III, when England had been dragged into war as a virtual dependency of the Dutch and their Stadtholder. Nevertheless Marlborough was only too well aware of the daunting nature of the undertaking bequeathed to him by William III.

For France's population numbered some 19 millions as against the Dutch Republic's mere 2 millions, and $7\frac{1}{2}$ millions each for the Habsburg Empire and Britain (the two as yet separate kingdoms of England and Ireland, and Scotland). She was the most highly

The Hall of Knights in the Binnenhof, The Hague, as it was in 1651. It was little changed when Marlborough addressed the assembled members of the States-General there in 1702. Painting by Dirck van Delen (1605–1671)

organized state in Europe; a military machine single in its obedience to the royal egotist of Versailles. Geographically France enjoyed a commanding central position in regard to every theatre of war – the Low Countries, Germany, Italy and Spain. Like Imperial Germany in the First World War she could switch forces from one theatre to another more easily and over shorter distances than her opponents, spaced as they were round her frontiers. Furthermore Spain, under 'Philip v', lately the Duke of Anjou, was now a French satellite; a French fleet dominated the western Mediterranean.

Nec Pluribus Impar – 'Not unequal to many' – ran the French royal motto. It was not so much a boast as a plain statement of fact.

On the other hand, the alliance of small or middle-sized powers which Marlborough must lead enjoyed few obvious advantages. The Elector of Brandenburg, at the price of being recognized in a grander incarnation as King Frederick I of Prussia, was to hire out his troops to them. The King of Denmark as well as some lesser German principalities were also to supply soldiers on contract; Baden, under its Margrave Louis, was an ally. Thanks largely to Marlborough's diplomacy in 1701, Charles XII of Sweden, that ferocious warrior-king, had lapsed from friendship with France into neutrality. Nevertheless, no man could say how long Charles XII, an impulsive and unpredictable monarch, might remain neutral, or on whose side he might one day elect to intervene.

Geography, too, hardly favoured the allies. The sea – tide and wind, tempest – divided England from the Netherlands. The length of Germany separated the Dutch and English armies from those of Baden and the Habsburg Monarchy. And northern Italy lay even more out of reach beyond the Alps.

Moreover, divergent war aims threatened the coalition from the very start with potential disintegration: the English wanted to secure their Protestant succession and win exclusive trade and colonial advantages; the Dutch too wanted much the same trade advantages, together with an impregnable barrier of fortresses along the French frontier; the Habsburgs wanted Spain and northern Italy; none was prepared to fight long for the objectives of other allies once his own had been secured. Merely to keep the coalition in being would take unceasing care and skill on Marlborough's part.

Yet there *were* factors that helped to redress a balance apparently so much in favour of France – factors perhaps more easily apparent to posterity than to Marlborough and his colleagues. In the first place the France of Louis XIV, outwardly so formidable, was now past the prime of her strength. She had been waging war for some thirty-five years with only relatively short respites. Even France's vast national resources were becoming strained by the cost of maintaining great armies and fleets for decades at a time; and by the need to make good the constant wastage of men, beasts and equipment. This debilitating attrition was William III's great achievement; an achievement obscured by his failure to win the kind of dramatic victories that men remember. Thanks to William's dogged campaigning, Marlborough now faced a France with tired muscles, her cutting edge already dulled. Then again, it was Marlborough's good fortune that the outstanding generation of French generals and administrators which William III had had to fight

Parties to the Grand Alliance:
LEFT TO RIGHT *Frederick I of Prussia (1657–1713), painting by Antoine Pesne (1683–1757); Charles XII of Sweden (1682–1718), painting by David Schwartz (1678–1710); Louis of Baden (1655–1707), engraving; Frederick IV of Denmark (1671–1730), pastel by Rosalba Carriera (1675–1757) and their enemy: Louis XIV of France (1638–1715), painting by Hyacinth Rigaud*

had now given place to mere competent second-raters. Louvois, the brilliant and ruthless minister of war who had created the French military machine, had died in 1691; Marshal Turenne in 1675; Condé in 1686; Luxembourg in 1695.

England and the Dutch Republic, on the other hand, were far stronger than the faction and localism of their politics and administration, so opposite from the centralized order of France, might suggest. Both countries were immensely rich and successful trading nations. The Dutch Republic had been the financial centre of the world for more than a century; England had already become her close rival, especially since the founding of the Bank of England in 1694. For this was the lusty springtime of English commercial capitalist enterprise – great risks undertaken in the hope of great rewards; a ferment of individual endeavour. Moreover, English methods of raising both taxes and credit were far more flexible and efficient than the cumbrous fiscal machinery of France. And in the early eighteenth century, as in any era, economic and financial resources were the key to victory in a long war.

Although in the long term English policy and grand strategy lay at the mercy of the ferocious party strife between Whig and Tory, the English had at least entered the war as a united people. This was one of the more notable achievements of Louis XIV's statecraft. For when James II died in exile at St-Germain in September 1701, just after the signing of the grand alliance, Louis XIV had recognized James's son as James III, King of England. By this action Louis made the English angry; always a dangerous thing to do. It was a flagrant breach of the last peace treaty, in 1697, by which Louis had accepted William III as King of England. But this was not all. 'James III' was, like his father, a Catholic. All Englishmen, whatever their party prejudice, henceforward knew that a French victory would mean a Catholic monarch in England; would mean that England would once again decline into the French satellite she had been under Charles II and James II. The Protestant succession was the one issue over which all shades of English opinion other than a small minority of Jacobites were united.

It was Louis XIV, in his ambition, arrogance and bad faith, who no less had provided the grand alliance as a whole with a *raison d'être* which transcended the divergent war aims of its members. For at base England, the Dutch Republic and the Habsburg Monarchy went to war in order to settle one question: was Europe to be nothing more than France writ large?

Later that same day on which Marlborough had taken leave of Sarah with such reluctance 'by the water's side', he landed in the Netherlands for the second time in hardly more than a month; on this occasion not for a passing diplomatic visit, but to open his first campaign as leader of a great army in the field. Yet before he was able to join the allied forces five more weeks were to elapse. For when he arrived at the Mauritshuis, the residence at The Hague originally provided for him by the Dutch during the negotiations for the grand alliance in 1701, he discovered that it was still in dispute who should be formally appointed allied generalissimo.

CHAPTER TWO

THE SUSPICIONS OF
THE DUTCH

Now in the lofty, wainscoted rooms of the Mauritshuis there began tense and anxious meetings between Marlborough and his old friend and colleague Anthonie Heinsius, the Grand Pensionary of Holland (who, as Governor of this, the largest of the seven Dutch provinces, which contributed some sixty per cent of the national budget, was the most powerful man in the Republic: in essence, head of the Dutch government), and other allied representatives. For while Marlborough had been accepted as William III's heir as moving spirit of the alliance, such an exalted post as allied generalissimo demanded, according to the custom of the time, a prince to fill it. Even Queen Anne, who had so

BELOW LEFT The only known representation of Anthonie Heinsius (1641–1720), the Grand Pensionary of Holland. Engraving by L. A. Claessens (1764–1834) after an original painting by Gerbrand van den Eeckhout (1621–1674)

proudly and readily confirmed Marlborough in his post as Captain-General of the English forces, had another candidate in mind for allied generalissimo. This was her own adored husband, Prince George of Denmark, whom she at the same time proposed as Captain-General of the Dutch forces, a post also left vacant by William III's death. Unfortunately Prince George was one of nature's colonels, brave enough under fire as a young man, good natured, harmlessly stupid, and now corpulent and asthmatic.

Marlborough himself could hardly have been placed in a more false position. Duty now compelled him to renew his advocacy of Queen Anne's blockheaded husband for a post which he must have desperately wanted for himself, as much for the sake of the public service as of private ambition. Yet he may have reflected that he would be better able to act through a compliant dummy like Prince George than through some other prince with pretensions of his own to generalship. In the middle of June such a candidate turned up at The Hague to complicate matters, in the person of King Frederick I of Prussia.

News from the allied army made Marlborough the more impatient to get this question of the command settled, and quit The Hague for the field. On 10 June the main body of the army, under the Dutch general Ginckel (ennobled by William III as Earl of Athlone),

The great audience hall at The Hague where members of the States-General received foreign ambassadors. Engraving by Daniel Marot (c. 1663–1752)

GENERAL GINCKEL,
CREATED EARL OF ATHLONE.

Godart, Baron van Reede-Ginckel, Earl of Athlone (1644–1703): until Marlborough's arrival, the acting commander of the allied army, who had nearly been caught and destroyed by the French under Boufflers. Painting by Sir Godfrey Kneller

had escaped encirclement at the hands of Marshal Boufflers only by the undignified speed of its retreat to the sheltering guns of the fortress of Nijmegen. It was a setback only partly redeemed by the capture of Kaiserswerth, below Düsseldorf on the Rhine, five days later by another allied force.

And still the impasse over the appointment of a generalissimo remained unsolved; no one would have Queen Anne's husband, and she would have nobody else. Perhaps Marlborough privately hoped that the impasse would open the way for himself, the unprincely outsider. By the end of June, however, he had had enough. He left The Hague by water for Nijmegen, where he could at least take up his command as Captain-General of the English forces. But while his 'yacht' was sailing along a dike between The Hague and Utrecht a courier brought him news that the Dutch had at last come to a decision – of a kind. They were not going to make a formal appointment of Captain-General of their forces after all; nor, as a consequence, of allied generalissimo either. Instead they would recognize Marlborough as being at the head of the allied armies. In the words of Adam de Cardonnel, Marlborough's personal secretary, 'The States have given directions to all their Generals and other officers to obey my Lord Marlborough as their General.'[1] However, this recognition did not go so far as conferring a title, pay or clear authority. There was no written patent. Moreover, Marlborough was to enjoy the power and right actually to give orders to the Dutch generals at such times only as the Dutch army was joined with his own in action. At all other times he was to depend on their voluntary collaboration, and the consent of the Dutch Field-Deputies, or political representatives of the States-General with the army.[2]

So Marlborough found himself about to occupy the role of allied generalissimo *de facto* and by default; a supreme commander only by the sufferance of his colleagues. His ability to direct allied strategy would depend almost entirely on his own tact and powers of persuasion, on his own personal force of character. He would have to carry a heavy handicap such as William III had never known, nor his French opponents now, and which must impose a tremendous extra strain on top of all the inevitable burdens and anxieties of high command. Marlborough gave a hint of his private feelings at this grudging and ambiguous appointment in a letter written twelve days later to his close colleague and friend at home, Sidney, Earl of Godolphin, the Lord Treasurer and the Queen's chief minister:

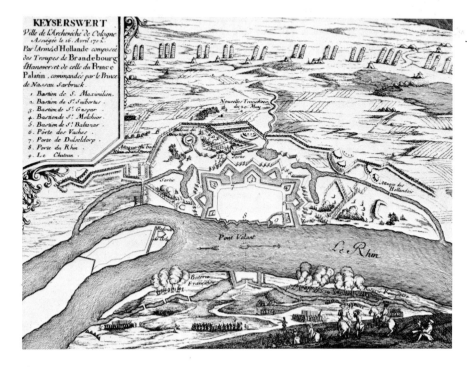

The siege of Kaiserswerth, which fell on 15 June 1702. Engraving

I am obliged to you for the compliment you make me for the station I am now in. It would have been a great deal more agreeable to me, if it could have been without disputes, and a little less trouble; but patience will overcome all things.[3]

In the evening of 3 July 1702 Marlborough disembarked at Nijmegen and went forward to the vast tented camp where 60,000 men awaited his direction. When he made his entry amid a mounted escort, fanfares pealing and salutes of musketry crashing, he had reached at long last that exalted, lonely place towards which he had been climbing ever since he first donned an ensign's scarlet coat thirty-five years earlier.

The ensuing councils of war presented Marlborough with his first challenge in his new role. He had to establish a personal ascendancy over his allied colleagues; to make his own ideas, his own will prevail. The Dutch generals, however, displayed the coldness and reserve, resentment even, of veterans required to defer to a foreign courtier-general. Athlone in particular was one of those Dutchmen whose preference by William III over Englishmen had provoked Marlborough's public resentment in the 1690s. It was Athlone too who had been in acting command of the army until Marlborough's arrival, and who had nearly been caught and destroyed by Boufflers. For Marlborough this was a delicate situation, uneasy with undercurrents of personal feeling. He therefore made no attempt immediately to assert himself, but instead listened tactfully while others had their say; content to observe and appraise.

The strategic position itself seemed grim enough. Marlborough found waiting for him a discouraged, baffled army, lying passively in front of the Dutch fortress of Nijmegen on the River Waal. Of the fortresses along the Maas, only Maastricht, now far in the rear of the French, remained in Dutch hands; and in that epoch, when roads were so bad, rivers served not only as barriers to armies but also as their principal supply routes. In the Electorate of Cologne, one of the three hundred and fifty principalities into which Germany was then divided, other French forces lay athwart the main allied line of communication via the Rhine between the United Provinces and the other allied powers, Baden and the Habsburg Empire.

Marlborough found waiting for him a discouraged, baffled army, lying passively in front of the Dutch fortress city of Nijmegen, shown here. Engraving

To the cautious, conventional minds of the Dutch generals, grown old and stale over decades of long sieges and lost battles, it seemed that the United Provinces themselves stood in acute danger from the vast military power of France. They could not forget the catastrophe of 1672 when the French had overwhelmed their frontier fortresses in a devastating surprise offensive, and very nearly conquered the entire country. At all costs, they believed, Boufflers must be prevented from taking Nijmegen and unlocking the invasion route into the heart of the country. Therefore the sound and proper course of action was to stand on the defensive at Nijmegen and in other fortresses along their borders.

But Marlborough did not believe that the French were as formidable as they seemed. Far off in Italy French strength was being bled by the bitter struggle with Imperial forces under Prince Eugène. Another French army was being pressed on the Upper Rhine by the Margrave of Baden. Much of the remaining French strength lay scattered in covering forces or locked up in fortresses in the Spanish Netherlands. Boufflers himself had under command an army only slightly larger than Marlborough's: a hundred and thirty squadrons of cavalry to a hundred and twenty; eighty battalions of infantry to seventy-six; and a hundred and thirteen guns to seventy.

And Marlborough reposed complete confidence in the superior fighting qualities of the allied troops, and in particular his English contingent, which constituted a fifth of the total. His pride in the English soldier, his passionate belief in that soldier's ability to outfight the French, was longstanding. In 1691, when he was commanding the English troops in Flanders, he had shown off his men to a Prussian officer, Count von Dohna, who indeed found them, in his words, 'fine troops and very alert'. According to Dohna

> Churchill asked me if I did not think them invincible and if, with such men, we were not sure to beat the French. Sir, I said to him, you see on the other side troops who believe themselves to be equally invincible, and if that is so, there's a clash of opinions.[4]

Marlborough's present confidence in his army rested on more than faith in its morale; he believed that its tactical methods were better too. While French cavalry relied on the firepower of their long-barrelled horse pistols, the English and their allies were trained for shock action, in the tradition of Cromwell's Ironsides, trusting to the weight and momentum of horses and men riding at a steady trot to smash down the enemy line. In the case of the infantry – now in all armies armed with the new flintlock musket and the bayonet – the French musket ball was lighter, weighing twenty-four to the pound against the English sixteen. And whereas the French fired in rotation by rank, the English fired by platoons grouped in 'firings' – far more concentrated volleys, and better directed and controlled by the regimental officers. Marlborough and his officers believed that the combination of a heavier ball and firing by platoons would shatter the French.

There was another factor which inclined Marlborough towards an offensive strategy, and perhaps the most important of all: his own temperament. The coolness and calm which so impressed observers like Lord Chesterfield were misleading. For Marlborough was a man of action; passionate, virile, dynamic. This was, after all, the man who had

A page from The Exercise of the Firelock and Bayonet, *a drill manual in use in Marlborough's day*

satisfied Barbara Castlemaine; who had won and held the love of Sarah Jennings; and between Marlborough the lover and Marlborough the soldier there was much in common.

The strategy which he now put forward to the council of war was bold and unorthodox enough to stop the stoutest Dutch heart. Leaving the fortress of Nijmegen to defend itself with the aid of part of the allied army, the main body would cross the River Maas and, outflanking Boufflers to the west, march on into the province of Brabant, in the Spanish Netherlands; a province which Boufflers, by his own advance, had left uncovered. At a stroke the French threat to Nijmegen and to the heart of Dutch territory would be ended, because, as Marlborough expressed it later, the French 'must then have had the dis-advantage of governing themselves by our motions' – in other words, by falling back in haste to defend Brabant.

The dismay of Marlborough's Dutch colleagues at this risky gamble contrary to all the sound rules of war was complete. That Marlborough had won Heinsius's consent to his strategy weighed nothing with them. They stood fast in dour, implacable opposition; and the Englishman discovered for the first time the tortures of arguing with Dutch generals. And while the arguments wearyingly revolved, the army hardly moved; a circumstance from which Boufflers benefited by sending a large detachment off to the aid of the French army opposed to the Margrave of Baden on the Rhine. Boufflers was now numerically inferior to the allies. On 20 July Marlborough furiously wrote to Heinsius:

> . . . it is soe shamefull our lyeing idle letting the Marshall Boufflers make his detachements for the Upper Rhyn, that I have noe patience. Besides if the two armys remain this side of the Meuse [Maas], you will find it very difficult to suport (sic) your troops in winter quarters, when you may be assured that the next campagne must begin in sight of Nimegne [Nijmegen]. Will not Prince Luis of Baden have great reason to be angry, when a superior army dose (sic) not hinder the enimy from sending detachements nor send more themselves? Till wee act ofensively all things must go ill. . . .[5]

Yet this dispute over strategy was only one among Marlborough's cares. He was more than the commander-in-chief of an army; he was virtually England's resident foreign minister in Europe; the crown wheel of the whole alliance. As he told Sarah in a letter at this time, after an envious reference to the current fine weather ripening the fruit in their garden at Holywell House, St Albans,

> I am a-horseback or answering of letters all day long; for besides the business of the army I have letters from The Hague, and all places where her majesty has any minesters (sic).

And he added with a sardonic humour characteristic of him:

> . . . and if it were not for my Zele to her service, I should certainly desert, for you know of all things I doe not love writting.[6]

On 22 July he at last won Dutch consent for a lunge at Boufflers's communications. Despite further delays because of rain which turned the roads into swamps, he was over the Maas by 27 July and driving south. Now, in the saddle with a marching army,

Marlborough was happy; tensions released, totally absorbed, supremely confident. 'From day to day,' wrote Field-Deputy Geldermalsen, 'he makes it the more felt that he is Commander here; whereas at Nijmegen he sought to do nothing that was not decided by the generals.'[7]

Already Marshal Boufflers was in full retreat, striving to reach Brabant before Marlborough got across his communications. He was too late. By the beginning of August Marlborough was some twenty miles south of Eindhoven, and so placed that Boufflers would have to make a flank march across the front of the allied army, if he wished to get back into Brabant. This march would take him over a wide stretch of heathland near the village of Peer – the perfect arena for a battle.

The hapless Boufflers was discovering that war was not so easy against Marlborough as it had been against Athlone. If he stayed where he was, he would be cut off from his base in Brabant. Moreover Brabant would lie at Marlborough's mercy. But if he made a dash for Brabant, he risked a battle under an immense disadvantage. Flustered, Boufflers decided to seek escape by commencing his escape march at night, hoping by sending out foraging parties to deceive Marlborough into thinking that he meant to stay put. But with that intuitive ability to read an opponent's mind which is the mark of the great general, Marlborough ordered his troops to sleep on their arms that night. He was no longer content to manœuvre Boufflers back from Nijmegen; he intended to smash him in battle and so straightaway transform the whole face of the war. Perhaps to

Marlborough's campaigns of 1702 and 1703

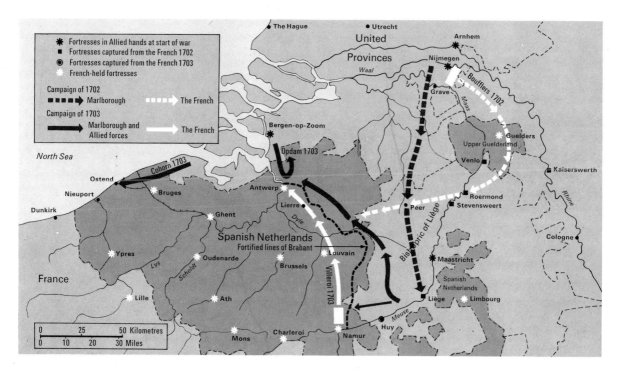

Marlborough's surprise the Dutch generals and field-deputies nerved themselves to consent to this purpose.

At first light on 2 August 1702 Marlborough began to deploy his army. When his cavalry reported that the French army was beginning to march straight across his front it was clear that Boufflers was doomed. At this moment, however, the Dutch leaders elected to lose their precarious nerve, and plead with Marlborough to call off the attack.

Marlborough faced a choice as difficult as it was urgent. Should he now exercise that authority to command the Dutch army in time of action which the States-General had vested in him – and insist that the battle take place? For otherwise he would be deprived of the almost certain victory he had arranged with such skill, and which the alliance so badly needed. Yet in all battles there must be an element of chance. Supposing the Dutch army, shield of the Republic, was destroyed or wrecked in execution of his orders? And even if the day ended well, would it still be wise to stand formally on his authority so early on in the war? Dutch resentment at being overruled could deprive him of that voluntary co-operation on which his effective direction of allied strategy must normally depend.

Swallowing his chagrin, he decided to yield to Dutch wishes, and ordered the tents and baggage to be brought up so that the army could encamp again. Nevertheless, he had no intention of allowing the Dutch leaders to congratulate themselves on their prudence. He asked them to ride forward with him so as to observe the French army pass over the heath.

> . . . which they and most of the general officers did and saw them [the French] hurrying over it in the greatest confusion and disorder imaginable; upon this day they all acknowledged that they had lost a fair opportunity of giving the enemy a fatal blow.[8]

What it cost Marlborough to renounce his battle is conveyed by two expressive understatements in a letter to Sarah on 3 August:

> Thes(e) last three or four days have been very uneasy, I having been oblig'd to *take more pains than I am well able to endure.*

And:

> Pray give my humble duty to the Queen. I was in hopes the Day before yesterday I might have done her some service. . . .[9]

· This was to be by no means the only occasion in the campaign when Dutch obstructive- ness robbed him of the chance of attacking an enemy wide open to the lunge of his blade. The Dutch leaders have been much censured for this by English historians. Yet they were being asked to confide the army of the Republic, the very safety of the state, to Marlborough's military judgment. What, after all, they might fairly ask, was there in Marlborough's past military record that would merit such unbounded and unhesitating trust?

'. . . Churchill's desire to become a soldier had been fired when he accompanied his master to watch the Guards at exercise.' Drill on Horse Guards Parade. Detail from a painting by Peter Tillemans (1684–1734)

CHAPTER THREE

SO LITTLE SERVICE

Marlborough's career as a soldier had begun thirty-five years earlier, on 24 September 1667, when as John Churchill, just over seventeen and a page to Charles II's brother James Duke of York, he was gazetted as an ensign into the King's Regiment of Foot Guards (today the Grenadier Guards). The original commission is still preserved at Blenheim Palace. According to a traditional account, Churchill's desire to become a soldier had been fired when he accompanied his master to Hyde Park to watch the Guards at exercise – officers as gaudy as parakeets; pikemen and musketeers performing slow, stately evolutions while the fifes squealed and the drums rattled. When the Duke of York noticed the boy's excited admiration and asked him what profession he meant to follow, Churchill is said to have dropped to his knees and begged 'a pair of colours [that is, a commission] in one of those fine regiments'.

Scandalmongers of the period and priggish and prurient historians since have suggested, their breath indrawn with disapproval, that Marlborough owed his commission to the fact that his elder sister Arabella was the Duke of York's mistress; if true, then it was fortunate for England and Europe that the Duke of York found her person so agreeable.

A year later, in 1668, Churchill joined the garrison of Tangier, which had come to the English crown as part of the dowry of Charles II's Portuguese queen, Catherine of Braganza. Here Churchill had remained for three years, skirmishing with the Moors in summer dust and the winter rain. The Moors, mobile, brave and cunning, masters of the ambush, had provided first-class tactical training and field experience for a young officer – rather as the tribesmen on the north-west frontier of India were to do for later generations of English soldiers. For a time in 1670 Churchill was seconded for service with the troops on board the Mediterranean fleet and took part in the blockade of Algiers, the principal base of the Barbary pirates.

The French army in action in the era of victory during which John Churchill saw service with it in the Royal English Regiment. Detail from a painting by Robert Bonnart (1652–1729) after an original by Pieter van der Meulen (1638–1685) and Charles Le Brun (1619–1690)

Two years later, after an interlude at court which witnessed the opening of his dashing campaign with Barbara Castlemaine, he had gone to sea again, at the beginning of the Third Dutch War. In March 1672 he was present when, before war had even been declared, the English fleet attacked the Dutch merchant convoy from Smyrna off the Isle of Wight; an operation which received its just reward in a rebuff at the hands of the Dutch escort. At the Battle of Sole Bay, in June, off the little Suffolk town of Southwold, Churchill and his company of the Guards (the senior company of the army) were in the

Royal Prince, flagship of the Lord High Admiral of England, Churchill's royal patron the Duke of York.

It was an experience which had taught Churchill even more about the hazards and uncertainties of sea warfare, for the French fleet (in the round dance of European politics England was then allied to France against the Netherlands) misread York's signal and sailed off on the wrong tack, leaving the English to bear the brunt of the Dutch attack under that tough old seaman De Ruyter. The *Royal Prince*, at the heart of a desperate, bloody fight, was beaten into a wreck, but Churchill remained on board even though the Lord High Admiral himself transferred his flag to the *St Michael*. Nothing is known of Churchill's own part in the fighting, but it must have been courageous and efficient enough, for afterwards he was promoted two ranks at once, from ensign in the Guards to Captain in the Lord High Admiral's Regiment.

Marlborough was one of the few generals of his era to have taken part in a great sea battle. He was never to fall into Napoleon's error of thinking that fleets, at the mercy of wind and tide, could be directed to and fro with the punctuality and exactitude of armies. As he was to tell an Imperial minister in 1708, 'Operations at sea are not as easily governed as those on land. There are many more precautions to be taken, and you and I are not capable of judging in the matter.'[1]

It had been in 1673 that Churchill had enjoyed his first experience of Continental warfare – when England was still France's ally – as an officer in the French army's Royal English Regiment, commanded by Charles II's bastard son the Duke of Monmouth.

Louis XIV's army was then at the peak of its fighting excellence. Two great ministers of war, Le Tellier and his son Louvois, had completely reorganized the French military system – pay, supply, discipline, administration. Churchill was now seeing this unrivalled army in action at close hand; another vital strand in his professional development.

John Churchill's commission as ensign in the King's Regiment of Foot Guards

'Louis XIV's army was then at the peak of its fighting excellence.' LEFT TO RIGHT *Michel de Louvois, Le Tellier (1603–1685), French Minister of War, engraving; François Le Tellier, Marquis de Louvois (1641–1691), engraving – as Minister of War he completed the task begun by his father of reorganizing the French military system; Henri de La Tour d'Auvergne, Vicomte de Turenne (1611–1675), Marshal of France (John Churchill served under him as a young officer), study for a tapestry by Charles Le Brun*

In 1674 he was fortunate to serve in Alsace and southern Germany under one of the most able French commanders, Henri de La Tour d'Auvergne, Vicomte de Turenne.

As a regimental officer in the French service Churchill had distinguished himself both for ability and personal courage. After the battle of Enzheim, where the fighting was so fierce that half Churchill's officers were killed or wounded, his leadership was praised in Turenne's official dispatch. Turenne is also said to have spoken warmly of Churchill as 'my handsome Englishman'. During the siege of the great Dutch fortress of Maastricht the year before, Churchill had been the first to plant the fleur-de-lis flag of France on an outer defence work attacked by Monmouth's Royal English Regiment. It was Monmouth and Churchill together who had later repelled a sudden Dutch sortie by their unhesitating action in leading a handful of men in a counter-attack across open ground swept by fire. Churchill, himself wounded in the action, was later honoured by the thanks of Louis XIV in person.

Next year, before joining Turenne, Churchill had again enjoyed the honour of meeting Louis, this time being received amid the cold formality of Versailles as a preliminary to receiving a promotion in his service. Here was another strand which went to the weaving of Marlborough, the relentless enemy of the French monarchy. He had seen that monarchy, and the monarch, at first hand; he had personally looked tyranny in the face. Moreover, he had got to know the French military system at first hand, its tactics and its methods. He had met some of the men he would one day fight – Tallard; Boufflers, who as a colonel was also at Enzheim; Villars, another veteran of the siege of Maastricht.

So far it had been a promising enough military career – active service for six out of the seven years, varied experience, hard fighting, European war with the best army of the era. But, although the war had continued until the Peace of Nijmegen in 1678, Churchill, unlike his future Dutch colleagues, or French enemies, had seen no further service in it.

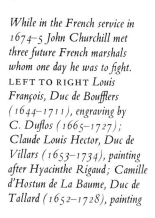

While in the French service in 1674–5 John Churchill met three future French marshals whom one day he was to fight. LEFT TO RIGHT *Louis François, Duc de Boufflers (1644–1711), engraving by C. Duflos (1665–1727); Claude Louis Hector, Duc de Villars (1653–1734), painting after Hyacinthe Rigaud; Camille d'Hostun de La Baume, Duc de Tallard (1652–1728), painting*

John Churchill's meeting with Louis XIV in the field would have been at a ceremony similar to this royal visit to the French fortresses in Flanders in 1680. Engraving

Instead, in 1675, now Gentleman of the Bedchamber to the Duke of York, he had been sent to Paris on a private mission. It had marked the beginning of his other career as a man of tact, manners and discretion apt for delicate diplomatic assignments. While he was in Paris he had arranged for his campaign silver plate to be sent home free of duty. The warrant lists the domestic items which a seventeenth-century colonel of moderate means found necessary for life in the field:

> one basin, 2 great dishes, 12 small, 2 massarines, 3 doz of plates, 2 flagons, 4 candlesticks, 2 ewers, 2 stands, 2 chafing dishes, 1 vinegar pot, 1 sugar pot, 1 mustard pot, 1 pair of snuffers and its case, 4 salts, 6 cups, 12 spoons, 12 forks, 12 hafts, one great spoon, one chamber pot, one tea pot, one chocolate pot, one great cup, one skillet and 2 Turkey cups.[2]

In 1676 Monmouth recommended Churchill for command of the Royal English Regiment, but Courtin, the French ambassador in London, reported to Louvois the

Part of Marlborough's campaign silver: ABOVE *a wine bottle for slinging on a mule or horse;* BELOW *a wine fountain*

Minister of War that Churchill had a competing interest. 'I assure you', he wrote, 'that he is hard in pursuit of Mme de Hamilton's sister [Sarah Jennings], who is the prettiest of the maids [Courtin added 'of honour', but in the interests of accurate reporting, crossed it out] of Madame the Duchess of York.'[3] Louvois doubted from this whether Churchill was really the man for the post, writing to Courtin loftily and for the sake of discretion partly in code that 'M de Churchil (sic) is too concerned with his pleasure to be able well to acquit himself of the responsibility intended for him. . . .'[4] Nevertheless, since Courtin reckoned that Churchill was the best-qualified candidate, he was offered the command – only to turn it down. As Courtin explained to Louvois, 'Churchill has preferred to serve Mme de Hamilton's sister, who is very pretty, than to be Lieutenant-colonel of the Duke of Monmouth's regiment.'[5]

Instead, after another two years' wait, Marlborough had got his colonelcy in the English service, when it seemed as if England was about to enter the war again – this time on the Dutch side – and new regiments were being raised. The new colonel, still only twenty-eight years old, was now entrusted by the Duke of York with a highly responsible mission, at once military and diplomatic. He was to negotiate with the Dutch and with the Spanish authorities in the Spanish Netherlands the size of the relative contributions of the new allies in ships of war and soldiers; and to arrange the details of military co-operation in the field. After a successful visit to Brussels, capital of the Spanish Nether-lands, he journeyed on to The Hague. Here he had met William of Orange for the first time, and in the course of tough but successful discussions, the two men had got on well together. William himself was highly impressed by the shrewdness and courtesy with which Marlborough had negotiated with him. For Churchill this successful diplomatic mission had served as far more valuable experience than just another campaign; already he was developing a breadth of understanding and expertise that mere soldiers like Athlone were never to achieve.

In May 1678 he had been promoted to brigadier of foot, charged with the enlistment of recruits; and in September he was with the troops in Flanders. However, as he had correctly prophesied to Sarah, then his wife of a few months, there was no war after all. Instead, the Peace of Nijmegen led to the shrinking of the English army to a small nucleus of 'guards and garrisons'; and the prospects of its officers had shrunk likewise.

Churchill himself, however, as a close and confidential associate of the Duke of York, had been fortunate, for while his military career was languishing, his other career, as high-level diplomatic go-between, had prospered. He had hardly returned to England when he found himself back in Brussels again, this time in the Duke of York's company. For the Duke, a devout Catholic, had been forced into temporary exile by the anti-Catholic hysteria which had exploded after the melodramatic but mendacious revela-tions of Titus Oates about a 'Popish Plot' to murder Charles II, massacre prominent Protestants, and place the Duke on the throne. While the Duke of York was residing in Brussels, Churchill had acted as his roving confidential envoy. He journeyed to Paris; he visited London in order to plead for his master's return. In 1680, when the Duke had

View near the Bierkade in The Hague. Painting by J. ten Compe (1713–1761)

exchanged Brussels for the granite, calvinistic gloom of Edinburgh, he recommended Churchill as ambassador either to France or the Netherlands. William of Orange, too, had wanted him as ambassador at The Hague. But nothing came of either appointment. In the wake of the popular panic caused by the Popish Plot, a ruthless political offensive was under way to force the Duke of York's exclusion, as a Catholic, from the succession to the throne. With merciless party witch-hunters at work, and the nation demented with rumours of treason and plot in high places, it had been no time for Charles II to appoint a prominent member of his brother's household to a key diplomatic post.

But after Charles's complete victory over the exclusionist party in 1681, and the Duke of York's triumphant return to London, Churchill's career had begun to prosper again. In December 1682, he was made Baron Churchill of Aymouth, in the peerage of Scotland; in July 1683 was chosen to escort the Princess Anne's fiancé Prince George of Denmark to England; in December 1683 he was promoted Colonel of the Royal Dragoons.

And when in 1685 his patron, the Duke of York, succeeded to the throne as James II, Churchill's career had seemed for a time to bowl along like a coach-and-six on a broad highway. In the list of the new King's nine Gentlemen of the Bedchamber Lord Churchill's name stood second only to the Earl of Peterborough, another distinguished soldier, and he was immediately dispatched to Paris secretly to negotiate a subsidy from Louis XIV on James's behalf. His journey had been wasted, however, for Louis got in

first, offering James the money through the French ambassador in London. At the coronation Churchill was rewarded with an English peerage as Baron Churchill of Sandridge.

In the same year of 1685 had come his first campaign for eleven years, against his old commanding officer the Duke of Monmouth and the ill-armed West Country peasantry who followed him in his luckless attempt to depose James II and make himself king. It had not been a campaign to weigh in the scales of European war. Brigadier Lord Churchill had ridden out for the West Country with just eight troops of horse and five

companies of infantry behind him – the sum of regular troops immediately available for the field.

He had moved fast, reaching Bridport, in Dorset, in two days. Once there he had ruthlessly commandeered draught beasts and wagons, and scoured the country to locate Monmouth's main body. This done, he had clung with his tiny force to Monmouth wherever the rebel leader moved, like a mastiff to the flank of a bull, until reinforcements eventually reached him. His letters to colleagues and to the King in London crackled with energy and decision. Then had come a disappointment. Along with the reinforcements arrived a new commander-in-chief, Lord Feversham, a Huguenot refugee, appointed by the King over Churchill's head. Feversham was all that Churchill was not – lethargic, slow, indecisive. As Feversham let one opportunity after another slide out of his limp hands, Churchill's letters had begun to reflect his bitterness and impatience. From Frome in Somerset he wrote to Sarah: 'We have had an abundance of raine which has very much tired our soldiers, which I think is ill, because itt makes us not presse the Duke of Monmouth soe much as I think he should be, and that itt will make me be the longer from you. . . .'[6] To Lord Clarendon he had confided sourly that 'I see plainly that the trouble is mine and that the honour will be another's.'[7]

At last Feversham had closed on Monmouth's army of peasants at Bridgwater. On 5 July 1685 he halted for the night near the village of Weston Zoyland, three miles away. During the night, however, Monmouth had advanced to attack the royal army – a final desperate gamble. In broken ditch-seamed country, the attackers lost their paths and their cohesion. Nevertheless, it was Churchill who had been instrumental in their final repulse and destruction. He himself brought up the guns to silence a rebel battery; shifted infantry from a quiet sector to a hard-pressed part of the line; and finally led his own Royal Dragoons in a charge which sabred down the rebel gunners. Yet, as he had feared, Feversham got the credit for the victory; and not only the credit but also the Garter.

Miniature though the campaign of Sedgemoor was, it had displayed Churchill at a turning point in his development as a soldier. The bravery, energy and resourcefulness in the thick of a fight which he had shown at Maastricht and Enzheim had become something more; a finger-tip feeling for how a whole battle was going, for where the danger points were, or would be. And his operations before the battle – rapid, decisive – had shown that the able regimental officer was maturing into a general of quick and complete strategic grasp, well able to bear the moral weight of independent command in the field.

Three years later Churchill was again riding westwards, this time as Lieutenant-General of the royal army, to meet the far more dangerous threat posed by William of Orange's landing at Torbay; with Dutch veterans as opponents instead of brave peasants. And once more Churchill had found himself serving under the feeble-spirited Feversham, a man with more appetite for his dinner than a battle; once more therefore slighted by James II. At a crucial council of war in Salisbury on 4 December 1688, Churchill had urged the King to advance and fight; Feversham, on the other hand, had recommended a retreat behind the Thames. James found Feversham's advice the more congenial. This council of war had marked the end of Churchill's brief direct military contribution to the events of the Glorious Revolution, for that night he had ridden over to William of Orange's camp, and under the impact of his and so many other distinguished desertions, James's will and his cause alike had collapsed.

William of Orange, for his part, had not come to England out of an altruistic desire to provide the English at their request with a new ruler, but in order to add England's weight to his fresh coalition against France, the League of Augsburg. Yet, although the War of the League of Augsburg lasted from 1688 to 1697, Churchill himself (made Earl of Marlborough in 1689) only saw three years' service in the field, and then mostly in subordinate commands. It was this brevity of active service between 1688 and 1697 as much as anything that his resentful Dutch colleagues in 1702 were to remember and hold against him.

It was William's own preference for trusted Dutch veterans which had accounted for Marlborough's relatively minor part in the war. Immediately after the Revolution Churchill was confirmed in his rank of Lieutenant-General, and given the task of reconstituting the army after its dispersal by James II. This not only called for high talent as an organizer but also for a leader who enjoyed the trust of the rank and file. Marlborough tackled the task with the same restless energy which he displayed on the battlefield. One of his colleagues wrote to a friend: 'My Lord Churchill proposes all. I am sent for to say the general consents, and Monsieur Bentinck is the secretary for to write all.'[8]

But in 1689 the chief command in Ireland – where James II and a contingent of French troops had joined the native Catholic Irish in an attempt to conquer the whole country – had been given to the Duke of Schomberg, who had accompanied William to England the year before. Marlborough himself was sent to Flanders in command of the English contingent of 8,000 men in the allied army under the Prince of Waldeck, possibly in order that he should not have to fight against his old master. Nevertheless, that year Marlborough and his English troops had brilliantly distinguished themselves at the Battle of Walcourt, when they had sustained the main weight of an attack by a French army under the command of Marshal d'Humières. Just as at Sedgemoor Marlborough had fought his battle line in person. When the French, with their frontal attack brought to a standstill, had sought to outflank the English position, Marlborough, clear-thinking amid the noise, smoke and confusion, perceived that in so doing they had exposed themselves to counter-attack. He himself had led this attack at the head of the Household Cavalry, bundling the French back in disarray.

For his part in the Battle of Walcourt Marlborough had won high praise. Waldeck wrote to King William that 'the Earl of Marlborough is assuredly one of the most gallant men I know', and that 'Marlborough in spite of his youth had displayed in this one battle greater military capacity than do most generals after a long series of wars.'[9] And William himself acknowledged to Marlborough that: 'It is your care which has undoubtedly much contributed to it (the success at Walcourt), and for which I am greatly beholden to you.'[10]

In 1690, while William was campaigning in Ireland with his Dutch colleagues, Marlborough had been left to mind military affairs at home as commander-in-chief of the forces in England. This appointment reflected William's growing confidence in Marlborough's ability, for the safety of the realm itself in the face of a threatened French invasion was entrusted to his hands. Coupled with his reconstitution of the army in 1688–9, it gave Marlborough administrative experience of supreme value for the future. He came to know the English military system in all its warrenous illogicalities and divided responsibilities, and learned how nevertheless to make it work; moreover, he himself had a major share in shaping the army which one day he would lead to victory. Another Marlborough now began to emerge alongside the diplomat and the hard-driving leader in the field – the methodical, painstaking organizer.

But even at this period Marlborough had created his own opportunity for service in the field. He proposed that an expedition be dispatched to take the Irish ports of Cork and Kinsale, thus disrupting the principal line of communications between France and the French forces in Ireland. The project had been the more bold because of the very real danger that the French were about to invade England in the wake of the victory they had recently gained over the English fleet off Beachy Head. It had been altogether too bold for the Privy Council, which refused to think of sending troops out of the country at such a moment. Queen Mary, however, had insisted on referring the plan to her husband in Ireland, who, to the dismay of the Council, approved it.

So, in the last week of August 1690, Marlborough had set about organizing and carrying out his first operation in independent command, and the only combined operation of his career. No form of warfare is more difficult or more prone to confusions and failure than a seaborne expedition. Although of all nations the English ought to have been masters of its techniques, English history is littered with the wrecks of combined operations launched in high hope. Marlborough's expedition to Cork and Kinsale in 1690 is one of the more rare successes. Speed and secrecy were the keynotes of the planning. Not even the Admiralty was told where the force was going, while the French were gulled by carefully spread rumours that their own coast was about to be attacked. In just ten days Marlborough was ready to sail from Portsmouth.

However, bad weather and contrary winds had then kept him fretting in harbour for nearly a fortnight. Now the Navy had begun to grow nervous, fearing to expose its ships-of-the-line to the hazard of autumn gales roaring in from the Atlantic. But Marlborough had been adamant: and so, on 27 September 1690, the fleet, with eighty-two men-of-war and transports, had sailed for Cork, the vessels rolling and plunging in heavy seas, Marlborough himself desperately seasick in his cabin.

On 1 October the expedition had arrived off Cork harbour; on the fourth, after a maddening delay, this time owing to lack of wind, the troops were put ashore near the city; on the seventh Marlborough's guns were smashing the walls; on the eighth a breach was opened and his assault troops waded through the River Lee at low tide to storm the breach. Four thousand Irish troops had unconditionally surrendered. Then it

William III's victories over James II in Ireland, 1690. Engraving by Romeyn de Hooghe

was Kinsale's turn. The siege and assault was pressed with the same furious urgency. The town surrendered on 26 October 1690. In just twenty-three days Marlborough had made a major contribution to the final victory in Ireland, and his success was all the more popular in England for being English. It was this which had prompted William III's comment that 'No officer living who has seen so little service as my Lord Marlborough is so fit for great commands.' English historians (such as Winston Churchill) have taken exception to the condescending nature of this remark. Nevertheless, the condescension was not unjustified. The defences of Cork and Kinsale were feeble and primitive compared with the elaborate fortresses designed by such Continental engineers as Vauban. And Marlborough's besieging troops, even as reinforced from the main allied army in Ireland, had only numbered some 9,000 men. Yet these two minor sieges were to be Marlborough's last experience of operations in the field until he became head of the allied forces in 1702, except only for the 1691 campaign in the Low Countries, in which he had commanded the English contingent, and which was one of barren marching.

For it was in the following year, 1692, that he had been dismissed by William III from all his offices. For the rest of the war Marlborough had remained in England, a sword in its scabbard, while his future Dutch colleagues were fighting in five grim campaigns: the bloody and unsuccessful battle of Steenkirk and Neerwinden in 1692 and 1693, and the ultimate triumph of William III's career, the great siege of Namur in 1695.

It was hardly unreasonable therefore that now, in 1702, when Marlborough was campaigning for the first time for eleven years and for the very first time as a commander-in-chief, the Dutch leaders hesitated to entrust their army and their country to his confident belief that, if he attacked the hitherto almost invincible French, he would beat them.

Yet, since Marlborough did not enjoy the authority of an allied generalissimo, the trust of his Dutch colleagues was the key to the future conduct of the war. Only a success could earn that trust. For personal and professional reasons as well as political and strategic, Marlborough in that late summer of 1702 hungered for a battle.

After the lost opportunity of 2 August 1702, when he was forced to watch Boufflers's army scurry to safety in Brabant through his unsprung trap, Marlborough set about clearing the line of the Maas fortress by fortress up to the now isolated Dutch stronghold of Maastricht. He began with Venlo. Almost at once, however, he found his purpose clogged by the sluggishness of his Dutch subordinates; men long accustomed to make war with the deliberation, not to say the dignified ritual, of a church service. Cohorn, the famous Dutch engineer, was so long in even beginning the siege of Venlo that Marlborough, in a fresh anguish of thwarted dynamism, bluntly warned Heinsius, the Grand Pensionary: 'If that [the siege] be not pressed soe that you may be masters at Venlo, you will lose all the frute of this campagne.'[11] Four days later he wrote again: 'The accounts wee have from Grave and the farther demands of stores which are made by M. de Cohorn considering how farr the season is advanced, gives mee the spleen....'[12]

As the 'spleen' worsened with the cumulative frustration of the campaign, with days filled without respite with military and diplomatic business, he looked to Sarah, far away in St Albans or London, for strength and comfort. Almost every night, when the camp had grown quiet after tap-to, he would draw the candle near and cool his mind by writing to her. During one of the most crowded episodes of the campaign he employed 'the onely time I have to myself this seven or eight days' in writing 'to you and my dear Children, the pleasure of which has refreshed mee for I have noe mind to goe to bed. . . .' And he asked Sarah 'how my garden is, which I have not forgote'.[13] Sarah herself sometimes wrote him two letters in the same day – but all of them afterwards destroyed by Marlborough at her wish; a tragic loss. 'I doe assure you,' he told her in a letter during that summer, 'that your letters are soe welcome to mee that if thay shou'd come in the time I were expecting the enemy to charge mee, I cou'd not forbear reading them.'[14]

In the second half of August, however, his spirits lifted. Boufflers, prodded by Louis XIV, emerged from his fortified lines and marched north-eastwards to intercept a supply convoy bound for the besiegers of Venlo. Marlborough moved swiftly to force on the battle he so much wanted. Once again the hapless Boufflers, not the most agile of military minds, found himself manoeuvred into the last kind of place he would wish to fight – a desolate stretch of open heath near Helchteren, in Brabant, with his left wing stuck in a bog. His troops and horses were exhausted by incessant marching, famished for want of provisions.

Even the Dutch agreed – though not without earnest discussion – that this time Boufflers was at such a disadvantage that he ought to be attacked. That afternoon Marlborough issued his orders: the Dutch under General Opdam were to open the attack by advancing against Boufflers's left wing, cramped as it was in marshy ground. Minutes passed; hours passed; still Opdam failed to move. Nothing would propel him forward until the state of the ground was exactly to his satisfaction. Dusk at last extinguished Marlborough's hopes of a day otherwise wasted in long-range cannonading. For Boufflers this was a respite for which he could never have hoped; a respite in which to recover his own balance and rest and reorganize his troops. In the morning it was the turn of the Dutch field-deputies, De Heyd and Geldermalsen, to paralyse the allied army: was it wise, they asked, to go on with the attack now that the initial surprise had been irretrievably lost?

So a day of fruitless argument began, while the armies stared motionless at each other and the guns boomed away. An eye witness has left a glimpse of Marlborough at this time. Lord Ailesbury, an old friend of his, had sent his secretary, Mr West, to him with a letter. When the secretary, together with a companion, eventually came up with Marlborough, he was standing in a cluster of generals and staff officers in the open field. Unperturbed by the enemy cannonballs which were bounding or soaring past, Marl-borough, who knew West, turned to him with his usual graceful courtesy: 'Mr West, my humble service to my Lord. You see I cannot write, but I will send an express to Aix [Aix-la-Chapelle where Lord Ailesbury was residing].' The secretary strolled away a short distance with his companion. At this moment his companion's head was smashed clean away by a cannonball. The secretary decided, not unreasonably, that it was time he departed. In Lord Ailesbury's words, 'not being used to such hot work, no doubt but he was sufficiently affrighted'.[15]

At last the Dutch were induced to consent to an attack at first light the following morning. But by then Boufflers had gone, his army struggling away under cover of darkness. Yet even now, Marlborough made a desperate effort to retrieve this second discarded opportunity of the campaign for a decisive battle. He personally led twenty squadrons of cavalry in pursuit of the retreating French. It was too late; he caught a few squadrons of the enemy rearguard, and that was all.

Under the mortification of seeing Boufflers saved for a second time in a month by the Dutch, the crust of Marlborough's patience and politeness cracked, and the feelings of a desperately thwarted man of action began to erupt to the surface. He reported to his friend the Lord Treasurer:

I have but to(o) much reason to complain, that the ten thousand men upon our right did not march as soon as I had sent the orders, which if thay had I beleive (sic) wee shou'd have

Fort S.! Michael Storm'd by y.' Lord Cutts Sep.! 31.1702.! Kill'd & drownned 600 men & took 2,00 prisoners in less y.' an Hours time

Lord Cutts taking the fort of St Michael, Venlo. From a contemporary pack of cards

had a very easy victory, for their whole left was in disordre. [And he added:] I am in soe ill houmer (humour) that I will not trouble you, nor dare I trust myself to write more; but beleive this truth, that I honor and love you, my Lady Marl, and my children, and wou'd die for the Queen.[16]

Four days later he was pouring out to Godolphin his contempt at the paralytic slowness of the Dutch at the siege at Venlo.

England, that is famous for negligence, should any they employ be guilty of half what I see here, it would be impossible for them to avoid being justly torn to pieces by the Parliament.[17]

To Heinsius he wrote savagely on 4 September:

The troupes has (sic) been before Venlo thes eight days, and thay now talke of opening the trenches two days hence. If this be zele, God preserve mee from being so served as you are my friend . . . I write this by candlelight, soe that I know not if you will be able read itt.[18]

On the 14th the deliberation with which the Dutch engineer Cohorn continued to conduct the siege inspired Marlborough to remark to Godolphin that 'It is not to be imagined the backwardness and sloth of thes(e) pepell, even for that which is for their own good.'[19] However, on 18 September English troops under General Lord Cutts (nicknamed 'Salamander' because of his appetite for the hottest fire) took the outlying fort of St Michael by storm; a spectacle which Venlo's defenders found so discouraging that the fortress surrendered four days later.

Now it was the turn of the fortresses of Roermond and Stevensweert. For Marlborough

The hazards of water transport. Engraving

was determined to clear the Maas before the end of the campaigning season. But the fine weather broke, and, as he sarcastically noted, 'The very ill weather gives too reasonable an excuse that the sieges do not go so fast as could be wished. . . .'

Marlborough himself was already looking beyond the fall of Roermond and Stevens-weert. He meant to force the French in Brabant back behind their fortified lines before the winter. However, as he commented to Heinsius,

> I foresee that the ill weather and the great sickness that is amongst the troupes will be the excuse for not doing itt. The French have the same weather and have as many sick; but this is noe argument to men that will not venture to doe any more.[20]

But he was determined that they should do more. With a new self-confidence born of success he had put aside his accustomed patience and courtesy. Field-Deputy Gelder-malsen for example reported to Heinsius that

> It is impossible to express the contempt in which he holds the Earl of Athlone, his indecision, his weakness in confiding in men of no account and following their advice regardless of resolutions already determined upon.[21]

Stevensweert fell on 2 October; Roermond, besieged simultaneously, on the 7th. It was now growing late in the campaigning season. Still Marlborough was not content. He gave immediate orders for an advance up the Meuse (as the Maas is called in the French-speaking territories south of Maastricht) on the great fortress of Liège, the bishop of which was an ally of the French. The capture of Liège would cut the shortest French line of communication between the Spanish Netherlands and the Rhine; uncover the province of Brabant to an allied invasion. As Marlborough thrust towards Liège, the French in his path scattered with a precipitation unseemly in troops of the *grand monarque*; in Tongres (Tongeren) they even left behind the wheelbarrows and pickaxes they had been using to construct fortifications. Boufflers himself, with the main body of the French army, manfully marched to protect Liège; but, a puzzled man, he again found himself effortlessly placed in the wrong place to fight a battle; was again preserved by Dutch caution; and fell back gratefully behind his fortified lines of Brabant.

On 13 October Marlborough's advanced guard saw ahead of it the smoke pall which marked the northern suburbs of Liège, set ablaze by the French. That same evening the city of Liège itself surrendered. On 19 October fifty battering cannon and forty-eight heavy mortars began to open a breach in the ramparts of the citadel. On 23rd Marl-borough in a hastily added postscript to a letter to the Secretary of State, Lord Nottingham, was able to report: 'by the extraordinary bravery of the officers and soldiers, the citadel has been carried by storm, and for the honour of her Majesty's subjects, the English were the first that got upon the breach.'[22]

On 29 October, after the siege guns had been laboriously shifted over ground rendered sodden by autumn storms, it was the turn of the fort of the Chartreuse, the last centre of French resistance in Liège. From secret intelligence Marlborough had received, he did not expect it to last long, as he informed Godolphin. With his letter he enclosed one written by Boufflers, which, in Marlborough's words, 'was brought mee last Saturday by a spye of his, which I gain'd some time agoe, so that he has had an opertunity ever since of cheating us both.'[23] Here was a glimpse both of Marlborough's care and skill in gathering operational intelligence, and of his sardonic sense of humour.

As he had predicted, the defenders of the Chartreuse were not in the mood for heroics. At the very first salvo they hung out flags all round the ramparts in token of surrender.

When the garrison marched out hands in pockets according to the terms of capitula-tion, he was there to watch them – the easy grace of a courtier in the scarlet and gold of a general. It was the crowning moment of this, his first campaign as commander-in-chief, for the army was about to disperse into winter quarters. Although the Dutch had denied him the battle which could have changed the face of all things, his achievement was such as William III had never seen in a single campaign. Perhaps the most important success of all was the least tangible – the moral domination Marlborough had achieved over the enemy commanders and their troops.

His campaign glowed the more brightly against the dark setting of defeat and failure elsewhere. Prince Louis of Baden had lost the fortress of Landau; a Habsburg army had been routed by Marshal Villars at Friedlingen in southern Germany; and a great Anglo-Dutch seaborne expedition to Cadiz had ended in the fiasco that history has so often reserved for such exercises.

Yet the campaign very nearly proved his last. He was on his way back to The Hague by water, when his boat was ambushed on the Meuse one night towards twelve o'clock by a French raiding party. The French grabbed the towrope, dragged the boat to the bank, overcame the guard to the flare of muskets and the flash and stink of grenades, and scrambled aboard in search of loot and prisoners.

Luckily for Marlborough, one of his clerks, Stephen Gell, had in his pocket a French passport made out in the name of Marlborough's younger brother, General Charles Churchill (it was the courtesy of the age to issue such safe conducts to enemy personages wishing to travel on private business). Gell handed it to Marlborough, who, with the same kind of sang-froid he had displayed when surprised by Charles II in Barbara Castlemaine's bedroom, passed himself off in the dim lantern light as his brother. Marlborough was later to reward Gell generously enough with a pension for life, but, being a man much aware of the value of money, the price of his deliverance remained in his mind; two years afterwards, in a letter to Sarah, he was to remark that Gell 'has cost me 50L a year ever since'.[24]

About five in the morning the French patrol, having ransacked the baggage and enriched themselves with silver plate, returned to the river bank, and left Marlborough's party free to sail on.

When Marlborough at last arrived at The Hague he was surprised, and touched, by the warmth of the Dutch people's welcome, by their evident relief that he was safe. From five o'clock in the afternoon till after ten at night musket fire resounded between the tall,

'. . . it was fortunate for England and Europe that the Duke of York found her person so agreeable.' John Churchill's sister, Arabella, mistress to James, Duke of York, later James II. Painting from the studio of Lely

scrolled gables of the city; 'which', Marlborough remarked, 'is their way of rejoicing'. It was difficult for him even to reach the Mauritshuis from the boat because of the dense press of cheering citizenry. A famous victory could hardly have done more for his popularity. As he wrote to Godolphin:

> Till thay saw mee, thay thought mee a prisoner in France, soe that I was not ashore one minut, before I had great crowds of the common pepell, some endeavoring to take mee by the hands, all cryeing out welcome, but that which moved mee most was to see a great many of both sexes crye for joye.[25]

At the beginning of December Marlborough, with an escort of warships – he was taking no chances now – sailed for England. Those Kentish cliffs which in the spring he had searched so vainly with his 'perspective glass' for a distant glimpse of Sarah rose again out of the grey rim of the sea; and there, at Margate, she was waiting for him.

In London an address by the House of Commons expressed the nation's pride: 'The wonderful success of your majesty's arms, under the conduct of the Earl of Marlborough, has signally retrieved the ancient honour of the nation.'

Queen Anne herself, however, had already found her own way of expressing her regard. On 22 October, while Marlborough was still besieging Liège, she wrote to her dear friend, Sarah Marlborough:

> It is very uneasy to your poor unfortunate faithfull Morley to think that she hath so very little in her power to showe how truly sensible I am of all my Lord Marlborough's kindness, especially at a time when he deserves all that a Rich Crown could give. But since there is nothing else at this time, I hope you will give me leave as soon as he comes to make him a Duke. . . .[26]

It was a letter which in all its warmth, its informality and kindness, bore witness to the intimacy of the friendship that had come to exist between Anne and the Marlboroughs. So strongly did Anne wish to preserve this friendship that, at her suggestion, the three of them, together with Godolphin, had adopted nicknames in their correspondence, so that in a fictional equality they might forget the gulf of rank that separated them. Anne herself became 'Mrs Morley'; the Marlboroughs 'Mr and Mrs Freeman', Godolphin 'Mr Montgomery'.

Now in the dukedom Mrs Morley was offering Mrs Freeman and her husband a gift which she hoped would come as a surprise and a delight; something personal from her, a token of her overflowing affection and admiration.

But while the Queen's letter certainly came as a surprise to Sarah Marlborough, it did not at all give the pleasure for which the fond Anne had arranged with such care. In Sarah's own words, '. . . when I read the letter first . . . I let it drop out of my hand, and was for some minutes like one that had received the news of the death of one of their dear friends. . . .'[27]

And she wrote off to her husband not solely to acquaint him of the Queen's offer of a dukedom, but to urge him to decline it.

'The Dutch Republic had been the centre of the financial world for more than a century . . .'
Detail from a painting of 1682 by Gerrit Berckheyde (1638–1698) of the Hofvijver, the ornamental water flanked by the ancient government buildings of The Hague.

CHAPTER FOUR

FOUNDING A FAMILY

Since all her letters were dutifully destroyed by her husband as she wished, exactly what Sarah wrote to Marlborough on the topic of the offered dukedom cannot be known, but that it was characteristically forthright can be inferred from Marlborough's reply:

> You know I am very ill at compliments, but I have a heart full of gratitude; therefore pray say all you can to the Queen for her extraordinary goodness to me. As you have let me have your thoughts as to the dukedom, you shall have mine in short, since I shall have the happiness of being with you so soon, when I may advise with you more at large on this matter. But be assured that I shall have a mind to nothing, but as may be easy to you. I do agree with you that we ought not to wish for a greater title, till we have a better estate. Your other objection is also very just, that this promotion might bring great solicitations upon the Queen, which I am sure I would not give occasion for. The Queen's goodness in being desirous to establish my family, answers the first since that may be done this winter; for I agree with you, that it should be done before the title.[1]

It was a letter which said much about John and Sarah Marlborough. There was the strength of his feelings towards the Queen both as a person and as a monarch; a compound of that romantic loyalty the Stuarts so often evoked in their entourages and of an almost religious sense of reverence. For Marlborough was an old-fashioned monarchist, a royal servant all his life, and a deeply religious Church of England man. Yet the letter also shows him caught between the Queen and Sarah; Sarah on whose love and strength he so much depended, and to whose wishes he always deferred if he could; moreover, whose judgment he so much respected.

For in a society where most women, however high in rank, were domestic and social appendages to their husbands, Sarah Marlborough was a shrewd, hard-minded businesswoman. She possessed a powerful self-taught intellect devoid of subtlety or imagination; ultimately disastrous in all matters of human relationships, but superb with money, property and all matters relating to her own and her husband's joint careers through the world. In that era all went by rank and status; and rank and status depended on possession of landed property in due proportion. If the Marlboroughs were to take their place without ridicule among the established ducal families, they too must have their broad acres. And all their life together the driving ambition of these two had been to achieve high social rank and the independence and security that went with it – to found a great family that would carry their name on down the generations. For both

John and Sarah in their childhoods and young years had known what it was to be poor and dependent.

Marlborough himself was born (on 26 May 1650, Old Style) in the house of his maternal grandmother, Lady Drake, and had spent the first nine years of his life under her stern and frugal regime. His father, Winston Churchill, had fought for Charles I in the Civil War. But Charles I had lost his stubborn and devious head on 30 January 1649; lopped off by his Parliamentary conquerors. Winston Churchill, like so many other cavaliers, was now made to pay for his conspicuous service to a defeated cause by a fine; in his case of £4,446. This was a crippling sum for a modest country gentleman such as he to find. He was only able to raise it by selling his estate, thus leaving himself penniless with a young wife and two small children. So his mother-in-law took them in. Lady Drake, however, had been on the other side during the Civil War, a staunch Puritan and Parliamentarian. Here was just one example of how deep that war hacked through English society.

John's father, Sir Winston Churchill. Painting by Sir Peter Lely

By an irony, the very house in which the ruined cavalier and his family now took refuge, and where his third son John was born, Ashe House, near Axminster in Somerset, had been pillaged and partly burned down by Royalist troops. So to all the personal tensions and difficulties that go with living with in-laws was added the bitterness of remembered personal wrongs inflicted by the opposing sides to which father and mother-in-law had belonged. Moreover Lady Drake, a widow, was herself so poor that it was many years before she could repair the roof over the fire-damaged part of the house. In this childhood without a parental home, cramped by want of money and soured by domestic tension, there were lessons for John Churchill: the corroding effects of poverty

'. . . this childhood without a parental home, cramped by want of money and soured by domestic tension . . .' Ashe House, belonging to John Churchill's grandmother, where he was born and spent the first nine years of his life

and dependence; the need to guard one's thoughts and tongue; the catastrophic consequences of being caught on the losing side in the conflicts of a society profoundly sundered by political and religious enmities.

Even after the Restoration of Charles II in 1660, Marlborough's father still remained far from prosperous, although he was appointed a Commissioner of the Court of Claims in Dublin two years later, and in 1663 knighted and made Junior Clerk Comptroller of the King's Household at Whitehall. It was partly Sir Winston's own fault, for he was always in a muddle over money and died heavily in debt (a lesson here which his son never forgot); partly because Charles II was himself too pressed for money to recompense old cavaliers for all they had lost in the royal cause. What he could offer them, because it cost nothing directly, were places at his court for their sons and daughters; honour and employment. So it was that in 1665 Sir Winston Churchill's daughter Arabella became a maid of honour to the Duchess of York (and eventually mistress to James Duke of York, the heir to the throne); to be joined some months later in the same household by her younger brother John, as page to the Duke. The lesson of childhood at Ashe House was now repeated amid the tawdry elegance and routine lechery of Charles II's court: dependence for daily bread on pleasing others; the need for self-effacement, compliance and tact. Marlborough's upbringing makes a striking contrast to the Duke of Wellington's family background and childhood, so spacious, so socially assured.

Sarah Jennings too (born on 29 May 1660, the day of Charles II's entry into London on his return from exile to the throne, but where is not known) came from modest country gentry. This close kinship of social origin was one of the strongest elements in a relationship so close as to amount to fusion; they knew and perfectly understood all that

John Churchill as a very young man. Miniature by an unknown artist

Charles II's court when John Churchill made his appearance there

Frances Thornhill, Sarah's mother. Painting by Sir Godfrey Kneller

had gone to form each other's outlook on life; they had nothing to explain to each other. Sarah's father, Richard Jenyns (to give the spelling of the time) sat in the House of Commons as burgess for St Albans; her mother, Frances Thornhill, was the daughter and heir of another squire, Sir Gifford Thornhill, Bt, of Agney Court in Kent. Richard Jenyns's house in the town of St Albans, Holywell House, was later to be the Marlborough's home. He also owned a property in the country at Sandridge, six miles from St Albans; just such another gabled and mullioned Jacobean manor house as Lady Drake's Ashe House – a little grander, but still a house which bespoke dogs and horses, careful housewifery and quiet dinners with country neighbours rather than fashionable state and show. When Sarah was eight years old, her father died, leaving his widow, encumbered with debt, to bring up Sarah and her two elder sisters, Frances and Barbara.

Thus Sarah's childhood, like John Churchill's, was blighted by the grey mildew of poverty. For her as for John, as for all the able-bodied – or beautiful-bodied – poor but gentle born, the court was the only source of indoor relief. She came to London in 1672, and in the following year, at the age of only thirteen, became one of the Duchess of York's maids of honour. Again like John when a page to the Duke, she now felt what it was to be poor and obscure and yet mix with the great.

Here then, in these experiences of childhood and youth, was the keen goad of John and Sarah Marlborough's ambition; the explanation too of that 'avarice' and 'meanness' of which their own world as well as later historians were to accuse them. For it was only by iron thrift, by shrewd and careful management, that a couple so poor as they were could hope to amass the wealth which would bring them independence, security and consequence.

Sarah's father's house in St Albans, Holywell House, which was later to become the Marlboroughs' home

The starting point of John's fortune was an annuity of £500 which he bought when he was twenty-four from Lord Halifax for £4,500. Since he was to live long in an age when men died early, it proved a good enough investment. Gossip said (in all likelihood correctly, although there is no proof) that the £4,500 was a present from Barbara Castlemaine, as exuberantly generous with Charles II's cash as she was with her own affections; gossip even specified that she gave it as a reward for John Churchill's quick thinking in jumping out of her window when surprised by the King.

Careful though Marlborough was with money, he could not compare with his wife in sheer financial flair. As Sarah herself put it,

> Soon after my marriage, when our affairs were so narrow that a good degree of frugality was necessary, Ld Marlborough though his *inclination lay enough that way*, yet by reason of an indulgent gentleness that is natural to him he could not manage so as was Convenient for our Circumstances, this obliged me to enter into the management of my family.[2]

Gradually, as John Churchill had risen in rank both as a soldier and as a courtier, and Sarah had shrewdly invested the surplus she created by her good management, their affairs had ceased to be quite so 'narrow'. Yet even sixteen years after their marriage they had badly felt the loss of his salaries and perquisites when in 1692 William III dismissed him from all his offices, for their own fortune, even together with Sarah's salary as Mistress of Princess Anne's household, was not large enough to support his earldom with the state proper to it.

Now, in 1702, rich as they were, in sight of their ambition's goal as they were with the Queen's offer of the highest title in the peerage, they still hesitated to risk over-extending themselves – or even their descendants.

Nevertheless Marlborough managed to persuade Sarah that they should accept the dukedom, partly on the grounds that it would enhance his standing with the allies. They hoped, however, that instead of the Queen's grant of £5,000 a year out of the Post Office revenues for Marlborough's own lifetime, Parliament might award this sum in perpetuity to his descendants in the title.

Their friend the Earl of Godolphin, the Lord Treasurer, duly laid the proposal before Parliament, but with something of the effect of prodding a wasp's nest with a short stick. The party political battle, already enough of a nuisance to a government trying to carry on a European war, gratefully latched on to a new issue. The proposal had to be withdrawn, much to Marlborough's mortification. Yet the whole episode contributed to the view that the Marlboroughs were too pushing, and, moreover, becoming too grand. As John Evelyn noted in his diary in December 1702:

> After the excess of honour conferred by the Queen on the Earl of Marlborough by making him a Knight of the Garter and a Duke, for the success of but one campaign, that he should desire £5,000 a year to be settled on him by Parliament . . . was thought a bold and unadvised request, as he had, besides his own considerable estate, above £30,000 in places and employments, with £50,000 at interest. . . .[3]

John and Sarah were Duke and Duchess of Marlborough now; they had arrived at last. Not for *their* daughters marriages to penniless soldiers of obscure family, like Sarah's own marriage, but into great families. The eldest, Henrietta – warm, headstrong as her mother, fashionable – had married Lord Godolphin's son Francis in 1698, thus tying the two families together into the next generation. Within a year the young Godolphins produced a son, William – 'Willigo' – to the delight of the grandparents. When Lord Godolphin was staying with the Marlboroughs at Holywell House, he sent his sister news of the eighteen-month-old Willigo.

> All here are very well at present and Willigo begins to make a noyse which he is pleased with himself because he takes it for speaking, but it's a language not much understood in the world hitherto. . . .[4]

Alas for the proud and hopeful families, Willigo grew up to be a wastrel and a drunk.

In 1700 the Marlborough's second daughter, the sweet and gentle Anne, had married Lord Spencer, an ambitious, virulently Whig politician, widower son of the Earl and Countess of Sunderland. At the beginning of 1703, just after the Marlboroughs got their dukedom, their daughter Elizabeth became betrothed to the Earl of Bridgewater; to be followed in the summer by an engagement between Mary Churchill, whom some said was her father's favourite, and Lord Monthermer, heir to the Earl of, and later the first Duke of, Montagu, a man of immense possessions and political influence.

The bustle of arranging these grand matches, with the attendant settlements of land and property, found Sarah Marlborough in her element; and the results were gratifying enough. Yet John's and Sarah's hopes of founding a great family of their own reposed in their eldest and only surviving son John ('Jack') Churchill, who had become Marquess of Blandford on his father's dukedom. He was now aged sixteen, and had left

John's and Sarah's daughters and two of their sons-in-law: Henrietta (1681–1733), painting by Sir Godfrey Kneller, married Francis Godolphin (1678–1766), painting by Sir Godfrey Kneller; Anne (1684–1716), painting by Sir Godfrey Kneller, 1710; Elizabeth (1687–1714), painting by Sir Godfrey Kneller; Mary (1689–1751), painting by Sir Godfrey Kneller, married John Montagu, Lord Monthermer, later Duke of Montagu (1690–1749), painting by John Shackleton (d. 1767)

Their son, John, Marquis of Blandford (1686–1703) aged sixteen. Painting by Sir Godfrey Kneller

Eton for King's College, Cambridge. Young Jack wanted to serve abroad with his father, but his mother would not agree to hazard her boy, the future of the Marlboroughs, to the discomforts and dangers of the field at so young an age. So, lovingly, anxiously, his parents watched him as he made his way along the lethal obstacle course of disease which constituted childhood in that epoch.

Jack would often ride over from Cambridge to Newmarket to stay with Lord Godolphin, whose passions were horses, racing and gambling. After one such visit Godolphin was able to write to Jack's parents just the kind of thing parents love to hear of their offspring:

> He is tractable and good humoured, and without any ill inclination, that I can perceive. And I think he is grown more solid than he was, and has lost a great deal of that impatience of diverting himself all manner of ways which he used to have.[5]

Some time later Godolphin wrote again:

> My Lord Churchill is now at Cambridg (sic), but today he comes hither for 5 or 6 days . . . tho the small-pox is in this town, yett he going into no house but mine, will I hope bee more defended from it by ayr and riding . . . than possibly he could bee anywhere else.[6]

On 13 October 1703 after Godolphin had come back to London, he had more compliments for Sarah Marlborough about her 'pretty son':

> I do assure you without flattery or partiality that he is not only the best natured and most agreeable, but the most fore-thinking and reasonable creature that one can imagine of his age. . . .[7]

In the New Year, however, Jack, for all his admirable qualities, got into some unexplained trouble at Cambridge; and in February 1704 wrote asking his parents to forgive him:

> Dear Mama, I received a letter from Mr Godolphin [his sister Henrietta's husband Francis] last post and the joy I had when I found I had some hopes of being friends with my Dear Mama is not to be expressed, but I can't think myself so happy till my Dear Mama can find some time to lett me have a letter from her, & I am sure there can be no greater pleasure than would be to my Dear Mama, your most Dutyfull son, Blandford.[8]

It was his last letter to them. Within days he was down with a fever; soon it proved to be that most terrible of all scourges, smallpox. For his family the news brought a dread that caught at the stomach and dried the throat; began a nightmare of frantic, useless effort. Sarah herself – Francis and Henrietta Godolphin as well – hastened to Cambridge as fast as horses could pull a heavy coach. The Queen, who had lost a son of her own from smallpox only three years beforehand, sent her own doctors in one of her own coaches.

Marlborough, who had not had the disease, stayed in London. He could only wait in trepidation for news, and relieve his pent anxieties by writing to Sarah:

'He was on his way to The Hague by water, when his boat was ambushed on the Meuse one night . . .' In that era, when roads were so bad, rivers served as the principal means of communication. Detail from a river scene by moonlight. Painting by Aert van der Neer (1603/4–1677)

OVERLEAF The Marlborough family. Painting by John Closterman (1660–1713). 'He [Closterman] painted the Duke and Duchess of Marlborough and their children . . . on which subject however he had so many differences with the duchess that the duke said "it has given me more trouble to reconcile my wife and you than to fight a battle."' (Vertue)

Thursday, 9 in the morning:— I hope Dr Haines and Dr Coladon got to you this morning. I am so troubled at the sad condition this poor child seems to be in, that I know not what to do. I pray God to give you some comfort in this great affliction. If you think anything under heaven can be done, pray let me know it; or if you think my coming can be of least use, let me know it. I beg I may hear as often as possible, for I have no thought but what is at Cambridge. Medicines are sent by the doctors. I shall be impatient to the last degree until I hear from you.[9]

In his agony of mind, he wrote again that same night:

I writ to you this morning, and was in hopes that I should have heard again before this time, for I hope the doctors were with you early this morning. If we must be so unhappy as to lose this poor child, I pray God to enable us both to behave ourselves with that resignation which we ought to do. If this uneasiness which I now lie under should last long, I think I could not live. For God's sake, if there be any hope of recovery let me know it.[10]

But there was no hope; Jack died on 20 February, just as his father, who had been sent for by Sarah, finally arrived from London. John and Sarah Marlborough had lost not only a dearly loved son, but also the keystone of their patient ambition.

They went to Holywell for a week or so and shut the door on their grief. But the alliance was waiting for Marlborough to take the field again; in Flanders, along the Rhine and in Bavaria, in Italy, the armies were stirring out of their winter quarters like hibernating animals that feel the spring. And this year the alliance would face a new enemy, Bavaria, under its Elector, Max Emanuel, who had entered the war on France's side towards the end of the last campaign.

So, bearing his own grief and leaving Sarah to hers, the Duke set off for the Netherlands at the beginning of March. Already a French army under Villars had captured Kehl, on the Upper Rhine, and it was evident that French strategy was to join with their new Bavarian allies and mount an offensive in southern Germany against the Habsburg Empire, while the French army in Italy pressed towards Vienna from the south.

At The Hague the Duke and his Dutch colleagues considered how best they could relieve the pressure on the allied forces in Germany while at the same time containing the French forces in the Spanish Netherlands, now under Marshal the Duke of Villeroi. The Dutch, whose minds ran much on fortresses, proposed that the allies should open the campaign by taking Bonn, on the Rhine, and so free communications up the river with Baden and the Habsburg Empire. This could be followed by an offensive in the Spanish Netherlands. Marlborough fell in with these proposals, although without relish; it may be because, with grief still fresh upon him, he was not in the mood either to invent a strategy of his own, or to embark on wearisome arguments.

While Overkirk faced Villeroi with a covering force, therefore, the Duke set off for Bonn. But even now, despite the anodyne of work and responsibility, grief kept tugging at his mind. On 20 April, when he was at Cologne, there was a public holiday, with a procession in which thousands of priests took part; and afterwards he wrote to Godolphin:

'... an anxious, efficient bureaucrat more at home with racehorses than women ...' Sidney Godolphin, Earl of Godolphin (1645–1712), Lord Treasurer and Chief Minister, and Marlborough's closest friend and colleague. Painting, copy after Sir Godfrey Kneller, 1710

I have this day seen a very great procession, and the thought how pleas'd poor Lord Churchill wou'd have been with such a sight has added very much to my uneasyness. Since itt has pleased God to take him, I doe wish from my soull I cou'd think less of him.[11]

A week later the methodical Cohorn, whose guns and ammunition had at last arrived, was ready to open the siege of Bonn, a circumstance which provoked a flicker of the Duke's old sardonic humour, for he remarked to Godolphin:

The name of Cohorn frietens all the ladys of Bon, which has given mee an ocation (occasion) of obliging them; for I have refused noe one a passe to go to Collogne, amongest which are all the Nuns of a Monestry. . . .[12]

On 18 May, with Bonn in his hands, Marlborough rejoined Overkirk, who, heavily outnumbered by Villeroi, had abandoned Liège and fallen back near Maastricht.

Now the Duke had to plan the main business of the campaign. It was no easy task. The opposing armies were roughly equal in size, while Villeroi enjoyed the protection of the extremely powerful Lines of Brabant, a system of field fortifications and water obstacles stretching from Antwerp to the Meuse near Namur. Nevertheless the Duke was confident he could outmanœuvre Villeroi and break through the Lines. The main objective of the plan he now evolved, which he dubbed the 'Grand Design', was the fortress and port of Antwerp, the western hinge of the Lines. He himself was to lure Villeroi to the opposite end of the Lines, near the Meuse, and hold him there. Cohorn was further to confuse the French by attacking down the coast on Ostend. Finally the Dutch general Opdam was to launch the offensive against Antwerp. But the 'Grand Design' began to go wrong from the beginning. Cohorn first delayed his advance while he argued over his orders, then went off on a pillaging expedition instead of going for Ostend. Villeroi, thus alarmed for his western flank, began to march towards Antwerp despite the presence of Marlborough's own force opposite him. The Duke, hastening after Villeroi, began to have forebodings of disaster.

If M Opdam be not upon his guard, he may be beat before we can help him, which will always be the consequence when troops are divided, so that the enemy can post themselves between them.[13]

Yet it was, after all, Marlborough's own plans which had so divided the troops. He reopened his letter to Godolphin in order to add the gloomy postscript: '. . . we have a report come from Breda that Opdam is beaten. I pray God it be not so, for he is very capable of having it happen to him.'[14]

But it was so. Despite Marlborough's warnings that he was in danger, Opdam advanced unsupported to Eeckeren, north of Antwerp, allowed the French to take him by surprise, and then himself departed the field, leaving his troops to fight their way out under the command of others.

The 'Grand Design' had ended in a fiasco for which English historians have blamed Cohorn and Opdam. It was not entirely their fault, however. Marlborough's plan had

The Maas at Rotterdam.
Painting by Abraham Storck
(1644–c. 1704)

been complicated, dependent on the punctilious timing and performance of generals in whom he had no reason to place much confidence. He had divided his forces, so exposing them to the defeat in detail which had occurred. His own feint near the Meuse had failed to deceive Villeroi. And lastly his plan prevented him from taking personal command of the key operation, the attack round Antwerp.

Undeterred he set about rebuilding his campaign. This time he intended to breach the Lines of Brabant between Antwerp and Lierre. But now he ran once more into the obstruction and suspicion of his Dutch colleagues. The army remained virtually para-lysed by the ever-more bitter dissensions within its high command; the paralysis and dissensions alike moved the Duke to a rage of despair. He wrote to Heinsius on 21 July:

> It is impossible the warr can goe on with success att this rate, if measures must be taken between two armys, and the quarrels and animositys of privatt pepel shall make a delay which hinders the whole. It is in my opinion impossible to avoyde in length of time some great misfortune; which gives mee soe much trouble, that I know not if I shall outlive this campagne, but I am sure I have not coridge to make another. . . . I own to you that I have the spleen to a very great degree, which may make mee judge ill of what I write in this letter. I wish it may prove soe. . . .[15]

But only two days later a flat Dutch refusal to obey his instructions to attack deprived him of the chance of fighting Villeroi, whom he had enticed into poking his head out of the Lines like a nervous hedgehog. The Duke gave up, marched back to the Meuse and laid siege to the small fortress of Huy, although as he wrote to Godolphin, 'I know that Huy will make very little noise in the world.' Yet he had still not abandoned hopes of a battle, 'by which God may give us more success in three or four hours' time than we dare promise ourselves . . .'.[16] In a council of war on 24 August, two days before Huy fell, the Duke put forward a fresh plan for breaking through a sector of the Lines of Brabant north of Namur, which was known to be weaker than elsewhere. But the meeting only saw the divisions within the allied command come to an open split; and ended in the drawing up of a memorandum signed by Marlborough himself, three English, two Danish and seven German generals, pointing out that the entire war situation demanded an attack on the Lines, and asserting that such an attack enjoyed a good chance of success. The Dutch generals for their part wanted to go off and besiege Limbourg. 'I am sure you will observe,' the Duke told Heinsius by letter two days later, 'all thay say is to incline us to act defensively, which I take to be destruction.' As he was sealing this letter came news that Huy had surrendered. 'For God's sake,' scribbled Marlborough in a postscript, 'take a vigorous resolution, for the enemy is frightened and we shall beat them whenever we see them.'[17]

Vigorous resolutions, however, proved a luxury beyond reach. On 30 August the Duke was writing to Godolphin of the possibility of his early return to England, because, as he put it with savage sarcasm, 'I shall not be very fond of staying with an Army that is to doe noe more but eat forage.'[18] Four days later, in a letter to Heinsius, the Duke gave vent to his utter desperation:

'. . . the meeting only saw the divisions within the allied command come to an open split . . .'
Resolutions of the Allied Council of War, August 1703, signed by Marlborough and twelve generals protesting against Dutch caution and calling for an offensive; the Duke's signature is at the foot.

. . . if I might *have millions* given mee to serve another yeare and be obliged to doe nothing but by the *unanimous consent* of the Generals, I would much sooner dye; for besides that nothing can be a secritt, all disciplin after the maner wee now live must be lost, it not being in the power of anyone to punish. . . .[19]

Marlborough therefore suggested 'as the only expedient I can think of', that he should simply command the English forces, together with such Dutch troops as the Netherlands authorities might decide should serve with the English under him. Had the command been so organized from the start of the campaign, 'I am veryly persuaded with the blessing of God I should have made a glorious campagne, for wee have had occasions to have made use of the bravarie of the troupes. . . .'[20]

The strain of command under such circumstances had now wound his nerves taut to snapping point. In his own words, 'the unreasonable opposition' he had met with so heated his blood that he was 'almost mad with the headache'.[21]

All this time he was also desperately worried about Sarah's health. In the early summer she had thought she might be pregnant again, for the first time in thirteen years. A fresh hope for a son! In an undated letter, he told her that 'What you say to me of yourself gave me so much joy, that if any company had been by, when I read your letter, they might have observed a great alteration in me.'[22] But then it became clear that Sarah's symptoms were due to ill-health; that the shock of losing her son had profoundly affected her mentally and physically. Far off in the field and unable to help her, Marlborough poured out his concern through his pen.

> . . . I shall have no rest till I hear again from you, for your health is much dearer to me than my own. . . . For God's sake let me know exactly how you are; and if you think my being with you can do you any good, you shall quickly see you are much dearer to me than fame. . . .[23]

On 2 August, when the army was on its march back from Antwerp to the Meuse:

> It was a great pleasure to me when I thought that we should be blessed with more children; but as all my happiness centers in living quietly with you, I do conjure you, by all the kindness I have for you, which is as much as ever man had for woman, that you will take the best advice you can for your health, and then follow exactly what shall be prescribed for you, and I do hope you will be so good as to let me have an exact account of it, and what the physicians' opinions are. . . .[24]

On 27 September 1703 the surrender of Limbourg, besieged at Dutch insistence, brought a dismal and nearly barren campaign to an end. But already the Duke had formed a resolution far-reaching in its consequences: next year he would campaign not in the Spanish Netherlands, but in Germany.

I LOVE YOU
SO TRULY WELL

*'France had been closing in on the
Habsburg empire . . .' A French
army crossing the Rhine.
Engraving by J. Maussard after
an original by P. D. Martin
(1663–1742)*

All through 1703, while the allied army in the Spanish Netherlands was doing little
more than, in the Duke's scornful words, eat forage, France had been closing in on the
Habsburg Empire both in Germany and in Italy. A French army under Marshal
Tallard had captured Breisach, on the eastern bank of the Upper Rhine, and recaptured
the fortress of Landau. Marshal Villars had led another army through the steep, winding
defiles of the Black Forest to link up with the Elector of Bavaria. In September Villars
and the Elector beat an Imperial force at Höchstädt on the Danube. There now seemed
nothing to prevent the Franco-Bavarians from entering Vienna in the course of 1704 and
dictating a peace to the Emperor Leopold in his own palace of the Hofburg. The Empire

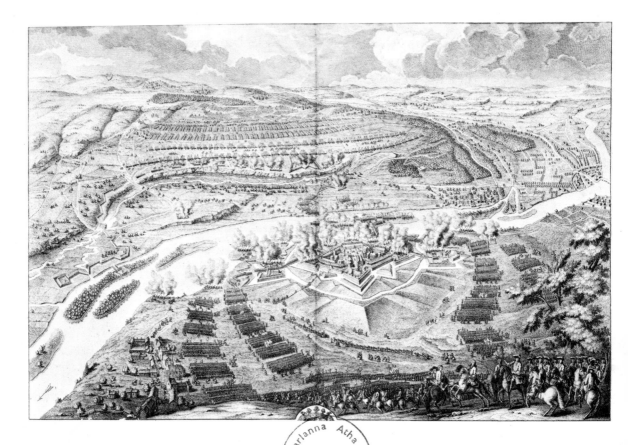

alone could not hold off its enemies, weakened as it was by defeat and by the other menace to Vienna offered by its rebellious Hungarian subjects. Only in Italy had Habsburg fortunes taken a turn for the better, with the entry of the Duke of Savoy into the war on the allied side.

Marlborough well understood that if the Emperor were forced to make peace, the highly probable consequence would be that the grand alliance would collapse. This was why he had dispatched some twenty battalions and eight squadrons to the aid of the Empire at the beginning of the 1703 campaign, a weakening of his own army which had contributed not a little to his own difficulties. The need to take French pressure off the Empire had provided one of the strongest motives in the Duke's efforts to carry out the 'Great Design' against Antwerp, and later to raise the Dutch imagination to larger enterprises than the siege of petty fortresses.

The fundamental idea of leading his own army into Germany in order to save the Empire was in his mind at least as early as midsummer 1703. On 22 June, for instance, the Duke gave Heinsius as alternatives that 'wee either attack Antwerp or Ostend, or else put ourselves upon the defensive and send the rest into Germany for two months, which may save the whole in Germany. . . .'[1] A campaign in Germany, moreover, offered the further advantage that it would physically remove him and his army from Dutch shackles.

The political situation at home in England no less than the state of the war demanded some decisive stroke, best of all a great victory. The opening of the annual winter session of Parliament (the campaigning season for politicians began with the retirement of the armies into winter quarters) unleashed a party battle between Whig and Tory which was violent and rancorous even for that era. As Dean Swift commented, 'I observe the very dogs in the street much more contumelious and quarrelsome than usual. . . .' The principal focus of the party battle, and the great stimulus to party hatred was sectarian prejudice: the Tories strong for the claims and doctrines of the Church of England; the Whigs broad Church or Nonconformist.

Godolphin as chief minister had to steer an uneasy course between Parliament on the one hand and the Queen on the other, a woman of fixed opinions and stubborn will. For it would be impossible to carry on without either her confidence or the support of a majority of the House of Commons. The Queen was adamant that she and her government must not fall prisoner of one or other of the political parties; a desire no less shared by Godolphin and Marlborough. But the drawback of the present middle-of-the-road administration lay in that it was all too exposed to buffeting from either side – or even both sides together, as now, when extreme Whigs and extreme Tories joined in censuring Marlborough's lack of success in the 1703 campaign. What made Godolphin's position even more acrobatic was that, in the interests of non-alignment, the Queen's government itself comprised both Whig and Tory ministers. The rows in the Houses of Parliament, the coffee-house debates, the ceaseless warfare of political pamphleteering, were all paralleled at the cabinet table itself.

'The coffee-house debates, the
ceaseless warfare of
pamphleteering . . .' A coffee
house in Marlborough's day.
Engraving

Thus the Duke was conducting the war from an all-too-narrow and fragile base of political power. It was a weakness and a worry such as Wellington was not to know. This winter, as every winter, Marlborough had to exchange the cares of command for those of politics – 'these uneasy and troublesome broils', as he put it.

Worse still, the party battle had spread from religion to grand strategy. In May 1703 the allies had concluded a treaty of alliance with Portugal. This treaty was largely the work of the extreme Tory Secretary of State, Lord Nottingham, nicknamed 'Dismal' on account of his grave demeanour. For the Tories believed that the quickest and cheapest way of defeating France was to concentrate English resources on maritime warfare and on a campaign in Spain. They argued that Continental land warfare in the Low Countries or Germany against the main French armies was slow, costly and indecisive. The Whigs on the other hand believed – like Marlborough himself – that a great land power like France could only be brought down by the defeat of her principal armies in the central theatre of war. This debate between a 'continental' and a 'maritime' school of strategy was a recurring theme in English history from the reign of Elizabeth I down to 1940 and beyond.

But in 1703–4 it had immediate and urgent political implications. Lord Nottingham, for example, had even diverted 2,000 English troops from the Netherlands to Spain in October without even informing Marlborough, an act which enraged an already over-strained commander-in-chief.

In April 1704, after a parliamentary session of ceaseless tumult, mostly over religion, and a cabinet crisis, 'Dismal' Nottingham resigned, while other high Tory ministers were sacked by the Queen, to the renewed fury of their party. They were replaced by 'moderate' Tories, middle-of-the-road men like Robert Harley, the new Secretary of

State, and until now Speaker – this time to the rage of the Whigs, who had vainly hoped for further offices. Godolphin's administration, under assault from all sides, was a beleaguered fortress with crumbling bastions; looking, as was the Habsburg Empire, to Marlborough's sword to save it.

Yet it was one thing for the Duke himself to come to the conclusion that he must fight the next campaign in Germany; it was quite another to obtain the sanction of his colleagues and the Queen, let alone the timorous Dutch, for so risky an undertaking. For the Dutch in particular it would mean the distant removal of the army which stood between them and French invasion. Marlborough even feared they might threaten to make a separate peace. The diplomatic preliminaries to the campaign saw Marlborough deploy all his skill as a man of affairs, his capacity for patient and persistent effort.

At the end of January he sailed to the Netherlands on a preliminary visit to discuss future strategy. His was the first ship to venture across the North Sea for six weeks, so fierce were the gales and so bitter the cold. Voyages such as this were among the incidental hazards of eighteenth-century generalship. To Heinsius and his colleagues Marlborough urged the need to rescue the Habsburg Empire; and proposed an offensive up the Moselle – which at that time was all that he had in mind.

By late March, however, Count Wratislaw, the Habsburg envoy in London, had convinced him that a campaign on the Moselle would not be enough to save Vienna from the Elector of Bavaria and his French allies; it must be the Danube. A secret bargain was struck: Marlborough would come, with or without the Dutch, if the Habsburg Empire would supply him with siege guns on his arrival, and – most important of all – if it would release Prince Eugène, then at the Ministry of War in Vienna, to command an Imperial army in Germany as his colleague.

On 2 April, with Marlborough's and Godolphin's connivance, Wratislaw presented Queen Anne with a formal memorandum dilating on the desperate peril in which the Empire stood. The Queen thereupon by Order in Council commissioned the Duke, in concert with the Dutch, 'to send a speedy succour to His Imperial Majesty and the Empire'.[2] Marlborough had now secured both a free hand and the Queen's authority for whatever strategy he finally chose to carry out. The responsibility was now all his.

Once more at The Hague, he cut short the renewed objections of the Dutch to his proposed march 'to the Moselle' in his grandest and most peremptory manner, laying the Queen's Order in Council on the table before their astonished eyes, and, declaring, in his own words, that he had made a resolution to go to the Moselle, and that he would leave The Hague on the following Monday. The Dutch crumpled, promising their full support; there was little else they could do. Yet in making use of the Queen's general authority in this fashion to bludgeon the Dutch into acquiescence, Marlborough assumed a further immense responsibility. As he reported to Godolphin: '. . . I am very sensible [aware] that I take a great deal upon me. But should I act otherwise, the Empire would be undone, and consequently the confederacy [alliance].[3]

He had indeed taken nothing less than the fate of Europe upon him.

He therefore needed to be sustained by Sarah's fierce love and loyalty now perhaps more than ever in his life. But instead, their last weeks together had seen their marriage come to its crisis. When he left England this time there had been no heartfelt parting by the water's side, but a letter handed to him by her. In this letter she had set down, with the brutal impact of the studied word, accusations she had been levelling at him for a month and more past.

Neither her letter nor his reply have survived; both burned by the recipients. However, letters written by Marlborough to Sarah earlier while he was in England reveal the substance of her accusations: he no longer loved her, indeed had come to hate her; he had fallen in love with another woman; he had made this woman his mistress.

Sarah's suspicions were not rational, not in any way justified by evidence. They were the symptoms of a personal breakdown. The shock of her son Jack's death in the previous spring had hit her desperately hard. One observer thought that it had affected 'not only her heart, but her brain'; another that it 'hath near touched her head'.[4] While she was still so much unbalanced by grief had come the summer's false hope that she was pregnant; a hope that soon gave way to the certainty that her child-bearing years were over for ever. And to that certainty, with all the implications which it bore for a woman, was added the profound physiological changes of the menopause.

Marlborough strove to convince her that she was wrong about this unnamed other woman; even more important perhaps, that she still possessed all his love.

> When I do swear to you as I do that I love you, it is not dissembling . . . I can't forbear repeating what I said yesterday, which is that I never sent to her in my life . . . may I and all that is dear to me be curs'd if I ever sent to her, or had anything to do with her, or ever endeavoured to have.[5]

Yet at the same time his own anguish at Sarah's behaviour towards him was intense. He told her, in his words, that while her suspicions as to 'this woman' would vanish, it could never go out of his mind the opinion she must have of him, since she refused to believe him even after his 'solemn protesting and swearing'.

At that moment it must have seemed to him all too likely that except as a social façade their life together was over; that he had lost her. Knowing that in so short a while he must leave for the Continent and the most daunting enterprise of his career, he wrote to plead:

> . . . If the thought of the children that we have had, or aught else that has ever been dear between us, can oblige you to be so good natur'd as not to leave my bed for the remaining time, I shall take it kindly to my dying day, and do most faithfully promise you that I will take the first occasion of leaving England, and assure you that you may rest quiet from that time you shall never more be troubled with my hated sight.[6]

These letters from a man of fifty-three to an unhappy woman of forty-three curiously resemble in their sheer desperation of feeling those that John Churchill, in his mid-twenties, wrote to Sarah Jennings, in her mid-teens, during their courtship:

My Soull, I love you so trully well that I hope you will be soe kind as to lett me see you some wher(e) to-day. . . . You are, and ever shall be, the dear objecte of my love, for by heavens I will never love annybody but yourselfe.[7]

And another letter, also written some time between 1675 and 1677:

. . . my soull, there is noe paine soe greatt to me, as that when I fear you doe not love me; but I hope I shall never live to see you less kind to me than you are. . . .[8]

On Sarah's part too their relationship had begun as it now seemed it might be ending. Those few of her letters which survive from the time of their courting display her then, as now, challenging his fidelity, and threatening him with emotional exile:

As for seeing you I am resolved I never will in private nor in publick if I could help it. . . . But surely you must confess that you have been the falsest creature upon earth to me. . . .[9]

I am as little satisfied with this letter [from him] as I have been with many others, for I find all you will say is only to amuse me and make me think you have a passion for me, when in reallity there is no such thing.[10]

Nevertheless, she had had better reason to bristle with suspicion in those days.

She was only fifteen when they had first met at the end of 1675; her sole guide and protector a widowed mother with whom she quarrelled ferociously. John Churchill was a soldier who had already won a name for bravery, and also – more important from young Sarah's point of view – as an accomplished rake. Bringing down pretty maids of honour was the fashionable sport at Charles II's court. For a girl like Sarah, who did not see herself as a kind of partridge to help fill a lecher's game bag, few men's attentions could appear more alarming than John Churchill's, handsome as he was, graceful as he was, Barbara Castlemaine's lover as he was. That Sarah must have felt herself falling swiftly and deeply in love with him could only have made the dangers appear to be the greater. She had therefore to be convinced that she was not intended as just another trophy of seduction; that he was sincere; she had to make sure that marriage and not another court 'great belly' was to be the outcome.

If it were true that you have that passion for me which you say you have, you would find out some way to make yourself happy, it is in your power, therefore press me no more to se(e) you, since 'tis what I cannot in honour allow of. . . .[11]

Sarah Jennings (see page 20) and Barbara Villiers (see page 19)

For two years, with a self-control and a shrewd instinct for self-preservation astonishing in a girl of her age, she held him floundering on the hook of his love for her.

It was a love which seems to have come upon him like a kind of secular conversion; a vision seen amid the sweaty finery of some crowded room at Whitehall or St James's. Accustomed as he was to the somewhat shop-worn lovelies of that court, she must have struck him like sunlight after candleflame – 'so clear an emanation of beauty', as she appeared to Colley Cibber, the playwright, even some thirteen years later, 'such a commanding aspect of grace'.[12]

John Churchill's courtship was painful and prolonged. He had to disentangle himself from Barbara Castlemaine. He could not afford to marry Sarah; she suspected the worst when he failed to propose; his parents recommended a sensible match to an ugly heiress. In November 1676, when their courtship had lasted about a year and was deep in difficulty, Courtin, the French ambassador, reported to Paris:

> There took place on Friday a small ball at the Duchess of York's, where the sister [Sarah] of Mme Hamilton, who is exceedingly pretty, had more desire to cry than to dance. Churchill who is her gallant says that he is attacked by the blight of consumption, and that he must take the air in France. I wish however that I were as well as he. . . . His father . . . does not at all wish to consent to his marriage with Mlle Jennings.[13]

Nevertheless, in the face of all difficulties and Sarah's own rebuffs John Churchill struggled on – meetings snatched or hoped for amid the bustle of the court and their own duties to the Duke and Duchess of York. His courtship displayed little of his talent for stratagem and subtle manœuvre; it was as if his need for Sarah was so overriding that he could think of nothing but a straightforward march on his objective, like a battalion advancing doggedly up to the muzzles of the guns it meant to capture.

> I fancy by this time you are awake, which makes me now send to know how you doe. . . .

> . . . pray lett me hear from you, and I beg that I may be blessed this night in being with you. . . .

> I was last night att the balle, in hopes to have siene what I love above my owne soull, but I was not soe hapy, for I could see you noe where, soe that I did not stay above an hour. . . .

> I beg that I may then have leave to see you to night att 8, for believe me, my love persuades me that itt is an age since I was with you.

One evening when she parted from him in anger in the Duchess of York's drawing room and failed to come back, he trailed off disconsolately to see if there was a light in her chamber, 'but I saw none':

> Could you see my hart you would not be soe cruell as to say that I doe not love you, for by all that is good I love you and only you. If I may have the hapyness of seeing you tonight, pray lett me know. . . .[14]

There is no record of where or exactly when they were married. Since the match was encouraged by the Duchess of York, who was fond of them both, it is likely that it took place in her palace lodgings, and probably in the winter of 1677–8. For some months it was kept a secret. They embarked on married life with no home but rooms at court, and little money. They were often parted – John accompanying the Duke of York to his exile in Holland and Scotland in 1678–81; Sarah in attendance on the Duchess and later on Princess Anne whenever they journeyed out of town. For him, it was still a time of longing, but a longing now springing not from frustration but from fulfilment. He wrote from Edinburgh in 1680: 'I swaire to you the first night in which I was blessed in having you in my armes was not more earnestly wished for by mee than now I doe to be againe with you. . . .'[15]

In 1684, when Sarah was at Tonbridge with Princess Anne, he wrote to let her know that his master the Duke was to visit the Princess there the day after tomorrow.

> . . . and I hope there will be roome in the cotch (coach) for me to com. The Duke will stay but on(e) night, and if I com with him, I must be forced to goe backe with him, soe that I hope you will take itt kindly my coming a 100 miles for the hapyness of one night.[16]

The lack of surviving correspondence from Sarah except those few cold and controlled notes written during their courtship conveys a misleading onesidedness of feeling. One short letter, written some time after 1690, is all that remains of the hundreds he must have received from her during their married life. Yet it is enough to demonstrate the force of her love for him; a force which the fact of marriage released like the breaking of a dam:

> Wherever you are, whilst I have life, my soul shall follow you, my ever dear Ld Marl; and wherever I am I should only kill the time, wish for night that I may sleep and hope the next day to hear from you.[17]

The Duke of Marlborough presents no more interesting contrast to the Duke of Wellington than in his marriage and emotional life. For Wellington married out of a gentlemanly sense of obligation a woman for whom he had almost no feeling; and did so at thirty-seven, on the verge of middle age. His wife Kitty was insipid if quaint, totally lacking in self-confidence, in awe of her husband, a hopeless muddler over money and household management. So whereas Marlborough's relationship with Sarah was the central fact of his life, Kitty was not much more to Wellington than a peripheral irritation. Wellington was – or had to school himself to be – emotionally dependent on no one. Perhaps as a consequence of this, there was a hardness of fibre to Wellington that was lacking in Marlborough.

In April 1704, however, as Marlborough read and re-read Sarah's unhappy accusations before locking the letter in his strong box, he must have wondered whether henceforth he would have to walk alone. 'Whatever becoms of mee,' he wrote to her on 25 April, 'I wish you with all my heart, all hapyness.'[18] It had the sound of a farewell.

Then at the beginning of May, while he was still at The Hague, he received a letter very different in tone from Sarah. Clearly she had realized, in a return to rationality, just how catastrophic might be the damage inflicted by her on them both; and now she sought as best she could to repair the perhaps already irreparable, even to suggest that she should come over and join him. Marlborough's reply was as if from a man reprieved:

> Your dear letter of the 15th came to mee but this minute. . . . I would not for any thing in my power that it had been lost; for it is soe very kind that I would in return lose a thousand

lives if I had them to make you happy. Before I satt downe to write this letter, I toke (took) yours that you write at Harwich out of my strong box and have burnt itt; and if you will give mee leave, it will be a great pleasure to mee to have itt in my power to read this dear, dear letter often. . . .[19]

Nevertheless, he had to tell her tactfully that it was impossible for her to join him, for he was 'going up into Germany'.

. . . love mee allways as I think you now doe, and noe hurt can come to mee. You have by your kindness preserved my quiet, and I believe my life; for till I had this letter, I have been very indifferent of what should become of my self.[20]

The strategic factors underlying his proposed march to the Danube were simple enough. Hitherto the allied armies had fought in two widely separated principal theatres of war, in the Netherlands and in southern Germany. France, with her commanding central position, had been able to concentrate against one group of allies, Baden and the Habsburg Empire, while standing on the defensive against the other group under Marlborough's command. Now Marlborough proposed that the allies should themselves stand on the defensive in the Netherlands with the Dutch army under Overkirk alone, and concentrate their main strength in southern Germany, the decisive theatre in the coming campaign.

But while the strategic conception might have been simple enough, to carry it out, in the conditions of the era, was a tremendous undertaking. It meant a flank march right round the eastern frontiers of France, with an ever-longer line of communications exposed to French counter-thrusts. It meant crossing great rivers, as yet unbridged; traversing an immense tract of difficult and poorly roaded country. Marlborough had to feed, water, shelter and move more than two hundred and fifty miles some 40,000 men – a third more than the populations of Norwich or Bristol, then the largest cities in England after London. In the latter stages of the march, when other contingents had joined him, it would be 60,000 men. Such roads as there were could prove to be either mudbaths or dustbowls, depending on the hazard of the weather.

With the aid of only a small personal staff under his Quartermaster-General, William Cadogan, the Duke had to plot the line of march, and select suitable places for the nightly camps; arrange for the baking of bread, the army's staple ration; set up depots along the line of march to be stocked ahead of the army's arrival with food and other supplies – even fresh shoes to replace those worn out by marching. He had to organize the army's transport – 1,700 wagons and some 4,000 draught beasts to hire, boats to collect for the moving of bulk supplies by water up the Rhine. He had to ensure that there was sufficient fodder to supplement the green forage in the fields. Since there were more than 14,000 horses in the cavalry alone, quite apart from the 5,000 artillery horses, all the draught animals and the beef ration on the hoof, this amounted to more than a hundred tons of oats a day. (The author is obliged to Lt-Colonel H. D. A. Langley, the Life Guards, for informing him of the weight of oats necessary to maintain chargers in the

'. . . sixty battalions of infantry tramping to tap of drum with the battalion carts grinding along behind . . .'; Marlborough's army on the march. Detail from a tapestry woven by De Vos after L. de Hondt

field.) He had to make advance arrangements for the construction of bridges of boats at selected points.

All these preparations depended on cash or credit being available at the right places and the right time. Finance was not the least of Marlborough's cares; nor the least aspect of his capacity as a general. On 29 April 1704, for example, while Sarah was much on his mind and when he was about to give his ultimatum to the Dutch that he was going into Germany, he was writing sternly to complain to Mr Lowndes, of the Treasury, that cash to pay the foreign troops in English hire and 'subsist' the English army had not arrived as he had arranged before he left England.

> This puts us into such distress, that I shall find it a very difficult task to get the forces out of garrison, though it be absolutely necessary they should take the field within these three or four days.[21]

Moreover, since becoming Captain-General in 1701, Marlborough had himself had to improvise his army's entire administrative and supply organization; a formidable test of resourcefulness. For England's permanent military system was so sketchy and chaotic as hardly to exist. French commanders, on the other hand, found ready to their hands the elaborate administrative machine bequeathed by Louvois.

It was an international army that Marlborough was about to lead to the Danube. The concentration of all the various contingents therefore itself called for careful planning; and Marlborough had begun to tackle the problem back in the winter in his correspondence to European governments. The main body of his army – the English, German troops in English pay, some Dutch – was to concentrate at Bedburg, near Cologne. The Prussians and Hanoverians were to join at Coblenz.

It was impossible to conceal advance preparations on this scale from the French. However, Marlborough's long-discussed and now privately discarded project for an advance up the Moselle provided the perfect cover plan, explaining all his arrangements, including the junction of the Prussian and Hanoverian troops at Coblenz, where the Moselle flowed into the Rhine. It was up the Moselle that the Duke's own allies, the

Dutch, fondly expected him to march; the Moselle which figured in his correspondence with such personages as Frederick I of Prussia. Only Queen Anne, Godolphin, the Habsburg Emperor, Wratislaw and Prince Eugène knew Marlborough's true destination. Even Sarah was only told that he was going 'higher up into Germany', and then not until just before he left The Hague for the army.

The French, therefore, made ready to meet an advance into their eastern province of Lorraine via the valley of the Moselle. Villeroi, in particular, in the Spanish Netherlands, watched with nervous anticipation for the Duke to move, for his instructions from Louis XIV were to follow him wherever he went.

Meanwhile in southern Germany the French were preparing for their own offensive on Vienna. In a fortified camp near Ulm on the Danube lay the Elector of Bavaria and Marshal Marsin, who had replaced Villars after Villars had quarrelled with the Elector, with an army of 40,000 men, as against the 30,000 which was all the Habsburg Empire could rake together to defend its capital. Early in May Marshal Tallard brought Marsin a reinforcement of 10,000 recruits, under escort of his own army, and then himself returned

'... the fortress of Ehrenbreitstein, humped on its rocks, guarding the confluence of the Rhine and Moselle ...' Coblenz and Ehrenbreitstein. Engraving

to the Rhine at Kehl to keep watch on the Margrave of Baden's forces. An attempt by the Margrave and the Habsburg commander on the Danube, Styrum, jointly to interfere with this operation utterly failed owing to sluggishness and muddle.

To Louis XIV therefore, as he sat of an evening on his close-stool chatting to Madame de Maintenon after a hard day writing strategic directives to his marshals, it seemed that nothing could now stand in the way of an early victorious conclusion to the war, and a properly French peace.

On 18 May 1704 the Duke of Marlborough, accompanied by the English train of artillery and the English troops under the command of his brother General Churchill, rode down into Bedburg, twenty miles north-west of Cologne, where his army now lay concentrated. It was a modest enough starting place for one of the decisive marches of history: a little cluster of gabled houses nestling in a fold amid a desolate sweep of upland, and now engulfed by tents and horse lines, by wagon and artillery parks; the little open space in front of the church and inn a-bustle with men and beasts.

'To Louis XIV . . . it seemed that nothing could now stand in the way of an early victorious conclusion to the war, and a properly French peace.' But this Dutch cartoon of Louis with Mme de Maintenon and Philip of Anjou is entitled 'Prophetic dream of the Sun's Eclipse'; and a verse printed with it suggested that peace would not be on French terms.

Two days later, on 20 May 1704, at first light, the army struck camp and marched: sixty battalions of infantry tramping to tap of drum with the battalion carts grinding along behind; forty-six squadrons of cavalry tracing the route in fresh dung; bread wagons; ammunition wagons; sutlers' carts; guns.

For the Duke himself this was a moment of relief and release, perhaps of exhilaration. Ever since arriving at The Hague five weeks earlier he had been suffering from continual headache, always with him a sign of emotional strain; and from which, as he wrote to Godolphin, he did not expect to be free until he was with the army. Now as the long columns wound through the freshness of a May morning towards the far-off Danube, his frustrations and vexations faded behind him: the Dutch, the Whigs and the Tories, Sarah even.

Yet he had measured soberly enough what lay at stake in this enterprise which had now begun; at stake not only for Europe, but also for him personally. If he should fail to save the Empire, he told Count Wratislaw, 'so would he be in England and Holland lost for ever.'[22]

CHAPTER SIX

THE LONG MARCH

Without word of the enemy, Her Majesty's army marched south⁄southeast; through black⁄and⁄white half⁄timbered villages where the sound of its passing was caught and amplified by the narrow streets, and the dogs barked, the children jumped and cheered in the gateways, and the old men stared.

In the ranks the mood was bright with anticipation; there was a cheerful confidence that under a chief like theirs they could beat any Frenchmen out of the field. The quality and morale of his soldiers were basic factors in Marlborough's calculations. 'The troups I carry with me,' he told Sarah, 'are very good, and will doe whatever I will have them.'[1] The Duke himself was in all likelihood riding in his great coach that day, since there was no early prospect of action, and since only ten days earlier he had been complaining that 'not having been on horseback for some time, I am soe weary that I can say noe more'.[2]

On the 22nd, when the army reached Kuhlseggen, south⁄west of Cologne, the Duke received reports that part of Villeroi's army had begun to follow him, just as he had calculated; and taking a parallel route about one hundred miles to his westward. But both surprising and disquieting was the size of the detachment Villeroi had made: thirty⁄six battalions and forty⁄five squadrons, including the Maison du Roi, the French household cavalry. It was an army not so very much smaller than Marlborough's own. Moreover, it was being led by Villeroi himself; another surprise. Marlborough confessed in a letter to Overkirk, the allied commander in the Netherlands: 'I had not thought that they would detach so many troops, nor that M de Villeroi would march in person, as I am informed he has orders to do. . . .'[3]

What was more, according to Marlborough's source of intelligence (and it must have been a source very high up in the French government machine), Villeroi had been ordered not to halt on the Moselle but to follow him wherever he went.

The Duke therefore wrote immediately to Heinsius to point out that if Villeroi was taking 'soe strong a detachment, thay [the French] will hardly be able to leave behind the name of an army', and that since as a consequence the Netherlands no longer stood in danger, the Dutch could and should send him reinforcements. 'I am sure I need not tel (sic) you that if we should be overpowered by numbers of troupes and consequently beaten you would feel the effects of it.'[4]

Two days after this laconic understatement came further disquieting news: in southern Germany Tallard had joined Marsin with 26,000 men. In fact the report was inaccurate, exaggerating the 10,000 recruits which Tallard had escorted to Marsin three weeks earlier, before himself returning to the Rhine. But what with Villeroi *and* Tallard, it began to look to the Duke as though he were heading into dangers on a scale he had not foreseen. That same day he communicated his sharpening anxieties to Godolphin: '. . . if the Dutch doe not consent to the strengthening the troupes I have, we shall be overpowered by numbers.'[5]

At the same time the Duke feared that the Margrave of Baden and Prince Eugène might be beaten before he could even reach them. He therefore decided to press ahead himself with the cavalry, leaving his infantry and guns to follow at their own pace. Yet it was no use bringing into Eugène's camp an army of blown horses and exhausted men. Henceforward Marlborough had to hold a balance between the urgent strategic need for haste and the no lesser importance of preserving his army's fighting power.

Every aspect of the organization of the march bore witness to the Duke's forethought and thoroughness. The army set off each day as soon as possible after first light, so that the day's march was completed by nine o'clock in the morning, before the sun grew hot. The daily distance averaged some twelve to fourteen miles, a comfortable span for men and draught animals alike. Marlborough's soldiers found that their chief seemed to have forgotten nothing. In the words of Captain Parker, of Hamilton's regiment,

As we marched through the countries of our Allies, commissaries were appointed to furnish us with all manner of necessaries for man or horse; these were brought to the ground before we arrived, and the soldiers had nothing to do, but pitch their tents, boil their kettles, and lie down to rest. Surely never was such a march carried on with more order and regularity, and with less fatigue both to man and horse.[6]

To the troops, trudging with shouldered firelock through the sunshine and the dust, the march was therefore just a jolly adventure. They were glad enough to see the back of the Low Countries, dreary and all-too-familiar campaigning country. Here in the Rhineland the fruit trees were in blossom. Moreover, some of the German girls, as the keen-eyed Captain Pope of Schomberg's regiment of horse noted, 'were much handsomer than we expected to find in this country'. As the army neared Sinzig, they saw the first vines on the hillsides; and down the valley ahead of them, hazy with distance, the jutting buttresses of rock, castle-crested, which marked the Rhine. Sergeant Millner, of Hamilton's regiment, noted that in camp that day they enjoyed 'plenty of wine and spaw water' for the first time. Next morning, 25 May, they were marching beside the Rhine, as it swirled its way in the opposite direction down into the Netherlands whence they had come.

As Marlborough's soldiers swung along from foot to foot, chatting, joking, swapping rumours, swearing in a manner horrifying to the Presbyterian Scots Colonel Blackader, of the Cameronians, the governments and princes of a Europe at war – even the Great King at Versailles – were eagerly studying the course of their humble footfalls. Already the French plans for an offensive against Vienna had been paralysed by the uncertainty created by Marlborough's march. Nevertheless, the French felt no great anxiety as yet.

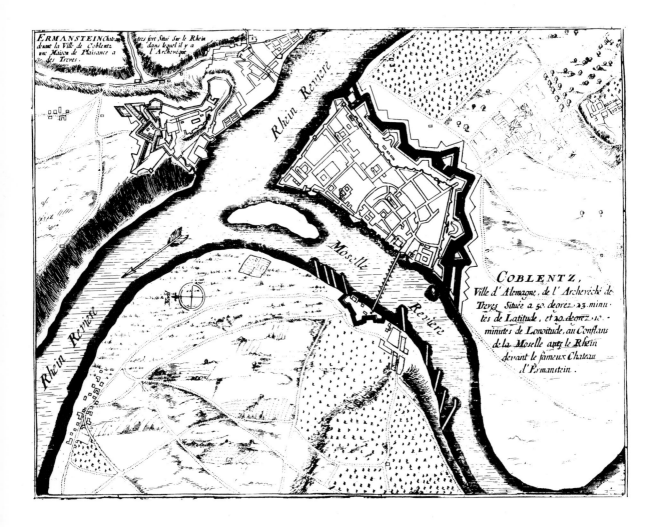

On the map:

ERMANSTEIN Chateau tres fort Situé Sur le Rhein
devant la Ville de Coblentz dans lequel il y a
une Maison de Plaisance a l'Archevesque
des Treves.

Rhein Riviere

Moselle Riviere

Rhein Riviere

COBLENTZ,
Ville d'Alemagne, de l'Archeveché de
Treves Située a 50. degrez 23. minutes de Latitude, et 20. degrez 10.
minutes de Longitude, au Conflans
de la Moselle apres le Rhein
devant le fameux Chateau
d'Ermanstein.

'So it was not to be the Moselle after all. But where was he taking them?' The confluence of the Rhine and the Moselle at Coblenz. Engraving

After all, Villeroi was marching parallel to Marlborough, only two days or so behind him, while Tallard lay at Landau. If, as expected, Marlborough changed direction at Coblenz up the valley of the Moselle, Villeroi and Tallard would unite on that river and meet him with superior forces. Then, with all the uncertainties removed, Marsin and the Elector of Bavaria, on the Danube, could proceed to dispose of the outnumbered armies of the Habsburg Empire and the Margrave of Baden.

On 25 May the Duke, riding ahead of the infantry and guns, saw the spires of Coblenz, slender and sharp as bodkins, ahead of him; the fortress of Ehrenbreitstein humped on its rock guarding the confluence of the Rhine and the Moselle.

He was in the very heart of the German wine country now, and from his camp at Coblenz he wrote to Godolphin that 'I doe with all my heart wish you and Lady Marl some Moselle that I have this day tasted, for I never drank any like it, but I do not know how to send itt. . . .'[7]

Both the French high command and Marlborough's own army expected him now to turn along the northern bank of the Moselle towards France. But instead the army crossed *over* the Moselle by the medieval stone bridge, past the old Burg, or castle, and on through Coblenz. The ranks buzzed with surprise and speculation. So it was not to be the Moselle after all. But where was he taking them? Soon they were back on the shore of the Rhine again, on the south side of Coblenz. Here, where the river was narrower and the current slacker than downstream of the Moselle, Marlborough had had bridges of boats constructed by the local prince – one of the results of his ceremonious correspondence during the winter with the rulers of the German states through whose lands the army was to pass.

While the Duke himself went off to view the fortress of Ehrenbreitstein, the cavalry picked its way over the pitching, snaking surface of the bridges of boats, to be followed two days later by the infantry, guns and wagons. Like a line of busy and laborious scarlet ants the army climbed the long slope up the cliff under the shadow of Ehrenbreit- stein and disappeared southwards.

Louis XIV and his generals had now to think again. An answer soon occurred to them. Marlborough was on his way to invade Alsace, starting with the recapture of Landau. The construction of another bridge of boats across the Rhine at Philippsburg convinced the French that this was his plan. Why else would he wish to cross back again to the west of the Rhine, and at a point so far to the south?

Between Versailles and the French armies the couriers bearing fresh instructions galloped on lathered horses. So Villeroi too went over the Moselle and plodded on to the south, while Tallard, who had been lying at Kehl, crossed to the west bank of the Rhine and marched to defend Landau. And still the French plan to advance on Vienna remained paralysed by uncertainty.

At Braubach, a day's march beyond Coblenz, Marlborough received the welcome news from Overkirk that the Dutch, as he had requested, had now dispatched after him reinforcements of eight regiments of infantry and twenty squadrons of cavalry, all Danish mercenaries. The Duke was now forced to abandon the Rhine shore for want of a road, and head into the Taunus mountains. While the Taunus presented little problem for the cavalry it was otherwise for the guns and transport. The fine weather had now given way to relentless, saturating summer rain, turning the bottom of the steep valley up from Braubach into a quagmire. The guns and wagons had to be manhandled the entire way to the crest; draught beasts straining while their drivers cursed and cracked their whips; men hauling on the draglines and shouldering the wheels round by main force. The march was not so gay now. 'A very steep hill and a tedious road,' Sergeant Millner called it. 'This', opined Colonel Blackader, 'is like to be a campaign of great fatigue and troubles.'

To the Duke himself it meant fretting delay, at a time when he was in urgent haste to reach Eugène and the Margrave before they could be overwhelmed. On 2 June he reported to Heinsius from Weinheim:

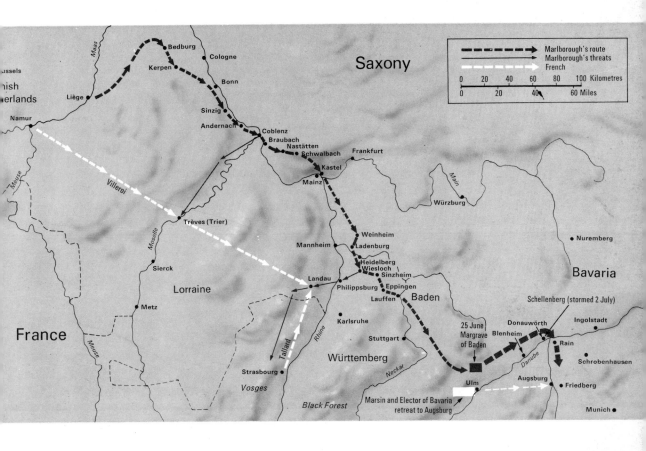

ABOVE *The march to the Danube*

There have been soe great rains that the artillerie and bread wagons were two hole (sic) days getting up the mountain this side of Coblence called Brouback, soe that I intend . . . to make a halt to give time to the foot and cannon to come nearer to me. . . .[8]

On the same day he wrote to Sarah turning down with the utmost gentleness and tact her renewed suggestion that she should join him: 'Besides, my dear soul, how could I be at any ease? For if we should not have good success I could not put you into any place where you would be safe.'[9] At Weinheim he was lodged in the castle of Windeck, high on a wooded peak above the town, and he told Sarah in the same letter:

I am now in the house of the Elector Pallatine that has a prospect over the finest country that is possible to be seen. I see out of my chamber windoe the Rhyne and the Neiker (Neckar), and his two principel towns of Manhem (Mannheim) and Heidelberg; but cou'd be much better pleased with the prospect of St Albans, which is not very famous for seeing farr.[10]

LEFT *Eppingen, where Marlborough's army camped on 7 June 1704, on the march to the Danube*

At Ladenburg, in the plain of the Neckar and the Rhine, he halted for three days to give guns and infantry time to close nearer to him; rest the cavalry's horses; and to make far-reaching arrangements for the next phase of the advance. To the Dutch States-General he wrote finally to break the news that he was really bound for the Danube. To the commanders of various German contingents which had not yet joined him, he sent letters allotting different rendezvous. To the Duke of Württemberg, commanding the Danish reinforcements dispatched by the Dutch, he wrote instructing him not to follow him directly but strike south-eastwards from Cologne to Frankfurt, where he would send him fresh orders. He added some typical Marlburian advice:

> It will be necessary . . . always to send ahead some officer to warn the countryside of the line of the march, so that forage will be ready in camp on their [the troops] arrival, in order to prevent disorders. . . . I recommend particularly that express orders be given that officers and men alike observe the strictest discipline so that there are no complaints whatsoever.[11]

Such tactful politeness yielded to the terseness of command when he wrote to his brother, General Churchill:

> I send this by express on purpose to be informed of the conditions you are in both as to troops and the artillery, and to advise you to take your march with the whole directly to Heidelberg, since the route we have taken by Ladenburg will be too difficult for you. Pray send back the messenger immediately, and let me know by him where you design to camp each night, and what day you propose to be at Heidelberg that I may take my measures accordingly.[12]

The Duke's earlier anxieties that he might be overwhelmed by sheer numbers or that he might arrive too late to save Prince Eugène and the Margrave of Baden seem to have faded by this time. He now expected to join them in eight days. Moreover, his letters exude confidence that the French were submitting helplessly to his initiative. He indeed knew from intelligence reports that Marshals Tallard and Villeroi, fascinated by the apparent threat to Alsace, were converging on Landau; Villeroi from the north-west, Tallard from the south.

On 6 June, the Duke reached Wiesloch, south of Heidelberg, some one hundred and fifty miles from his starting point. Next day he would change direction from south to east, east for the Danube, and at long last the French would know his true destination. The trickiest part of the whole operation therefore lay ahead of him; a complex calcula-tion of time and space involving several armies. Marlborough had to arrange for his junction with Prince Eugène and the Margrave of Baden while at the same time prevent-ing Tallard or Villeroi, or both together, from coming to the rescue of his designated victim, the army under Marsin and the Elector of Bavaria. The Duke wrote to the Margrave of Baden emphasizing that the Margrave must prevent Villeroi (the nearer of the French marshals) from crossing to the east of the Rhine, for this would directly threaten Marlborough's own communications. On 7 June 1704 the Duke and the cavalry began the last lap of the march, riding eastward out of Wiesloch up on to the broad hogsback which carries the road to Sinzheim and Eppingen. It was another miry puddle of a road, and from his next camp at Eppingen the Duke sent some good advice back to his brother with the infantry and guns: 'We came most of the way up hill, so that you must take care beforehand to ease your artillery horses all you can. . . .'[13]

The Marksburg, Braubach. It was here that Marlborough left the Rhine bank and led his army into the Taunus Mountains.

It was an example of a mind which even in the middle of grand strategic combinations never lost sight of detail; detail which might make all the difference between a successful march and a gruesome hold-up. On the following day, hot sun now instead of rain-clouds, he had more good advice for his brother: 'I hope this warm weather you take care to march so early as to be in your camp before the heat of the day.'[14]

While Marlborough, the moving centre of the whole war, rode on towards the east, consternation had laid cold fingers on the French marshals and on the Elector of Bavaria. For they knew now that Marlborough was bound for the Danube; they knew that they had been completely gulled; they knew that as a consequence they had diligently marched into exactly the wrong places whence to take prompt countermeasures. The Elector of Bavaria in particular saw his role suddenly change from that of executioner to that of victim. Isolated as he was on the Danube, far from Villeroi and Tallard, he perceived all to clearly that he was to be destroyed by Eugène and Marlborough. The Elector and his French colleague, Marsin, therefore dispatched repeated and heart-rending appeals to Versailles for aid and succour. Tallard and Villeroi, stuck on the far side of the Rhine, puzzled away at the problem. They well realized that with that broad river as a defensive obstacle, vastly inferior allied forces could hold them off while a catastrophe was arranged and consummated on the Danube. Seeing no solution them-selves, they laid the problem in Louis XIV's lap. Earnest discussion, conducted by galloper at several days' delay, now ensued, and lasted a fortnight.

Finally on 23 June Louis decided that Tallard should make a long southward detour, cross the Rhine at Kehl, which was in French hands, traverse the mountains of the Black Forest yet again, and thence march north-eastwards to the Danube. Villeroi was to keep watch on the allied forces on the Rhine, but march to join Tallard if these forces departed. The Sun King's new strategy failed to kindle any warmth of enthusiasm in his two marshals. It was depressingly apparent to them that, while their enemies were now operating in a central position, in easy touch with each other, they themselves were about to be scattered widely over the face of southern Germany. Tallard in particular was unhappy about the size of the force now allotted to him by his royal master, especially in cavalry. However, the marshals, though far from keen, obeyed. On 1 July Tallard's army recrossed the Rhine at Kehl and began to sweat its way up through the pines and firs of the Black Forest.

But while Louis XIV and his marshals had been corresponding, the Duke had been marching. On 9 June he camped at Mundelsheim, well to the south-east of Stuttgart, and only a few days distant from the armies of his allies near Geislingen. It was here, at Mundelsheim, that one of the most famous and influential friendships in European history began, when at about five o'clock on the following evening Prince Eugène of Savoy rode down into Marlborough's camp with Count Wratislaw to concert future strategy. Now in this humble Württemberg village nestling amid tiny vineyards steeply terraced in the local yellow-grey stone, an English duke played host to an Imperial prince with all the ceremony of the baroque age. Military pomp and splendour were

Rheingaustrasse, Ladenburg. Here Marlborough, with the cavalry, halted for three days for his guns and infantry to draw nearer to him.

The church at Gross Heppach

followed by a banquet: table magnificent with Marlborough's campaign silver plate; the Duke's silver candlesticks in profusion as the light faded; and the two great person-age themselves, one the most famous of living soldiers, the other with a reputation still to make, exchanging smiling compliments and shrewdly appraising each other from beneath their wigs.

Next morning Eugène rode with Marlborough on the day's march to Gross Heppach; a further opportunity to get to know one another. Each was impressed. Eugène wrote later of Marlborough:

He is a man of high intelligence, of gallantry, well-disposed, and determined to achieve something, all the more so because he would be discredited in England if he returned there having accomplished nothing. With all these qualities he knows well enough that one does not become a general over-night, and is unassuming about himself.[15]

Marlborough for his part reported to Sarah that

Prince Eugène . . . has in his conversation a great deal of my Ld Shrewsbury [a man Marlborough much liked, and who was known as the 'King of Hearts' because of his pleasant nature], with the advantage of seeming franker.[16]

Prince Eugène of Savoy (1663–1736). Painting by Sir Godfrey Kneller, 1712

Prince François Eugène of Savoy was in his forty-first year; thirteen years younger than Marlborough. He had been born in Paris and brought up at the French court; his mother was the niece of Cardinal Mazarin, Louis XIII's chief minister. As a child and youth he suffered from a poor physique and it was for this reason that Louis XIV had forced him to enter the Church rather than become a soldier in the French army as he wished. His father was twice exiled from France because of court intrigues. It was his mother's grief at such injustice that had inspired in Eugène his bitter hatred of Louis XIV and the French monarchy. When his father died young, Eugène left France swearing that he would never return but sword in hand. He and his brother settled in Vienna, and Eugène joined the Imperial army. He first saw war at the age of twenty, when the Turks were besieging Vienna; and the bare record of his career bespoke his military talent: colonel at twenty, major-general at twenty-one, general of cavalry at twenty-six. A crushing victory over the Turks at the Battle of Zenta in 1697 first established his European reputation.

The sign of the Lamb Inn, Gross Heppach. In the yard of this inn the three allied commanders, Marlborough, Prince Eugène and the Margrave of Baden, finally met.

It was with some pride therefore that when they reached Gross Heppach Marlborough paraded all nineteen squadrons of his English cavalry for Eugène to review. The water meadows between the river and the jumbled roofs of the village were scarlet with more than 2,000 horsemen. After Eugène had ridden slowly along their ranks he expressed himself, according to an eye witness,

very much surprised to find them in so good condition, after so long a march, and told his Grace that he had heard much of the English Cavalry and found it to be the best appointed and the finest he had ever seen. But, says he, Money (which you don't want in England) will buy fine clothes and fine horses, but it cannot buy that lively air which I see in every one of those troopers' faces. . . .[17]

Marlborough's reply showed that when it came to compliments he was already master of the field:

That must be attributed to . . . the particular pleasure and satisfaction they had in seeing your Highness.[18]

Three days later Louis, Margrave of Baden, rode into Gross Heppach, and there, on the gravel yard before the spreading gable of the Lamb Inn, all three allied commanders finally met: more sweeping off of hats and deep bows; more ceremony; another great feast; a conference which decided urgent questions of command and strategy. Eugène was to go to the Rhine to prevent the French marshals marching to the rescue of the Elector of Bavaria: a role calling for high skill and boldness since his forces would be numerically much inferior. Marlborough and the Margrave together were to tackle the Elector of Bavaria. Marlborough would personally have preferred to have had Eugène with him, for the Margrave was an unimaginative plodder, prickly over rank, and not altogether trustworthy. Eugène indeed had privately warned Marlborough about the Margrave: 'He has been very free with me', wrote the Duke to Sarah, 'in giving me the character of the Prince of Baden, by which I find I must be much more on my guard than if I was to act with Prince Eugène.'[19]

On 22 June, near Lauensheim, the Duke linked up with the Margrave of Baden's army. It was a day bleak with scudding rain. Marlborough wrote to Sarah:

> As I was never more sensible of heat in my life then (sic) I was a fortnight agoe, we now have the other extreamity of cold; for as I am writing I am forced to have fyer in the stove in my chamber. But the poor men, that have not such conveniences, I am afraid will very much suffer from these continnual rains. . . .[20]

On 27 June, after a final struggle against mud and gradient, the English infantry and guns joined Marlborough at Giengen, near Ulm. The Dutch battalions which had been serving in Germany under General Goor ever since the beginning of the previous year also joined, together with other contingents. The march was completed. Marlborough had now concentrated one hundred and seventy-seven squadrons and seventy-six battalions, the largest army to take to the field in the present war. They were now in a region of vast open landscapes rolling away into the distance – ideal for marching and fighting.

The Elector of Bavaria lay in a fortified camp only a few miles off near Dillingen, on the Danube. However, Marlborough first had to establish a new line of communications north-eastwards into the friendly states of central Germany, in place of his existing highly vulnerable two-hundred-and-fifty-mile-long supply route from the Netherlands. But to secure this new supply line and at the same time unlock an invasion route across the Danube into the heart of Bavaria, he needed the town of Donauwörth.

Donauwörth was strongly protected by the adjacent hill of the Schellenberg, partly fortified and strongly garrisoned. As the army neared the town, the Margrave of Baden meditated a protracted formal siege, which, since he had failed to provide a siege train, was likely to be even more protracted. On 2 July, however, at three in the morning, the Duke proceeded to march swiftly upon the defenders. He bridged the River Wörnitz to the west of the town about midday, got his field guns over the river and up the lower slopes of the Schellenberg, and at about six in the evening launched a furious attack on the defenders before they could complete their defences.

After two years of war Marlborough at last saw the action for which he had craved.

The principal sovereigns and commanders of Europe in the year of Blenheim, with allegorical figures. Engraving

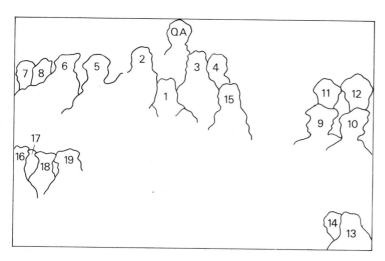

QA Queen Anne
1 Emperor Leopold I
2 King of the Romans
3 King of Spain
4 King of Portugal
5 Duke of Marlborough
6 Prince Eugène
7 Landgrave of Hesse
8 Lord Cutts
9 Tsar of Russia
10 King of Poland
11 Johann von Patkul
12 King of Prussia
13 Marshal Tallard
14 'Lamenting Spaniard'
15 Louis of Baden
16 Admiral Rooke
17 General Dopff
18 General Hompesch
19 Admiral Leake

The Franco-Bavarian garrison fought stoutly, repelling Marlborough's first assaults with devastating volleys at close range, followed by counter-attacks. But then the English foot guards and other English and Dutch infantry regiments drove the defenders back in a storm of musketry. By now the main strength of the garrison was locked in struggle with the English and Dutch, leaving their perimeter almost undefended further to the west. Imperial troops led by the Margrave of Baden now burst through this sector, and took the defenders in the flank. The English and Dutch advanced again, this time bearing their colours over the enemy parapets; and the defenders gave way in panic flight, many of them to be driven into the Danube by the allied cavalry. Out of 15,000 men in the garrison of the Schellenberg, only some 3,000 escaped. The trophies of victory included thirteen colours, sixteen guns and all the garrison commander's silver plate. But the victory had not been cheap, for Marlborough had lost 1,500 killed and 4,000 wounded.

The attack on the Schellenberg was the prototype Marlburian battle – the immediate assertion of moral ascendancy by unhesitating attack; the smashing blows on one sector

Taking the Schellenberg, 2 July 1704. Engraving

of the enemy line which, kept up despite fearsome casualties, forced the enemy to drain his forces from the sector where finally the victory-winning assault was delivered.

With Donauwörth in his hands, Marlborough had Bavaria wide open before him, for its Elector withdrew his army to Augsburg, well out of his way. As he wrote on 9 July:

> I have great reason to hope that every thing will goe well, for I have the great pleasure to find all the officers willing to obaye without knowing any other reasons then that it is my desire, which is very different from what it was in Flandres, where I was oblig'd to have the consent of a Councel of War for every thing I undertooke. . . .[21]

Yet the battle of the Schellenberg was followed by a curious, dragging anti-climax. Instead of marching straight on the Elector of Bavaria's capital of Munich, in order to force him either to give battle or make peace, Marlborough first besieged the minor fortress of Rain, and then spent the rest of July meandering about the country burning towns and villages, in the hope that the Elector would be persuaded by the sufferings of his people to desert the French. As layings-waste went, it was a fairly half-hearted operation. Marlborough's letters to Sarah reveal why. 'This is so contrary to my nature,' he wrote on 13 July, 'that nothing but absolute necessity cou'd have oblig'd me to consent to it.'[22]

By the beginning of August even Marlborough's own officers were growing restless at the indecision and waste of time. Cardonnel wrote home to Matthew Prior on the 7th:

> We have made no progress since our success at the Schellenberg, except that it be in burning and destroying the Elector's country . . . our last march was all in fire and smoke. We are now going to besiege Ingolstadt, and I wish to God it were all over that I might get safe out of this country.[23]

The Duke had been much handicapped during July by lack of a siege train, which the Margrave of Baden had still failed to supply as promised. Moreover, as the Duke expressed it in his dry fashion:

> Our greatest difficulty is that of making our bread follow us, for the troops I have the honour to command cannot subsist without it, and the Germans that are used to starve cannot advance without us.[24]

Yet despite these real problems, it was Prince Eugène's professional judgment that Marlborough's leadership had been wanting since the Schellenberg:

> They amuse themselves laying siege to Rain and burning a few villages instead, according to my opinion, which I have made known to them clearly enough, of advancing directly upon the enemy and, if they can't attack them, to station themselves half an hour away, being so superior in cavalry in open country. . . .[25]

It was as if the Duke had run out of ideas – or as if, perhaps, that the carnage among his own troops at the Schellenberg, the very violence of his first battle for fourteen years, had shaken him and drained him of vitality. Certainly he confessed to Sarah in a letter of 13 July that 'My blood is so heated that I have had these two last days a very violent headache. . . .'[26]

Meanwhile Tallard, who had started from the Rhine on 1 July, joined Marsin and the Elector of Bavaria at Biberach, south of Ulm, on 5 August. Marlborough seemed therefore to have let slip the opportunity which he had arranged with such finesse in the final stages of his march to the Danube. The situation was retrieved by Eugène. As soon as he learned that Tallard was on the move through the Black Forest at the beginning of July, he had straight away marched to join the Duke, leaving part of his army behind him on the Rhine to bluff Villeroi into remaining in place. The bluff succeeded: Villeroi decided that staying put, and waiting and seeing, constituted the wisest course to pursue.

Throughout Eugène's eastwards march from the Rhine, he and the Duke remained in constant touch by messenger. On 6 August, only a day after Tallard had joined Marsin and the Elector, Eugène rode over from his army to Marlborough's camp at Schroben-

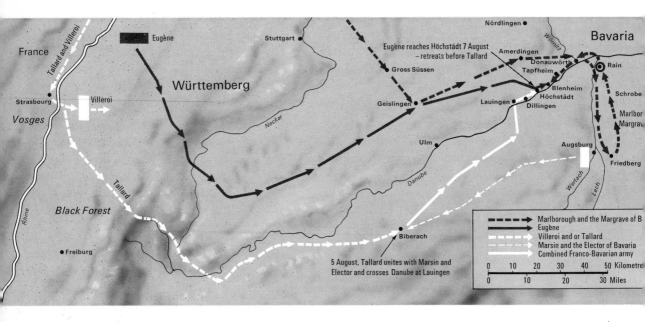

Within the map:

France

Tallard and Villeroi

Eugène

Stuttgart

Nördlingen

Bavaria

Eugène reaches Höchstädt 7 August
– retreats before Tallard

Amerdingen

Donauwörth
Tapfheim

Rain

Württemberg

Gross Süssen

Blenheim
Höchstädt

Schrobe

Strasbourg

Villeroi

Neckar

Geislingen

Lauingen
Dillingen

Marlbor
Margrav

Vosges

Ulm

Augsburg

Danube

Wertach

Friedberg

Black Forest

Tallard

Biberach

Lech

Freiburg

5 August, Tallard unites with Marsin and
Elector and crosses Danube at Lauingen

Legend:
— Marlborough and the Margrave of B
— Eugène
— Villeroi and or Tallard
— Marsin and the Elector of Bavaria
— Combined Franco-Bavarian army

0 10 20 30 40 50 Kilometre
0   10   20   30 Miles

Manœuvres before the battle of Blenheim

hausen. Next day both generals went out to reconnoitre the surrounding country, for the opposing groups of armies were now only some twenty miles apart. In the evening the Duke, Prince Eugène and the Margrave of Baden conferred. It was agreed that the Margrave should go off and besiege Ingolstadt. Two days later he proceeded to do so, taking 20,000 men with him. So large a detachment from the allied army when a battle was imminent was a curious decision. It argued either that Eugène and the Duke had enormous confidence in themselves; or little in the Margrave.

Tallard, Marsin and the Elector had been conferring too. They decided that they would advance on Eugène's heavily outnumbered army which now lay at Höchstädt, on the northern bank of the Danube, crush it if they could, and, if not, march eastwards along the Danube towards Donauwörth to threaten Marlborough's communications. This, according to the rules, would compel him to evacuate the Elector's territory. They did not realize how closely Eugène and Marlborough were in touch; how quickly their armies could unite.

At eleven o'clock in the evening of 10 August the Duke, now at Rain, received an urgent signal from Eugène:

Sir: The enemy have marched. It is virtually certain that their whole army has crossed the Danube at Lauingen ... the plain of Dillingen is full of them. I have held on here all day, but with only 18 battalions I dare not stay the night. . . . Everything, milord, depends on haste and that you get moving straight away in order to join me tomorrow, otherwise I fear it will be too late. . . . While I have been writing this I have [received] certain news that their whole army has crossed. Therefore there is not a moment to lose. . . .[27]

The Duke issued immediate orders to march. Only three hours later – a short time indeed to get the orders out to all commanders, and for them then to strike camp and assemble their troops in columns of route – the Duke's brother General Churchill started off to Eugène's assistance with twenty battalions. At three that morning, 11 August, Marlborough followed with the main body of the army. By eleven in the evening the last of the long columns had crossed to the north bank of the Danube at Donauwörth or other bridging points and come into camp alongside Eugène's little army. Early next day the Duke and Eugène rode forward together with forty squadrons of cavalry to reconnoitre the ground between themselves and the French. At Tapfheim the two commanders climbed the church tower; spread out before them was the whole plain that lay between the Danube to their left and wooded hills to their right, with the position of each village marked by its church. And there, to the westward towards Höchstädt, on a broad treeless swell of higher ground between the villages of Blenheim and Lutzingen, they could see through their telescopes the combined Franco-Bavarian armies about to make camp, 'whereupon', in the Duke's words, 'we resolved to attack them.'

'At Tapfheim the two commanders climbed the church tower . . . there to the westward . . . they could see through their telescopes the combined Franco-Bavarian army about to make camp, "whereupon," in the Duke's words, "we resolved to attack them."' The church at Tapfheim

CHAPTER SEVEN

BLENHEIM

That night the Duke's and Prince Eugène's armies camped side by side some four miles from the enemy, with one flank on the Danube, the other on the woods which swept down the hillsides to the edge of the plain, and their front protected by the Kessel stream.

It was a night that began with busy preparation: bridges to be built across the Kessel for the armies to advance over in the morning; firearms to be cleaned; swords and bayonets to be sharpened. Then all grew quiet, as men who tomorrow must face maiming or extinction lay down to sleep, if they could. As the night hours went on, the air grew cooler, and a mist began to form and thicken round the orderly rows of tents, a damp smell of earth and growing things, spiced with the tang of woodsmoke from the dying cook fires.

The Duke himself fell on his knees and prayed before lying down on his campaign bed. This was an hour when the most able and the most resolute man could feel himself small and alone. For Marlborough knew too well that tomorrow would decide the entire course of the war; that defeat would bring with it immeasurable catastrophe; and that not only Louis XIV but also powerful political factions in England were hoping to see him fail.

An army encamped. Detail from a tapestry after L. de Hondt

The bible given to Marlborough by William III

So, in the quiet of the night, as the mist wreathed and billowed, he prayed.

Next morning, 13 August 1704, at about two o'clock, before the day had even broken, the bugles summoned the allied armies out of their blankets. The bustle began of preparing for the advance to battle: men and animals to be fed; horses to be harnessed and draught beasts to be put to carts or guns; all the baggage to be packed up so that it could be sent back to Donauwörth for safe keeping; sixty-six battalions and a hundred and sixty squadrons – some 56,000 men and sixty-six cannon – to be organized into columns of route.

Meanwhile the Duke went to confer with Eugène in his tent. It was only a few weeks since their first meeting, and they had been able to spend little enough time together. Now they had jointly to conduct a great battle. But the six weeks of anxious manœuvre which had led up to this present morning had only served to strengthen the mutual liking, the trust and understanding, which each seemed to have felt at their first meeting.

It was dawn when the armies marched off westwards in eight great columns; a dawn white with mist, chilling to men physiologically at their lowest ebb. The columns converged close together to pass through a defile where the hills tumbled down close to the marshes of the Danube; then spread out again, like a hand about to grasp the enemy. Beyond this defile the Duke halted in order to form a ninth column on the extreme left, of twenty battalions and fifteen squadrons under General Lord Cutts. Then the army moved on again through the mist.

Ahead of the main body rode the Duke and Prince Eugène with 'the grand guard', or advanced force, of twenty squadrons, some 2,500 horsemen; the Duke on his white charger and wearing the silver star of the Garter which he had specially asked Sarah by letter to request Lord Cutts to bring over with him from England. Towards six in the morning, full light now, the mist beginning to thin in the warmth of the early sun, they reached rising ground near the village of Wolperstetten; and there, less than a mile distant, lay the enemy Marlborough had marched across Europe to find and destroy. The Duke and Eugène could see Tallard's tents stretching for nearly five miles across a broad swell in the plain. Yet in the enemy camp all remained sunk in repose.

The Duke now personally reconnoitred the enemy position at close range. It was immensely strong. The French right wing rested on Blenheim, beside the Danube; a spacious, sprawling village of stone farmhouses separated by patches of orchard and grazing. Each house was a potential strongpoint; the whole village a potential fortress. From Blenheim to the next village in the French line, Oberglau, a distance of over three miles, stretched a treeless expanse of stubble field sloping down almost imperceptibly from the French tents and up again. Here was an ideal arena to deploy the unwieldy masses of an army, and fight a battle. However, a stream, the Nebel, ran through the shallowest part of the ground, protecting the entire length of the French front. Today the Nebel is diked and dry-banked; a man could jump it. But in 1704 it was twelve feet wide, flowing sluggishly with marsh on both sides of it. The Nebel was impassable unless bridged; and even then would be a difficult enough obstacle for an army to

Lord Cutts of Gowran (1661–1707), nicknamed 'Salamander' because of his relish for the hottest fire. Painting attributed to Thomas Murray (1663–1734) or Sir Godfrey Kneller

negotiate in the face of the enemy. The village of Oberglau, standing like a bastion on a slight rise, commanded Tallard's left centre: another potential fortress. From Oberglau the French line swung back to Lutzingen, two miles distant, the anchor of its left flank. Broken, ditch-seamed ground, woods and thickets, dense brambles, extending for a mile and more in front made this sector difficult to approach and attack.

Taken all in all, Tallard's position was so strong that one of Marlborough's senior commanders, Lord Orkney, confessed afterwards that had he been in command, he would never have dared to attack it.

The Duke and Eugène had no detailed 'master plan' for the battle. They would fight by eye and ear and tactical sense, like swordsmen gradually overcoming an opponent in the cut-and-thrust of a brawl. Their deployment of their armies was itself largely dictated by the ground. Eugène, with the smaller army (eighteen battalions of infantry, seventy-four squadrons of cavalry), was to attack the French left flank, between Oberglau and Lutzingen, a front of less than two miles. Eugène's function was to pin the French opposite him in their place, and prevent them from sending reinforcements elsewhere.

The Duke decided to draw up the main strength of his own army opposite the French centre, that three-mile-wide expanse of stubble across the Nebel between Blenheim and Oberglau. After his engineers had bridged the Nebel in several places, and laid causeways of bundles of straw and brushwood across the marshy ground, seventy-one squadrons of cavalry and twenty-eight battalions of infantry would advance over the stream and form up beyond. Yet the Duke realized that once across his troops would

Tallard's view towards Unterglau. The allied army was deployed in the stubble in front of the village.

be exposed to flank attacks from the French in Oberglau and Blenheim. He was particularly concerned lest the French in Blenheim strike deep in the rear of his centre as it was advancing. So Lord Cutts, with his twenty battalions and fifteen squadrons, was to attack Blenheim while the Prince of Holstein-Beck with ten battalions was to assault Oberglau.

It was soon after seven o'clock when the columns of the main body of the army began to come up, 'both officers and soldiers,' according to Dr Hare, the Duke's chaplain, 'advancing cheerfully and showing a firm and glad countenance, and seeming to be confident to themselves of a victorious day'.[1] Now began the long and laborious business of deploying masses of men and horses from long columns into a line of battle. For precise, standard drill movements had not yet been invented. Wheelings had to take place at the halt. Sergeants pushed and jostled their men into line, dressing the ranks with their half-pikes or 'spontons'. Moreover, the armies of the era, although usually divided on the battlefield into a centre and two wings, further suffered from lack of flexibility because the two-battalion brigade was the only formation between regiment (or battalion) and the unwieldy body of the whole army. To Wellington's officers a hundred years later, or to a modern drill sergeant, Marlborough's deployment would have appeared something of a shambles.

All the time the Duke and Eugène and their staff were reconnoitring the enemy position, the French camp had remained in tranquil slumber. For the very last thing Tallard was expecting that morning was to be attacked by both allied armies, even though he –

Lord Cutts's view across the Nebel stream towards the village of Blenheim

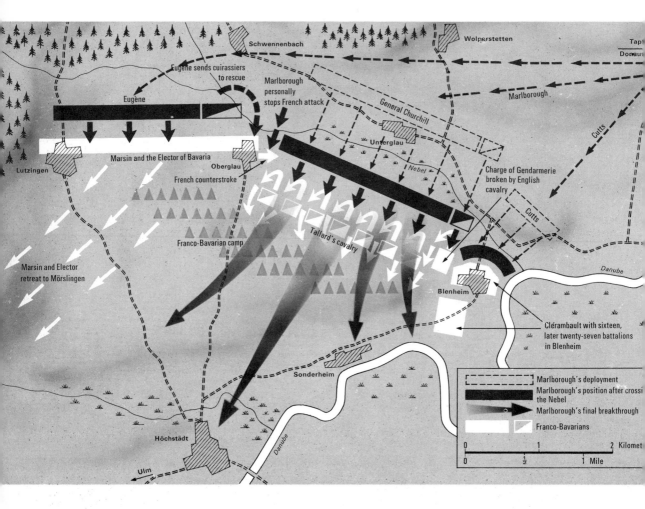

The labels on the map include: Schwennenbach, Wolperstetten, Tapt, Donau, Eugène sends cuirassiers to rescue, Marlborough personally stops French attack, General Churchill, Marlborough, Cutts, Eugène, Unterglau, Nebel, Marsin and the Elector of Bavaria, Oberglau, Charge of Gendarmerie broken by English cavalry, Lutzingen, French counterstroke, Cutts, Franco-Bavarian camp, Tallard's cavalry, Danube, Marsin and Elector retreat to Mörslingen, Blenheim, Clérambault with sixteen, later twenty-seven battalions in Blenheim, Sonderheim, Danube, Höchstädt, Ulm

Legend: Marlborough's deployment / Marlborough's position after crossing the Nebel / Marlborough's final breakthrough / Franco-Bavarians

0 ... 1 ... 2 Kilomet
0 ... ½ ... 1 Mile

The battle of Blenheim,
13 August 1704

or his picquets – had heard the allied bugles and trumpets sounding at two o'clock and again at three; even though his picquets had later observed the allied armies drawn up ready to march from their camp. For all this had simply served to confirm Tallard and his colleagues in their comfortable delusion that Marlborough and Prince Eugène were about to retreat north-eastwards towards Nördlingen, in order to save their communications from his, Tallard's, advance. Tallard in fact wrote a report to this effect to Louis XIV that very morning. Hardly had he sent off the messenger when the Duke's and Eugène's columns began to appear opposite his camp, on the rising ground beyond the Nebel. The Comte de Mérode-Westerloo, one of Tallard's generals, recounts how he was sleeping soundly in a barn when his servant roused him and blurted out that the enemy was there.

> Thinking to mock him, I asked 'Where? There?' and he at once replied, 'Yes – there – .' – flinging wide as he spoke the door of the barn . . . the door opened straight on to the fine, sunlit plain beyond – and the whole area appeared to be covered by enemy squadrons. I rubbed my eyes in disbelief. . . .[2]

Mérode-Westerloo, riding out later through the camp, met Tallard himself at the gallop, but otherwise found 'everyone snug in their tent – although the enemy was already so close that their standards and colours could easily be counted.'[3] They did not remain snug in their tent for long. Suddenly two cannon shots boomed out across the peace of the morning; a signal to the French foragers to come in. Now the urgent blare of trumpets and bugles all through the French encampment began a frantic bustling – neither militarily nor psychologically the best prelude to a battle. 'We saw', wrote Sergeant Millner, 'all their camp in a motion, their Generals and their Aid de Camps galloping to and fro to put all things in order.' Marlborough and Eugène had already won their first advantage. It was only indeed because Prince Eugène had a much longer approach march to make than the Duke, and through difficult terrain, that the French were accorded the grace they needed to scramble through their own deployment.

A cavalry trumpeter. Detail from a tapestry

Tallard and his officers, gazing westward into the brilliance of the early morning sun, found the advance of the allied army an oppressive spectacle. 'I could see', wrote Mérode-Westerloo, 'the enemy advancing ever closer in nine great columns of cavalry and deployed battalions, filling the whole plain from the Danube to the woods on the horizon.'[4]

Even now, however, there were French officers who, observing Eugène's columns beginning to work their way along the edge of the woods towards the line Oberglau–Lutzingen, declared that these columns were in fact retiring on Nördlingen.

About eight o'clock a French battery near Blenheim fired the first shot in the battle – a distant puff of dark smoke, a pause, a bang, and an iron ball flying in a shallow arc over the stubble, to bounce and bound through the deploying troops with horrible momentum. The Duke ordered his chief gunner, Colonel Blood, to establish counter-batteries; and he himself visited the guns to check the fall of shot.

As the morning hours passed, the cannonade grew fiercer. The air grew hazy and acrid with powder smoke, which, fortunately for the allies, was blown by the prevailing breeze into the eyes of the French. But the enemy, with ninety guns to the allies' sixty-six, had the best of the exchange of fire. A French artillery commander recounted:

> One was excited by the extraordinary effect it (the French fire) produced, every shot cutting through their battalions, some of them raking obliquely; and from the very way in which the enemy was deployed, not a round was wasted.[5]

Yet the French guns could only hinder, not halt, the allied deployment. Opposite the French centre 14,000 infantry and over 5,000 horsemen gradually formed up in four lines stretching three miles across the plain, two of cavalry sandwiched between two of infantry; a novel formation ordered by the Duke. Along the Nebel the Duke's engineers worked away at their bridges and causeways. Nevertheless, except for their guns the French made no attempt to interfere with this operation; Tallard's cavalry remained ranged on the distant skyline, tiny figures like blackfly along the edge of a leaf.

It was high morning now. The vast plain of stubble over which the battle was soon to be fought glared yellow in the August sun. Cuirasses and accoutrements winked and flashed as the sun caught them; colours and standards, rich with embroidery, stirred in the breeze. Behind the allied line smoke towered up into the sky from the villages set ablaze by the French covering parties before they withdrew. Divine service had now been said in every regiment of the Duke's army. With men's souls at peace, it was time to kindle their fighting spirit with martial music. The bands of both sides struck up in turn; the kettledrums beat out their thunder; fanfare answered fanfare; and everything waited for Eugène, far away on the flank.

Meanwhile, according to an eye witness:

> His Grace now rode along the lines to observe the posture and the countenance of his men, and found both them and the officers of all nations of all the Allies very cheerful and impatient of coming to a closer engagement with the enemy. And as he was passing in front of the first line a large cannon ball . . . grazed upon a plow'd land, close by his horse's side, and almost covered him with dust. He never halted his pace for this, but moved on. . . .[6]

Of the allied army's 56,000 men, only 9,000 were English or Scots. Yet it was only because of those 9,000 redcoats and their Captain-General that all the other contingents were there on that German field – Imperialists from Austria; Prussians from the sandy heaths of Brandenburg; Hanoverians whose Electress Sophia might one day be an English queen; Hessians and other German mercenaries; Danes, mercenaries too; the Dutch, whom Marlborough had virtually kidnapped from their government. Now an Englishman who had once served at the courts of Charles II and James II when England was a paid French satellite was about to lead a European army into battle against Louis XIV's super-state.

The Duke's opponent, Marshal Tallard, nevertheless awaited the Duke's and Eugène's attack with confidence, despite the haste with which he had been forced to deploy his army. To defend his five-mile line, Tallard had eighty-four battalions and a hundred and forty-seven squadrons, amounting, since they were well below establish-ment, to some 60,000 men. Because of shortage of time, he had had no alternative but to make his order of encampment the order of battle; that was, instead of a combined single army (with a centre and two wings), two armies side by side – Tallard's own, and that of Marshal Marsin and the Elector of Bavaria. As a result, the centre of the French line, the wide-open expanse between Blenheim and Oberglau, was defended not by infantry but by the almost unsupported cavalry of Tallard's and Marsin's adjacent wings. This was to have important consequences.

Moreover, Tallard had not posted his squadrons close behind the marshy course of the River Nebel, in order to prevent Marlborough crossing it and redeploying; indeed to prevent Marlborough's engineers even bridging it. He posted them instead more than half a mile back from the Nebel, on the crest of the barely perceptible slope between the stream and the plain where he had pitched his camp. It was Tallard's cunning intention to lure Marlborough forward over the Nebel in strength, then attack him in both flanks from Blenheim and Oberglau. Finally, the French cavalry would complete

Marlborough after the battle of Blenheim receiving Tallard's surrender. Detail from a tapestry woven by De Vos after L. de Hondt

Marlborough's destruction by charging down the slope and driving him into the Nebel marshes. It was an ingenious plan which did credit to Tallard's subtlety of mind, all the more so because of the speed with which he had had to think it up. But in view of the strength of Marlborough's centre, which Tallard could judge for himself as it deployed, it was a risky one if events failed to conform exactly with the scenario.

Tallard was particularly concerned with the Blenheim sector, not only because its garrison was to launch the flank attack against the advance of Marlborough's centre, but also because he had observed Lord Cutts's column marching over the plain towards it. And Cutts's column was conspicuous with the scarlet coats of the English who had led the ferocious assault on the Schellenberg. If the English were to take Blenheim, Tallard realized, it would knock the hinge out of his entire line. He would be rolled up from right to left; driven away from his communications over the Danube at Höchstädt. Tallard therefore garrisoned Blenheim with no fewer than sixteen battalions of infantry, with eleven more posted in the open nearby. During the morning his troops, working at desperate speed, turned the village into a formidable redoubt, linking the stout farm-houses with a perimeter barricade of carts and wagons, barn doors, and even furniture.

Between Oberglau and Lutzingen Marsin's and the Elector of Bavaria's army, whose front was also protected by the Nebel and buttressed by villages on both flanks, was as strongly posted, in Tallard's judgment, as his own.

There were other, less tangible, reasons for Tallard's confidence. After all, France was the greatest military power in the world. The French army had forty years of conquest behind it, conquest unmarred by so much as a single major defeat.

But despite the imposing appearance, this was no longer a French army of the quality of the great days of the 1660s and 1670s. The supply system and the discipline had decayed since Louvois's death. Trained manpower was running short in France after so many years of war. Tallard's and Marsin's battalions numbered only three hundred and fifty each as against the five hundred men in Marlborough's and Eugène's battalions, with all the consequent damage to morale and fighting power. Even more serious was the crippling shortage of good horses of the right breed to replace those killed during Louis XIV's past exercises in glory. To mount their cavalry the French had had to make purchases all over Europe, and of any kind of animal. Moreover, Tallard's and Marsin's horses were currently being decimated by an infectious disease, and twelve squadrons of Tallard's dragoons were forced to fight dismounted.

Nor was Tallard of the same calibre as a leader in a decisive battle as Turenne or Luxembourg. He was a rather gentlemanly dilettante of war. The Comte de Mérode-Westerloo describes how Tallard, during the march through the Black Forest, invited him into the castle where he was lodging to share his breakfast chicken:

> He was very partial to the fine martial air imparted by receiving from a page a chunk of cold meat or a smoked tongue merely wrapped in a napkin with a hunk of bread. . . . We were standing before a window devouring chicken and watching the army roll by beneath, when he suddenly emerged from the pensive mood that had gripped him for some time

Prince Eugène. Painting by J. van Schuppen (1670–1751)

and remarked, 'Unless I am very mistaken, there will be a battle before three weeks are out; if one does take place – it will be a very Pharsala [the battle in 48 BC where Caesar's victory over Pompey decided the mastery of the Roman Empire].'[7]

Now Tallard stared into the sun at the blue and red masses of Marlborough's army opposite him, and waited for the battle to start which he had prophesied so accurately.

A mile away over the Nebel, by the village of Unterglau, the Duke was also waiting – for news of Eugène. Somewhere over there to the right, in the hazy distance towards the hills, hidden by folds in the ground, Eugène's army was struggling towards the French left flank. But how far had he got? Had he run into unforeseen trouble? By late morning there was still no news. In his mounting anxiety and impatience Marlborough sent off his Quartermaster-General in person, Colonel Cadogan, to find Eugène and report back.

But, as Cadogan found, Eugène was pushing on his troops as fast as was practicable through extremely difficult terrain. There was nothing for the Duke to do but wait while the cannonballs smashed and mangled their way through his patient ranks as they lay or sat on the shelterless stubble. About midday the army – the Duke and his staff in their midst – ate their rations. Then, about half-past twelve, an officer galloped up from the direction of Lutzingen: a bow; a message from Eugène to say that he was deployed and ready to attack at last.

The Duke called for his horse. To Cutts he dispatched an ADC with the order to launch the assault on Blenheim. He instructed his brother, General Churchill, commanding the centre, to begin the advance over the Nebel. Then, Blenheim village being invisible below the skyline from the centre of his line, the Duke galloped over to his left to observe the progress of Cutts's attacks.

It was led by a brigade of five battalions of English infantry under the command of Brigadier Rowe, with a Hessian brigade in echelon to the rear. Rowe had ordered that no one was to fire until he struck his sword on the French barricades. The French defenders too held their fire; Rowe's redcoats marched up to the grey gables of Blenheim in an ominous silence. Then, when they were only thirty paces away, the fences and barricades ahead of them spurted flame and black smoke. Rowe himself fell mortally wounded; his brigade recoiled as the volley struck them. At this moment French cavalry attacked them in the flank. The scarlet ranks began to melt in confusion. The supporting brigade of Hessians came up and poured a volley into the French horsemen. While the French in their turn were recoiling, they were charged and thrown back by English cavalry. But now a French counter-charge in much greater strength, swinging wide round Blenheim, threatened the flank of Cutts's entire advance.

It was the Duke himself who parried the danger, by ordering five fresh squadrons of English cavalry under General Palmes forward over the Nebel. When Tallard saw Palmes's five squadrons advancing, he launched eight squadrons of the Gendarmerie, one of France's most ancient and renowned cavalry regiments, to throw them back into the stream. But instead, in one of the most significant episodes of the battle, Palmes's

Prince Eugène attacking the French wing at Blenheim. Detail from Laguerre's oil sketch

outnumbered troopers, advancing at a steady trot with drawn swords, broke and routed the Gendarmerie like a fist going through a rotten plank. It was a spectacle which profoundly shook Tallard's own confidence, as he was later to admit.

The struggle round Blenheim, visually isolated from the rest of the field by a gentle rise in the ground, now became a battle of its own – a furious, swaying scramble and scrum in a billowing fog of powder smoke. To the right of the village more allied cavalry, ordered forward by the Duke, defiled over the narrow crossing points across the Nebel under furious French cannon fire. Beyond the stream they struggled and squelched onwards over boggy ground, charged in front by French cavalry and raked in the flank by fire from Blenheim itself. But under the Duke's personal supervision, the allied bridgehead gradually widened and deepened.

Meanwhile Cutts's infantry brigades, with those ferocious English yells that so chilled the enemy at Schellenberg, attacked the village again and again. Steadily and despite the crumpled heaps of torn flesh and cloth that more and more littered the ground, they fought their way over and through the fences and barricades of carts and doors and furniture, and on in between the farmhouses. Each of these houses – built of stone, shuttered windows, one roof covering living quarters, byre, barn and wagonshed – was a strongpoint; the open spaces between them raked with crossfire.

But now the commander of the French right wing, the Marquis de Clérambault, an excitable and now over-excited man, lost his head. With the rest of the battlefield out of sight and possibly out of mind over the skyline to his left, he became obsessed with the local struggle for Blenheim. When he saw Cutts's soldiers beginning to fight their way into the village, he ordered the eleven battalions of French infantry near the village to join the garrison: the very mistake Marlborough would have wished him to make.

There were now twenty-seven battalions packed into Blenheim. As the Comte de Mérode-Westerloo wrote:

> The men were so crowded in upon one another that they could not even fire, let alone receive or carry out any orders. Not a single shot of the enemy missed its mark, whilst only those few of our men at the front could return the fire.[8]

Thanks to Clérambault's misjudgment Tallard now had only nine battalions of infantry, all recruits, available to support his cavalry facing Marlborough's centre along the three-mile front between Blenheim and Oberglau. And Tallard was no longer himself near Blenheim to rectify Clérambault's mistake, having ridden over to the other end of his line to see how Marsin and the Elector of Bavaria were faring against Prince Eugène. From that distance not only was Blenheim itself invisible, but the smoke and noise of the fighting there was blotted out by the intervening smoke and noise of the entire line of battle. In any case Tallard was short-sighted, his clear vision limited to twenty paces. The situation at Blenheim, having dropped out of Tallard's sight, seems to have equally dropped out of his mind – just as the situation elsewhere had dropped out of Clérambault's.

The Duke, on the other hand, though himself now back in the centre of his line, kept close touch with Cutts by galloper. When he learned that the French had been driven back into Blenheim, and that it was now packed with enemy troops, he ordered Cutts to cease his attacks, and limit himself to preventing the French from breaking out.

Meanwhile, Marlborough's centre had been steadily crossing the Nebel by the bridges or causeways built by his engineers, and redeploying in the sweeping expanse of plain beyond; first the infantry and then, behind their protecting line, the cavalry. While this delicate operation was going on, Tallard's cavalry still remained on the skyline three-quarters of a mile away, content to watch in supine inaction. In the words of one French officer, Marlborough 'was forming up a complete battle array at his leisure in the very centre of our army'.[9] 'We neglected', wrote a French commander at Tallard's own side, 'the great double lines forming at the foot of that fatal hill.'[10] For at this period of the battle Tallard was down in Blenheim, and in the words of the same French officer, 'by that means, the hill was neglected, he not being able to perceive what passed at the foot of it.'[11]

Around three o'clock in the afternoon the Prince of Holstein-Beck with ten battalions advanced on the right of Marlborough's line towards Oberglau, a cluster of farmhouses round a church on a slight rise in the ground. His task, like that of Cutts at Blenheim, was to pen up its French garrison. But when only two of Holstein-Beck's battalions had crossed the Nebel, they were counter-attacked by nine French battalions from Oberglau, with Irish émigré regiments in the French service (the 'Wild Geese') in the van. Holstein-Beck himself was wounded and taken prisoner, and his troops were thrown back towards the stream.

It was the most dangerous moment of the entire action. In Tallard's words, 'I saw one critical instant when the battle was won. . . .'[12] The very danger Holstein-Beck's attack on Oberglau was intended to prevent had now occurred: the right flank of Marlborough's main body lay wide open to the French. Moreover, the French counterstroke equally threatened the junction opposite Oberglau between Marlborough's own army and Eugène's. As the exultant French pressed on towards the gap in the allied line, only an instant decision, and a right decision, could save the allies from disaster.

Once again the Duke was present at the one point in his three-mile line where he was most needed. When he saw Holstein-Beck's shattered battalions falling back to the Nebel with the French after them, he galloped up and personally organized a combined force of infantry, cavalry and guns to block the French advance. Then he rallied Holstein-Beck's battalions and led them forward again. Yet the danger was not yet over. The French launched a fresh attack with cavalry from the right of Oberglau, riding in towards the flank of Marlborough's hastily organized defence. The Duke, with no more reserves available, could only send an urgent appeal for help to Prince Eugène.

But Eugène himself was in the thick of a desperate fight all along his line. His Prussian and Danish troops had been repeatedly but vainly attacking the strongly posted enemy ever since the battle began. Nevertheless, in an instantaneous decision that was no less an instantaneous gesture of total comradeship, he ordered Fugger's Imperial Cuirassiers on the right of Oberglau to change front and charge the flanks of the French cavalry menacing Marlborough.

The crisis had passed; the Duke brought up more infantry and guns and drove the enemy back; and thereafter the French garrison of Unterglau was left as bottled up and impotent as that of Blenheim.

It was probably during this period of the battle that the Duke halted an officer retreating with his unit and told him with ironic politeness: 'You are under a mistake; the enemy lies that way; you have nothing to do but face him and the day is your own.'[13]

It was by such personal leadership that the Duke imposed his will on the vast, sprawl, ing confusion of the battle. Time and again the trim figure on the white charger would ride up through the eddying smoke and take direct command; the calm voice with the court drawl contrasting with a visage taut with nervous energy being poured out at full power. The Duke, according to Lord Orkney, 'had been everywhere from one attack to another and ventured his person too/too much'.[14] But his soldiers, black as miners from powder grime, eyes stinging from the smoke, their musket barrels as hot as flatirons from constant firing, found fresh courage in the sight of 'Corporal John', as they nicknamed him.

Tallard, on the other hand, was allowing the battle to slip gradually from his grasp. The French army fought on unit by unit, sector by sector, in a struggle without a theme.

It was now almost four o'clock in the afternoon. From one end to the other of the five, mile line the firing remained continuous. The afternoon sun glared down on the armies through a stinking shroud of powder smoke. More smoke still reeked into the sky from the villages and mills set ablaze by the French in the morning. Across the undulating plain the masses of men still swayed and struggled, tiring, thirsty, garments foul with sweat; the ground more and more encumbered by dead or maimed men and animals, by riderless horses wandering with hanging reins. The crash of cannonfire and the rattle of musketry provided the percussion to shouts and yells, to the screaming or whimpering of those lying torn open, eviscerated, with smashed or splintered bone.

Yet beneath the apparent chaos the design of victory was taking shape, moulded by Marlborough's professional intuition out of the plastic material of battle. In that decisive arena in the centre, on the French side of the Nebel, he now had deployed twenty/eight battalions of infantry, some 14,000 men, and seventy/one squadrons of cavalry, over 5,000 horsemen; but Tallard, with so much of his infantry drawn into Blenheim, had only nine battalions of infantry, all recruits, and sixty/four squadrons of cavalry to face him.

Tallard's only remaining hope was to launch his too/long withheld cavalry. The Duke and his troops saw the dark specks close/lining the long horizon ahead of them begin to move; grow larger and larger until they became horsemen by the thousand sweeping towards them; with the Marquis d'Humières, commander of the French centre, and brilliant in a magnificent gilt cuirass, riding at their head.

Before this onset the first line of allied cavalry gave way and retired through the intervals in the line of infantry battalions behind them. Now the purpose of Marlborough's unorthodox tactical formation, with cavalry and infantry interlined, became clear. As the French cavalry sought to press home their attack, the volleys crashed in succession up and down the long line of allied infantry, English, German, Dutch; blue coats and red. Field guns blasted away at close range with 'partridge shot'. As the fresh billows of smoke went drifting up and away, it could be seen that the French cavalry had been brought to a halt in a shambles of fallen horses and riders. A French general observed with dismay what now followed:

The attack on the French right wing at Blenheim. Detail from Laguerre's oil sketch

... our men were forced to shrink back, and throw themselves on our second line, which, being at some distance, gave the enemy time to gain ground which they maintained by their numbers, and their slow and close march.[15]

In desperation Tallard sent to Marsin for aid. But Marsin told Tallard's messenger that it was all he could do to hold off Prince Eugène's Prussians and Danes; he had no troops to spare. As the Duke's infantry, cavalry and guns, working in combination, began to press Tallard's almost unsupported cavalry back yard by yard up the slope, Tallard himself galloped down to Blenheim to try to retrieve some of the infantry he had allowed Clérambault to cram into the village. He found them, however, so packed together, so boxed in on three sides by Cutts, that it was impossible to extricate them in time.

It was now clear to Marlborough that the battle was almost won. Only near Oberglau were the French cavalry supported by infantry – the nine battalions of recruits, standing in squares. English guns and Hanoverian infantry smashed open the squares, and allied cavalry cut down every man in his place.

At about five o'clock the Duke rode right along the line of battle. He could see that Tallard's cavalry were spent. He could see that beyond them there was nothing. He gave the order to sound the charge.

The soldiers of both armies heard the trumpets calling from squadron to squadron all the way from Oberglau down to Blenheim; a beautiful and terrible sound. Then, in a double line of squadrons three miles long, Marlborough's cavalry moved forward, first at a walk, then at a trot. They came up the hardly perceptible gradient packed knee to knee; a vast flail sweeping over the ground in a cloud of dust.

Tallard's cavalry waited for them uneasily at the halt. As they sat their horses waiting, the stubbled earth under them reverberated with the pounding of the 24,000 hoofs which were carrying their enemy towards them with ever greater momentum.

Then the allied cavalry was upon them, charging home with the sword. The French fired one wavering volley with their long horse pistols; swung their horses' heads round; and fled, even the Maison du Roi, the French household cavalry. And as they broke, so broke with them Louis XIV's ambitions of universal monarchy.

Pursued by Marlborough's squadrons, the French cavalry galloped frantically through their own camp and on to Höchstädt, bearing the hapless Tallard away with them. A great French army had dissolved into a panic-stricken swarm of fleeing individuals, many of them even riding their horses straight over the bank of the Danube in their frenzy to escape.

Between Oberglau and Lutzingen, Marsin, threatened in the flank by Tallard's collapse, only escaped destruction himself by retreating in utmost haste away from Höchstädt, towards Mörslingen, followed by Eugène's exhausted but still game troops until the light faded.

Somewhere in the press of fugitives round Höchstädt Hessian troopers took prisoner Marshal Tallard himself.

Only the French in Blenheim, now completely encircled, still fought on, as the roofs of the blazing farmhouses collapsed over their heads. Tallard, though now a prisoner, sent a message to Marlborough offering to prevent any further firing by the French in Blenheim, if the Duke 'would let those poor fellows alone and suffer them to retreat'. The Duke's comment on this proposal was frosty: 'I wonder Monsieur de Tallard does not consider, that he has no command where he now is.'[16]

Two French regiments, Provence and Artois, tried to cut their way out, but failed. Now the allied troops – Cutts's indomitable redcoats among them – fought their way into the heart of the village, round the churchyard and its stone wall. Clérambault himself was not there to see the final tragedy of the gallant troops he had led so incompetently, for, in a fit of desperation, he had ridden straight into the Danube and drowned. Battalion by battalion, the surrounded French began to surrender. Then General Lord Orkney persuaded the acting French commander in Blenheim, the Marquis de Blanzac, to capitulate. As the sun was going down, 10,000 men marched into captivity, and the Battle of Blenheim was over.

But even before the firing had stopped, the Duke, an utterly spent man after seventeen hours in the saddle, had scribbled his first report on the battle. He scribbled it in pencil on the first piece of paper that came to hand, the back of a tavern reckoning; and it was to Sarah that he sent it:

I have not time to say more but to beg you will give my duty to the Queen, and let her know Her army has had a Glorious Victory. Monsieur Tallard and two other Generals are in my Coach and I am following the rest. . . .[17]

The note Marlborough wrote to Sarah in the saddle and on the back of a tavern reckoning to give her news of the victory. It took Colonel Parkes eight days to carry it to Sarah and on to the Queen.

CHAPTER EIGHT

ANNE AND SARAH

There had been no such victory since the great Gustavus Adolphus of Sweden had triumphed at Lützen and Breitenfeld in the 1630s. It eclipsed even the victory by Condé over the Spaniards at Rocroi in 1643 which had established France as the foremost military power in Europe.

The French losses were immense: some 30,000 killed, wounded and missing. The spoils too were colossal: forty-seven guns, twenty-five standards and more than forty colours; generals' coaches; cases of silver; more than 3,000 tents; and, perhaps most immediately welcome to the allied rank-and-file, 'about a hundred fat oxen ready skinned'. Moreover, the extent of the disaster was not to be measured by numerical or material loss alone, but by the fact that, in the Duke's own words, Tallard's army was 'quite ruined'.

Marlborough and Eugène had saved the Habsburg Empire, and thereby preserved the grand alliance from collapse. They had wrenched out of Louis XIV's grasp the initiative he had enjoyed for forty years; snapped in pieces his hopes of an early and victorious peace. Moreover, they had destroyed the myth of French invincibility; destroyed it both in the eyes of an astounded Europe, and in the eyes of the French themselves. Blenheim indeed brought an era of European history to an end.

There was still no rest for Marlborough, even when the firing had at last stopped that evening. As his chaplain narrates:

> ... His Grace gave orders about dressing the wounded men and putting them under cover. Then he made a separation of the French prisoners, which amounted to eleven or twelve thousand men. . . . These prisoners, with their generals, being divided and disarmed, were ordered to adjacent villages in the rear of our army. . . .[1]

Ahead of the wounded there lay the tortures of eighteenth-century surgery: the knife through the unanaesthetized flesh, the saw grating on the live bone, the boiling tar to cauterize the stump; and afterwards perhaps eventual recovery, for the healthiest and luckiest, but more probably gangrene and death. And in any case, this being an era which trained more clergymen than surgeons, there were only seventeen doctors with the English contingent at Blenheim, roughly one to every six hundred men, and these lacking the support of any kind of nursing services.

On the night after the battle the Duke slept for three hours in a mill near Höchstädt while his army bivouacked on the battlefield. Next morning when the Duke rode back over the field, the bodies of the dead had already been stripped by the victors; good shoes or sound breeches were valuable commodities to soldiers on a shilling a day. From Blenheim to Lutzingen the naked corpses lay white and stiff as bone, scattered like the litter left behind by some departed fair.

When Marlborough and Eugène paid a visit to their most distinguished prisoner, Marshal Tallard, for whom the agony of the previous day had been rendered terribly complete by the death of his own son at his side, they found him wounded in one hand and 'very much dejected'. Triumph found the Duke magnanimous, understanding and courteous towards his unhappy foe: 'His Grace desired to know how far it was in his power to make him easy under his misfortune, offering him at the same time the convenience of his quarters, and to take him thither in his coach.'[2]

Tallard declined the Duke's offer, preferring to stay where he was until he could have his own coach, so Marlborough dispatched a 'trumpet' to Marsin's army to ask for it to be sent over under a safe conduct.

The last page of the official dispatch Marlborough wrote to Robert Harley the day after the battle, with its apology for not writing the whole in his own hand

Marlborough's triumph portrayed on the roof of Blenheim Palace by Grinling Gibbons (1648–1721), showing the British lion savaging the French cock

While other French general officers in the room crowded round to look at and to listen to the two commanders who had destroyed their army, Tallard turned the conversation to the battle itself, and remarked that 'if his grace had deferred his visit (meaning the attack) a day longer the Elector and he would have waited him upon his grace first'.[3]

The Duke's bearing towards his prisoners at this time was to do much to foster his legend among his French enemies. For while Eugène, who had his own reasons for hating the French, was harsh towards the officers in his hands, the Duke displayed 'all possible consideration, kindness, the most obliging civility, and a modesty perhaps superior to his victory'.[4] He ordered the guard to turn out and pay Tallard the same honours as himself whenever the French commander called at his quarters. As a further kindness to the broken Tallard, the Duke enabled him promptly to write his own report on the battle, and provided a French officer with a safe conduct so that it could be dispatched straight to Louis XIV at Versailles.

On 17 August the whole allied army, which had now advanced to Steinheim, observed a day of thanksgiving for the victory; the hymns and prayers of a Te Deum followed by a triple discharge of all the artillery and small arms. But by now the Duke himself was overcome with the moral and physical prostration that followed the total exertion of conducting a battle; the spiritual hangover after so much violence and bloodshed. As he admitted to Godolphin in a letter on the day of the Te Deum,

> Ever since the battaile I have been so employ'd about our own wounded men and the prisoners, that I have not one hour's quiet, which has so disorder'd mee, that were I in London I shou'd be in my bead (bed) in a hie feavour.[5]

To Sarah next day:

> I have been soe very much out of order these four or five days, that I have been oblig'd this morning to lett blood, which I hope will sett me right, for I shou'd be very much troubled not to be able to follow the blow we have given . . . my dearest life, if we cou'd have another such a day as Wensday last, I shou'd then hope we might have such a Peace that I might injoye the remaining part of my life with you. . . .[6]

But five days later he was still complaining to Godolphin:

> I am suffer'd to have so litle time to my self, that I have a continual feavour on my spirits, which makes me very weak, but when I go from hence I am resolved to keep in my coach til I come to the Rhine.[7]

He was now feeling not only the reaction from the battle itself, but also from the anxieties and efforts of the entire march to Blenheim. As he expressed it in the same letter:

> . . . nothing but my Zeal for Her majesty's service cou'd have enabled me to have gone thorow (through) the fatigues I have had for these last three months; and I am but to(o) sure when I shall have the happyness of seeing you, you will find me ten years older than when I left England.[8]

Meanwhile Colonel Parkes had been riding for the North Sea coast with the Duke's battlefield note to Sarah and the Queen; other couriers had been carrying official reports of Tallard's destruction to the courts of Europe; and all men began to measure the revolution which had taken place in the affairs of the Continent.

From Frankfurt the English representative, Henry Davenant, gleefully wrote to Stepney, the ambassador at Vienna:

> Yesterday Colonel Parkes came here with the agreeable news of the victory we have gained over the enemies. This battle will in all appearance put an end to the war in the Empire, and give the means of assisting the Duke of Savoy who is very near his ruin. The Duke of Marlborough has beyond all dispute saved the Empire. . . .[9]

At The Hague the splendid news brought by Parkes roused the English envoy from the glum and fearful mood into which earlier reports from Germany had cast him:

> We cannot speak of anything else but these glorious advantages. There has not been in our age or scarce to be found in story so complete a victory as Prince Eugène and our Duke have gained. . . .[10]

On 21 August, Parkes at last landed in England and headed for London and Windsor Castle, spreading the news as he went. As he clattered up to the Marlboroughs' town house, the guns of the Tower were saluting the victory and the city bells were ringing.

At Windsor Castle Parkes, on bent knee, handed Marlborough's message to the Queen; his gift of a victory which had made her one of the greatest sovereigns in Europe

By a curious mischance, at the moment that France was sustaining one of her greatest defeats, Louis and the French court were celebrating the birth of a grandson with a great fête in Paris where the Seine was shown triumphing over the other rivers of Europe. Engraving

instead of queen of an offshore island. When Parkes had departed, Anne sat down and wrote to Sarah for the second time that day:

> Since I sent my letter away by the messenger, I have had the happiness of receiving my dear Mr Freeman's by Colonel Parkes, with the good news of this glorious victory, which, next to God Almighty, is wholly owing to dear Mr Freeman, on whose safety I congratulate you with all my soul. May the same Providence that has hitherto preserved, still watch over, and send him well home to you. . . .[11]

By evening the broadsheet vendors in the streets of London were selling printed copies of Marlborough's note in thousands to eager passers-by. The news buzzed from shop to shop, from household to household, tavern to tavern, and Englishmen began to celebrate their first great victory on land against a European power since Agincourt nearly three hundred years before. According to an eye witness the coffee houses were packed with 'Loyal, honest Englishmen' with 'real satisfaction in every face'. But coffee and tea were soon found inadequate beverages for the occasion: 'Away they adjourned to the tavern, every bumper was crowned with the Queen's or the Duke of Marlborough's health and the loyal citizens emptied the cellars so fast I think two-thirds were foxed [drunk] next morning.'[12]

When night fell, a city normally sunk in darkness except for the occasional torch's flare or lantern's glimmer was gay with 'illuminations' – thousands of candles placed in windows; and high above the bells pealed on and on in rejoicing for the Duke's victory.

It was not until 21 August that Louis XIV received news of the battle, and then only a bald message from Villeroi that Tallard's army had been all killed or taken prisoner. The message gave no word as to the fate of Marsin and the Elector. Villeroi himself knew nothing more, for his information came from a 'trumpet', or messenger under flag of truce, sent over by the troops which had been left on the Rhine by Eugène when he departed to join the Duke. For six days the King dwelt in agonizing suspense, with everything a mystery beyond the simple and terrible fact that all was lost in Bavaria. Gradually, letter by letter, the nature and dimension of the catastrophe became clearer. Then, on 29 August, one of Tallard's officers, released on parole by Marlborough, arrived in Paris with Tallard's own report on the battle.

At first Louis and his courtiers, the French public at large, found it hard to take in that a French army could have suffered so immense a defeat. As the Duc de Saint-Simon remarked, 'One was not accustomed to misfortunes.'[13] Then the shock wore off and the pain set in.

> It can be guessed [wrote Saint-Simon] what was the general consternation, when every illustrious family, without counting the others, had kinsmen dead, wounded or prisoner; what was the predicament of the ministry of finance and the ministry of war at having to make good the loss of an entire army; and what was the anguish of the King, who had held the Emperor's fate in his hands, and who, with this ignominy and loss, saw himself reduced to defending his own lands. . . .[14]

Marlborough was desperately weary; longing for Sarah. But he recognized that France was too powerful to be forced to make peace by a single victory, however devastating. During the remainder of the current campaigning season, therefore, he meant to lay the foundations for an invasion of France itself in 1705, via the valley of the Moselle. So as the summer mellowed into autumn he drove himself and his army onwards – to the Rhine; to Landau, which the Margrave of Baden was left to besiege; and north-westwards to Trèves (Trier). It was October now; the terrain, in his own words, 'very terible mountagnes. Had we had any rain it wou'd have been impossible to have gote forward the Canon.'[15]

And still there was no slackening in the daily drudgery of running a war: correspondence with princes, generals, diplomats, supply contractors. It was little wonder that he wrote to Sarah on 10 October:

> For thousands of reasons I wish myself with you. Besides I think if I were with you quietly at the Lodge, I should have more health, for I am at this time so very lean, that it is extreame uneasy to mee, so that your care must nurse me this winter. . . .[16]

Sarah was sufficiently worried by his evident exhaustion to urge him to give up his responsibilities at the end of the campaign, and retire to Holywell. But the Duke answered:

> What you say of St Albans is what from my Soull I wish, that there or somewhere else we might end our days in quietness together: and if I considered only my self, I agree with you, I can never quit the world in a better time, but I have too many obligation (sic) to the Queen to take any resolution, but such as Her Service must be first consider'd.[17]

'. . . a lively old lady . . .' The Electress Sophia of Hanover (1630–1714), who was delighted with the Duke when he visited her in 1704. Painting by Andreas Scheits (d. 1735)

So the Queen's Captain-General soldiered on. On 29 October he won a race with the French into Trèves, on the Moselle. Almost immediately he opened the siege of Trarbach, further down the river; then himself travelled all the way back over the barren hills of the Hunsrück in order to infuse the Margrave of Baden's siege of Landau with the dynamism it had so far lacked. On 8 November Landau fell; in the middle of December Trarbach. Marlborough now had his base on the Moselle ready for an offensive next spring. Yet Marlborough himself had already departed on another exhausting mission, this time to Berlin, nearly four hundred miles distant in the heaths and forests of Prussia, in order to persuade the Prussian king not to withdraw his contingent from the war, but to hire out 8,000 more soldiers for service in Italy, where the allied cause was far from prospering.

From Frankfurt he reported to Godolphin on 16 November that 'I have been on the road yesterday from 4 in the morning til dark night, and am now going into the coach before daylight. . . .'[18] It was a gruesome journey for a tired man, for, in the Duke's words, 'The ways have been so bad I have been oblig'd to be every day 14 or 15 hours on the road, which has made my sides very sore. . . .'[19]

By the beginning of December he was on his way back from Berlin, after tough and ticklish negotiations which had taken all his patience and skill to bring to a successful end. At Hanover he called on the Electress Sophia, who stood to inherit the English throne if Queen Anne should die, in order to arrange Hanover's military contribution in 1705 with her ministers. While there he wrote to Sarah that 'I long extremely to be with you and the children, so that you may be sure I shall lose no time when the wind is fair.'[20] Cumulative fatigue did not, however, impair the Duke's ability to charm. The Electress Sophia, a lively old lady, was delighted with him: 'Never have I become acquainted with a man who knows how to move so gracefully, so freely, and so courteously. He is skilled as a courtier as he is brave as a general.'[21]

Even when he reached The Hague, there were still the customary end-of-campaign discussions with Heinsius and the other Dutch leaders. It was not until 22 December that he at last set sail from Rotterdam in one of the royal yachts, and accompanied by thirty-six captured French senior officers, including Marshal Tallard himself and sixteen generals.

On 25 December 1704 [14 December by the Old Style calendar in use in England] he landed at Greenwich, under the long colonnades of Wren's new hospital. While all

'From the day of her accession in 1702, at the age of thirty-eight, she carried the role of queen with superb dignity.' Queen Anne in her robes of state. Painting by Sir Godfrey Kneller

the colours and standards he had captured at Blenheim were lodged in the Tower, the Duke himself went to St James's Palace to pay his duty to the Queen; and then he was with Sarah at last.

Next day he took his seat in the House of Lords, and heard the Lord Keeper, in the name of the Peers, offer a long and elaborate thanks for 'the great and signal services Your Grace has done her Majesty this campaign' and for 'the immortal honour you have done the English nation. . . .'[22] The Duke's reply was brief, plain and modest:

> . . . I must beg, on this occasion, to do right to all the officers and soldiers I had the honour of having under my command; next to the blessing of God, the good success of this campaign is owing to their extraordinary courage. . . .[23]

In the first days of January 1705 the thirty-four captured French standards and the hundred and twenty-eight colours were borne in procession from the Tower to Westminster Hall. The Queen herself was at a window in St James's Palace to see the procession pass by into St James's Park, where forty guns were fired twice in salute. Then it was the City of London's turn to honour the Duke's victory, with a banquet in Goldsmiths' Hall.

There was still more to come. In February 1705 the Queen, with the consent of Parliament, made the Duke a grant of the royal manor of Woodstock, in Oxfordshire, with some 16,000 acres, so that he could build, as a further gift from a grateful crown, a palace majestic enough to commemorate a victory over the royal owner of Versailles.

All this sudden adulation was in its way as much a test of character as the campaign itself. John Evelyn, the diarist, and an old acquaintance of the Duke's, met Marlborough by chance at this time in the Lord Treasurer's room. The Duke, he recorded,

> came to me and took me by the hand with extraordinary familiarity and civility, as formerly he used to do, without any alteration of his good nature. He had a most rich George in a sardonyx, set with diamonds of very great value; for the rest very plain. I had not seen him for some years, and believed he might have forgotten me.[24]

An allegorical representation of Queen Anne presenting the grant of the royal manor of Woodstock to Marlborough for military merit. Painting by Sir Godfrey Kneller

Yet party politics fly-spotted the splendour of the hour, and soured the Duke's pleasure in the nation's gratitude. It was perceived by the Tories that the Battle of Blenheim, being fought in central Europe, must be a Whig victory, and therefore to be diminished as much as possible. On the other hand a fumbling and indecisive action by Admiral Sir George Rooke off Malaga, being maritime warfare, must be a Tory victory, and therefore to be magnified at least into an equality with Blenheim. Conversely, Marlborough became the unwilling object of Whig enthusiasm. The Duke's own opinion of both the parties, as expressed in a letter to Sarah in October 1704, was that 'I know them so well that if my quiet depended on either of them, I should be most miserable', and he added a sarcastic reference to leaving a good name behind him in 'countrys that have heardly any blessing but that of not knowing the detested nams of Wigg and Torry'.[25]

As in the previous year strategy and religion were strangely intermixed as focuses of party rancour. A High Church pamphlet attacked both Godolphin and Marlborough as Whig sympathizers who were betraying the Church, which led Godolphin to remark that a discreet clergyman was almost as rare as a black swan.

In March 1705 the Queen dissolved Parliament, and the spring saw the country deep in the pleasures of a general election: lies, bribery and beer. However, the squires who paid the land tax had at last seen a victory for their money; Blenheim routed not only Tallard but also the High Tories. In place of the Tory majority in the last Parliament there were now, so Godolphin calculated, one hundred and ninety Tories of one kind or another, and one hundred and sixty Whigs, with one hundred 'Queen's servants', or members loyal to the court, holding the balance.

The Queen, in her dread of party government, insisted to Godolphin that 'you will do all you can to keep me out of the power of the merciless men of both parties'.[26] The administration therefore was still to rest not on a reliable majority of its own, but on the goodwill of the moderates in both parties; to remain in office by a continual act of political levitation. In so precarious a parliamentary situation Godolphin and Marlborough – who in any case regarded themselves as royal servants – were utterly dependent on the Queen's support; on 'Mrs Morley's' affection for and trust in 'Mr Montgomery', and 'Mr and Mrs Freeman'. One of the pivots round which the affairs of Europe turned was therefore a unique personal relationship between sovereign and three subjects.

The relationship had originated in the passionate crush conceived by a plain, podgy and timid teenage princess for one of her stepmother's maids of honour who was all that the princess was not. Princess Anne and Sarah Churchill had occasionally played together when Anne was still a child being brought up in seclusion and the Church of England at Richmond. But it was the exile of the Duke and Duchess of York's household to the Netherlands in 1679–80, during the Popish Plot, which had really acted as the midwife of friendship. For here in the intimacy of a small group in a foreign land, living in an atmosphere of danger and crisis, the fourteen-year-old Anne began to nourish for the nineteen-year-old Sarah the feelings of a dull and lumpy fourth-former towards a beautiful, brilliant and masterful head girl.

The Glory of the Allied Armies illustrated by an emblazoned description of 128 flags and 35 displayed standards captured from the French and the Bavarians by the allied troops of the Empire and her Britannic Majesty and the United Provinces on 2 August 1704, carried in triumph from the Tower through the City of London to Westminster Hall. Engraving by R. Spofforth

When Princess Anne married Prince George of Denmark in 1683, an honest, faithful and kindly bore who was to make her very happy, it was Sarah's husband who had been entrusted with the mission of escorting the prince to England. Now Anne was to have her own household, at the Cockpit, a residence across the street from the Palace of Whitehall. Who but Sarah could be her Lady of the Bedchamber? In the closeness of household life, the friendship between the two young women had thickened. Anne the homely and Sarah the glittering shared the experiences of almost annual pregnancy, all the horrors of seventeenth-century childbirth, septic and agonizing, the early deaths of the young so painfully produced, so hopefully christened. Always there was Sarah's hard, incisive mind for the uncertain Anne to lean on for support and guidance; and

Sarah's vitality for the sluggish Anne to milk. And Anne had been insistent that no barrier of rank should stand between her and the affection and devotion for which she hungered:

> . . . let me beg of you not to call me your highness at every word, but to be free with me as one friend ought to be with another; and you can never give me any greater proof of your friendship than in telling me your mind freely in all things, which I do beg you to do. . . . I am all impatient for Wednesday, till when farewell.[27]

So after 1684 it had been no longer Princess Anne and Lady Churchill who talked of court affairs or of children and obstetrics over their tea or chocolate, but Mrs Morley

and Mrs Freeman, as if they were two City merchants' wives genteelly passing the time while their husbands were busy on 'Change'.

> As to the names Morley and Freeman [wrote Sarah many years later] the Queen herself was always uneasy if I said the word Highness or Majesty, and would say from the first how awkward it was to write every day in terms of Princess etc. And when she chose the name Morley for herself, for no reason that I remember, but that she liked it, or the sound of it, I am not sure that I did not choose the other with the same regard to my own humour [temperament], which it seems in some sort to express.[28]

In 1684 Sidney Godolphin, the Churchills' closest friend, joined the Cockpit circle under the pseudonym of Mr Montgomery. John and Sarah Churchill, for their part,

ABOVE LEFT *'Now Anne was to have her own household, at the Cockpit, a residence across the street from the Palace of Whitehall. Who but Sarah could be her Lady of the Bedchamber?'* A view of Westminster and Whitehall showing the Cockpit. Detail from a drawing by H. Danckerts (1634–1666)

had grown genuinely and deeply fond of the gentle, kindly and artless Anne. They were happy to act as her guides and protectors in an unquiet time. John Churchill himself with his strong chivalrous streak, his almost religious reverence towards royalty, seems to have cast himself in the role of her knightly champion.

But it was the brief and catastrophic reign of Princess Anne's father, James II, which fused the Cockpit friendships into a tight little league against a world of hazard and intrigue, where even a letter from a royal daughter to her sister might carry the taint of treason. Anne was devoutly Anglican, and therefore James II's ever more rapid march towards the conversion of England to Roman Catholicism had forced her to decide between her duty to her father, as a daughter and a subject, and her religion. Churchill and Godolphin too were Church of England men, but Churchill, like Anne herself, owed a special loyalty to James; in his case that of protégé to patron. By 1687 all three had nevertheless decided that their first allegiance must be to their religion. In the course of a long letter to her sister Mary, now married to William of Orange, Anne told her: 'The King has never said a word to me about religion since the time I told you of; but I expect it every minute, and am resolved to undergo anything rather than change my religion.'[29]

As the country moved towards revolution, and the disaffected looked to William of Orange for deliverance, Anne and her simple spouse Prince George had put their trust in the counsel of John Churchill, worldly, shrewd, subtle. When William of Orange's emissary, Dykvelt, visited England to sound out the extent and strength of opposition to King James, Anne, as she informed her sister in the same letter,

> never ventured to speak to him [Dykvelt], because I am not used to speak to people about business and this Lord [Sunderland, James's chief minister] is so much on the watch that I am afraid of him. So I have desired Lord Churchill (who is one that I can trust, and I am sure is a very honest man and a good Protestant) to speak to Mr Dykevelt for me. . . .[30]

Churchill, after his discussions with Dykvelt, had later confirmed the princess's resolve in a letter to William of Orange, in which he added on his own behalf that 'my places and the King's favour I set at nought, in comparison of being true to my religion. In all things but this the King may command me. . . .[31]

And when in November 1688 Churchill and Prince George of Denmark had ridden out with James's army to meet William of Orange's invading forces, with the intention of deserting the King in a day or so, when the opportunity best should serve, Churchill had left behind in Sarah's strong hands complete arrangements for securing Princess Anne's safety. On the night of 24 November 1688, about midnight, Sarah and Mrs Berkeley, another old childhood friend, later Lady Fitzhardinge, had conducted the Princess from her closet down a new set of back stairs specially built for the occasion so that no servant should know she was not safe in bed. There in the dark street a coach was waiting, and within it the Earl of Dorset and Bishop Compton of London, the latter wearing, as a sign of the times, a sword in place of his accustomed episcopal lawn sleeves.

Sarah Marlborough and Lady Fitzhardinge playing cards. Painting by Sir Godfrey Kneller

The garden front of St James's Palace c. 1690

They conducted us that night [wrote Sarah] to the Bishop's house in the city, and the next day to my Lord Dorset's at Copt Hall. From thence we went to the Earl of Northampton's and from thence to Nottingham, where the country gathered about the Princess; nor did she think herself safe till she saw she was surrounded by the Prince of Orange's friends.[32]

Such an adventure, even if more to Sarah's taste than to Mrs Morley's, could only wind tighter the bonds between protectors and protected. And the advent of a new reign had seen these bonds tightened even further, when the Marlboroughs (as they had now become) took Princess Anne's part in a dispute with King William and Queen Mary over money.

Anne wished to have her own Civil List income granted by Parliament, instead of being dependent, as hitherto, on a grant from the Sovereign's Privy Purse. King William – and even more so Queen Mary – had opposed the Princess's desire both in principle and because they thought the income named, £70,000 per annum, was excessive by £40,000. They tried to wheedle Anne into abandoning her wish. Anne, immovably obstinate – it was a portent – refused. The Marlboroughs used their influence; Sarah canvassed among the politicians. William and Mary sought to bend Sarah into recommending her mistress to give way. Sarah, embattled and aggressive, refused. Parliament ranged itself on the side of Princess Anne and voted her £50,000 per annum. Defeated

and mortified, the Queen asked Anne to choose between her and King William on the one hand, and the Marlboroughs on the other. But Anne, grateful for the staunchness of her friends – and for the final success they had helped to bring about on her behalf – had refused to give them up.

When William finally dismissed Marlborough from all his offices in 1692, Queen Mary had demanded that Princess Anne should also dismiss Sarah from hers. It would be, after all, anomalous if Marlborough, dismissed the court, should continue to live with Sarah at the Cockpit, which being a royal residence was really part of the precincts of the court.

Now it was Anne's turn to protect her protectors. She did so sturdily enough, by leaving the Cockpit herself rather than turn the Marlboroughs out, and taking her household (including the Marlboroughs) off to reside at Syon House, the Duke of Somerset's house by the Thames at Brentford. And when Marlborough found himself in the Tower as a result of a Jacobite plot (see p. 23), Anne had written to Sarah (who was in London to be near her husband) almost daily to comfort her. Her sympathy had been the warmer because Sarah had just lost her baby son Charles.

My dear Mrs Freeman was in so dismal a way when she went from hence, that I cannot forbear asking how she does, and if she has yet any hopes of Lord Marlborough's being soon

'. . . methinks it is a dismal thing to have one's friends sent to that place.' The Tower of London, where Marlborough was imprisoned for six weeks in 1692. Leonard Knyff (1650–1721) and Jan Kip (1653–1722)

at liberty. For God's sake have a care of your dear self, and give as little way to melancholy thoughts as you can.[33]

After a final stand-up quarrel with her sister (it was the last time they ever met), Anne had written to Sarah:

> ... if you should ever do so cruel a thing as to leave me, from that moment I shall never enjoy one quiet hour. And should you do it without asking my consent (which if I ever give you, may I never see the face of Heaven) I will shut myself up and never see the world more. ....[34]

Friendship could hardly be closer or more intense than this. And eleven years later when she was Queen and when the prisoner in the Tower had become her Captain-General, her feelings remained just as strong. When in the autumn of 1703 the Marlboroughs and Godolphin, under the weight of their foreign and domestic anxieties, spoke of retiring, Anne wrote to Sarah:

> ... give me leave to say you should a little consider your faithful freinds (sic) and poor Country, wch must be ruined if ever you should putt your melencoly thoughts in execution, as for your poor unfortunate faithfull Morly she could not beare it, for if ever you should forsake me, I would have nothing more to do with ye world, but make another abdycation, for what is a Crown when ye support of it is gon: I never will forsake your Dear self, Mr Freeman nor Mr Montgomery, but allways be your constant faithfull servant & we four must never part, till death mows us down with his impartiall hand.[35]

It was as if nothing had changed since they had all been living together in adversity at the Cockpit. Yet this was not really so. For Mrs Morley was Queen of England now. She was Mrs Freeman's sovereign lady. Moreover, although her father's doctrine of the Divine Right of Kings was dead under the Revolution settlement, Anne nevertheless remained true to its spirit. For her the sovereign stood in a special relationship to God; the responsibilities entrusted to her were religious as well as political; and kingship was tinged with the mystical. All through her reign she performed the traditional ceremony of 'touching for the King's Evil' – effecting magical cures of the scrofulous by laying the royal hand on them. Anne's outlook was understood by Marlborough; indeed it chimed exactly with his own sense of reverence towards the office of sovereign. For this reason he was able to hold the delicate balance between the friendship and familiarity due to (and demanded by) Mrs Morley and the distance and respect due to (and desired by) the Queen of England.

Nor was Anne as a person any longer the dull and timid adolescent who had once worshipped Sarah. Her happy marriage to Prince George had fulfilled her as a woman. The broils and intrigues of two reigns had matured her judgment of people and situations, and her personal confidence. Despite the homely language of her letters on public affairs, they display much shrewdness and wisdom. There was a stolid strength in her, a stubborn will.

From the day of her accession in 1702, at the age of thirty-seven, she had carried the role of Queen with superb dignity. Upon the news of King William's death, she received the privy council with a 'well-considered speech', and, according to a contemporary account:

> she pronounced this, as she did all her other speeches, with great weight and authority, and with a softness of voice, and sweetness in the pronunciation, that added much life to all she spoke.[36]

Because of Anne's natural sweetness of voice Charles II had ordered the actress Mrs Barry to train her in elocution. The result justified Mrs Barry's fee: 'I have heard the queen speak from the throne,' wrote Mr Speaker Onslow, '. . . I never saw an audience more affected: it was a sort of charm.'[37]

Queen Anne's first appearance before Parliament in 1702 had offered a vision of majesty. She was wearing an ermine-lined robe of red velvet, edged with gold. Round her thick, strong neck was a heavy gold chain, whence was suspended a badge of St George on the matronly bosom. On her head – full-cheeked, firm-jawed – she wore a cap of red velvet surmounted by the crown of England. When she announced that she was giving up for the public service £100,000 of the revenue voted to her by Parliament, the enthusiasm of that Parliament for their new sovereign was even more rapturous. A foreign diplomat reported: 'Since Queen Elizabeth there had been no instance of such graciousness. . . . The Queen had completely won the hearts of her subjects.'[38]

But Sarah, less sensitive to nuances than her husband, Sarah, with her powerful, practical, literal mind, was incapable of perceiving the subtle distinctions between Mrs Morley and the Queen of England: would indeed have been impatient of them if she *had* perceived them. Reverence was not Sarah Marlborough's line. And her own will to dominate, together with long habit, prevented her from perceiving too that she was now dealing with a woman whose own strength of will was no less than hers because less flamboyantly evident.

Sarah was a Whig; the Queen, though of no party preference, broadly in sympathy with the outlook of the Tories. Sarah set out to convert the Queen to her own enlightened views: 'I resolved therefore from the very beginning of the Queen's reign to try whether I could not by degrees make impressions in her mind more favourable to the Whigs. . . .'[39]

Unfortunately Sarah's only strategy in life was the frontal attack – in this case, of endlessly reiterated, and of course to her mind unanswerable, argument. She was a female politician before her time.

With the Duke away campaigning for two-thirds of each year, and Godolphin, the Lord Treasurer and chief minister, an anxious, efficient bureaucrat more at home with racehorses than women, there was potential danger in Mrs Morley's consequent exposure to Mrs Freeman's over-free treatment of her. For the Marlboroughs' friendship with Anne was still, as it had been in 1688 and 1701, the source of their power – that, and the Duke's continued military success.

CHAPTER NINE

SEE WHAT A HAPPY MAN HE IS

On 11 April 1705 Marlborough set sail for the Netherlands. The voyage was terrifyingly rough; his yacht went aground on the sandbanks of the Dutch coast; and the Duke finally reached haven after a four-hour pull in an open boat against wind and tide. It was not a good beginning:

> I have been so very sick at sea [he wrote to Sarah] that my blood is as hote as if I were in a feavor, which makes my head eake extreamly, so that I beg you will make my excuse to Ld Treasurer, for I can write to nobody but my dear soull, whome I love above my life. I am just now going to bed, although I know I cannot sleep. . . .[1]

The Duke intended that this campaign should complete the work of Blenheim and bring Louis XIV to make a reasonable peace. The means of persuasion was to be an invasion of France, which must prove a distasteful as well as a novel experience to a monarch who had spent his reign invading the territories of other people. Marlborough proposed to outflank the chain of powerful fortresses which blocked the invasion routes into France from the Low Countries by an offensive against her much more lightly guarded eastern frontier. While the Margrave of Baden besieged Saarlouis as a subsidiary operation, and Overkirk lay on the defensive in the Low Countries, the Duke himself, with the main strength of the allied forces, would strike up the Moselle valley towards Thionville. He calculated that his own offensive in Germany would force the French to drain troops from their army in the Spanish Netherlands, and so prevent them from falling on the outnumbered Overkirk. The Duke's strategy in 1705, as in 1704, absolutely depended therefore on his wielding the initiative from the very start of the campaign. And this in turn depended on the allied armies concentrating and taking the field before the French. But as soon as the Duke reached The Hague his timetable began to go awry.

He found that the Dutch were quite unready to take the field – and not merely unready, but unwilling to see their frontiers again denuded for the sake of another Marlburian gamble in Germany. On 21 April the Duke glumly reported to Godolphin:

> I cannot but say that almost all their business here is in great disorder, and their generals' desire of keeping 50 battalions and 90 squadrons on the Meuse is very unreasonable; for if this should be complied with, I should have on the Moselle but 60 battalions and 79 squadrons, to act offensively. . . . I am sure I shall never consent to what they desire; but how I shall be able to get the troops out of the country is the difficulty. . . .[2]

'The voyage was terrifyingly rough . . .' A squall at sea. Painting by Willem van de Velde (1633–1707)

This renewal of the half-forgotten tortures of protracted argument with the Dutch left Marlborough, so he confided to Sarah, 'like a sick body that turns from one part of the bed to the other: for I fain would be gone hence, in hopes to find more quiet in the army'.[3] Moreover, even a modest solace was denied him, for 'I can get no Tee that is fit to be drunk'.

On 26 May the Duke at last reached the army at Trèves on the Moselle, having first journeyed all the way down to Baden and back in order to confer with the Margrave. He found him full of difficulties; no wagons, no guns, a shortage of horses. The projected siege of Saarlouis was abandoned therefore. Instead the Margrave would join the Duke on the Moselle, but not until the third week of June. At Trèves Marlborough

'. . . the ablest living French general – flamboyant, brave, energetic . . .' Claude Louis Hector, Duc de Villars. Painting after Hyacinthe Rigaud

found more trouble. According to the arrangements he had made with German rulers during the winter, all the German contingents should by now have rendezvoused on the Moselle with the English forces. In fact the Prussians were not now expected until the 10th or 12th of June; the Palatines until the 6th. 'By all this you will see', reported the Duke to Godolphin, 'we want a third of our foot, and about half our horse, which makes it impossible for me to march.'[4]

This was by no means the sum of his problems. He had also arranged in the winter for supply depots to be fully stocked ready to nourish the army's advance up the Moselle. But instead the depots were half-empty because of the neglect, or, as the Duke suspected, even treachery of the local officers responsible. As a result, in the Duke's words, 'we are much more afraid of starving than the enemy'.[5]

Nevertheless, on 2 June Marlborough advanced towards the French frontier, one column winding along in the valley of the Moselle, and the other on the bleak heights above. So stark was the country that the need to find fresh forage for the animals compelled him to move in any case. Although the Duke's army was a third under strength, he had such confidence in his troops that he was still sure he could win a battle. And as precious time leaked away, and with it the initiative for which Marlborough had planned with such vain care, a battle again became his best, indeed his only, hope.

The French commander on the Moselle, Marshal de Villars, had, however, no intention at all of providing him with a battle. He was the ablest living French general – flamboyant, brave, energetic, loved by his soldiers because of his willingness to share their hardships; rather less loved at court and by his colleagues because of his vainglory, quick temper, and outspoken sarcasm. Villars had not at all been taken by surprise by Marlborough's advance. As long ago as September 1704, Louis XIV and his advisers had rightly guessed that Marlborough would seek to take Trèves and Trarbach that autumn, as the base for an offensive up the Moselle on Thionville in 1705. So Villars, well reinforced and completely prepared, sat tight in an immensely strong entrenched position at Sierck, with his left flank protected by the Moselle and his right by forests, and waited for hunger and events elsewhere to drive Marlborough away.

For a fortnight the Duke hung on in front of Sierck, waiting for the troops of his dilatory allies to arrive; hoping that Villars might give him the opening for a battle. But Villars, like Wellington in the Lines of Torres Vedras, was not to be tempted out of his defences. Every day Marlborough's situation became more precarious. 'We are in a country', wrote the Duke on 6 June, 'where there is nothing to be found, and if we should be without bread for a single day, we are ruined.'[6] Although it was now approaching midsummer there were hard frosts every night, a circumstance which, as he said, 'does hurt both to our men and horses'. Moreover, the frosts worsened his critical supply problem by killing the green forage in the fields. Under the stress of hunger and hardship, deserters began to slide away for the ports and home. It was no longer a question of brilliant manœuvres and decisive battles, but of bread and oats. Into this struggle for subsistence the Duke threw all his resources of personal leadership. He rounded up the bakers from the villages of the countryside and sent them in squads under escort to Trèves. He sent orders to his commissary at Trèves to 'Have the flour and forage sent forward from Mainz and Coblenz as soon as possible; get the biscuit with all speed to Trèves, because I shall need it soon . . .'; and added the urgent postscript: 'Send up the biscuit as fast as it is baked, . . . and distribute none without my orders.'[7]

But by 12 June he had to recognize that despite all efforts the supply situation remained so critical that 'this army may be ruined without fighting'.[8] Meanwhile Villeroi, once more commanding the French army in the Low Countries, had taken the little fortress of Huy, on the Meuse, and was advancing on Liège. Overkirk, his Dutch opponent, who was outnumbered two to one, abandoned Liège and fell back on Maastricht. The alarm of the Dutch was prodigious – just as the French intended. Marlborough's

Nassau.
gusgue

A market tent in camp, 1707. Drawing by Marcellus Laroon (1679–1774) who served throughout Marlborough's campaigns in Flanders

chagrin at the frustration of his own plans was the worse because he understood too well what the French were about. He wrote to Robert Harley, the Secretary of State, on 9 June:

> . . . it is plain his [Villars's] whole aim is to give time to the Marechal de Villeroi to act on the Meuse, where I find he had already alarmed them to such a degree in Holland, that I dread the consequences of it, and am apprehensive every day of receiving such resolutions from the States [General] as may entirely defeat all our projects on this side.[9]

His predictions were soon borne out. Frantic and repeated appeals for help arrived from the Dutch; appeals backed by the implied threat that they might have to make peace unless the Duke detached large forces to their rescue, or, better still, transferred his whole army from the Moselle to the Meuse.

LEFT '. . . *the one Dutch soldier with whom he enjoyed relations of mutual trust'. Henry of Nassau, Lord of Overkirk (Ouwerkerk) and Woudenburg (1640–1700), veldmaarschalk and commander-in-chief of the Dutch army. Painting by Sir Godfrey Kneller*

Still Marlborough hung on, refusing to acknowledge that his plans had crumbled beyond repair. For the first time since he had become commander-in-chief he knew what it felt like to lose control of the strategic situation; he knew the deep disquiet that came from a sense of impotence in the presence of unfolding calamity.

On 16 June 1705, with still no prospect of decisive action on the Moselle, the supply position ever more grim, and Overkirk at Maastricht in real danger from Villeroi,

Marlborough gave orders for the army to start the march back to the Low Countries the following night.

He had sustained a major strategic defeat. Far from making the French move to his initiative, they had forced him to move to theirs. The Duke himself laid the blame on the failure of his allies to provide troops and supplies at the promised time and place. 'If I had known beforehand,' he wrote to Sarah in his bitterness, 'what I must have endured by relying on the people of this country, no reasons could have persuaded me to have undertaken this campaign.'[10]

Although it was an explanation he was to elaborate to many people, it hardly amounted to the whole truth. For there was an inherent gamble in a strategy which entirely depended on a coalition being able to get its armies into the field before a single absolute monarchy. The gamble came off in 1704, but not in 1705. In any case, there was little of the usual Marlburian subtlety and psychological deception about the Duke's offensive plan. Unlike the march to the Danube, it failed to threaten alternative objectives, and so keep the enemy puzzled and paralysed until too late. Moreover, an advance up the Moselle was so obvious a gambit that Louis XIV and his generals had been expecting it ever since the previous autumn. It was not, after all, because of the defaultings of his allies that the Duke found Villars strongly entrenched across his path.

Marlborough, already fretted by a month of disappointment and worry, took the final collapse of his plans with less than Wellingtonian phlegm. He confided to Godolphin in a letter of 16 June, on the eve of the army's withdrawal, that he was writing mainly in order to 'ease' himself because 'my head and heart are so full'; and concluded by assuring his old friend that '. . . I think if it were possible to vex me so for a fortnight longer, it would make an end of me. In short, I am weary of my life.'[11]

But it was the last sentence of a letter written that same night to Sarah which gives the measure of his anguish: 'My dearest soul, pity me and love me.'[12]

On 17 June 1705, at midnight, the army slipped away, drums silent, the sounds of its furtive going masked by the mutter of pelting rain.

Within a fortnight the Duke had joined Overkirk at Hannef, near Liège; and Villeroi, with his mission of drawing Marlborough away from the Moselle accomplished, retired to Tongres, with orders from Louis XIV to stand on the defensive. Marlborough now found himself back again in the lush plains and long horizons of the Low Countries, the scene of all his frustrations in 1702–3; and in much the same company of Dutch generals. The pains of coalition warfare – command by councils of war – descended upon him once more. Yet with patient strength of purpose he began to plan a fresh campaign. He had now to regain the initiative he had lost on the Moselle; to make up for nearly two months' wasted time; to wipe out the political effects of failure. Once more the war situation demanded that he should seek a battle.

Marlborough's new strategy, born though it was out of disappointment and depression, was far more worthy of him than his original Moselle plan. Somewhere between the

'. . . his unhappy wife . . .'; Sarah Marlborough, after she had cut off her long hair in a fit of the 'spleen'. She holds the severed tresses in her hand. Painting by Sir Godfrey Kneller

small fortress of Léau (Zoutleeuw) and the Meuse he meant to break through the Lines of Brabant, which the Dutch had stopped him attacking in 1703. He therefore judged it better to confide his purpose only to Overkirk, *veldmaarschalk* and commander-in-chief, of the Dutch army, and the one Dutch soldier with whom he enjoyed relations of mutual trust. Marlborough's plan entailed deceiving not only the French but also his own allies; more, it was a bluff within a bluff. To the council of war he announced that he would advance with the English forces towards the Lines near Léau, and so draw Villeroi to this sector. This, he asserted – no doubt with his blandest expression – would open the way for the Dutch forces to break through the Lines near the Meuse, where the defences were weakest. He himself would then swiftly countermarch to join them.

The Dutch generals were not convinced. They argued that the Duke's feint near Léau would not deceive Villeroi, because that sector of the Lines was particularly powerful, and Villeroi would realize that no one could seriously intend to attack it. Instead, pronounced the Dutch, Villeroi would keep his army near the Meuse, behind the weakest part of his defences. Nevertheless, they kindly agreed to give the Duke's plan a try.

And just as they had so sagaciously predicted (and the Duke himself secretly expected), they found Villeroi opposite them when they advanced in the south. For Villeroi had judged that the Duke's advance in the north was no more than a feint – again just as the Dutch had sagaciously predicted. When the Duke began to march southwards, obviously to join the Dutch, Villeroi was confirmed in his conviction that this was where the danger lay.

But on the night of 17/18 July 1705, the Duke, having now completely taken in his allies and the enemy, suddenly reversed direction under cover of darkness, and marched at utmost speed back northwards. For he meant to launch his real attack on the very sector where he had feinted earlier. At first light Marlborough's advanced guard attacked the French defences between Elixhem and Léau; he did not even wait for his own main body to come up, let alone Overkirk and the Dutch army, who were now marching to join him. Indeed it was his hope and intention that the action would be all over before the Dutch could arrive.

Because this sector of the Lines was particularly formidable – ramparts, redoubts, inundations – Villeroi had garrisoned it more lightly than elsewhere. Taken now utterly by surprise by yelling redcoats storming out of the dawn, the defenders were swiftly rushed and overwhelmed on a three-mile front, and Marlborough's troops poured through to the west. The dreaded Lines of Brabant which had loomed so fearfully in the minds of Dutch generals had been broken as easily as a burglar jemmying a door – but only because Villeroi had been so completely tricked by the Duke's double bluff and by the speed of his marching.

The north gate at Mindelheim, Marlborough's principality as a Prince of the Holy Roman Empire

In the course of the morning, however, the French and their Bavarian allies (who had been an army in exile since Bavaria was occupied by the allies after Blenheim) regrouped their local reserves and counter-attacked. A ferocious mêlée ensued between enemy horsemen in black helmets and cuirasses and Marlborough's redcoated cavalry. The Duke was, as always, up with his leading troops. According to Lord Orkney:

My Lord Marlborough in person was everywhere, and escaped very narrowly; for a squadron, which he was at the head of, gave ground a little, though [it] soon came up again; and a fellow came to him and thought to have sabered him to the ground, and struck at him with that force, and missing his stroke, he fell off his horse. I asked my Lord if it was soe; he sayd it was absolutely so. See what a happy man he is.[13]

And Orkney added: 'I believe this pleases him as much as Hogstet [Blenheim] did. It is absolutely owing to him.'

In the exhilaration of that fight at Elixhem Marlborough found relief from his earlier anxieties and disappointments. He himself led the charge which finally routed the French counter-attack. When he rode up sword in hand to the head of his troops officers and troopers alike burst into cheers. It was a sight and sound which lifted Marlborough's tired spirit as much as the success of the day. For as well as commanders inspiring their troops, troops can also inspire their commanders. So it was with the Duke at Elixhem.

The kindness of the troops to me [he wrote to Sarah] has transported me, for I had none in this last action, but such as were with me last year . . . this gave occasion to the troops . . . to make me very kind expressions, even in the heat of the action, which I own to you gives me great pleasure, and makes me resolve to endure everything for their sakes. . . .[14]

Sarah, however, alarmed by his account of the action, implored him not to take unnecessary risks. He therefore hastened to assure her that

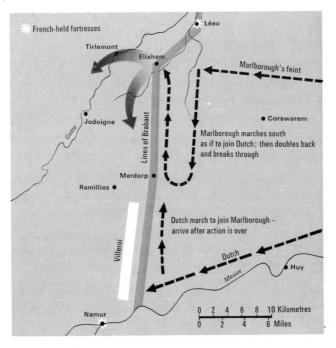

LEFT *Breaking through the Lines of Brabant*

RIGHT *Forcing the Lines of Brabant 17–18 July 1705. A very accurate topography with the village and bridge at Elixhem, and the castle of Wangen in the centre. Detail from a tapestry woven by De Vos after L. de Hondt*

I never venture myself but when I think the service of my queen and country requires it. Besides, I am now at an age when I find no heat in my blood that gives me temptation to expose myself out of vanity; but as I would deserve and keep the kindness of this army I must let them see that when I expose them I would not except myself.[15]

In the face of Marlborough's breakthrough, Villeroi fell back behind the River Dyle, with his left flank on the fortress of Louvain. But it was not so much the Dyle which saved him from Marlborough's pursuit as the Dutch. At the end of July and the beginning of August a fresh attempt by the Duke, in his words, to 'cheat them into success', failed amid disobedience and open dispute bordering on mutiny. The ringleader was, as on previous occasions, General Slangenberg, a man who, in addition to being a curmudgeon by nature, nourished a sour jealousy of the Duke. 'God forgive', the Duke wrote to Heinsius on 30 July, 'those that are better pleased when anything goes ill then (sic) when we have success.'[16] Three days later he warned him that unless the system of command was changed, there could be no hope of decisive success, because the endless councils of war 'intierly destroys the secrecy and dispatch upon which all great undertakings depend'; and, what was more, only provided a platform for all the differing views and 'the private animositys' among the allied commanders.

> . . . it is absolutely necessary that such a power bee lodged with the general as may enable him to act as he thinkes proper according to the best of his judgement, without being obliged either to communicate what he intends further then (sic) he thinkes convenient. The success of the last campagne with the blessing of God was owing to that power, which I wish you would now give for the good of the Publique and that of the States [of the Netherlands] in particular. . . .[17]

The Duke went on to tell Heinsius that he was perfectly willing to resign, 'if you think anybody can execute it better than myself'.

Towards the Dutch generals themselves, however, Marlborough still maintained an unruffled front of courtesy which must have cost him dear in self-control and inward strain. 'I dare not show my resentment,' he explained to Godolphin, 'for fear of too much alarming the Dutch, and indeed encouraging the enemy.'[18]

On 15 August, still undeterred by his vexations, he opened a new offensive, crossing the River Dyle and swinging wide to the south round Villeroi's army near Louvain. He had stocked his wagons with ten days' supply of bread, so for that period he could cut free from his communications and enjoy complete mobility. In three days he had reached Genappe, and turned north towards Brussels by the same route Napoleon was to take in 1815. He had dispatched ahead of him a powerful combined force of infantry, cavalry and guns under his brother General Churchill. This force skirmished with French covering parties at Waterloo and pressed on into the Forêt de Soignies, the sprawling green masses of which blanket the southern approaches to Brussels.

Villeroi and his colleague the Elector of Bavaria had now taken post facing south-east behind the little River Yssche and midway between Brussels and Louvain. With their

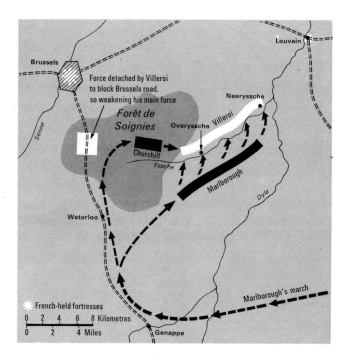

The lost victory on the River
Yssche, 18 August 1705

army already depleted by the need to find garrisons for the all-too-numerous towns of Brabant, Villeroi and the Elector found themselves placed by Marlborough's march in an exquisite dilemma. As Villeroi was later to explain to Louis XIV:

> Imagine, sire, if you please, the cruel moment when it was necessary to make up one's mind to march to Brussels in order to save it, at the price of abandoning Louvain, it not being possible to defend them both. Supposing the enemy were to avail himself of the opportunity which we gave him by quitting our post in order to save Brussels, and made himself master of Louvain and after that the whole of Brabant, it still seemed to us that the loss of Brussels was yet more important.[19]

Villeroi now received more and more reports that allied troops were pushing in great strength through the Forêt de Soignies towards Brussels. Still he and the Elector continued to dither. Finally they became convinced that Marlborough's objective really was Brussels; and they accordingly prepared to issue orders to their army to march westward to cover it. The fact that for the past hour they had seen a force of allied cavalry riding along opposite them on the far side of the Yssche did nothing to change their minds, because as Villeroi told his King, 'we regarded this as a feint on the Duke of Marlborough's part while he marched on Brussels with his entire army'.[20] But shortly Villeroi and the Elector observed 'very distinctly columns of infantry debouching from the woods', and following the allied cavalry. A revelation now struck them: 'beneath our very eyes the enemy army was marching in front of us'.[21] They had been helplessly delivered up to the last experience they desired – a battle.

For Marlborough had suddenly swerved eastwards off the Brussels road to grab them unawares. He now planned their total destruction. While the main body of the allied army attacked them across the Yssche, the detached force under his brother, now concealed deep in the forest south of Brussels, would emerge and strike into Villeroi's flank and rear. Marlborough was utterly confident of victory, for whereas at Blenheim he had faced superior numbers, he now outnumbered Villeroi by four to three; and he had no doubts that in morale and fighting power the allied army was immensely stronger.

Yet the Duke's request to the Dutch leaders for their consent to launch the attack turned out to be more than the polite formality he had this time expected in view of the enemy's plight. The field-deputies wished to confer with their generals. The generals wished minutely to inspect the ground. When they had done so, 'that beast Slangenberg', in the epithet of Marlborough's chaplain, and as ever the troublemaker, loudly asserted that to attack over the Yssche would be 'murder and massacre'.

It was true enough that the French position was strong, for the steep-banked Yssche was only passable by bridging, while a sunken road a little distance beyond it provided cover for defending infantry. Nevertheless, it was certainly no stronger than Tallard's position at Blenheim. In any case Villeroi's army was visibly too weak in numbers adequately to man the whole length of its front. It was no less obvious that the moral advantage lay with the allies, for agitated to-ings and fro-ings among the French formations gave evidence of the enemy's state of alarm and confusion.

But none of this weighed in the least with Slangenberg, who seemed more interested in picking a personal quarrel with the Duke, helpfully remarking that many agreed that the Duke's attack at Blenheim had been itself imprudent. Marlborough for his part at first tried flattering Slangenberg himself – 'I am happy to have under my command an officer of your courage and skill'. Slangenberg proving impervious to charm, the Duke then sought to win the consent of the Dutch leaders as a whole. According to his chaplain, who was an eye witness, he employed every tactic of persuasion:

> sometimes fair words and sometimes hard words, and at last told them that if they neglected this opportunity they could never answer it to God or their masters, and that this would be the last time he should lead them to the enemy.[22]

But they would not budge. Only Overkirk took his side. And so, instead of leading the army forward against Villeroi, it fell to Marlborough to issue orders for a retreat to his starting point at Meldert, south-east of Louvain. Next day he vented his mortification on Heinsius:

> I do before God declare to you, that I am persuaded that if Slanenbourg (sic) had not been in the army, at this day we might have prescribed to France what peace we might have pleased. . . .[23]

Yet even now, in drafting his official report to the States-General on the lost victory on the Yssche, the Duke felt that he must keep his language discreetly mild for fear of sharpening antagonism between the allies. 'I should have writ in a very angry style,' he explained to Sarah, 'but I was afraid it might have given an advantage to the French.'[24]

But even the Duke, with all his patience and determination, had had enough. He now went on a kind of general's strike, simply agreeing to whatever operation appealed to the Dutch military imagination, such as a petty siege. 'The resolution I have taken,' he told Heinsius, 'of being governed by your generals the remaining part of this campaign gives me a great deal of quiet, so that I am drinking the Spa waters.'[25]

However, he was not really enjoying as much 'quiet' as he made out to Heinsius, for he had already confessed in a letter to Sarah:

> I have so many things that vex me, that I am afraid the waters, which I think to begin tomorrow, will not do me much good. . . . It is impossible for me to express how much I long for the end of the campaign, for I have no prospect of any thing considerable that can be done. . . .[26]

He was right: nothing considerable *was* done; only the taking of Léau and the demolition of the captured Lines of Brabant. For the Duke the year, for all its repeated hopes, had proved almost entirely barren. His only consolation prize was provided by the Habsburg Emperor, who made him a Prince of the Holy Roman Empire and gave him as his principality the little Bavarian town of Mindelheim and its surrounding district. The Emperor had offered the Duke the princely title alone after Blenheim, but characteristically he would not accept it until a principality was found to support its dignity.

Why did Marlborough show such quite astonishing forbearance towards the Dutch? This was, after all, the third campaign which they had aborted by their obstructiveness. Yet on every occasion he had yielded to their wishes and abandoned his hopes of victory rather than assert the authority vested in him by the States-General to give orders to the Dutch army when it was united with his own in action. Was it, as his admirers have contended, all a proof of his wonderful self-command? Or was it a mark of weakness?

Marlborough had spent most of his adult life in deferential service at court, his thoughts concealed and his feelings masked. Except for the single, and disastrous, occasion when he had openly opposed William III, he had always pursued his ends obliquely rather than directly; reluctant to place all he had achieved in the world in jeopardy. Moreover, eager for battle though he was as a soldier, he shrank from conflict in other spheres of life such as politics and personal relations. Here his wife Sarah was the born fighter, not the Duke. It was only against an enemy in the field that he sought a decision by confrontation. At the core of the Duke of Marlborough there was more pliant metal than Wellingtonian iron.

Yet even Wellington went on his knee during the Talavera campaign in 1809 in his efforts to persuade his proud but incompetent Spanish colleague to fall in with his plans. Thereafter Wellington simply refused to have anything to do with the Spaniards; an option hardly open to Marlborough with regard to the Dutch. Appeasement of the

Dutch, even if temperamentally congenial, was the only possible course for Marlborough to pursue in view of his lack of the formal title and authority of allied generalissimo. Nothing would have been really served by a series of open rows with Dutch generals, or by attempting to issue categorical orders which would only have been disobeyed.

But why did not Marlborough force a general showdown with the Dutch government itself, by threatening to resign unless he were given full authority? After his débâcle on the River Yssche, the English government actually suggested to the Duke that they should make some such formal demand to the Dutch government, but he advised against it, characteristically preferring a more discreet and sideways approach by 'advising with such of our [Dutch] friends as I am sure are in the true interest'.[27] In fact, there was a single decisive reason for Marlborough's wish at all costs to avoid a showdown with the Dutch over the question of the command. It would, he recognized, inevitably lead to a major crisis in Anglo-Dutch relations. And such a crisis, especially over such an issue, would come as a godsend to the powerful anti-war factions in both countries, and equally to the no less powerful anti-Dutch faction in England. The very continuance of the alliance might be in danger. Marlborough's handling of his Dutch colleagues displays his ability to think as a statesman rather than a mere soldier; to subordinate military questions, however important, to the interests of high policy. He had indeed felt a nagging anxiety ever since 1703 lest the Dutch might be tempted to make a separate peace. As it happened, his motive in appeasing them was lent a fresh urgency during that very month of August when he was forgoing his battle on the River Yssche. For Louis XIV had made a peace offer to The Hague.

The offer was cunningly framed to divide the allies by appealing to the war-weary among the Dutch. Louis apparently conceded the principal Dutch war aim of security against French attack, by proposing that the Spanish Netherlands should become an independent buffer state between the United Provinces and France. The rest of the Spanish Empire, Spain itself, and the colonies with their rich trade potential were to go intact and entire to Louis's grandson, 'Philip v', while the allied candidate, 'Charles III', was to receive Naples and Sicily as compensation.

But Louis's proposed terms were quite unacceptable to England. As Marlborough reminded Heinsius on the day after his lost victory on the River Yssche, 'you know as well as I that England can like no peace but such as puts King Charles III in possession of the Monarche of Spain....'[28] In October 1705 the Queen's speech at the opening of Parliament proclaimed:

> If the French monarchy continues master of the Spanish monarchy, the balance of power in Europe is utterly destroyed, and he will be able in a short time to engross the trade and the wealth of the world. No good Englishman could at any time be content to sit still, and acquiesce in such a prospect....[29]

'No peace without Spain!' – it was to become the English, and even more so the Whig, rallying cry; one of those simple slogans which have the power to drive nations

Queen Anne in the House of Lords. Painted by Peter Tillemans between 1708 and 1714

at war onwards and onwards in the elusive search for victory. Yet 'no peace without Spain' was a war aim far beyond the scope of the original Treaty of Grand Alliance. The allies had then accepted that Louis's candidate should succeed to the Spanish throne, given only that Louis guarantee that the crowns of Spain and France should never be united, and that the Spanish Netherlands and Spanish lands in Italy went to the Austrian candidate.

The new English war aim was the consequence of buying a fresh ally with rash promises. The alliance with Portugal in 1703 had been concluded for the sake of Portuguese bases for the Royal Navy, the use of Portugal as a base for land operations in Spain, and the dubious assistance of the Portuguese army. The King of Portugal, however, stipulated as his condition for entering the war on the side of the allies that they must undertake not to make peace until the Austrian candidate, Charles III, was recognized as King of Spain and of her undivided empire. By signing this treaty of alliance, England committed herself to the policy of 'no peace without Spain', and thereby put aside almost all possibility of a compromise settlement with Louis XIV. Instead such a war aim could only be achieved by reducing Louis to a virtual state of surrender. And this in turn would demand military successes on a scale far beyond anything the allies had yet achieved, even Blenheim. The Portuguese alliance had transformed the whole nature of the conflict – and of Marlborough's task.

Nevertheless, the Queen's speech to Parliament in October 1705 asserted that 'at this time we have good grounds for hope that . . . a good foundation is laid for restoring the monarchy of Spain to the house of Austria.' The Queen and her ministers saw their good grounds for hope neither in Marlborough's own fruitless campaign, nor in northern Italy, where Prince Eugène had failed to link up with the Duke of Savoy, who was in ever more desperate straits under French attack, but in Spain itself. In the winter of 1704–5 Gibraltar, newly captured by England, had been successfully defended against a besieging French army. On 9 October 1705 an allied expeditionary force under the Earl of Peterborough captured Barcelona in a brilliant surprise attack. Catalonia, never friendly towards the Castilians who ruled Spain from Madrid, embraced the cause of 'Charles III'; and so too did Valencia. Glorious prospects now opened of Peterborough marching on Madrid from Catalonia while the Earl of Galway, the allied commander in Portugal, advanced on it from the west. When their forces converged, 'Philip V' would have to vacate the capital and the throne to 'Charles III'.

But already the Iberian Peninsula, which in Marlborough's grand strategy figured as no more than a subsidiary theatre, was coming to swallow up nearly as many allied resources as the Duke's own operations. The Spanish war could only be fed by long sea communications, and the wastage of men and beasts in transit in disease-ridden, storm-tossed ships was enormous. One force sailing no further than from Lisbon to Valencia lost half its strength of 8,000 men on the voyage. Militarily as well as politically, therefore, Spain was the whore's smile which seduced English policy from prudence into expectations the ultimate cost of which no man could foresee. Marlborough himself could not effectively control operations in the Iberian Peninsula from the Low Countries. He hoped for success in Spain; he did what he could to promote it; but for him the centre of gravity of the war remained the army of which he was at the head.

And so in the winter of 1705–6, while Louis XIV's peace feelers were coming to nothing, the Duke again followed the exertions of a campaign by a tour of European capitals in order to keep the alliance in good repair. In Düsseldorf he persuaded the Elector Palatine to supply troops for service in Italy next year. In Vienna, after a 'very tedious journey' of six days down the Danube by boat, he met the new, and young, Emperor Joseph, who had succeeded Leopold in May 1705. The Duke shrank, however, from the prospect of enduring the public formality of being a guest in one of the Emperor's palaces. 'I must entreat the liberty', the Duke wrote beforehand, to Stepney, the English ambassador in Vienna, 'when I come, to set up my field-bed in your house, and if you find that preparations are making to lodge me elsewhere, I pray you will let [them] know that I expect this retirement as a particular mark of the Emperor's favour.'[30]

After Vienna and a ceremonial investment with his Principality of Mindelheim by the Emperor, he was off to Berlin, to soothe the feelings of Frederick I of Prussia, who was full of grievances against the Dutch and the Emperor, and charm out of him a promise of 8,000 men for Italy next campaign. His second visit to Hanover, on the way back to The Hague, was as great a personal success as his first the year before. After his departure, the Electress Sophia gushed away in a letter to Sarah about 'the joy we felt in having had my Lord Duke here in person, and in having known that his manners are as obliging and polished as his actions are glorious and admirable.'[31] It was only on 11 January 1706 (31 December 1705, old style) that he finally reached London, after a 2,000-mile round trip.

Though he had given no hint to any of the rulers he had visited about the strategy he hoped to carry out in 1706, he had in fact begun to lay its foundations when he arranged for German contingents to serve in Italy. For his plan was nothing less than to transfer himself and the English army to northern Italy, there to unite with Prince Eugène and save Savoy from extinction, just as they had saved the Empire at Blenheim. It was a strategy of astounding boldness.

And given only that it could be carried out, its advantages were correspondingly great. The Duke would escape from the Low Countries where, with both the enemy and his principal ally apparently intent on avoiding battle, there seemed little hope of achieving the kind of far-reaching success the war demanded. It would enable him to fight alongside the only allied commander of ability and energy comparable with his own. If he and Eugène could beat the French in Italy and preserve Savoy from being overrun, the territory of Savoy, straddling the mountain passes between Italy and France, would serve them as a gateway into the heart of Louis XIV's kingdom. Or alternatively they might invade France along the Mediterranean shore, via Nice and Toulon, and with the support of English seapower.

Nevertheless, in proposing to transfer his army to Italy, Marlborough was accepting immense risks. It entailed a march through the length of Germany, across Austria, over the Alpine passes and down into the plain of Lombardy; twice the distance of the march to Blenheim. To keep the army in bread and forage would tax even his skill as a quarter-master. The contingents of allied and mercenary troops must reach the various rendezvous assigned to them by the Duke exactly on time, and in the promised strengths, or other-wise his strategy would be fatally dislocated. They had done so punctiliously enough on the march to the Danube in 1704; they had completely failed to do so on the Moselle in 1705. Was the Duke expecting too much? And if the Duke failed to draw the war after him, and the French were to launch a serious attack on the Dutch, he would be too far off to return in time to save them.

Everything turned, just as in 1704 and 1705, on the Duke's being able to seize the initiative from the very beginning of the campaign. But once again the French monarchy moved faster than a cumbersome coalition. In March 1706 a French army under Marshal Vendôme defeated a Habsburg army at Calcinato, in northern Italy. On 12 May, while Marlborough's various allies and hirers of troops were still chewing their lips over the riskiness of his strategy or defaulting on their promises, Marshal Villars, the French commander in Alsace, took the Margrave of Baden by surprise, captured Haguenau, and drove the Margrave back over the Rhine in disorder. The fortress of Landau, so often taken and retaken, submitted once more to a French siege.

Marlborough, to his intense disappointment, had now to accept that he must after all campaign in the Low Countries. All that remained of his ambitious hopes were the handmills he had issued to the troops so that they could grind their own corn on the long march to Lombardy. Yet perhaps it was as well. The Duke's Italian strategy was, despite its vision, a fearful gamble. It is hard not to sympathize with Godolphin's remark to Marlborough that 'I could never swallow so well the thoughts of your being so far out of our reach and for so long a time. . . .'[32]

In any case the Duke had totally miscalculated French intentions in the Low Countries. Far from standing on the defensive, Louis XIV had decided to attack in that theatre as well as in Germany and Italy. Although he wanted peace, he wanted it on reasonable terms. Before renewing peace feelers, therefore, he meant to convince the allies that there was more strength and fight left in France than they appeared to think. As a consequence, the French armies would everywhere go over to the offensive in 1706. From the Low Countries Marshal Villeroi informed his King on 8 May that he was persuaded that it could only be 'advantageous to accept a battle, especially if the enemy were obliged to come and attack us'.[33] His immediate objective, assigned to him by Louis XIV, was the fortress of Léau; and he was prepared to march and, if need be, fight, without even waiting for a strong force under Marsin from the Rhine which was to join him in June.

Marlborough arrived in the Low Countries that spring sunk in despondency. He found preparations even less advanced than in 1705 – a further indication that his Italian strategy would in any case have broken down. On leaving The Hague for the army he groaned to Godolphin: 'God knows I go with a heavy heart, for I have no hope of doing anything considerable, unless the French do what I am very confident they will not. . . .'[34] And to Sarah: 'I am very uneasy when your letters do not come regularly, for without flatterie my greatest support are the thoughts I have of your kindness.'[35]

At this time too he found himself caught as a father and a husband in the crossfire between Sarah, a righteous and indignant mother incensed at the lack of consideration shown her by her daughters, and the daughters themselves, for whom the Duke cherished an indulgent fondness.

> . . . hether too I really have not had time to write to my Children, but when I do be assur'd that I shall let them know my heart and soul, as to their living dutyfully, and kindly with You, and let mee beg for my sake of my dear Soull, that she will passe by litle faults and consider they are but very young. . . .[36]

On 17 May 1706 the English and Dutch forces concentrated near Tongres. The Hanoverians and Hessians had yet to arrive. Frederick I of Prussia was being awkward, and withholding his contingent until his various grievances were remedied; the Danish cavalry was still two days' march away. Nevertheless, the Duke decided to advance on Namur without delay, in the hope that this might provoke Villeroi out of his usual caution. But next day came intelligence reports that Villeroi needed no provocation, but had passed the Dyle and was advancing towards Tirlemont (Tienen). On 20 May, when the Duke was at Borchloen, held up by heavy rain, it became clear that Villeroi had turned southward through Jodoigne, heading for the gap between the headwaters of the Petite Gette stream and the River Mehaigne. The Duke sent a message to the Danish horse to join him as fast as possible, and ordered his own army southwards to meet the French. The miasma of despondency which had enveloped the Duke was now swiftly dispelled. He positively sparkled at the prospect of action. 'We shall be 122 squadrons, and 74 battalions,' he informed Godolphin. 'They pretend to be stronger both in horse and foot; but, with the blessing of God, I hope for success, being resolved to venture. . . .'[37] To M. Hop, a prominent Dutch statesman, he asserted, 'For my part, I think nothing could be more happy for the allies than a battle since I have good reason to hope . . . we may have a complete victory.'[38]

THE GREAT GLORIOUS SUCCESS

On 22 May the army camped near Corswarem, a straggling village of reddish-brown brick lying in a hollow in the shadow of its windmill. At 1 a.m. on the 23rd, a Sunday, the Duke dispatched Cadogan with an advanced guard to reconnoitre the high ground between the Mehaigne and the Petite Gette. All this was country well known to the Duke and his army from previous campaigns. It was fortunate that it was so, because after days of drenching rain, there was thick fog that night. At 3 a.m. the Duke followed with the main body.

Beyond Merdorp, another russet-brick village rich with middens, the ground gradually rises. Here about 8 a.m., full daylight, Cadogan bumped into a French patrol; there was a sound, damped by the mist, of scattered firing; the French retired; and Cadogan halted. Then, just as at Blenheim, the mist began to thin and lift in the strengthening sunshine. An immense sweep of open country, devoid of hedges and trees, opened up before Cadogan's gaze: broad undulations rolling away to the westwards. Through his telescope Cadogan could see, lit by the slanting sun, movement on high ground some four miles off: Villeroi's advanced guard. A galloper hastened back over lanes thick in mire to warn the Duke. At 10 a.m. the Duke rode up and joined Cadogan. There, to the westward beyond the village of Ramillies, he could see the horizon crawling with ant figures; the glinting of equipment. The army he meant to smash and scatter was deploying for battle.

But over in that army morale was high enough, as it marched into the eye of the morning sun in two great columns of infantry with the artillery rumbling along in between, and the cavalry in battle formation. According to a French brigadier, de la Colonie,

> . . . it would be impossible to view a grander sight. The army had but just entered on the campaign, weather and fatigue had hardly yet had time to dim its brilliancy, and it was inspired with a courage born of confidence. The late Marquis de Goudrin, with whom I had the honour to ride during the march, remarked to me that France had surpassed herself in the quality of these troops; he believed the enemy had no chance whatever of breaking them in the coming conflict; if defeated now, we could never again hope to withstand them.[1]

Now, before Marlborough's watchful, appraising gaze, the French were deploying over the green corn to defend a four-mile line between the village of Autre-Eglise on their left and the River Mehaigne, at Francqnée, on their right; and he had to make up his mind how to attack them.

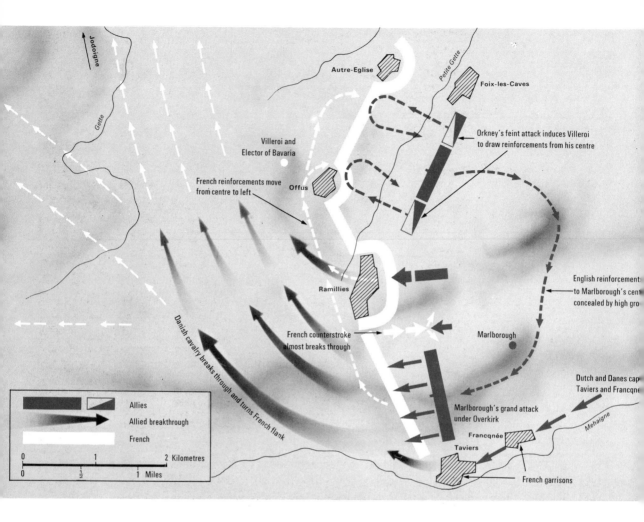

Autre-Eglise

Foix-les-Caves

Villeroi and
Elector of Bavaria

Orkney's feint attack induces Villeroi
to draw reinforcements from his centre

French reinforcements move
from centre to left

Offus

Ramillies

English reinforcement
to Marlborough's cent
concealed by high gro

French counterstroke
almost breaks through

Marlborough

Danish cavalry breaks through and turns French flank

Dutch and Danes cap
Taviers and Francqne

Marlborough's grand attack
under Overkirk

Francqnée

Taviers

French garrisons

	Allies
	Allied breakthrough
	French

0   1   2 Kilometres
0   ½   1 Miles

The battle of Ramillies, 23 May 1706

The battlefield of Ramillies is amazingly like that of Blenheim, for here too there is an immense arena of arable in which more than 100,000 men in rigid mass formations could align themselves against each other unimpeded by woods or hedges. And as at Blenheim the surface of this arena flowed in subtle and complex undulations, so that one part of it was hidden from another.

There were other, more particular resemblances. Whereas Tallard's right at Blenheim had rested on Blenheim village, by the Danube, Villeroi's right rested on Francqnée and Taviers, by the Mehaigne. And these villages, as Blenheim had been, were invisible except for their spires from the rest of the battlefield. Whereas Tallard's centre had been secured by the village of Oberglau, Villeroi's was secured by Ramillies itself, lying on a slight eminence which gave distant views to the north and east. However, there was no stream like the Nebel at Blenheim to hinder the movements of cavalry in the plain between Taviers and Ramillies. But Villeroi's left flank, like Tallard's, was protected by

'Lord Orkney, commanding the right flank, was to cross the Petite Gette with his English and Scots troops and advance on Offus . . .' The scene of Marlborough's diversionary attack during the battle of Ramillies, which induced Villeroi, the French commander, fatally to weaken the centre of his line. Offus from across the Gette

more close and broken country, and by a stream, the Petite Gette, the spring of which lay near Ramillies. Poplars stiff as grenadiers now mark the course of the Gette through its shallow valley in place of the sedge and reed which bounded the swampy stream of Marlborough's time. But even today, though diked and narrow, the Gette runs deep down between steep and slippery slopes; it would still be an obstacle to troops in clumsy parade formation. On the French side of the Gette the ground rises fairly sharply to Offus, the village which, together with Autre-Eglise further to the north, anchored Villeroi's left flank, as Lutzingen had anchored Tallard's.

When Marlborough rode along with his staff and allied officers to reconnoitre the French position, it was obvious to him, as it was to those with him, that the decisive collision must take place in the rolling plain between Taviers and Ramillies. Just as at Blenheim therefore his 'plan' was dictated by the nature of the ground. But whereas his colleagues urged him to concentrate all the allied cavalry opposite this sector, he never-

theless posted half on the slopes opposite the Gette. It was on this sector too that he chose to deploy his English infantry, their scarlet lines lurid against the lush green of the young corn, and as riveting to the eye and mind of Villeroi as they had been to Tallard's.

Villeroi himself sought diligently to avoid Tallard's errors of deployment. He put only a brigade of infantry into Taviers, with a smaller force forward in Francqnée. He packed the two-mile gap between Taviers and Ramillies with a hundred out of his hundred and thirty squadrons of cavalry, and interlined them strongly with infantry. He posted twenty battalions in and around Ramillies itself, and more infantry supported by cavalry behind the Gette from Ramillies to Offus and Autre-Eglise. In all, his army was about equal in numbers to Marlborough's, although the Duke had nearly half as many more guns. To Marlborough's professional eye the French army ranged before him under its standards and colours looked, as he told Bishop Burnet later, 'the best he had ever seen'. Villeroi was indeed strongly posted. But, by choosing to stand on the defensive, he had already presented the Duke with the initiative.

Marlborough's own deployment had taken three hours to complete. 'We began to make our lines of battle', he reported to Godolphin afterwards, 'about eleven o'clock, but we had not all our troops till two in the afternoon, at which time I gave orders for attacking them.'[2]

Lord Orkney, commanding the right flank, was to cross the Gette with his English and Scots troops and advance on Offus and Autre-Eglise; Overkirk, commanding the left, to clear the French out of Francqnée and Taviers with his Dutch and Danes.

Villeroi had posted himself near Offus, whence he could see down across the Gette to the scarlet English masses on the further slope. Had not Louis XIV warned him hardly a fortnight earlier 'to pay particular attention to that part which will bear the brunt of the first shock of the English troops'?[3] As he watched, the English infantry began to struggle through the marshes in the stream bottom despite cannon and musket fire. They clambered up on to firm ground, re-formed their ranks, and started up the slope, blasting the defenders back with their platoon volleys. Step by step, the red lines showed nearer and nearer through the smoke. Behind them English cavalry too could be seen floundering their way over the Gette.

It was plain to Villeroi that the impassable Gette was all too passable; that his left flank, which he had believed so naturally strong, was in growing peril. Soon the red-coats were close under the walls of the houses and farms of Offus and Autre-Eglise; driving their garrisons from building to building with that peculiar ferocity of English troops in attack. In rising alarm Villeroi sent to his centre between Ramillies and Taviers for strong reinforcements of cavalry and infantry. The struggle for Offus grew

LEFT *Sir William Cadogan, later Earl Cadogan (1675–1726), Marlborough's quartermaster-general and chief staff officer. Painting attributed to Louis Laguerre, c. 1716*

RIGHT *George Hamilton, Earl of Orkney (1666–1737). Painting by Martin Maingaud.*

fiercer yet. In the words of the English commander, Lord Orkney, 'I think I never had more shot about my ears.'

> . . . I endeavoured to possess myself of a village, which the French brought down a good part of their line to take possession of, and they were on one side of ye village, and I am on the other; but they always retired as we advanced.[4]

Orkney was on the very point of occupying Offus when an aide-de-camp rode up from Marlborough and told him to call off his attack and retire across the Gette. At this inexplicable order Orkney was understandably bewildered and angry – as the Duke well realized he would be. This was why, to make absolutely certain that his order reached Orkney and was obeyed, he dispatched no fewer than ten ADCs to him, and finally his Quartermaster-General, Cadogan, in person.

> I confess [wrote Orkney] it vexed me to retire. However we did it very well and in good order, and whenever the French pressed upon us, with the battalion of the guards and my own I was always able to make them stand and retire. Cadogan came and told me it was impossible I could be sustained by the horse if we went on then, and since my Lord could not attack everywhere, he would make the grand attack in the centre, and try to pierce there. . . .[5]

It had all been another Marlburian double bluff. Because the Duke had deceived Orkney into believing that his attack was seriously meant, it had carried a weight and power such as no mere feint could have emulated – and so, just as the Duke intended, completely took in Villeroi. For as Orkney's troops ebbed back across the Gette in obedience to the Duke's orders, Villeroi was congratulating himself on having repulsed a highly dangerous English advance. Nevertheless, Villeroi could still see the scarlet ranks lining the slope beyond the Gette; they might attack again; his left flank was not yet out of danger. So he failed to send back to the centre of his line the powerful forces he had withdrawn from it in order to meet Orkney's attack. Marlborough had achieved his first objective: he had induced the French commander to unbalance his dispositions. He had tricked him into thinning out those once deep and solidly packed lines of cavalry and infantry across the two miles of open plain between Ramillies and Taviers; the sector where the Duke intended eventually to launch his grand attack.

At the opposite end of the battle line, along the Mehaigne, the French had been driven out of Francqnée and Taviers by Overkirk. For the French this struggle on their right wing was becoming as much a self-contained action on its own as the struggle for Blenheim village in 1704, and for the same reason. Rising ground hid it from the French commander-in-chief's sight, posted as he was for most of the battle at the opposite end of his line near Offus, keeping an eye on the English redcoats.

But Marlborough, from a swell in the terrain midway between Ramillies and Taviers and half a mile to their eastward, enjoyed a panoramic view of almost the entire battlefield, from the spires of Francqnée and Taviers to the line of the Gette – four miles of smoke.

Now the firing along the Gette, over to the right, was beginning to slacken, as Orkney, in obedience to the Duke's order, brought his men back over the stream and took up a

The battle of Ramillies. Detail from an oil sketch by Louis Laguerre

defensive position. But the smoke was billowing thicker and thicker round Ramillies, the roar of the battle rising, as twelve battalions under the Dutch general Schultz – including Scots regiments in the Dutch service, and two English battalions – fought their way over the crest of the gentle rise in front of the village, and on into its straggle of dark-brown brick houses. Soon the French garrison were locked up in their own defence; unable to threaten the right flank of Marlborough's grand attack in the centre.

This was led by old Overkirk. The allied cavalry, supported by Dutch, German and Swiss infantry, began to move forward 'in four dense lines like walls', as they appeared to de la Colonie, extending from Ramillies to the Mehaigne. At a trot they crashed ponderously into the first line of French and Bavarian cavalry and tumbled it back. But when they rode onwards, the infantry which interlined Villeroi's cavalry volleyed them to a standstill. The Maison du Roi, the French household cavalry, thirteen squadrons strong, counter-charged them. Before the onset of these famous regiments – the Gardes du Corps, the Gens d'Armes, the Mousquetaires – Overkirk's squadrons recoiled in confusion. Just to the south of Ramillies, where a trough of low ground provided an avenue of advance eastwards, the Maison du Roi threatened to break clean through the allied ranks. But the Duke was there himself with four battalions of infantry to shore up the crumbling line. He rallied some of the Dutch squadrons and led them back into the mêlée. The furious press of horsemen strained for a time this way and that, shouting,

The Battlel of Ramillies where ȳ D of Marlbo voug.ˢ 8ᵗ: took 26. Standards & 83. Enfigns the French loßing 20000 men all their Baggage Amunition &c.

The cannonball shearing off the head of the Duke's equerry. From a contemporary pack of cards

grunting with exertion, hacking at each other like demented butchers at sides of beef. Then the allied cavalry gave way again. The French recognized the Duke in his scarlet coat with the sky-blue sash of the Garter and exultantly sought to ride him down. His horse stumbled at a ditch and threw him. In every way this was the critical moment of the battle.

> Major-General Murray [wrote an eye witness] who . . . was so near he could distinguish the Duke in the flight, seeing him fall, marched up in all haste with two Swiss battalions to save him and stop the enemy who were hewing all down in their way. The Duke when he got to his feet again saw Major-General Murray coming up and ran directly to get in to his battalions. . . .[6]

One of Marlborough's ADC's leaped off his horse and gave it to the Duke in order to speed him to safety. His French pursuers rode so furiously after him that some of them were unable to pull their horses up when they reached the Swiss infantry, and ran on to their bayonets.

A few moments later Colonel Bringfield, the Duke's equerry, brought him another of his own horses. While Bringfield was holding the Duke's stirrup and helping him to mount, a cannonball sheered off the equerry's head. According to one account the ball actually went between the Duke's legs as he was swinging his right leg across the saddle. No wonder an eye witness wrote afterwards that the Duke 'fulfilled that day all the parts of a great captain, except in that he exposed his person as the meanest soldier'.[7]

The cavalry battle in the centre had now become a slogging struggle. However, the Duke was steadily feeding into this struggle the cavalry from his right wing along the Gette, their movement concealed by rising ground from the French. The Duke, having by Orkney's attack on Villeroi's left induced the French commander to drain troops from his centre, was now strengthening his own. By late afternoon he had built up a superiority of eight to five in the decisive area, the open ground between the River Mehaigne and Ramillies. On his far left Danish cavalry beyond Taviers smashed away the French anchor on the Mehaigne and began to swing north to take Villeroi's line in flank. Gradually the French gave ground under the weight now pressing upon them inexorably from front and flank, their line bending back from the Mehaigne like an overstrained bow. About four o'clock the Duke judged it time to launch his final charge:

> I saw [wrote a French brigadier] the enemy's cavalry advance upon our people, at first at a slow pace, and then, when they thought they had gained the proper distance, they broke into a trot to gain impetus for their charge. At the same moment the Maison du Roi decided to meet them. . . . The enemy, profiting by their superior numbers, surged through the gaps in our squadrons and fell upon their rear, whilst their four lines attacked in front.[8]

While the Danish cavalry swept round the collapsing French from the south, allied infantry at last captured Ramillies and drove its garrison out on to the open plain or into the marches of the Gette.

As the French line broke so too did French morale. An Irish captain in the French service described how 'We had not got forty yards on our retreat when the words *sauve qui peut* went through the great part, if not the whole army, and put all to confusion. Then might be seen whole brigades running in disorder.'9

Too late Villeroi tried to employ his almost unused cavalry along the Gette. He ordered them to form a new line facing south, at right angles to the old, in order to cover the army's retreat. But as the spark of fear leaped from man to man all fifty squadrons rode in panic through the fleeing French infantry.

The whole plain now swarmed with the human wreckage of that proud army which had advanced across it so confidently in the morning sunshine. An immense jam of wagons and coaches blocked the muddy lanes north-westwards through Jodoigne to safety, damming up a tumult of fugitives. Marshal Villeroi and the Elector of Bavaria, stuck in the press, narrowly escaped being taken by Marlborough's pursuing cavalry. All Villeroi's fifty cannon had to be abandoned to swell the Duke's triumph. The fugitives took to the fields and woods like wild creatures, and all that evening and night the English cavalry, least engaged in the battle and therefore freshest of the allied horse, hunted them down with remorseless pleasure.

When the Duke was asked by Bishop Burnet the difference between the battles of Blenheim and Ramillies, he answered that 'the first battle lasted between seven and eight hours, and we lost above 12,000 men in it; whereas the second lasted not above two hours, and we lost not above 2,500 men.'10 Furthermore the Duke's judgment was that the French officers 'did not do their part, nor show the courage that had appeared among them on other occasions'.11

In the market square of Louvain, on the night after the battle, Villeroi's generals met in a brief council of war by the smoky flare of torches. They decided that Louvain, though a major fortress, must be abandoned, and all its stores dumped into the River Dyle. These unheroic decisions made, they spurred on again to Brussels.

Marlborough himself rode with the pursuit far into the night; then lay on the ground to snatch a little sleep wrapped in his cloak. He offered to share its shelter with a Dutch field-deputy, Sicco van Goslinga; a characteristic grace note. On the following morning, at eleven o'clock as the pursuit rolled on towards Louvain, the Duke found a moment for Sarah:

> I did not tell my dearest soul in my last letter the design I had of engaging the enemy if possible to a battle, fearing the concern she has for me might make her uneasy; but I can now give her the satisfaction of letting her know . . . that God Almighty has been pleased to give us a victory. I must leave the particulars to this bearer, Colonel Richards, for having been on horseback all Sunday, and after the battle marching all night, my head aches to that degree, that it is very uneasy for me to write. . . . Pray believe me when I assure you that I love you more than I can express.12

On 28 May the Duke rode into the Grand' Place of Brussels, a conqueror in English scarlet in the footsteps of such great captains of the past as Alva, Parma and Don John of Austria; and in the fourteenth-century Hôtel de Ville the city fathers made haste to acknowledge Charles III, the allies' candidate to the Spanish throne, as their sovereign.

Every day the magnitude of Marlborough's victory at Ramillies became clearer. The French had lost 15,000 men killed and wounded on the battlefield and as many again in prisoners: half their strength. But as a fighting force Villeroi's army was totally destroyed, the survivors a rabble ready to bolt at the first sign of the enemy. Villars characterized his brother marshal's defeat as 'the most shameful, humiliating and disastrous of routs'. He was the more enraged because Ramillies paralysed his own offensive in Germany, his army being now milked of troops to reinforce the unhappy Villeroi.

In Marlborough's own sober judgment, as expressed to Godolphin,

> The consequence of this battle is likely to be of greater advantage than that of Blenheim; for we have the whole summer before us. . . . I think we may make such a campaign as may give the queen the glory of making an honourable and a safe peace. . . .[13]

Yet the Duke confessed to Sarah from Brussels that he had 'not yet had all the pleasure I shall enjoy' in the victory, and for a familiar enough reason: 'I have been in so continual a hurry ever since the battle of Ramillies, by which my blood is so heated, that when I go to bed I sleep so unquietly that I cannot get rid of my head-ache. . . .'[14]

And still he drove the pursuit remorselessly onwards, renowned fortress cities surrendering at the first sight of his troopers.

> We are now masters of Ghent [he wrote to Sarah on 31 May], and tomorrow I shall send some troops to Bruges. So many towns have submitted since the battle, that it really looks more like a dream than truth.[15]

To Sarah again two days later:

> Every day gives us fresh marks of the great victory; for since my last . . . we have taken possession of Bruges and Damme, as also Oudenarde. . . . In short, there is so great a panic in the French army as is not to be expressed.[16]

Nevertheless, for Marlborough the real importance of the victory lay in its political effect. 'I am so persuaded,' he told Sarah, 'that this campaign will bring us a good peace, that I beg of you to do all you can that the house at Woodstock may be carried up as much as possible that I may have the prospect of being in it.'[17]

In England they were for the moment content to cheer, fire guns in joy, quaff brimming toasts in city taverns and country alehouses to the names of Marlborough and that gallant old Dutchman Overkirk; and, in more seemly fashion, to attend services of thanksgiving with wives and prayer books.

As for Mrs Morley herself, her gratitude was rapturous to the point of incoherence:

> The great Glorious Success wch God Almighty has bin pleased to Bless you wth, & his preservation of your person, one can never thank him enough for, & next to him all things

are owing to you; it is impossible for me ever to Say soe much as I aught in return of your great & faithful Services to me, but I will endeavour by all ye actions of my life to Shew you how truly Sensible I am of them. . . .[18]

And still the cities of the Spanish Netherlands were falling. At the beginning of June the fortress and port of Antwerp delivered up its keys to the Duke, receiving him not with the discharge of cannon but a feast in the bishop's palace; it had surrendered only once before in its history, and then after a siege of a hundred and twelve days. Ostend, further down the coast, resisted Marlborough for three weeks; a somewhat less resolute defence that it had offered the Spanish general Spinola a century earlier, when it held out for three years.

As the Duke swung south towards France, the entire structure of French power in the Spanish Netherlands, which at the beginning of May had seemed so invulnerable, so permanent, was collapsing like a house of which the kingpost had been shattered by a cannonball.

This process of collapse Villeroi was helpless to arrest, painful as it was to his royal master, and even though troops had been drained out of garrisons and from the French forces on the Rhine in order to make good his losses. For he knew his troops would never stand in the face of another onslaught by Marlborough. He was thankful enough to have got back under the guns of the French frontier fortresses, and there he stayed, occupying himself with composing dignified apologia to Versailles for his defeat. In August, when the Duke was laying siege to Menin, Villeroi, discredited in spite of his apologia, was replaced by Marshal Vendôme, the victor of Calcinato. Vendôme was staggered by the black defeatism in which he found his new command wallowing: '. . . everyone here,' he disgustedly wrote, 'is ready to take off his hat when one names the name of Marl-borough.'[19]

Yet Vendôme himself made no effort to relieve Menin, which, although one of the most elaborate fortresses in Europe, fell to Marlborough in less than a month. 'The Duke of Vendôme,' Marlborough observed drily, 'continues to talk more than I believe he intends to perform.' And so it was to prove.

For when Marlborough eventually closed down the Ramillies campaign in October he had completed the conquest of almost the whole Spanish Netherlands; a success beyond any that Turenne or the great Condé had ever won in a single campaign in that region. Now Louis XIV's own domains lay before his victorious sword.

He was fifty-six; formed by victory, tempered by five years of strain. Although the hair under the great wig had turned for the most part grey, the straight-nosed face was still surprisingly youthful. Sicco van Goslinga, who was at the Duke's side throughout the Ramillies campaign, has left this portrait of him:

He is above average height and with as fine a figure as you could see; he has a flawlessly handsome face; fine, flashing eyes, with a clear red and white complexion which could put the fair sex to shame; good teeth; in short, except for his legs which are too slender, one of the best-looking men you could wish to see. He has plenty of good sense and sensibility, shrewd and sound judgement, keen and deep understanding; is a good judge of men and can distinguish true worth from the bogus. He expresses himself well and pleasantly, even in French, which however he speaks very inaccurately; his intonation is warm and melodious; he is deemed one of the most attractive of speakers in his own language. He has a very gracious manner, and if his handsome and prepossessing countenance disposes everyone in his favour, his manners and gentleness captivate all those who are biased against him or displeased with him.[20]

Courtesy and consideration were central to his nature. They were bestowed not only on those people Marlborough needed for his professional ends, but also on the unfortunate or unimportant. There was, for example, the kindness he had shown to the broken Tallard after Blenheim. He made it easy after that battle and after Ramillies for captured French officers to return home on parole to settle their family affairs. A typical gesture was the sending of a case of wine in 1705 to an old acquaintance, the Duchess of Portsmouth, once Charles II's mistress and now living again in her native France.

> I must offer my excuses for the quantity, but good wine is very scarce in England at the moment because of the war. I hope you will not take it ill that I have shared my own campaign-store with you.[21]

Lord Ailesbury, a Jacobite in exile in the Low Countries, but an old friend of the Duke's and still welcome in his camp, recorded a vivid impression of the Marlborough charm in action, that charm which could make a man feel that he was the one person in Europe whose society and conversation the Duke really valued. When Ailesbury called upon the Duke in his camp at Tirlemont in September 1705, the Duke 'embraced me much and made me many protestations. At dinner, sitting by me, he would continually take me by the hand, but politickly (at which he was a great master) putting his hand under the napkin.' This was by no means the end of the courtesies, however. That night, while Ailesbury was the guest of General Lord Orkney 'at a vast supper' eaten to the music of the hautbois of the foot guards, the Duke called in uninvited. 'My Lord Orkney,' said Marlborough, pointing to Ailesbury, 'do not take it ill if I say I come here for the sake of this Lord.'

> He was perfectly merry, and for him ate much and drank heartily, and we all found the effects of the excellent wine and I never saw more mirth. The next day he asked me where I dined. I told him . . . at Count Oxenstierra's. 'I shall not be so happy,' said he, 'for I am condemned to dine with base company, and shall have as base dinner.' The three States Deputies of the [Dutch] Army had invited him, and that year they were three sad fellows and great pedants, and continually thwarting him.

The following morning the Duke, who had to go off and review Overkirk's troops, bid Ailesbury farewell, and began to climb into a one-horse chaise. But when he was

'The world saw imperturbable good temper; a mask of serene confidence which rarely slipped. To maintain this self-command in the face of all his worries and troubles . . . exacted a high price in terms of inward strain.' Marlborough. Painting by Sir Godfrey Kneller

OVERLEAF *The battle of Ramillies. British cavalry capturing the enemy's wagon train after the French army had dissolved in rout. Oil sketch for Marlborough House by Louis Laguerre*

half-way up he dismounted again and told Ailesbury that he had forgotten to show him the plans of his new house and garden at Woodstock. So inside they went again, and the plans were spread out. In Ailesbury's words, the Duke, 'in pointing out the apartments for him and lady, etc, laid his finger on one and told me, "*that* is for you when you come and see me there".'[22]

Nevertheless, courtesy and charm as genuine and spontaneous feelings shaded imperceptibly into a courtesy and charm calculated to further the Duke's professional purposes and mask his own mind. According to Sicco van Goslinga, the Duke was a man of 'deep dissimulation, all the more dangerous because he disguises it by a manner and a style of expression which appear to convey nothing but candour itself'.[23] It was a shrewd assessment. As one example, late in 1706 Marlborough wrote to Lady Peterborough, the wife of the English commander in Spain, to express the hope, as he put it in his most velvet style, of having the honour of waiting upon her in a few days himself, 'yet I would not omit in the meanwhile acknowledging the favour of your obliging letter, and of the packet of papers accompanying it from my Lord Peterborough, with whom you may be sure I shall readily embrace all opportunities to improve the friendship that has been so long between us.'[24] To Sarah, however, he placed a rather different valuation on his friendship with the Peterboroughs: 'I have observed . . . that the next misfortune to that of having friendships with such people is, that of having any dispute with them, and that care should be taken to have as little to do with them as possible.'[25]

Yet as Lord Chesterfield noted, despite all Marlborough's affability, 'no man living was more conscious of his situation, nor maintained his dignity better'.[26] He was not only a duke now, but also a prince: kings addressed him in their letters as 'Mon Cousin'. His outlook was becoming more European than mere English, for he was out of England for more than two-thirds of each year, moving amid the grand formalities of Europe in the baroque age; himself one of its most illustrious personages. If he were to exert the influence he ought with kings, princes and margraves, it was inevitable and essential that he should carry himself with that state, that consciousness of his own rank, which they respected. This was indeed his principal reason for accepting the principality of Mindelheim.

His critics at home nevertheless objected to such un-English manifestations as the title 'highness' which he had assumed on the Continent and which 'was given him by all the officers of the army'.[27] At the end of 1707 the Genoese ambassador was to report that the Duke affected an almost royal state, receiving the important on his bedchamber while he put on his shirt and shaved. The former page and gentleman of the bedchamber must have relished being the principal actor in such scenes instead of one of the supporting cast. But did he, as his critics suggest, relish it too much? Was the role beginning to usurp the man?

Yet while on campaign Marlborough lived very simply except when entertaining visiting grandees in the way of business. Instead of the lavish table kept by commanders such as Prince Eugène or the French marshals, he preferred to eat quietly with his

The thanksgiving service in St Paul's for the victory at Ramillies, attended by the Queen and members of both Houses of Parliament

Marlborough's chocolate cup made from a coconut with silver mounts, and his silver-gilt toothpick case

military 'family' – Cadogan, Cardonnel and a few others. On the march to Blenheim he dined each day at the table of one or other of his generals; as good a way as any of keeping his finger on the pulse of his army, and in turn transmitting his own ideas and spirit of command.

On the other hand he loved to play host by way of celebration; he loved to see others enjoying themselves.

> Lord Cadogan used to say that he remembered seeing the Duke completely out of humour one day, a thing very unusual with him, and much agitated; in the evening, however a messenger arrived who brought him some news which he liked. He immediately ordered the messenger to be placed in some place where no one could speak to him, [so as to keep the good news as a surprise] and ordered his coach to be opened, and some cantines to be taken out, containing some hams and other good things, and spread before some of the principal officers, he looking on and tasting nothing.[28]

There were not wanting those to say that the simplicity of the Duke's way of life in the field, his fondness for being a guest at other men's tables, were proofs of his meanness and avarice. That he *was* both mean and avaricious was widely accepted, both in England and on the Continent. He was said in 1692 to have had only three coats, one of which he saved for great state occasions; and to walk home from the Palace through streets thick with mud rather than spend money on a sedan chair. There is a more circumstantial version of this latter story, dating from after the Duke's retirement. When the Duke was staying in Bath, Lord Bath and his brother, General Pulteney, who had been Marl-borough's ADC, played cards with him at Lord Bath's lodgings.

> The Duke had lost some money, and on going away desired General Pulteney to lend him sixpence to pay his chair-hire. This he of course did, and when the Duke left the room, Lord Bath said to his brother, 'I would venture any sum, now, that the Duke goes home on foot. Do pray follow him out.' The General followed him and to his astonishment saw him walk home to his lodgings.[29]

Other stories of the Duke's meanness, if invented, seem to belong to that category of fond exaggerations which commanders of strong personality often inspire from their troops; if true, they reveal no more than a rather touching eccentricity. According to one anecdote, for example, when an officer brought an urgent message to Marlborough in the middle of the night, the Duke asked whether or not it was in writing. When he was told that it was verbal, he said, 'Then put out the light.' On another occasion, the story went, the Duke's linen gaiters got soaking wet while he was riding in the rain, so that they could not be removed without tearing. He therefore instructed the servant to take care to rip them down the seam, so that they could be sewn together again.

What is certain is that as the administrator of an army and as a private person Marl-borough hated waste, and practised the utmost thrift. Branded deep in his character was the memory of his impoverished early life, and the insecurity and ignominy that went with it. As Sarah, when an old lady of eighty-four defending his memory against the charge of avarice, was to write:

> The Duke of Marlborough never had any vanity, and therefore living so many years with great employments he left a great estate, which was no wonder he should do, since he lived long, and never threw money away, and money was for many years at 6 per cent.[30]

Nor was he necessarily mean because he saved gaiters and neglected to keep a magnifi-cent table for the free enjoyment of others in the style expected of a great man of the time. After his capture of Cork and Kinsale in 1690, for example, he made provision for the destitute Irish prisoners of war. Sarah Marlborough was to avow, and it has the ring of truth:

> He had a great deal of compassion in his nature, and . . . he gave money out of his own pocket to those that were poor. . . . For I was directed by him to pay some pensions when he was abroad, and have letters to prove the truth of it from the persons.[31]

Of his compassion there is no question, whether it be for the sufferings of his own or enemy wounded soldiers after a battle, or for individuals such as the widow and family of Colonel Bringfield, killed while holding his horse at Ramillies, whom he particularly asked Godolphin to commend to the Queen's care. On the eve of Ramillies, deprived though he was of Prussian troops by the awkwardness of the Prussian King, the Duke nevertheless found time to write a letter to the English ambassador in Berlin asking him to solicit a pension for the widow of a Prussian officer killed in the last campaign. Wellington too was compassionate, but he hid it behind a peremptory harshness; moreover he could be brutally cruel to his subordinates while in his fortunately rare icy rages. There was nothing of this about Marlborough, who was gentle to a degree possibly unique in a great commander.

> . . . for his natural good temper [wrote Lord Ailesbury], he never had his equal. He could not chide a servant, . . . and in command he could not give a harsh word, no not to the meanest Sergeant, Corporal or Soldier.[32]

Yet though he lacked the conventional panoply of authority there was about him a power which not only English soldiers, but also Dutch, Danish, Swiss and German recognized and responded to; they were ready to follow wherever he led them, certain that under Corporal John all would go well. For as with Nelson and his fleet the bond between Marlborough and his army was of a mutual trust which transcended mere authority and obedience. An insight into what Marlborough meant to his troops is offered by the army's state of mind when in October 1705 he had to quit it for a while in order to consult with the Dutch at The Hague. According to an eye witness:

> In his absence we were a body without a soul. The French having thrown down a little of their line, and laid bridges . . . for the purpose of forage, we were in perpetual alarms, as if an inferior dispirited army would leave their lines because the duke had left us.[33]

Marlborough for his part, a man of warm affections, felt the loneliness of his position; and in the absence of Sarah needed the society and support of his military 'family' the more. In August 1706 he was desolated when an officer from a foraging party brought him the news that

> . . . poor Cadogan is taken prisoner or killed, which gives me a great deal of uneasiness, for he loved me, and I could rely on him. I am now sending a trumpet to the governor of Tournay, to know if he be alive; for the horse that beat him came from that garrison. I have ordered the trumpet to return this night, for I shall not be quiet till I know his fate.[34]

Fortunately Cadogan had been taken alive, and the Duke made haste to arrange his exchange with a French officer in English hands.

Although in 1706 Marlborough and Prince Eugène had not campaigned together for two years, the Duke still cherished his comradeship. When in September he heard of Eugène's brilliant relief of the Duke of Savoy's capital, Turin, in the face of a far larger French army, he wrote to Sarah that 'it is impossible for me to express the joy it has given me; for I do not only esteem, but I really love that Prince.'[35] These feelings for Eugène were unalloyed by the slightest trace of professional jealousy. He made a point of telling Heinsius, for example, that 'I am assured that the French take more to hart (sic) their misfortunes in Italie, then (sic) thay did that of Ramillie.'[36]

He was, however, correspondingly hurt and angry if his friendship was abused. Early in 1705 Count Wratislaw, the Imperial minister, virtually accused him of betraying confidences to the English ambassador in Vienna from Wratislaw's private letters. Marlborough dispatched a formidably stern rebuke;

> . . . I must . . . confess to you . . . that I take it in very ill part that you could believe me capable of disclosing extracts from your letters. I had expected quite a different treatment from you. I see besides from all the rest of your letter that our correspondence is likely in the future to be very sterile, and as perhaps you have not kept a copy [of your letter] I send it back to you so that you may see the coldness with which you quit me.[37]

Yet such sternness was uncommon enough. The world saw only imperturbable good temper; a mask of serene confidence which rarely slipped. To maintain this self-command in the face of all his worries and troubles, to say nothing of the sheer burden of work, exacted a high price in terms of inward strain. 'It is most certain that upon many occasions I have the spleen, and am weary of my life. . . .'[38] Occasionally – as after the battle of the Schellenberg – he succumbed to a kind of prostration of will. He was dogged by headaches and eyestrain; perhaps the symptoms of migraine, more likely psychological, as he himself believed. 'I own to you,' he confessed to Sarah during the abortive Moselle campaign of 1705, 'that my sickness comes from fretting. . . .'[39]

Even if he had had the time to seek escape in reading, he lacked the inclination, despite an education at St Paul's School. The intellectually refined, such as Lord Chesterfield, politely despised the Duke for his want of culture and general knowledge. The Duke displayed his breezy unconcern for those matters when in 1705 the Professor of Greek at Cambridge brought an edition of Anacreon to the war department in the hope of dedicating it to him, and collecting, as was the custom of the time, a few guineas from him, the great man thus honoured.

> Mr St John, who was Secretary at War, was then in the room, the Duke comes up to him: 'Dear Harry, here's a man comes to me and talks to me about one Anna Creon, and I know nothing of Creon, but Creon in the play of Oedipus, prithee do you speak to the man.'[40]

His family, his house and his garden – these and his prayers provided his mental refuge from the stress of command. During his first campaign in 1702 he wrote wistfully to tell Sarah that 'We have now very hote weather, which I hope will ripen the frute at St Alban's. When you are there, pray think how happy I should be to be out of this crowd, and walking alone with you.'[41] And during his marchings near the Danube in 1704:

> You have forgot to order Hodges to send me a draught of a stable, as I directed him for the Lodge [Windsor Lodge, given to Sarah for life by the Queen on her accession, along with the Rangership of Windsor Park]; for it ought not to be made use of till the year after it is built; and as I see you set your heart on that place I should be glad all conveniences were set about it.[42]

From 1704 onwards it was the progress of the splendid palace slowly rising at Wood-stock, to be named Blenheim in eternal celebration of his victory, which took his mind

RIGHT '. . . *a great pleasure at my return, if I could see the walks in the park planted.' A plan for the grounds and gardens of Blenheim Palace, 1709*

BELOW '. . . *massive and masculine, it looms across the English countryside like the charge of a victorious army.' Blenheim Palace, Sir John Vanbrugh, architect*

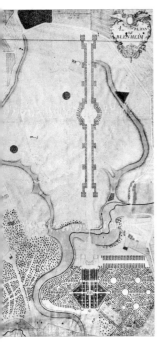

off his cares. In 1705, for example, when all was going wrong on the Moselle, he was urging Sarah: 'Pray press on my house and garden; for I think I shall never stir from my own home. . . .'[43] Two months later, in the midst of his vexations over Slangenberg:

> I hope some time this summer you will go down to Woodstock for three or four days, and that you will let me know if Mr Wise [the famous landscape gardener] be still of the opinion that he shall be able to make all the plantations this next season, which would be a great pleasure to me at my return, if I could see the walks in the park planted.[44]

During the heatwave of June 1707 he was to have more gardening advice for Sarah:

> If you have the same weather, it must make all sortes of fruit very good; and as this is the 3rd yeare of the trees at Woodstock, if possible, I shou'd wish that you might, or somebody you can relie on, taste the fruit of every tree, so that what is not good may be chang'd. On this matter you must advise with Mr Wise, as also what place may be proper for the ice-house; for that shou'd be built this sumer, so that it might have time to dry. The Hott weather makes me think of these things, for the most agreeable of all the presents I receive is that of ice.[45]

But the Duke was only to be cast down by Sarah's dutiful report of her discussions with Mr Wise:

> Your expression of the ice-house, that it can't be of use these three years, is a very melancholy prospect to me, who am turned on the ill side of fifty-seven.[46]

Now it was December 1706, and he was home again, an English general to an English triumph. Between the serried and cheering mouths of the humble, he jolted in a procession of coaches loaded with their betters, the horse grenadiers at the head escorting twenty-six gentlemen each bearing a French standard captured at Ramillies, and the foot guards in the rear escorting a hundred and twenty-six pikemen each bearing a French colour. He was ceremonially crammed at a banquet in Vintners' Hall given by the City of London. The Lords and Commons had already presented their addresses of congratulation; the Commons, not stinting the hyperbole, described Ramillies as a victory 'so glorious and great in its consequences, and attended with such continued successes . . . that no age can equal'.

More gratifying to the Duke than hyperbole, however well turned, was that both Houses willingly gave effect by act of Parliament to his request that his title might descend through the female line; that the estate and house at Woodstock should be rendered inseparable from the title; and that the pension of £5,000 a year, granted to him for life after the Battle of Blenheim, should pass to his heirs in perpetuity. So, triumphing over smallpox by act of Parliament, he founded his family – his dynasty – at last; and as long as the world endured, there would be a Marlborough at Blenheim Palace.

At the end of 1706, therefore, he seemed to have topped out the splendid edifice of his career. But in fact the foundations of that edifice were already beginning to shift and slide.

CHAPTER ELEVEN

A BACK WAY TO
THE QUEEN'S CLOSET

In midsummer 1706, during the euphoria of conquest that followed Ramillies, Marl-borough had convinced himself that 'this campaign will bring us a good peace'. If the Duke's conviction had come true, Ramillies would have been his Waterloo, washing him up like Wellington on to the safe high shore of final victory. Instead Ramillies was to prove more like his Austerlitz: the bright crest of a wave which for all its power still fell short of finality, and which, in breaking, left him and his career at the mercy of a dragging and an ever more dangerous undertow.

Yet the chance of 'a good peace' was there after Ramillies. In August Louis XIV put forward fresh peace feelers to The Hague. Stimulated by disaster, he offered to concede almost all that the allies had originally gone to war in order to secure. He would recognize Anne as sovereign of England instead of the Pretender 'James III'. He would acknow-ledge that he had no interest in the succession to her throne. He would even leave Spain

Louis XIV. The 30-ton marble
bust on the pediment of the
south front at Blenheim Palace.
Marlborough removed it from
Tournai after the siege in 1709.

to the allied candidate, Charles III, providing that his own candidate, the Duke of Anjou ('Philip V') might have Naples, Sicily and Milan as compensation. He would concede the Dutch their 'barrier' in the Spanish Netherlands.

Louis's proposals, as that astute monarch intended, levered a crowbar in between the English and the Dutch. For Marlborough's successes had left the Dutch with less and less cause to fight on. They were now in possession of their barrier of territory and fortresses, give or take a town or two. Therefore, as the Duke reported to Godolphin on 30 August 1706:

> It is publicly said at the Hague that France is reduced to what it ought to be, and that if the war should be carried farther, it would serve only to make England greater than it ought to be. In short, I am afraid our best allies are very fond of a peace.[1]

Nevertheless, the Duke seems to have felt a personal sympathy for the Dutch desire for a compromise peace:

> I . . . shal obaye your commands as far as I dare [he wrote to Heinsius on 21 August 1706], for as a good Englishman I must be of the opinion of my country, that both by treaty and interest, we are obliged to preserve the Monarque [monarchy] of Spain entier. At the same time as a friend I must own, that I believe France can hardly be brought to a peace, unless something be given to the Duke of Anjoue, so that he may preserve the tytle of king.[2]

This letter sums up what was to be Marlborough's attitude towards peace negotiations for the rest of the war: whatever his private doubts, he must submit to official English policy. It was an unheroic attitude for a man of his unique position. Perhaps he feared that the government (and even himself) might be brought down by the infuriated Whigs if it dared to propose settling for less than 'no peace without Spain – entire'. Yet if he had now thrown the full weight of his prestige on the side of compromise, he might well have brought his victory at Ramillies to its consummation in a peace. Instead, and not for the first or last time in his life, he seemed to shrink from making an open stand for an unpopular view, as if he found it more congenial to 'venture' in the field than off it.

In his role of passive servant of English policy, the Duke now induced the Dutch to fight on by dangling a bribe of a 'super-barrier' which would include as yet untaken French fortresses. The problem of peace would be solved by the sword.

The year 1707 opened promisingly enough with a successful diplomatic mission to Charles XII of Sweden, a warrior-king with the garb and manners of a trooper of the old school, who had invaded Saxony in the wake of victories over the Russians and the Poles. It was Louis XIV's hope that Charles might now care to join in the war of the Spanish succession on the side of France, and he lavished the skills and gold coin of French diplomacy to this end. It fell to Marlborough to go off to Charles XII's court at Altranstädt on behalf of the allies, and persuade Charles to keep to his own northern war. On being ushered into the Swedish King's presence the Duke blandly buried him in a cartload of Marlburian flattery of the ripest quality.

I present to your majesty a letter, not from the chancery, but from the heart of the queen, my mistress, and written with her own hand. Had not her sex prevented it, she would have crossed the sea to see *a prince admired by the whole universe*. I am in this particular more happy than the queen; *and I wish I could serve some campaigns under so great a general as your majesty, that I might learn what I yet want to know in the art of war.*[3]

The Duke correctly guessed, however, from all he gleaned at the Swedish court that Charles XII was not interested in fighting Louis XIV's battles, but rather in toppling the Tsar of Russia off his throne. It only remained therefore for Marlborough to distribute English pensions to Swedish ministers and return to the Netherlands.

Unfortunately this mission to Charles XII of Sweden was the Duke's only success in 1707. Far from bringing a victorious peace in the wake of fresh triumphs on the battle-field, as he hoped and expected, the year witnessed only stalemate diversified by calamity.

The Duke's strategy was once again ambitious and intricate, calling for punctilious timing by allied forces in Italy, Spain, Germany and the Netherlands; and once again it fell to pieces. Despite Marlborough's efforts to dissuade him, the Habsburg Emperor sent his forces in Italy off on a jaunt southwards to conquer Naples, so delaying an invasion of Provence and a siege of the French naval base at Toulon which Marlborough had designed as the major allied operation of the year.

Louis XIV caught between England and Holland, with William III looking on. Engraving 1706

During this delay catastrophe overtook the allied cause in Spain, when the Earl of Galway was routed by the Duke of Berwick at Almanza and his army completely destroyed. By a curiosity of the tangled religious and political loyalties of the time, Galway, the allied commander, was a Protestant French émigré, while Berwick, one of Louis XIV's most able generals, was a Roman Catholic Englishman, and, moreover, Marlborough's own nephew, being the bastard of his elder sister Arabella and James II.

When the Habsburg forces in Italy eventually marched on Toulon, Prince Eugène, their commander, who had never been as keen on the operation as Marlborough himself, displayed less than his usual energy. The French were ready for him; the siege was a failure; and by August the dustcloud of Eugène's army, winding slowly back into Italy along a thyme-scented road above the Mediterranean, was all that remained of Marlborough's great hope for the year.

In Germany the incompetent allied commander, the Margrave of Bayreuth, was surprised by Marshal Villars, who, to the immense alarm of the local princelings, raided deep into southern Germany.

And in the Netherlands the Duke himself achieved nothing in the face of a French army numerically stronger than his own, operating from the protection of the French frontier fortresses and skilfully handled by Marshal Vendôme. The weather that summer was remarkable even for the Low Countries. After being as scorching hot and dusty in June as the Duke remembered it in Tangier, it turned so cold by August that he had his winter clothes on and a fire in his room. Worse, so much rain had fallen that 'I can hardly stir out of my quarter, the dirt being up to the horse bellies.'[4] It did nothing to raise the Duke's spirits that Lord Peterborough, sacked from command in Spain at the beginning of the year, and a man of shallow and giddy mind, was then staying with him: '. . . the ill weather hinders me from going abroad [out],' he complained to Sarah, 'so that Lord Peterborough has the opertunity of very long conversation. What is said one day the next destroyes, so that I have desir'd him to putt his thoughts in writting. . . .'[5] Three days later came this sardonic cry from the heart: 'Lord Peterborough has said all that is possible to me, but says nothing of leaving the army. . . .'[6]

Despite all Marlborough's efforts to manœuvre or bait Vendôme into battle, the French marshal was not to be drawn. The campaign closed in the gloom of stalemate; the Duke himself, according to gossip in the army, was by now 'much out of humour and peevish'.[7]

When after Marlborough's return to England, the High Tory Earl of Rochester presumed to criticize his generalship in the House of Lords, he was stung to public anger; a rare occurrence which revealed how sensitive he was to his failure to fulfil the splendid promise of the Ramillies campaign. Denouncing Rochester as an armchair critic who knew nothing of the realities of war, he hotly asserted that once Vendôme had weakened his army by detaching troops for the defence of Toulon, he, Marlborough, had 'lost not a moment in dancing after them who retired from post to post and could not be brought to fight. . . . We cannot promise every day victories. . . .'[8]

'. . . veteran of many battles and renowned for his uncouth and dirty habits . . .' Louis Joseph de Bourbon, Duc de Vendôme (1654–1712). Detail of a painting by Jean Gilbert Murat (1807–1863), commissioned for Versailles by Louis-Philippe

Yet after the rebuff of Louis XIV's peace feelers in 1706, only victories would do. As it was, a peace on English terms was even more distant at the end of 1707 than 1706; and in the meantime Marlborough's own position at home and abroad was beginning to crumble.

Thanks to the Habsburg Emperor Joseph, the Duke's friendship with Anthonie Heinsius had lost something of its former warmth and candour. In June 1706 the Emperor, in the name of 'Charles III' of Spain, had offered the Duke the Governor-Generalship of the Spanish Netherlands, then swiftly falling to the Duke's forces. To a man as ambitious as Marlborough, it was a magnificent prize, conferring on him quasi-royal status and an income of £60,000 a year. Moreover, it would lend him still greater consequence in his dealings with kings and princes, and place in his hands the administration of a country now vital to his army's operations. Queen Anne and her ministers were happy that the Duke should accept the post. However, he realized that, in his own words, he must take care that the Dutch took no jealousy. They had, after all, their own interest in the occupied territories. Unfortunately, through Habsburg mismanagement or worse, Heinsius and the States-General only learned of the Emperor's offer after it had been made privately to the Duke. That the Emperor should have sought to settle the future government of the Spanish Netherlands without first consulting them, and done so in an apparently underhand fashion, deeply angered the Dutch. Marlborough, taken aback by the evident strength of Heinsius's feelings, hastened to try to put things right:

> I write this to beg of you to do me the justice to be fermly (sic) persuaded that I shall make no step in this matter but what shall be by the advice of the States, for I prefer infinetly their friendshipe before any particular interest to myself; for I thank God and the Queen I have no need or desire of being richer, but have a very great ambition of doing everything that can be for the Publick good. . . .[9]

The Duke was tugged between the wish at all costs not to forfeit the already jeopardized goodwill of the Dutch, and the hope that they might after all sanction his acceptance of the governor-generalship. But they refused to do so. Now it was Marlborough's turn to feel resentment, for their refusal implied a lack of trust in him personally which his past services to them hardly merited. Finally it was the Emperor's turn as well to have hard feelings, when he received Marlborough's letter formally declining his offer; feelings which also were to linger, for Vienna was never again to regard the Duke with quite the same trust and admiration.

Heinsius, for his part, cannot have relished the Duke's pointed warnings later in 1706 that the highhandedness of Dutch officials was fast turning the people of the Spanish Netherlands against the allies. Although justified by the facts, these warnings could only carry the implication that things would have been otherwise had the Duke been permitted to become governor-general.

So it was that the victory at Ramillies, instead of warming the friendship between Marlborough and Heinsius, touched it with frost.

In regard to Marlborough's relations with Queen Anne, however, it was not a question of a mere touch of frost, but of the approach of bitter midwinter.

All through 1706, while the Duke had been laying siege to the cities of Flanders, the Whig leaders had been laying siege to Godolphin. As their price for supporting the government in the next parliamentary session they demanded that a member of their 'Junto', or leadership, should be appointed as one of the two secretaries of state. The Whig Junto believed that they had made a cunning choice of candidate in the Earl of Sunderland – 'driving the nail that would go', as they exquisitely put it. For Sunderland was the Marlboroughs' son-in-law.

Unfortunately they could hardly have picked a more unsuitable nail for the timber. Queen Anne detested the thought of him, as a notoriously doctrinaire Whig. Moreover, she had heard that Sunderland was personally overbearing and intellectually arrogant. A monarch and a secretary of state saw much of each other. Anne did not wish to see much of Sunderland. 'I am afraid', she explained to Godolphin, 'hee and I should not agree long together; finding by experience my humour and those that are of warmer will often have misunderstandings. . . .'[10] Could she have been half-thinking here of Sunderland's mother-in-law, dear but formidable Mrs Freeman?

In any case Anne was fighting for a principle in resisting the Whigs. She was determined that she and her government should not fall into the hands of either political party. She wished to preserve the sovereign's right to choose the best men in the country as ministers, regardless of their party; she was not the only, or the last, of her countrymen to dream of such happy impossibilities. In 1705 she had reluctantly given way to Godolphin's and the Duke's insistence that something must be done to please the Whigs, and had agreed to appoint Sir William Cowper as Lord Keeper of the Great Seal. But that was enough; and with Sunderland as the next candidate, quite enough.

Between this royal obduracy and the pressure of the Whigs the harassed Godolphin was ever more uncomfortably squeezed, like an olive in a press.

At the same time it was Godolphin's judgment that the government must have Whig support if it were to survive the next parliamentary session. And so, with the utmost distaste and reluctance, Godolphin, under siege himself, set about laying siege to the Queen on behalf of the Whigs.

Sarah, however, being a Whig by conviction, a friend of members of the Junto, and mother-in-law to their candidate for office, joined in with enthusiasm, bombarding Anne with an immense weight of tiresome argument. This was Sarah at her worst: tactless and hectoring, and with more than a hint of the intellectually *haut* bringing enlightenment to the intellectually *bas*. With what relief must 'poor, unfortunate, faithful' Mrs Morley have sunk back on her cushions when the moment came for Mrs Freeman to sweep out of the royal closet in a grand rustle of taffeta and take her powerful personality elsewhere for a time; apply that no-nonsense – and no subtlety – mind to some other business in her very busy life.

For Mrs Morley, at forty-one, lacked the vitality to cope with Mrs Freeman's batterings. Pregnancies had left her a slow, crippled, sickly hulk.

> Her majesty [wrote a Scots visitor to the royal closet in 1706] was labouring under a fit of the Gout, and in extreme pain and agony, and in this occasion everything about her was in much the same disorder as about the meanest of her subjects. Her face, which was red and spotted, was rendered something frightful by her negligent dress, and the foot affected was fixed up with a poultis and some nasty bandages.[11]

Now perhaps more than ever since the early days of the Cockpit circle Mrs Morley looked for comfort and support from those close to her. Instead she found herself fighting off a prolonged political siege by those very friends of the Cockpit circle who had once been her champions against the world. And the more relentlessly Mr Montgomery and Mrs Freeman pressed their siege, the more Mrs Morley's resistance stiffened. For although her body may now have become feeble, her character was sturdy enough, particularly when she was under attack. As the year 1706 wore on, and Mr Montgomery and Mrs Freeman kept on and on at her, Mrs Morley therefore began to entertain a fresh emotion towards Mr Montgomery and Mrs Freeman – that of resentment. She not only entertained it, but she displayed it.

Mr Freeman, campaigning in Flanders, learned of Mrs Morley's growing coolness with alarm, for he realized at once all the personal, political, and international implications it held.

> I shall be very uneasy [he wrote to Godolphin on 16 September] til I hear from you that everything is easy between Mrs Morley and yourself: for without that I shall have no heart to act in anything, being sure that all things must go to distruction.[12]

Instead he learned from Godolphin some time later that 'The uneasiness between the queen and myself continues as it was. . . .'

In the case of Mrs Freeman, however, Mrs Morley's attitude had by October hardened from 'uneasiness' into profound affront, after the suppressed tensions between the two women had been exploded by a combination of bad luck and Mrs Freeman's tactlessness. She dispatched to the Queen a letter briskly summarizing the arguments she had been repeating all summer – 'But 'tis certain that your government can't be carried on with a part of the Tories, and the Whigs disobliged. . . .' The letter concluded by assuring Mrs Morley that

> Your security and the nation's is my chief wish, and I beg God Almighty . . . that Mr & Mrs Morley may see their errors as to this notion before it is too late; but considering how little impression any thing makes from your faithful Freeman, I have troubled you too much, & I beg pardon for it.[13]

The tone of this letter, impertinent, impatient, was in any case little calculated to warm Mrs Morley's feelings for its author. But unfortunately Mrs Morley misread Mrs Freeman's hasty handwriting, taking the word 'notion' as 'nation'. Mrs Freeman was impugning her entire conduct as Queen of England! It was insolence, an insult, not to be borne from anyone, especially an old friend against whom she now nourished a well-accumulated resentment. She therefore made Mrs Freeman no reply; a mistake, for it provoked Mrs Freeman into another salvo of argument. Mr Montgomery, upon learning of Mrs Morley's anger, made haste to point out that she had misread Mrs Freeman's letter. It signified little; Mrs Morley's reactions to Mrs Freeman had now become, and were to remain, those of a gouty toe to well-directed buffeting.

Nor could Mr Freeman in Flanders escape embroilment in the question of Sunderland's appointment. Both Godolphin and Sarah looked to him to intervene decisively with the Queen. But whereas Godolphin was content to implore him to use his immense personal influence, Sarah wanted him to bully Anne, as she herself was bullying her. Because the Duke refused to do so, Sarah nagged away at him as well as the Queen. This marred the Duke's enjoyment of the conquests which followed Ramillies. Despite his patience and his fondness for his wife, he began, like the Queen, to grow weary at Sarah's constant prodding and complaining. In his driest manner he wrote to Sarah on 7 October:

> I could wish with all my heart every thing were more to your mind; for I find when you wrote most of them [her recent letters], you had very much the spleen, and in one I had my share, for I see I labour under the same misfortune I have ever done, of not behaving as I ought to the queen.[14]

Marlborough was too fond of Queen Anne as a person, too conscious of the dangers of upsetting her, too full of reverence for the office of monarch, to relish bullying her. Instead he sought with a blend of tact, courtesy and firmness to convince her that she must give way:

> But madam [he wrote on 24 October], the truth is that the heads of one party [the High Tories] have declared against you and your government as far as it is possible without going into open rebellion. Now, should your majesty disoblige the others, how is it possible to obtain near five millions for carrying on the war with vigour, without which all is undone.[15]

It was unanswerable; but middle-aged ladies who have made up their minds are not to be swayed by anything so slight as an unanswerable argument. Only in November, after the Duke had returned to England, did the Queen finally surrender, and only then because the Duke and Godolphin intimated that they could not carry on unless she accepted Sunderland as secretary of state.

The Whigs were satisfied for the moment; in the parliamentary session of 1706–7 government measures for carrying on the war were voted through with alacrity; and Godolphin's political anxieties were temporarily eased.

But the besiegers' eventual success in their long siege of the Queen had been dearly bought. For the first casualty had been the Cockpit relationship, even though the ritual

of 'Mrs Morley', 'Mr Montgomery' and 'Mr and Mrs Freeman' was to continue for some time yet, along with an outward but ever more strained cordiality. It was a fateful development. The Marlboroughs had risen to greatness not least because of their intimacy with Anne. The Duke's present power rested, where it did not rest on his own prestige, on the Queen's continuing favour, for he was a royal servant, without a political base. Fortunately Anne displayed least coolness towards Marlborough himself, who was glorifying her reign with victory. Nevertheless, this could change; the resentment she felt for the Duke's friend Godolphin and even more for the Duke's wife could easily be displaced on to him.

LEFT TO RIGHT *Queen Anne, painting by Sir Peter Lely. Sarah Marlborough, painting by Sir Godfrey Kneller. A portrait thought at one time to be of Abigail Hill, Lady Masham (d. 1734) by an unknown artist c. 1700 (?)*

In the summer months of 1707, when Marlborough was trying in vain to bring Vendôme to battle, he was disquieted to receive reports from Sarah and Godolphin that a new menace had arisen at home. They feared that the Queen had found other confidential friends, who were covertly fomenting her hostility towards her old Cockpit intimates and their advice. Sarah had first begun to suspect as early as the winter of 1705–6 that there was a hidden and malign influence behind the Queen's growing alienation. By June 1707 she had divined who the villain was: Abigail Masham (née Hill), one of the Queen's bedchamber women. It was a sour irony that it was Sarah who had originally found Abigail her place at court, for she was Sarah's cousin. This act of kindness from Duchess Sarah towards a poor branch of the family Abigail was never to forgive.

Abigail was one of those meek who mean to inherit the earth; poor, obscure, mousy, red-nosed, sly, apt at dropping a curtsey – and her eyes – before her betters, and keeping her envies and jealousies of them to herself. As bedchamber woman, a semi-menial job even though discharged by the gentle born, it fell to her to act as nurse and companion to the ailing Queen; to plump the pillows and make the tea; to ease with gentle and self-effacing conversation the tedium of the sickbed and the discomforts of the gout; and to amuse the royal invalid with her tiny talent for mimicry. In this intimacy of the bed-chamber, the Queen, with her lifelong craving for absolute loyalty and affection, warmed towards the soothing, attentive Abigail. As the Queen saw less and less of busy Mrs Freeman, and then only to be nagged by her, so the friendship between the Queen and Abigail thickened, becoming almost a conspiracy against Mrs Freeman. Sarah describes how on one occasion when she was with the Queen, having gone to her bedchamber 'very privately by a secret passage',

> on a sudden this woman, not knowing I was there, came in with the boldest and gayest air possible, but, upon sight of me, stopped; and immediately, changing her manner, and making a most solemn courtsey, *did your Majesty ring*? And then went out again. This singular behaviour needed no interpreter *now*, to make it understood.[16]

In June 1707 Sarah found out that Abigail had got married with the Queen's knowledge, but without either of them telling her. Sarah was not pleased at this double deception, even though she had to recognize that Abigail's new husband, Samuel Masham, was exactly suitable for her, 'being a soft good-natured, insignificant man always making low bows to everybody, and ready to skip to open a door'.[17]

So the Duke had to take his mind off French marshals and consider how to out-manoeuvre a bedchamber woman. 'If you are so sure', he wrote to Sarah, 'that 256 [Abigail] does speak of business to 42 [the Queen], I should think you might speak to her with some caution [warning], which might do good, for she certainly is gratefule, and will mind what you say.'[18] After all, Abigail was politically nothing, no matter how close the intimacy of the bandage and the 'poultis' she might now enjoy with the Queen. But the Duke was out of touch with the realities of this particular battlefield. All too soon he learned that Sarah and Godolphin suspected that Abigail was only a tool, albeit a tool well adapted to its purpose; and that the real villain was Robert Harley, Secretary of State for the Northern Department, and a close government colleague of the Duke and Godolphin.

Insinuation into the Queen's confidence through the medium of such as Abigail was entirely congenial to Harley's temperament. In the nickname of 'Robin the Trickster' his countrymen paid tribute to his cunning as a politician. Harley, a secretive man, concealed himself behind halting and convoluted language. As Cowper, the Whig Lord Keeper, put it, the bias of his character was

. . . never to deal clearly and openly but always with Reserve, if not Dissimulation, or rather Simulation; & to love Tricks even where not necessary, but from an inward Satisfaction he took in applauding his own Cunninge. If any Man was ever born under a necessity of being a knave, he was.[19]

Paradoxically enough, however, Harley, a moderate Tory with a Puritan family tradition, was a man of political principle: the principle of balance and the middle road. Ever since the General Election of 1705 he had disagreed more and more with Godolphin's and the Duke's policy of wooing the Whig Junto. He was convinced that appeasing the Whigs would only whet their greed for office, and was, moreover, unnecessary. In his judgment it was still possible to rally enough moderates of both parties behind the 'Queen's servants' to assure the government's survival. By the end of 1706 Harley had come to believe that under Godolphin's leadership the Queen and her administration would fall into the hands of the Junto, and the worst of political horrors, party government, would have arrived. This the man of the middle road intended to prevent if he could.

Although Harley's aim was lofty, his method was characteristically devious. Instead of openly expressing his disagreement with his colleagues or resigning, he set himself up as an alternative, and secret, source of advice to the Queen; an oracle of the backstairs. Naturally enough, the Queen, with her own fear of falling prisoner of party and her own dislike of the Whigs, found Harley's advice more congenial than Godolphin's. It was a marvellous stroke of luck for Harley when he discovered that one of the Queen's bedchamber women, Abigail Hill, later Masham, was a distant cousin of his, so affording him, even if often only by proxy, access to the Queen at her most unguarded and receptive.

In August Marlborough learned that the Queen, without consulting Godolphin, though not (Godolphin guessed) without consulting Harley, appointed two Tory clergymen to vacant bishoprics, to the immediate fury of the Whigs. Although the Duke now realized the extent of the danger which he and Godolphin faced, he still thought that a brisk frontal attack would do the trick, telling Godolphin in a letter of September:

What you write concerning 239 (the Queen), 199 (Mr Harley) & 256 (Mrs Masham) is of that consequence, that I think no time should be lost in putting a stop to that management, or else to lett them have it entirely in their own hands.[20]

So Godolphin duly taxed the Queen in person about Harley's illicit counsels; Sarah had a go at her too; and the Duke dispatched her a magisterial letter. But again it proved not so straightforward a matter as the Duke had thought. The Queen, schooled by deceitful Abigail and cunning Harley, flatly denied that she had ever acted without the Duke's and Godolphin's advice; in particular she denied that her appointment of the Tory bishops was prompted by Harley. The choice of those entirely worthy clerics was, she argued, a perfectly proper exercise of her royal prerogative. As for Sarah's accusations

that she had 'an intire confidence in 4 (Mr Harley)', the Queen wondered how 41 (the
Duchess of Marlborough) could say such a thing, 'when she has soe often bin assured
from me, that I relyed entirely on no one but Mr Freeman and Mr Montgomery.'[21]

Here, evoked by the thick atmosphere of intrigue and expiring friendship, was mani-
fested in Anne a streak of characteristic Stuart shiftiness.

It was this royal shiftiness, coupled with the stealthy nature of Harley's backstair
offensive, which presented the Duke and even more so Godolphin, as chief minister
with a conundrum extraordinarily hard to solve. The Duke, for all his subtlety of mind
found it easier to state the problem than offer Godolphin an answer. As he wrote
Sarah on 29 September,

> . . . if he (Godolphin) stays in his place, and dose not intierly govern the Queen, he will
> dup'd by Mr Harley, and if he dose what is certainly best for him, quitt, he will do great h
> both to the business at home and abroad. . . .[22]

Godolphin decided on what was, in view of Harley's character, a desperate enoug
expedient: to have it out with him in a frank interview. The interview resulted in nothi
but slimy and unconvincing avowals of honesty and loyalty. '. . . you have not', Harl
assured Godolphin in a letter afterwards, 'a more faithful servant nor a truer nor m
zealous friend in the world than myself. . . .'[23]

Meanwhile Sarah too had been in action. She might perhaps have served her husban
interests best by trying to fan back into life the Queen's still lingering affection for her
kind gestures and nostalgic reminders, while at the same time avoiding embroilment wi
Abigail. But Sarah, true to form, preferred to attack them both head-on with much d
charge of reproaches and remonstrances. She accused Abigail to her face of seeing t
Queen in secret and turning the Queen against her. This ill-judged frontal assault mere
gave the sly and adroit Abigail the opportunity to inform Sarah patronizingly that 's
was sure the Queen, who had loved me extremely, would always be very kind to me'.

The Duke, though deep in his own problems over in the Low Countries, was ke
well informed by his indignant wife about Abigail's insufferable conduct, which t
sweeping of low curtseys whenever the two women happened to encounter each oth
only served to render the more galling. Nevertheless, the Duke, to whom indigna
letters from Sarah were no novelty, only answered her in his most fatalistic and worl
weary style:

> What you say of 256 (Mrs Masham) is very odd, and if you think she is a good weathercoc
> it is hie time to leave off strugling; for believe me nothing is worth rowing against wind a
> tyde; at least you will think so when you come to my age.[25]

But when Marlborough returned home soon afterwards, in time for the winter sessi
of Parliament, he found that unless he rowed, and rowed hard, against the wind of pa
attacks and the tide of Harley's and the Queen's purpose, the Godolphin administrati
was going to founder. The High Tories launched bitter criticisms of Marlborough

FAR LEFT *Henry St John, Viscount Bolingbroke (1678– 1751). Painting attributed to Jonathan Richardson (1665– 1745)*

LEFT *Admiral George Churchill, Marlborough's brother (1654–1710). Painting by Sir Godfrey Kneller*

failure to win the war in 1707 and demanded that 20,000 soldiers be transferred from the Low Countries to Spain. The Whigs, infuriated by the Queen's appointment of the Tory bishops, threatened to withdraw all support from the government, and in the meantime busied themselves with a ferocious attack on the Admiralty Board, which lay in the hands of the Queen's Tory husband, Prince George the Prince Consort, and of Marlborough's Tory brother, Admiral George Churchill.

All in all, the session afforded a convincing demonstration of the constructive purpose and public spirit of the nascent party system.

To Godolphin and the Duke inexorable logic pointed towards further wooing of the Whig Junto in order to win back their support. The Junto shared Marlborough's belief that Spain was only a military sideshow. They were full of zeal towards the prosecution of war. Indeed the Whigs had virtually adopted the Duke's victories as their own.

Yet the more Godolphin and the Duke urged on the Queen the necessity for fresh concessions to the Whigs, the more they pushed her into Harley's embrace. And Harley offered her what she most desired – to be saved from the Whig Junto, and to be put at the head of a 'national' government composed of moderates from both the parties. There would even be a place for the Duke of Marlborough in Harley's new administration, since the Queen still admired him, and Harley, in view of the Duke's immense prestige, could not do without him.

Harley's offer, demanding only that Marlborough betray Godolphin, was put to the Duke through Henry St John, the Tory Secretary at War, and formerly an admirer of his. The Duke did not accept Harley's offer. Instead he sought to persuade the Queen that she must dismiss Harley, on account of his 'false and treacherous proceedings' towards Godolphin and himself. But he sought in vain; Anne's mind was made up.

There was nothing left for the Duke and Godolphin but their own resignations. The letter which Marlborough now wrote to the Queen, apparently marking the end of more than a quarter of a century of friendship and service, was bitter enough:

> . . . I find myself obliged to have so much regard to my own honour and reputation, as not to be every day made a sacrifice to falsehood and treachery, but most humbly to acquaint your majesty that no consideration can make me serve any longer with that man. And I beseech your majesty to look upon me from this moment as forced out of your service as long as you think fit to continue him in it.[26]

Queen Anne took the resignations of her old friends with an equanimity which did her little credit. Her new friend Mr Harley bustled about, sounding politicians and trying to put together his moderate Tory administration. Unfortunately for Harley, Godolphin's belief that no such government was possible at that time proved correct; certainly not one which lacked the presence of the Duke of Marlborough.

On 19 February 1708, at the customary Sunday morning meeting of the Cabinet Council, the Queen took her usual place at the head of the long table. Amid the double row of periwigs which lined that table, there were two conspicuously empty chairs. Harley, as Secretary of State, nevertheless opened the business of the meeting. But the grave faces beneath the periwigs seemed restive rather than attentive; there were murmurs as if of protest. Realizing that no one was listening to him, Harley stumbled to a pause. In the silence that followed, ministers looked at each other and at the Queen and Harley in unease and uncertainty. Then the Duke of Somerset stood up and remarked: 'I do not see how we can deliberate when the Commander-in-Chief and the Lord Treasurer are absent.'[27] The Queen said nothing; Harley shifted in his seat. It was too evident to them both that Somerset had done no more than express the general feeling of his colleagues. After another awkward silence, Somerset said again that it was impossible to go on with the meeting without the Duke and Godolphin. The Queen saw that she was faced with a virtual mutiny at her own Council table. Flushing up her thick neck with anger and humiliation, she closed the meeting and hobbled from the room.

But even now it was not she who admitted defeat, but Harley. Next morning she summoned the Duke of Marlborough to inform him that Harley had resigned. So the Duke and Godolphin were back in power again after all. But the tears of anger, the bitter reproaches, with which the Queen accompanied her announcement made it all too plain what was to be the nature of their future relationship with her. And Harley, out of office though he was, still remained her confidential adviser, thanks to the kind offices of Abigail Masham. As Sarah Marlborough described years later:

> While she [Abigail] lived at her Little House over against the gate that goes into Windsor Castle, Harley and his friends saw the Queen as often as they pleased. Those that saw her who were not to be known, came in from the Park into the garden, and from thence Abigail carried them a back way to the Queen's closet. . . .[28]

CHAPTER TWELVE

THE INSTRUMENT OF
SO MUCH HAPPINESS

In contrast to the hope of great successes which had glowed upon him a year before, the Duke now approached the campaign of 1708 in a mood of weary pessimism. Although the crisis over Harley, with its wear and tear on the spirit, was over, the Duke and Godolphin were still as painfully caught between the Whigs and the Queen as ever. The antics of Parliamentary faction depressed him, especially when the Commons threw out by seven votes a provision in the new Recruiting Bill for a compulsory levy of men. Contemplation of the state of the alliance provided him with no comfort. The stresses between the partners brought it nearer and nearer to collapse with every year the war went on. When Heinsius dilated upon the exhaustion of Dutch resources, the Duke retorted that if the Grand Pensionary knew the true state of English finance and trade, 'you would not think our conditions to differ much from that you represent Holland to be in. . . .'[1] And when it came to shifting burdens on to others, the Habsburg Empire had no rival, as Marlborough reminded Heinsius:

> I confess it is very melancholy to reflect how little the Empire have done this warr for their own preservation and little they seem disposed to exert themselves at present, when their all is at stake. . . .[2]

The strategic prospects for 1708 were equally glum. In Spain the French must be expected to press home their victory at Almanza the year before. 'My fears for Spain are as great as yours,' the Duke confessed to Heinsius in January. Nevertheless, he told the Dutch leader that if he could defeat the French in Flanders, he 'should hope to gain Spain by France'.[3]

Flanders, then, was to be the decisive theatre this year. The Duke was sure that the French themselves meant to go over to the offensive, in order to win a better bargaining position in any fresh peace talks; 'but that which I most fear,' he confided to Heinsius at the beginning of March, 'is that they will endeavour to be in the field before us.'[4]

At The Hague in April, the Duke, Heinsius and Prince Eugène decided that the allies should deploy in three armies: the Elector of Hanover, with the smallest, to watch the French in Alsace and guard southern Germany; Eugène on the Moselle, to threaten the French with a repetition of Marlborough's 1705 invasion plan; the Duke in Flanders. But Eugène's presence on the Moselle was intended only as a bluff to dupe the French into diverting strong forces from Flanders. Eugène was then to slip away and march at utmost speed to join the Duke. As soon as Eugène arrived in Flanders, so Marlborough informed Heinsius, 'we shall move directly upon the enemy and bring on a battle, trusting in God to bless our designs. . . .'[5]

So the Duke was again seeking battle – not because he 'believed' in battles, but, as always, because a battle seemed in the circumstances the best, perhaps the only, solution to all the political problems which beset the allies.

Both sides, however, were delayed in taking the field by the wetness of the spring. Meanwhile intelligence reports gave Marlborough a more and more disquieting picture of French strength and intentions. Louis XIV had sent his grandson the Duke of Burgundy to take titular command of Vendôme's army, the presence of a prince of the blood arguing a great purpose and greater hopes. As the Duke laconically informed Godolphin on 14 May, the French 'continue to threaten us with the Duke of Burgundy and a vast army, I hope the Duke of Burgundy will come; and as for their army, I can-not see how it is possible for them to be stronger than they were the last campaign.'[6] In fact Burgundy's army numbered 100,000 men; larger than the Duke's, and a tribute to French ruthlessness in recruitment and in stripping other fronts.

Burgundy and Vendôme were not all that was on Marlborough's mind. He was uneasily aware that the people of the Spanish Netherlands would probably welcome French deliverance from Dutch administrators. A French plot to seize the citadel of Antwerp by surprise was discovered; the Duke feared a sudden lunge at Brussels. When on 26 May Burgundy and Vendôme advanced to Soignies, south of Brussels, he began to think that they were really about to 'venture'; and, as he reported to Godolphin two days later, 'by their having sent no troops to the Moselle, they are certainly a good deal stronger than we are'.[7] For Marlborough's intended deception on the Moselle had utterly failed of its purpose. Because of the usual kind of delays, Eugène's army was only now beginning to assemble. Eugène himself was held up in Vienna on government business. 'I would not willingly blame Prince Eugène', wrote the Duke, 'but his arrival at the Moselle will be ten days after his promise.'[8] In any case, however, Berwick, now commanding the French army on the Moselle, had guessed that allied preparations on that river were only a blind.

The Duke now lay in considerable danger from Vendôme's larger army, and would continue to do so until Eugène at last arrived with his forces. On 1 June Vendôme and Burgundy began to move again; another false alarm, for after a brief flurry of manœuvre in pouring rain, the armies came to rest again, the French near Braine-l'Alleud, south of Brussels; the Duke just west of Louvain. 'I am in my health, I thank God', he assured Sarah on 11 June, 'as well as one of my age, and that has not his mind very much at ease, can be. . . .'[9]

In fact, his mind was far less at ease than he cared to indicate to his wife. That same day he dispatched an urgent message to Eugène, who at last was on his way from the Moselle, asking him to hasten on with his cavalry alone, since their hopes of launching a surprise attack on Vendôme depended entirely on Eugène's speed.

The pinnacled roof of the late medieval Town Hall of Oudenarde, with gilded Habsburg double eagle. After the battle of Oudenarde the market square beneath was crammed with French prisoners under guard – a welcome sight to the Duke and Prince Eugène when they rode in next morning to the cheers of their soldiers.

If you can gain only forty-eight hours, I will make my dispositions for the moment of your arrival; and with the blessing of Heaven, we may profit so well by those two days, as to feel the good effects of it the rest of the campaign. You will order the infantry to hasten as much as possible. . . .[10]

But it was the French who, on 13 July 1708, broke the long lull, and while Eugène's troops were still between the Moselle and Flanders. Their plan – daring, swiftly accomplished – took the Duke totally by surprise. From Braine-l'Alleud, they suddenly marched westwards towards the cities of Bruges and Ghent, while advanced guards raced on ahead of them. As soon as the French appeared before these two cities, fore-warned French sympathizers among their populations opened their gates. Bruges fell immediately into French hands; in Ghent, however, three hundred English soldiers managed to hold out in the citadel for a few days. At a stroke the French had undone much of the work of Ramillies; they dominated West Flanders, and were on the verge of completely cutting Marlborough off from his North Sea coast base at Ostend.

For the first – and, as it was to prove, the last – time, the French had inflicted on Marl-borough the kind of sudden, stunningly unexpected strategic disaster he so often inflicted on them. The impact came after weeks of stress and anxiety; for the moment, to the amazement and dismay of those about him, he was shattered by it. Count Grumbkow, Prussian commissary at the Duke's headquarters, reported to his king:

> The blow which the enemy dealt us did not merely destroy all our plans, but was sufficient to do irreparable harm to the reputation and previous good fortune of Mylord Duke; and he felt his misfortune so keenly that I believed he would succumb to this grief early the day before yesterday, as he was so seized by it that he was afraid of being suffocated.[11]

According to General Natzmer, commanding the Prussian cavalry, '. . . there was deep depression in the army. Mylord Duke was inconsolable over these sad happenings and discussed with me in touching confidence this sudden turn in events. . . .'[12]

Prince Eugène, riding furiously ahead of his army to join the Duke, was astonished by the state in which he found him at Assche, west of Brussels on 9 July, two days after the fall of the citadel of Ghent had completed the French coup. He reported to the Emperor in Vienna: '. . . I did not remain in Brussels, but passed straight through the town to the army in order to discuss with the Duke of Marlborough what is to be done. I have found him also in full march and pretty consternated.'[13] Then, according to Grumbkow's account,

> While Mylord Duke was writing to the Queen, the Prince drew me aside and asked me what exactly all this meant. The Duke was incomprehensibly exhausted and talked as though everything was lost . . . this morning Mylord Duke had a severe fever and was so ill that he had to be bled. He is very exhausted. . . .[14]

From the gateway of the citadel of Lille, the royal arms of France looked down on the Sun King's troops marching out in surrender on 9 December 1709.

Nor did the arrival of trouble-loaded letters from the Queen and Sarah help the Duke, weakened as he was by fever, to ride the shock of the French *coup*. On the same day that Eugène was reporting to the Emperor on Marlborough's condition, the Duke himself explained to Godolphin:

> ...the treachery of Ghent, continual marching, and some letters I have received from England [from the Queen and Sarah] have so vexed me, that I was yesterday in so great a fever, that the doctor would have persuaded me to have gone to Brussels; but I thank God I am now better....[15]

Sweating out the fever helped; so too did the arrival of the faithful Cadogan from Ostend, full of cheerful confidence. But it was the sight of Eugène which did most to restore Marlborough's morale and the morale of the army. And depression, even despair, now served with Marlborough just as on earlier occasions as the unlikely prelude to outstandingly dynamic feats of leadership.

On 8 July reports arrived that the French were on the move again, marching south from Alost (Aalst) towards Lessines, an important crossing point over the River Dender. The Duke correctly guessed that the French wanted Lessines in order to cover a siege of Oudenarde, the fortress town on the Scheldt. If the allies lost Oudenarde, they would be completely fenced off from the Flanders coast.

At two in the morning on 9 July, the Duke set out to race the French to Lessines,

French recruits joining their regiment. Painting after Antoine Watteau

heading down the dead-straight road that leads from Assche to Enghien. 'If I get the camp of Lessines before them', he reported to Godolphin, 'I hope to be able to hinder the siege, being resolved to venture everything, rather than lose that place [Oudenarde].'[16] By midday he had reached Herfelingen, near Enghien, 'where we shall only halt till about seven in the evening, and then pursue our march towards Lessines . . . in order to attack the enemy'.[17] At four that afternoon he ordered eight squadrons and eight battalions to make a forced march to Lessines and seize the town. At midnight the cavalry of this force clattered into the sleeping streets: no French. At four in the morning the infantry joined them. The main body of the army, starting from Herfelingen at seven the previous evening, marched all night and through the morning. By about noon the Duke's whole army was encamped at Lessines; a march of thirty miles in thirty-six hours. It was an outstanding performance for an army of the period and it totally disrupted French plans. Vendôme and Burgundy halted near Ninove to hold an anxious council of war; then swerved away westward towards Gavere, on the Scheldt north of Oudenarde. Meanwhile, a French siege train had been making its way towards Oudenarde from Tournai. Nevertheless, the Duke thought that the French might now abandon their project of besieging the fortress; 'if they persist', he wrote to the Secretary of State, 'it may give us the opportunity of coming soon to battle.'[18]

Manœuvres before the battle of Oudenarde

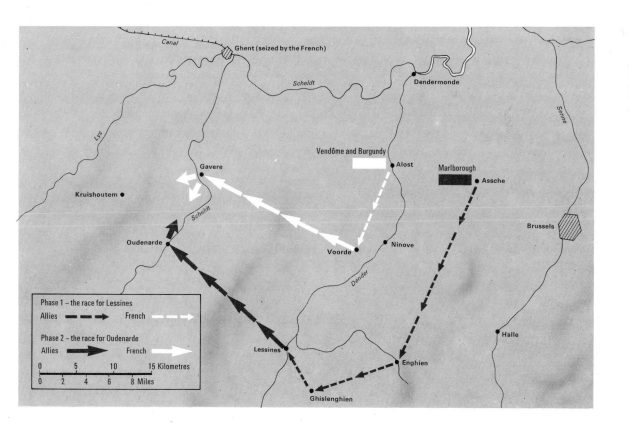

For now that Vendôme and Burgundy had ventured so far out from their frontier fortresses, Marlborough meant to catch them in the open and destroy them – and even though he still had only Eugène and not Eugène's army with him.

At daybreak on 11 July 1708 the Duke dispatched Cadogan to Oudenarde with an advanced guard of fifteen squadrons, twelve battalions, thirty-two guns, and all the army's pontoons, or 'tin-boats', for making temporary bridges. He was to cross the Scheldt near Oudenarde, seize the high ground beyond and erect bridges over that river for the passage of the army. Once again the Duke was racing Vendôme and Burgundy for a vital crossing point; and this time hoping to get across their line of march and trap them into battle. By 10.30 in the morning Cadogan was bridging the Scheldt just north of the sunlit zig-zags of Oudenarde's ramparts, his cavalry advancing up the rising ground beyond.

When the cavalry reached a gentle crest about a mile north of Oudenarde, they saw French foraging parties busy among the barns and villages of the rather English-looking countryside on the far side – hedgerows, copses, lush fields. They had arrived just in time.

Meanwhile Burgundy and Vendôme, in happy ignorance that the allied advanced guard had got to Oudenarde before them, had been crossing the Scheldt at Gavere in no great haste and heading down the west bank towards Oudenarde. Relations between Burgundy, young, high-mettled, royal, and Vendôme, a veteran of many battles and renowned for his uncouth and dirty habits, were not smooth. Vendôme had wanted to fight for Lessines, but he had been overruled. His mood that day was sour and un-cooperative. When, about two in the afternoon, they received reports that the Duke's

LEFT *Raising the militia in the vicinity of Orleans. Drawing*

RIGHT *The battle of Oudenarde, 11 July 1708. Detail from a tapestry woven by De Vos after L. de Hondt. The troops are shown in the foreground marching up in column of route, and in the distance deploying into line of battle. The topographical details were drawn under the Duke's personal supervision.*

forces were already between them and Oudenarde, between them and France indeed, their readings of the situation did not agree, except on the one point that they had been left no alternative but to fight. Vendôme judged – correctly – that at the moment they were only facing an advanced guard, which they should fall upon without delay and march straight on to Oudenarde. But Burgundy again overruled him, ordering the French army to form into line of battle along an irregular east–west ridge to the north of a stream, the Norken. From this ridge and its villages – Wannegem, Lede, Huise – they could see the spires of Oudenarde about three miles distant below them to the south and, in the middle ground, the rise occupied by Cadogan's advanced guard.

About ten in the morning the Duke, on the march with the main body, received Cadogan's report that he had safely reached Oudenarde ahead of the French, but that the enemy were crossing the Scheldt in force further north at Gavere. The Duke ordered the troops to step out so as to reach Cadogan before the French could attack him in overwhelming strength. The troops stepped out; there was an excitement in the ranks that morning as if they were racing to head off a fox or a hare. 'It was not a march', recalled Field-Deputy Goslinga, 'it was a race.'[19]

The Duke and Eugène crossed the pontoon bridges with the leading troops about midday and rode north to join Cadogan. They found that he had already been in action against the cavalry of the French advanced guard under de Biron near the village of Eyne. About a mile further to the north the Duke could see the French army deploying along a low, partly wooded ridge crowned with three villages. It was, in his judgment, 'as strong a post as is possible to be found'.[20] His own troops were only now scrambling over the pontoon bridges; most of them still in long waiting columns on the far side of the Scheldt. He knew that in any case Vendôme and Burgundy must outnumber him. In holding fast to his decision to attack them, he was therefore running enormous risks, as he recognized only too well.

> . . . but you know [he wrote to Godolphin afterwards] when I left England I was positively resolved to endeavour by all means a battle, thinking nothing else would make the queen's business go on well. This reason only made me venture the battle . . . otherwise I did give them [the enemy] too much advantage . . . I am very sensible [aware] if I had miscarried, I should have been blamed. . . .[21]

In Cadogan's immediate front at the moment there were only seven enemy battalions (actually Swiss mercenaries). These had been sent forward by Vendôme when that general had been bent on attack, and, by an oversight, never recalled. Just before three, with the allied army crowding across the bridges and beginning to come up in support, Cadogan, with the Duke's consent, attacked the Swiss – English redcoats to their front; Hanoverian cavalry to their flank and rear. Within an hour the attack had been, in the Duke's words, 'executed with much success; one of the brigades having defeated and killed or captured seven enemy battalions, and thereby given time for part of our army to come up while the enemy were deploying. . . .'[22]

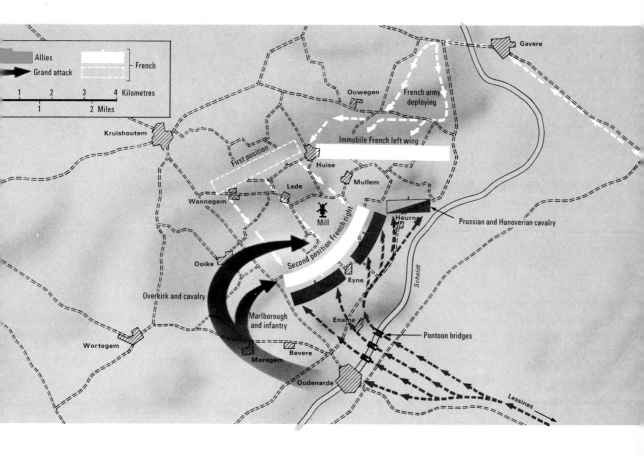

The battle of Oudenarde, 11 July 1708

It was the destruction of the Swiss, visible from the main French positions behind the River Norken along the Wannegem–Huise ridge, that caused Burgundy to change his mind about how to fight the battle. Young and ardent spirits among his entourage persuaded him to advance and attack while the allied army was still crossing the Scheldt and deploying, and while the allied fighting front was still weak and narrow. Vendôme, who earlier had favoured attacking, now opposed the decision as coming several hours too late. He was overruled again. The French right wing began to wend its way down the slopes, over the Norken, and forward over the close countryside, all streams, hedge-rows, copses and brambles, which lay between them and the allies round Eyne. However, by a misunderstanding, if nothing worse, between Vendôme and Burgundy the French left wing stayed put on the high ground.

About five o'clock the enemy right wing smashed into Cadogan's force, overlapping it to the west, and threatening the fragile allied line with envelopment and collapse. A battery posted by the Duke himself (the only guns to get across the crammed bridges that day) banged away at the advancing French troops, while Cadogan changed front to his left to meet them. In this close, cut-up countryside, there was no scope for cavalry; instead an infantry battle of a fierceness unique in the war began to develop. Only on

Cadogan's right was there open ground for cavalry – and here Prussian and Hanoverian horse, as yet unsupported by infantry, faced the whole left wing of the French army. Vendôme, in the thick of the infantry fight, therefore sent an order back to Burgundy to launch the left wing against the Prussians and Hanoverians, so that Cadogan could be crushed on both flanks as if in a clenched hand. But Burgundy failed to pass on the order; his staff assured him – wrongly – that there was a morass in the way; and the French left wing continued to remain passive spectators of the battle.

Just as Vendôme's attacks were beginning dangerously to overbear and overlap Cadogan's line the Duke brought up twenty battalions under the Duke of Argyll and extended his flank westwards. Twenty English and sixteen German battalions now faced nearly fifty French in a desperate fight among the thickets and hedgerows. Once again the French began to overlap the allied left; once again fresh troops came up just in time for the Duke to extend his front to meet the new menace. So it went on, the struggle swaying from minute to minute as each side fed in reinforcements; the rattle and smoke of musketry stretching always further westwards.

Such a battle could all too easily slide into shapeless confusion. The Duke, cool-headed and clear-thinking amid the turmoil and the racket, controlled it by a display of energy and dominating will remarkable in a man still suffering from the aftermath of fever. 'Mylord Duke', wrote Grumbkow, 'shone in battle, giving his orders with the greatest sangfroid and exposing his person to danger like the commonest soldier. Prince Eugène showed much spirit under the heaviest fire. . . .'[23] It was a rare demonstration of teamwork in command: Marlborough holding the supreme responsibility, Eugène at his side willingly acting as his adviser and agent, and riding off as necessary all over the field, 'as if', wrote an eye witness, 'he had been aide-de-camp to some or all of the generals'.[24]

The danger that Vendôme might overwhelm the allied front before the Duke could bring his main strength into action had now passed. The line was holding despite Vendôme's repeated onslaughts – and the Duke still had in reserve all the Dutch infantry and cavalry under Overkirk, whom he had directed to cross the Scheldt via Oudenarde itself, in order to relieve pressure on the pontoon bridges.

The shape of victory now began to emerge. Leaving Eugène in command of the right flank, Marlborough rode over to take personal charge of operations on the left. To his westward the Duke perceived a rim of higher ground, bald of surface and perfect for cavalry, which swung west and then north round the close countryside where the infantry of both armies were struggling among the hedgerows. Between six and seven the Duke launched Overkirk's troops along this broad and open hogsback; a combined force of cavalry and infantry to go wide and deep for the enemy rear, another force of infantry alone to make a tighter turn against the flank of the French infantry line.

In the French command no such clear, simple pattern was evolving. Vendôme, like Ney at Waterloo, was fighting in the front line, pike in hand, as if he could beat a way to victory by his own physical efforts. Burgundy – inexperienced, beset by advice, bewildered

– stared at the distant, smoking confusion of battle from the mill at Royegem, well behind the front. The French left wing, blocked by an imaginary morass and in default of other orders, still remained stationary on the slope behind the Norken, while a mile to the south-west their comrades of the right wing struggled against ever-increasing odds.

The Duke had now completed preparations for the double encirclement of the enemy. He had transferred twenty battalions of infantry and seventeen squadrons of English cavalry from his centre to shore up Eugène's hard-pressed line on the right. He himself was up with the Dutch infantry on his left centre; on his extreme left Overkirk lay a mile further to the north along the hogsback, poised to strike down into the French right rear. From the ridge the Duke and Overkirk enjoyed a commanding sideways view of the whole battlefield, as if they were watching the action on the stage of a theatre from a vantage point in the wings. It was now between seven and eight in the evening; only an hour or so of daylight left. The Duke sent orders to Overkirk to begin his attack.

With the westering sun behind them, the masses of infantry and horsemen began to surge in a slow flood down the slopes. It was a spectacle which transfixed the Duke of Burgundy and his staff at Royegem with a pang of fear. The Maison du Roi, already spent after a grim but successful collision with Prussian cavalry on the opposite flank, wheeled to form front to the new danger. But Overkirk brushed them aside and rode deeper and deeper into the French rear. Except for its still inactive left wing north of the Norken, the French army was now almost surrounded, under attack from west, south and east. As the light faded, Marlborough drew his noose of fire tighter and tighter round the doomed French infantry. 'We drove the enemy', wrote Sergeant Millner, 'from ditch to ditch, from hedge to hedge and from out of one scrub to another in great hurry, confusion and disorder.'[25] The volleys were now flaring luridly against the oncoming dusk. To distinguish friend from foe was fast becoming impossible; indeed Eugène's and Overkirk's troops, completing the ring round the French, actually fired on each other. About nine o'clock, with the last of the light, the battle died away.

'If we had been so happy as to have had two more hours of daylight', Marlborough was to write, 'I believe we should have made an end of this war.'[26] As it was, many of the encircled French filtered through the allied cordon under cover of darkness, some fleeing south to Tournai, others north to Ghent. It was to Ghent too that Burgundy and Vendôme themselves made off with the troops of their intact left wing; a flight the panic and ignominy of which was only emphasized by a furious public quarrel between the two commanders.

That night Marlborough's soldiers lay down where they were on the battlefield and slept on their arms. A gentle rain began to fall on the living, the dead, the dying and the wounded; and where mass violence had resounded, there was now only a whispering of raindrops amid the leaves.

Next morning about nine o'clock, after an unsleeping night in the saddle, ready to renew the battle at dawn if necessary, the Duke and Eugène rode down into Oudenarde.

There in the main square, under red-bricked crow-stepped gables and the soaring Late Gothic filigree of the Hôtel de Ville, they climbed off their horses to the cheers of their soldiers. The square was packed with droves of disconsolate French prisoners; there were already 6,000 of them in the town, and the number was finally to rise to 9,000, including eight hundred officers. The total French losses in dead, wounded, prisoners and deserters amounted to some 20,000 men. Forty French battalions had ceased to exist as formed bodies. 'I have given such a blow to their foot', exulted the Duke, 'that they will not be able to fight again this year.'[27]

Among the French prisoners was the Comte de Biron, commander of the French advanced guard, who, being entertained almost as an honoured guest according to the civilized custom of the age, recorded a glimpse of his distinguished captors in the afterglow of their victory:

> He noticed an almost royal magnificence at Prince Eugène's quarters, and a shameful parsimony at the Duke of Marlborough's, who most often ate at other people's quarters, the closest co-operation between the two in regard to business, of which the detail turns much more on Eugène, a deep respect on the part of all the general officers for these two chiefs, but a tacit preference on the whole for Prince Eugène, without the Duke of Marlborough being jealous of it.[28]

Later in the day after the battle, while he was suffering from his customary excruciating post-victory headache, Marlborough wrote to tell Sarah of his success. But this time his letter was, for him, cold and curt; eloquent of exhausted patience with both her and the Queen, and with their quarrels and complaints.

> I have neither spirits nor time to answer your three last letters; this being to bring the good news of a battle we had yesterday, in which it pleased God to give us at last the advantage . . . I do, and you must, give thanks to God for his goodness in protecting and making me the instrument of so much happiness to the queen and *nation, if she will please to make use of it.*[29]

As it happened, neither the victory nor even this letter from the Duke to Sarah was to serve as the instrument of much happiness to Queen Anne. The Queen's first reaction to the news of Oudenarde was to exclaim: 'Oh Lord, when will all this bloodshed cease!' The very thanksgiving service served as the occasion for a furious quarrel between Anne and Sarah. Sarah, as the Queen's Mistress of the Robes, had laid out the royal clothes and arranged the royal jewels for the Queen to wear. When the two ladies were seated opposite each other in the state coach, and it was lumbering from St James's to the City, Sarah saw that Anne was wearing no jewels at all; perhaps as a gesture of wifely concern for Prince George, who was bedridden and slowly failing with asthma. It says much about Sarah's state of mind that she should instantly leap to the conclusion that this was a deliberate insult to herself and the Duke, and, moreover, the work of Abigail Masham. It says just as much for Sarah's judgment and self-control that she should blurt out this conclusion there and then, as the two of them rode through the

cheers. They were still wrangling about it as they climbed the steps into Sir Christopher Wren's vast and still unfinished cathedral of St Paul's, amid bowing throngs of dignitaries. Sarah, beside herself with self-righteous anger, actually went so far as to tell her sovereign in public to be quiet.

It says even more for Sarah's judgment that upon returning home she committed the cardinal error of writing – and posting – in hot blood. Off to the Queen went a letter making her case all over again. To this indiscretion she added another: she enclosed the Duke's letter to her expressing his private hope that the Queen would make good use of his victory.

Queen Anne and Sarah Marlborough would have travelled to St Paul's in a coach rather like this one in which the Queen is here going to the Houses of Parliament. Painting attributed to Alexander van Gaelen (1676–1728)

> I cannot help sending your Majesty this letter, to show how exactly Lord Marlborough agrees with me in my opinion that he has no interest with you; though when I said so in church on Thursday, you were pleased to say it was untrue. And yet I think he will be surprised to hear that when I had taken so much pains to put your jewels in a way I thought you would like, Mrs Masham could make you refuse to wear them in so unkind a manner, because that was a power she had not thought fit to exercise before.

Sarah, having assured the Queen that she was going to make no comment on these transactions, then immediately proceeded to do so:

> ... only I must needs observe that your Majesty chose a very wrong day to mortify me, when you are just going to return thanks for a victory obtained by Lord Marlborough.[30]

So it was that 'Mrs Freeman' and 'Mrs Morley' too were casualties of Oudenarde. The Queen made no answer to this explosion of uncontrolled emotion except a brief note returning, not 'Mr Freeman's' letter, but 'the Duke of Marlborough's'. To the Duke himself she wrote asking him to explain what he meant by the expression 'if she will please to make use of it [the victory at Oudenarde]'.

> I am sure I will never make an ill use of so great a blessing, but, according to the best of my understanding, make the best use of it I can, and should be glad to know what is the use you would have me make of it. . . .[31]

Wearily the Duke, in full campaign, had now to explain a remark which he had never meant the Queen to see. He told her yet again that she must reconcile herself to the Whigs, since it was clearly impossible for her government to rest on the Tories. Making good use of his victory meant following Godolphin's advice, 'for any other advisers do but lead you into a labyrinth, to play their own game at your expense'.[32]

But the Queen was to take no heed of this warning against Abigail and Harley. She continued to resist Whig demands for office, even though the General Election of July 1708 returned a House of Commons with a strong majority in support of Whig policies. The Whigs, in their unappeased craving for office, kept up their attacks on the Admiralty Board, so further alienating the Queen, whose slowly dying and Tory husband headed the Board as Lord High Admiral, and also the Duke, whose Tory brother Admiral Churchill ran it. The Duke and Godolphin found themselves ever more uncomfortably placed between the demands of the Whigs and the unbudging resistance of the Queen. To complete their troubles, the Tories, who looked upon them as mere Whig puppets, endeavoured, in the Duke's words, all they could to vex them.

Although after six years it was hardly a novelty to Marlborough to have to conduct a war with this kind of thing going on behind his back, the mean-spirited opportunism of the parties was at last beginning to get him down. His letters strike a deeper and more insistent note of weariness and disgust at the attacks he and his family had to endure from enemies and alleged friends alike. Tory criticisms of his conduct of operations after Oudenarde, for instance, moved him to bitter sarcasm:

> By some letters from England, I find in all manner of ways I am to be found fault with; for when I am lucky, I am negligent, and do not make use of the occasion; and if I should ever prove unfortunate, no doubt I should run the risk of being a fool or a traitor. . . .[33]

Throughout this year, moreover, he was suffering from grumbling ill-health of a not always specific nature; a further cause of his spiritual fatigue, or even possibly a consequence of it. He talked more and more in his letters to Sarah of his yearnings to escape into retirement:

> I am doing my best [he wrote on 20 August] to serve England and the Queen, and with all my heart and soul, I pray for God's protection and blessing; but I am so tired of what I hear, and what I think must happen in England. . . .[34]

Godolphin too yearned for escape. The Queen did not, however, welcome their talk of retirement, for she and Harley had come to recognize that they were indispensable for the time being. She therefore appealed – successfully – to their loyalty and sense of public duty:

> . . . I hope you will both consider better of it, and not resort to an action that will bring me and our country to confusion. . . . You may flatter yourselves that people will approve of your quitting; but if you should persist in these cruel and unjust resolutions, believe me, where one will say you are in the right, hundreds will blame you.[35]

The Queen asked much in pressing them to stay in office, while at the same time denying them her confidence and backing. The Duke himself felt deeply the loss of the royal support and affection which in the past had done so much to sustain him amid his troubles. He was also torn between the political need to coerce the Queen over the Whigs and his own desire never to hurt her 'who I can't but love and endeavour to serve her as long as I have life; for I know this is not her fault, otherways then by being to(o) fond of 256 (Mrs Masham), who imposes upon her.'[36]

Nor was this the only inner conflict to disturb him in the summer and autumn of 1708. There was Sarah, whom he loved and needed so much, and yet who kept on bombarding him with fresh grievances about the Queen's conduct and fresh examples of outrageous behaviour on the part of Abigail. For Sarah, as she neared fifty, was undergoing a slow and terrible transformation from a beautiful, high-willed woman of magnetic personality into a strident and self-righteous virago to whom all the world – including her own daughters – were, firstly, in the wrong, and secondly, intent on doing her down. It was hardly surprising therefore that Sarah came to quarrel with many people. But it was her vendetta against the Queen and Abigail Masham which most disturbed the Duke's peace of mind, and tested his love and loyalty.

In these demands and reproaches the Duke was invited to join at long distance, so pulling him between two loyalties. Though he did from time to time write to the Queen on the topics so interesting to Sarah, in order to appease her, he regarded it as a useless exercise; and he tried to persuade his wife to show some discretion and self-control herself:

> I am sure that the interest of Mrs Masham is so settled with the queen, that we only trouble ourselves to no purpose; and by endeavouring to hurt, we do good offices for her; so that in my opinion we ought to be careful of our actions, and not lay everything to heart, but submit to whatever may happen.[37]

But this advice was far too wise to be heeded by anyone as unsubtle and impatient as Sarah. The quarrelling and the nagging in the Queen's closet went on; letters full of woe and indignation continued to arrive at the Duke's headquarters. If Sarah had had more insight into the minds and feelings of others, she might have refrained from adding to the burdens of the husband she loved so much, at a time when he was, as she well knew, conducting in the wake of the Battle of Oudenarde one of the most exacting campaigns of his career.

After the battle the Duke rested his army for two days, 'the troops having need of some ease after their great fatigue'.[38] Then he moved south-west to Wervicq, on the River Lys, only ten miles from Lille, the principal city of French Flanders and a major fortress. At Wervicq Marlborough, Eugène and the Dutch conferred on future strategy.

> It is most certain [wrote the Duke to Godolphin] that the success we had at Oudenarde has lessened their army at least 20,000 men; but that which I think our greatest advantage, consists in the fear that is among their troops, so that I shall seek all occasions for attacking them.[39]

But how to bring the French to battle again? How best to exploit the moral ascendancy the allies now enjoyed over the enemy troops and commanders alike?

Marlborough proposed that the allied army should ignore the French frontier fortresses and march deep into France. In his view this operation 'certainly, if it succeeded, would put a happy end to the war'. He had it in mind that a seaborne force already assembled to launch a 'descent' somewhere on the French coast (one of several such projects during the wars against Louis XIV, none of which ever came to fruition) should seize the port of Abbeville in co-operation with his own advancing army. With Abbeville as a base and a supply port, Paris itself would lie within his reach. Meanwhile the French frontier fortresses and their garrisons could be left to wither on the vine.

It was a bold and brilliant conception which lay far outside the military orthodoxy of the period. Moreover, it had strong practical advantages. For while, in the Duke's words, the allies were 'masters of marching where we please . . .',[40] they were not masters of taking what fortresses they pleased, because they had no siege train with them, and the canal and river lines of communication for transporting it up to the French frontier were blocked by the isolated French-held fortress of Ghent, at the junction of the Lys and the Scheldt, where Vendôme and the surviving part of his army had taken refuge.

The Duke's proposed strategy aroused much trepidation among his allies. Once again he found himself up against the special problems of commanding an international army: '. . . were our army all composed of English', he wrote to the Earl of Halifax on 26 July, 'the project would certainly be feasible, but we have a great many among us who are more afraid of wanting provisions than of the enemy.'[41] The project was certainly far too risky for the Dutch to relish, especially since they were beginning to look again towards a peace. On the same day that he wrote to Lord Halifax, the Duke reported to Godolphin that he was afraid the States-General 'will not willingly give their consent for the marching their army into France. . . .'[42]

Weighing more heavily with the Duke than Dutch fears were the objections of his comrade-in-arms, Eugène, a soldier of immense experience and a man not in the least timorous.

ABOVE LEFT *Plan of the citadel at Lille*

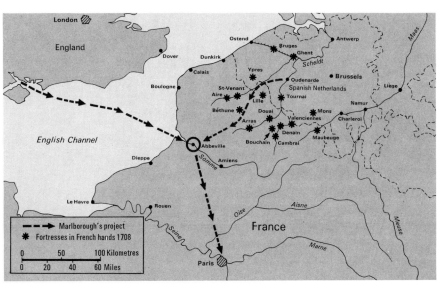

ABOVE RIGHT
*Marlborough's project for a deep
invasion of France after the
Battle of Oudenarde, 1708*

I have acquainted Prince Eugène [ran the same letter from the Duke to Godolphin] with the earnest desire we have for marching into France. He thinks it impracticable, till we have Lille for a *place d'armes* and magazine. . . .

It was Eugène's belief, the Duke went on, that without a fortified base such as Lille, 'we may make a very great inroad, but not be able to winter, though we might be helped by the fleet.'[43]

English historians have tended to brush aside Eugène's objections as simply displaying his inferior vision. Yet he was probably correct in judging the Duke's strategy to be too great a gamble. The allied army would have risked a fate similar to that which actually overtook Charles XII of Sweden in the following year, when after a daring march deep into the heart of Russia, his army, by then worn down by hunger, fatigue and ambush, was destroyed at the Battle of Poltava. And curiously enough the criticisms which Marlborough himself had made of Charles XII's army when he visited it in 1707 – and completely borne out by the event – were applicable to his own proposed invasion of France. The Swedish army, he observed, had 'no hospitals, no magazines. It is an army which lives on what it finds, and which in a war of *chicane* would soon perish.'[44] A war of *chicane*, or delay and evasion, was exactly the course the French government might have been expected to follow against the Duke. Louis XIV's officials would have stripped the towns and countryside of the food and forage on which the allied army, lacking secure supply lines and magazines, must have depended. Moreover, as Eugène argued at the time, it is highly doubtful whether the ships of the era could have maintained adequate cross-Channel supplies through all the gales of winter.

In any case the Duke gave up his project, although it is not known whether because he came to think that Eugène might be right, or whether simply because he felt he had to yield to the wishes of his allies. Instead the allied army would first lay siege to Lille.

But this in itself was a grand and hazardous enough operation. Lille was the most elaborate of all Vauban's fortress cities; a masterpiece of geometry in stone. Zig-zagging outer ramparts studded with huge, sharp-jutting bastions enclosed a broad moat fed from the River Deule. Within the moat itself were triangular island defences, or demi-lunes, from which the defenders could pour fire into the flanks of attackers who had managed to break through the outer defences. Finally, on the far side of the moat rose yet another mighty wall of ashlar flanked at frequent intervals by more bastions. On the north-west of the city lay the star-shaped citadel, the defences of which were even more formidable still: two lines of outer ramparts and two moats for the attackers to cross before they could even reach the main wall and bastions.

To crumble a breach through such defences would demand an immense weight of cannonball – and of powder to project it. But Vendôme in Ghent still blocked the strategic waterways. Marlborough and Eugène therefore proposed to bring the siege train from Brussels by road; by no means a routine operation. For the convoy comprised ninety-four guns and sixty great mortars, 3,000 wagons loaded with powder and shot, and was dragged along by 16,000 horses. Since it occupied no fewer than fifteen miles of road, it offered a splendid target to Vendôme's army to the north of the route, and Berwick's (he had now arrived from the Moselle) to the south. Nevertheless, the Duke and Eugène (his army too had arrived from the Moselle) successfully covered the convoy from attack, like anxious geese protecting a gaggle of monstrous goslings from marauding foxes, while it rolled slowly over the seventy miles from Brussels to Lille.

On 13 August the Duke was able to report to Godolphin: 'This day Lille is invested; I pray to God to bless the undertaking. What I most fear is the want of powder and ball for so great an undertaking; for our engineers fear we must take the town before we can attack the citadel.'[45] The siege itself was to be Eugène's responsibility; the Duke's to cover the siege with the field army against any attempt by the French to relieve the city. On 20 August the lines of circumvallation – earthworks entirely surrounding the city, to prevent the garrison breaking out, or attacking the besiegers – were completed, and the besiegers began to dig their trenches forward towards the ramparts. Fortunately – since this was Flanders in August – the sun shone and the ground was dry; a circumstance which provoked the Duke to remark to Sarah that day in a letter otherwise occupied with the Queen and his own wish to retire:

> You say nothing of going to Blenheim, but the weather is so fine I could wish you there, by which the finishing within doors, I believe, would go on the faster. If it were possible, I would flatter myself that I might be so happy to see it next summer, especially if M de Vendôme keeps his word in endeavouring the relief of Lille. . . .[46]

On 27 October the guns began to lob their twenty-four and thirty-two pound balls of iron against Vauban's masonry on the two sectors selected for making the breaches.

'This was his chosen monument . . . Yet he took a simpler and more domestic pleasure in the mansion too; choosing the furniture, the looking glasses and the pictures. . . .' The Second State Room at Blenheim Palace showing a portrait of Louis XIV and one of the battle tapestries woven by De Vos after L. de Hondt, under the Duke's personal supervision

The engineers hoped that this work would be completed in ten days. Instead the days dragged into weeks and still the guns failed to pound a breach; a reflection equally on the competence of Vauban and his masons, and the incompetence of the allied engineers. Such was the subtlety of Vauban's geometry that the besiegers in their trenches always found themselves exposed to flanking fire, try as they might to avoid it.

Meanwhile Vendôme with his field army had left Ghent and joined Berwick near Tournai. Since part of the allied army was engaged in the siege operations, Vendôme's and Berwick's combined army outnumbered the Duke's covering force. While the guns battered on, the French army sidled round Lille this way and that, trying in vain to get past Marlborough's agile shield, but always refusing the battle Marlborough so much hoped for. It was a time of constant strain for him, and, as the siege dragged on into the middle of September and beyond, the strain grew worse. On 20 September the Duke confided in a letter to Godolphin:

> It is impossible for me to express the uneasiness I suffer for the ill-conduct of our engineers at the siege, where I think everything goes very wrong. It would be a cruel thing, if after we have obliged the enemy to quit all thoughts of relieving the place by force . . . we should fail of taking it by the ignorance of our engineers, and the want of stores; for we have already fired very near as much as was demanded for the taking of the town and the citadel; and as yet we are not entire masters of the counterscarp [outer defences]. . . .[47]

That evening the besiegers launched yet another assault, and achieved a further lodgement on the defences, at the cost of 1,000 casualties. Eugène, in the thick of the fight as usual, was himself wounded in the head; and so Marlborough had to take over responsibility for carrying on the siege itself as well as covering it. It was now that he made a highly alarming discovery, as he reported to Godolphin:

> Upon the wounding of Prince Eugène, I thought it absolutely necessary to inform myself of every thing of the siege; for, before, I did not meddle in any thing but the covering of it. Upon examination I find they did not deal well with the prince, for when I told him there did not remain powder and ball for above four days, he was very much surprised. I own to you, that I fear, we have something more in our misfortunes than ignorance.[48]

The Duke was indeed finally to become convinced that though 'I cannot prove what I am going to say . . . I really believe we have been from the very beginning of that siege, betrayed; for great part of our stores have been embezzled. . . .'[49]

With only four days' supply of ammunition left, the siege was on the point of collapse. The Duke therefore sent orders for a convoy of powder and shot to make its hazardous way overland from Ostend; dispatching forces under General Webb to Thourout and Cadogan to Roulers to cover it from French attack. At Wynendael, between Thourout and Roulers, the French general de la Motte, seeking to intercept and destroy the convoy, attacked Webb's covering force. But Webb, although outnumbered one to three, handled his force so skilfully and his troops fought so stoutly that de la Motte retreated in some haste, leaving all his guns behind. Although Wynendael was a local action rather

Marlborough's horse housing with silver-mounted flintlock pistols in the holster caps; and some of the mathematical instruments traditionally believed to be owned by him

than a battle, if Webb had not succeeded, the Duke freely admitted, 'and our convoy had been lost, the consequences must have been the raising of the siege the next day'.[50]

On 1 October the besiegers finally made themselves masters of all the counterscarp, despite such hazards as boiling pitch, tar, oil and scalding water tipped from above. Layer by layer Vauban's protecting masonry was gradually being eaten away. But now that the siege was at last going smoothly, the Duke's anxieties about affairs at home began to deepen again. The winter session of Parliament, with all its promise of political turmoil and crisis, was again in sight; the Whigs were already beating the charge; and the Duke's brother Admiral Churchill was their objective. On 19 October the Duke wrote a forbiddingly stern letter to tell him 'plainly, with all the kindness of a brother and the sincerity of a friend', that unless he resigned before Parliament met,

> You will certainly do the greatest disservice imaginable to the queen and prince, the greatest prejudice to me, and bring yourself into such inconveniences as may last as long as you live, and from which it is wholly impossible to protect you.[51]

By 22 October a practicable breach had at last been battered through the defences of Lille. Before the final assault could be launched, however, Marshal Boufflers (Marlborough's old comrade-in-arms at Enzheim thirty-four years earlier, and his opponent in the Netherlands campaigns of 1702–3), who commanded the garrison, surrendered the town in order to save the population from the plunder and rapine customary if besiegers were put to the cost of storming the breach. Boufflers now retired into the enormously powerful defences of the citadel and the besiegers began all over again. Nevertheless, Lille, which back in 1668 had been the most splendid trophy of all Louis XIV's young manhood of conquest, was doomed.

It was therefore with a fine sense of timing that on 30 October, eight days after Boufflers had retired into the citadel, Marlborough wrote privately to his nephew the Duke of Berwick on the topic of peace.

The battle of Wynendael,
28 September 1708. Detail from
a tapestry woven by De Vos
after L. de Hondt

A VERY MURDERING BATTLE

Marlborough was well aware that the French government had been in discreet contact with the war-weary Dutch during the summer. He himself, for that matter, had also touched on the topic of peace to Berwick before, in the course of the routine correspondence about such things as passports and exchanges of prisoners then usual between opposing commanders. Nevertheless, this letter of 30 October 1708 was very different; nothing less than a private and unofficial peace initiative:

> In my judgement, it is at this time in our power to take such steps as could lead to peace before the next campaign. . . . My opinion is therefore that, if the Duke of Burgundy [nominally the French commander-in-chief in Flanders] had the King's permission to put forward proposals by means of letters to the deputies [Dutch field-deputies], to Prince Eugène and myself, calling upon us to communicate them to our masters, which we could not omit to do, this would make such an effect in Holland that for a certainty peace would follow.[1]

At this point in his letter Marlborough linked the grand subject of European peace to a point of more personal concern:

> You can be assured that I will be wholeheartedly for peace, not doubting at all that I shall find the goodwill which was promised me two years ago by the Marquis d'Alègre. . . .

This promised 'goodwill' was a sum of two million livres which d'Alègre had offered him in Louis XIV's name at the time of the abortive peace feelers in 1705–6. D'Alègre, captured at Elixhem and temporarily released on parole, had acted as a go-between in these discussions. The two million livres were not a bribe, but a *douceur*, or present, of a kind then customary. The *douceur* was to be given without strings *after* the successful conclusion of a peace in gratitude for Marlborough's good offices.

What thoughts, what motives, lay behind the Duke's attempt to bypass his own and other allied governments by writing direct to Berwick can only be guessed at. This was the Duke at his most subtle, oblique, and stealthy. He may, for example, have been well aware of his own reputation for avarice, and therefore have reminded Berwick about d'Alègre's offer in order to convince the French that he must be in earnest over peace – while at the same time putting himself in line for the two million livres again. As for his motive, it may be that he was telling no more than the simple truth when in the same letter he assured Berwick that 'I have no other aim but swiftly to bring a wearisome war to an end.'

His own personal reasons for desiring peace could hardly have been stronger, what with cumulative fatigue and ill-health, all his political troubles, and the swift decline of his influence with the Queen. Political considerations too were all in favour of making a decisive move now to end the war. The allies would negotiate from the firm base of a victorious campaign. On the other hand, if the conflict went on, the alliance was all too likely to collapse. Marlborough knew that the Dutch were exhausted. If a general peace were long delayed, they might well be tempted into separate negotiations with France. At home, moreover, it was plain that the winter Parliamentary session would see the Whigs finally take over the government – and the Whigs were the war party, the party of 'no peace without Spain – entire'. The Duke may have wanted, therefore, to present the incoming Whigs with a *fait accompli*, by producing in collusion with the French 'such an effect in Holland that peace would certainly result'.

But to start such an irresistible tide for peace required pressure on France as well as the allies. Five days before his letter to Berwick, the Duke wrote to urge Heinsius to lose no time in announcing an increase in the Dutch forces for next year; 'This resolution', he asserted, 'in the circomstances (sic) we are now in would bring France even this winter to reason.'[2]

Nothing could have been more in Marlborough's character than so to work his purposes invisibly through the manipulation of others. And there was one other point: under the proposal he put to Berwick, he himself and Prince Eugène would be at the commanding centre of the negotiations.

There was in any case a precedent for Marlborough's approach to Berwick. In 1697, when negotiations before the previous peace treaty had become bogged down, William III had sought to give them a new impetus by opening direct contacts with the then French commander-in-chief in the field.

But on 5 November Louis XIV instructed Berwick to turn down the Duke's proposal on the grounds that France's apparently grim military situation might easily be transformed in the future. His attempt at bringing about this transformation was not long in coming. On 22 November a French force made a dash for the weakly garrisoned city of Brussels and began to lay siege to it. The outcome, however, was only a further French defeat, for Marlborough and Eugène, without relinquishing their grip on Boufflers in the citadel of Lille, pounced on this French raiding force so swiftly and from so unexpected a direction that it had to abandon its wounded and its guns in its scramble to safety.

On 9 December Marshal Boufflers was at last forced to yield the citadel of Lille which he had defended so stoutly; and from the grandiose pediment over the gateway of the fortress the carved sun-ray symbol of Louis XIV's glory looked down on the Sun King's troops marching out in surrender. From first to last the siege had cost the allies 15,000 casualties (of which some 1,000 were British) – five times their losses in the Battle of Oudenarde.

Louis's rebuff of Marlborough's peace proposal had therefore proved a sad misjudg-ment. It was also to prove a tragic missed opportunity. For the month of November 1708 marked a turning point in the course of the war, and in Marlborough's own career. On 7 November Queen's Anne's beloved and long-ailing husband died. For several weeks grief prostrated the Queen's stubborn will, and during that time Tories fell from office like autumn leaves to make way for a Whig springtime. The Junto had come to power, and Marlborough and Godolphin, already alienated from the Queen, had become their prisoners: a doubly precarious existence. The Queen was also the Junto's prisoner. But she could hope and plan for her eventual escape, thanks to Robert Harley, her backstairs adviser.

And for Europe too the coming of a Whig administration in England was a fateful event. The Whig leaders were hot for the exaction from Louis XIV of 'no peace without Spain – entire', without any compromise whatsoever. Yet in the winter and spring of 1709 even such inflated war aims began to look practicable. Before the Duke at last closed down the Oudenarde campaign in January 1709, long after the normal time for going into winter quarters, he had retaken Bruges and Ghent. And the siege of Ghent witnessed the onset of an enemy even more terrible to France than Marlborough. In the last days of 1708 cold of unimagined bitterness closed on Europe like a trap. At Ghent the sentinels of besieged and besieging forces alike were frozen to death at their posts. And this was only a beginning: after a short and deceptive thaw in January, the cold set in like another ice age, the people of Europe cringing month after month under a bruise-coloured sky heavy with snow. On the frozen Thames at London Bridge there was an ice fair; a

A frost fair on the Thames in the winter of 1683–4. Detail from a painting by A. Hondius (1638?–1691)

little city of booths and stalls stretching from bank to bank, and bonfires twinkling across the ice in the polar gloom. From Brussels Marlborough was reporting to Heinsius in February:

> The continuall snow as well as hard frost will, if it continues, kill al the cattel of this country and bee very inconvenient for our garrisons, for even in this town we have no forage but what we bring dayly by carts. . . .[3]

The port of Harwich was ice bound; so were the Dutch ports. There were ice floes in the Channel. Even the mouth of the Tagus at Lisbon was frozen. It was fortunate indeed that the Duke had not carried out his post-Oudenarde plan to invade France, or his army might now have been lying somewhere between Abbeville and Paris, with sea-borne supplies cut off by ice, and dependent for subsistence on what it could find in the French countryside.

And in France, already impoverished by war as she was, famine had come in the wake of frost. The cattle died; the vines split. In the towns and the country the starving wandered in search of food in ragged, despairing packs. The very fabric of French society seemed in peril from the effects of the cold.

In the face of these calamities Louis XIV acknowledged that France must have peace. In February he secretly made touch with the Dutch government; in April the French foreign minister himself, the Marquis de Torcy, arrived at The Hague to open formal negotiations with the allies. By now, as the cold yielded to an appallingly wet spring hardly less damaging to French agriculture, the allied governments realized the full extent of the catastrophe which had overtaken France. In May the Whig Junto appointed their own man, Lord Townshend, as principal British representative at the peace talks. Townshend and the Junto now held the reins of British policy, and Marlborough, though officially Townshend's colleague at the talks, was relegated to the box beside the coachman.

In their desperation the French seemed ready to concede anything the allies – whose appetites were whetted by knowledge of France's plight – cared to demand. By 18 May the Duke was assuring Godolphin that 'M. Torcy has offered so much that I have no doubt it will end in a good peace.'[4] He even asked Sarah to have a chair and canopy of state made for his use during the treaty ceremonies, adding a characteristically house-wifely suggestion that she should take care to have the canopy made 'so that it may serve for part of a bed, when I have done with it here, which I hope will be by the end of the summer'.[5]

On 28 May the allies presented Torcy with their preliminary conditions for peace: a formidable catalogue of forty demands, together with an ultimatum that if Louis XIV failed to accept them by 4 June, they would take the field again. Nevertheless, Louis conceded every demand except one – even that the entire Spanish Empire should go to the allied candidate Charles III; even that he, Louis, should immediately yield up a whole string of fortresses in Flanders and on the Rhine as a pledge of good faith. But he

RIGHT *Jean Baptiste Colbert, Marquis de Torcy (1665–1746). Engraving by M. Dossier (1684–1750) after Hyacinthe Rigaud*

FAR RIGHT *Charles Townshend, Viscount Townshend (1675–1738). Painting after Sir Godfrey Kneller*

would not accept the article which stipulated that his grandson Philip V must quit Spain within two months, or the armistice between France and the allies would come to an end. For it was simply not within his power to guarantee this; Philip V and the Spanish people had their own views on the matter.

The allies had now to decide whether or not to give way on this one article. The Duke himself had no doubt it ought to be scrapped; Eugène likewise. Townshend and his Whig colleagues in London, however, were resolved to stuff it down Louis XIV's throat. The Duke therefore found himself at odds with the Whig ministers over no less an issue than that of peace and war. It was more than a dilemma; it was a moral challenge. If he openly threw the full weight of his prestige against the Whig insistence on this article, he would explode a political crisis that would make all earlier political upsets of the reign like a mere rattling among the chocolate dishes. In view of the enthusiastic support Whig peace terms enjoyed in Parliament, he could well bring about his own fall.

But in the event the Duke chose to go no further than the discreet and wholly ineffective proffering of advice behind the scenes. Since the allies refused to yield over the disputed article, the preliminary peace conference broke down.

There is a clue in a letter to Godolphin as to why the Duke elected to follow so indecisive a course. He owned that it had been his opinion that Louis's agreement to surrender fortresses was in itself enough to secure allied aims, and added: 'but I do not love to be singular, especially when it was doing what France seemed to desire'.[6] It was a curious and self-revealing remark. Was this confessed dislike for being 'singular', or the odd man out, the true explanation for other episodes of his life, such as his appeasement of Dutch generals and field-deputies? Was he here acknowledging that he lacked the moral strength to stand alone on a question of principle, and risk the personal consequences? It is interesting that as long ago as the Sedgemoor campaign in 1685, he confided to a correspondent that despite his disagreements with his superior, Feversham, 'I am afraid of giving my opinion freely, for feare that itt should not agree with what is the King's intentions, and soe only expose myselfe. . . .'[7]

When, despite the collapse of the peace conference, negotiations still continued between the allies and France via letter and go-between for the rest of the year, the Duke came to disagree with Whig policy more strongly than ever. He was convinced that conditions would never be so ripe as now for concluding a good peace; and that the Whigs' refusal to abate their extreme demands on France was utter folly. But even now, rather than embark on open opposition to his Whig colleagues, he preferred simply to brush himself clean of any personal responsibility for English policy. In the summer and autumn of 1709 he deliberately diminished himself into the role of public servant wholly obedient to the directives of his political masters, and with no right officially to advocate a view of his own. When Heinsius, for example, asked him for his comments on a letter from Torcy, the Duke replied:

> . . . whatever you desire of mee will always be complyed with, otherwise I should not care to write on this subject, being sensible of the warmth England has for the carrying on of the warr, soe I might begg of you that what I now write may be known to nobody, and that you will be pleased to tare [tear] or send me back my letter for fear of accidents. . . .[8]

He might have been a junior clerk in trepidation of his superiors rather than My Lord Duke of Marlborough, Prince of Mindelheim and Her Majesty's Captain-General. And for the remainder of the year he contented himself with private warnings about the exorbitant and impractical nature of allied demands, coupled with anxious reminders to his correspondents that

> . . . I can as you may well believe, have no other opinion on a matter of this consequence, whatever my own privat notions may be, then what is agreeable to the instructions I have received with Lord Townshend from England. . . .[9]

Marlborough equally believed that the Whigs were inflicting great damage on English interests by pressing negotiations with the Dutch for a barrier treaty, the purpose of which was to bribe the Dutch into supporting Whig peace terms. But here again he lay low; in this case for fear of upsetting the Dutch as well as the Junto. His most forceful action in the matter was to obtain the Queen's permission not to have to sign the treaty, which bore Townshend's Whig signature alone.

It is hard to recognize in this performance the man who at the outset of the Blenheim campaign five years earlier had been willing to take the destiny of Europe on himself. But at that time the Queen, strong, affectionate, trusting, had been behind him; now he was alone, except for poor worried Godolphin. For the paradox was that the Duke, outwardly still the greatest figure in the alliance, was no longer in control; he was a prisoner of the Whigs. Moreover, he was a man deeply uneasy about his own future; troubled by the return, after so much honour and success, of the insecurity which had dogged his early years. Far from putting at risk the posts and emoluments which stood for status and security, his urge was to cling to them at all cost. Under the compulsion of this urge he was moved to commit the one outright blunder of his life. He asked to be appointed Captain-General for life.

In May, when the peace talks were coming to their climax, the Duke sent one of his entourage to search unobtrusively in the Privy Seal office for a precedent for such an appointment. None was to be found. The Duke then wrote directly to Lord Cowper, the Lord Chancellor. But Cowper discouragingly replied: 'I cannot find it was granted at any time otherwise than during [the sovereign's] pleasure.'[10] During the rest of the summer and autumn, while the Duke was dispensing his carefully unofficial views on peace terms and being studiedly obedient to Whig instructions, the idea nevertheless lingered in his mind. Not only would it give him the immediate security in his post for which he craved, but it would also place him above and beyond the party strife he so much detested. In October, fortified by his fresh victory at Malplaquet, he sat down and wrote to the Queen formally to request the Captain-Generalship for life. Since he was well aware that relations between the Queen and Sarah were currently stormier than ever, for him to choose this moment to solicit such a favour is a further sign of how strongly anxiety about his future was preying on his mind.

The Queen's inevitable, and justified, refusal stung and humiliated him into a deeper uneasiness; and he now gave way to uncharacteristically outspoken reproaches. The nature of these is suggested by a subsequent letter from the Queen, which is all that survives of their correspondence on this topic:

> I saw very plainly your uneasyness at my refusing ye mark of fayvour you desired, and beleived by another letter I had from you on ye subject you fancied ye advice came from Masham; but I assure you you wrong her most extreamly, for upon my word she knows nothing of it . . . what I said was my own thoughts, not thinking it for your service or mine to do a thing of ye nature. . . .[11]

It is also clear from the Queen's letter that Marlborough, goaded by Sarah, had at the same time reproached her for her treatment of Sarah.

> . . . you seem to be dissatisfyed with my behaviour to the Duchesse of Marlborough. I do not love complaining, but it is impossible to help saying on this occassion I beleeve no body was ever so used by a freind as I have bin by her ever since my coming to ye Crown. I desire nothinge but that she would leave off teasing and tormenting me, and behave herself wth ye decency she ought both to her freind and Queen, and this I hope you will make her do. . . .[12]

When Marlborough read these royal comments on Sarah's conduct, temperate as they were, he must surely have recognized their justice. This recognition could hardly have afforded much relief to his uneasy sensation that his world was tilting and sinking beneath him.

The execution of deserters during the 1707 campaign. Drawing by Marcellus Laroon

at Albert Camp. 1707.

A Execution of Deserters in Flanders 1707

The army, with its order and discipline, its obedience to his direction, must have seemed to him a spiritual refuge; and more and more he was to keep himself to his purely military role as commander-in-chief. But in the army too there had been intense disappointment when the peace was lost which everyone had taken to be as good as signed. When the Duke had taken the field in July 1709 after the breakdown of the peace talks, the army was as loyal and formidable a fighting force as ever, but it no longer followed him with the same keen edge of enthusiasm as of old.

Because of continual rain and roads reduced to mud wallows, it was not until the last week of June that the Duke completed the concentration of the allied forces near Lille.

Their strength, at 120,000 men, was 25,000 men greater than at the start of the Oudenarde campaign, thanks largely to the Duke's undiminished skill at cajoling Europe's hirers of mercenaries. He assured the prickly King of Prussia, for instance, that 'the excellence of your troops makes me prefer them to all others'[13]; a compliment worth 5,000 extra men. The Duke's own Anglo-Dutch army numbered one hundred and ninety-seven squadrons and one hundred and twenty-nine battalions, of which only fourteen squadrons and twenty battalions were native British; Eugène's army one hundred and twenty-three squadrons and sixty-six battalions. Both commanders agreed that this year there was no political or strategic need to 'run so great a hazard' as seeking a battle. It was a question of applying relentless pressure on the French while peace contacts continued. Nevertheless, if the French, in their desperation, sought a battle, as the Duke believed they well might, he was ready to oblige them.

He knew from the reports of his spies to what straits France and the French army were now reduced. However, these reports failed to make clear to him that despite frost, wet and hunger, there had been a great resurgence in French morale, inspired by the new commander-in-chief in Flanders, Marshal the Duc de Villars. For now Marlborough was up against the one living French soldier in the same class as himself and Eugène. It was Villars who had won the dashing victory over the Margrave of Baden at Friedlingen in 1702; defeated a Habsburg army at Höchstädt in 1703; and rushed the lines of Stollhofen in 1707. It was Villars too who, by his canny defensive on the Moselle in 1705, had inflicted the first strategic reverse ever sustained by Marlborough. And Villars's personal qualities – wit and humour, flamboyant bravery, a quick temper, a flair for rhetoric and braggadocio – were exactly those to warm the enthusiasm of the French soldier.

Yet the new fighting spirit was not limited to the army; the French nation felt it too. The allies had only themselves to blame for this. When Louis XIV turned down the allies' outrageously humiliating preliminary peace terms, he appealed to his subjects for their support in fighting on for a just peace. The French people responded. In 1709 the allies were no longer merely fighting the machine of absolute monarchy; they were fighting France herself.

Now Villars was waiting behind the water obstacles and earthworks of his defensive lines between St Venant and Douai for the Duke and Eugène to attack. On 23 June the allied army struck camp and trudged into the sodden flatlands south of Lille, heading south-west towards Villars's lines apparently to launch an attack, as Villars expected. But Marlborough's advance was only a feint. In one of his favourite night marches he suddenly pounced in the opposite direction, investing the fortress of Tournai, east of Lille, before Villars could shield it or throw reinforcements into it. The Duke had won the first gambit of the campaign.

The siege of the town and citadel of Tournai lasted from late June to 3 September: a grim affair where the besiegers were up to their thighs in mud and water, and where a peculiarly horrific struggle took place in the close darkness of galleries dug to plant mines

The siege of Tournai, 8 July 1709. Engraving

and counter-mines, and in the underground tunnels with which Tournai's defences abounded. Though Villars made valiant gestures with his army, he knew he was too weak to risk a battle to save the city. Nevertheless, the length and bloodshed of the siege had its effect on the morale of the allied troops. The more thinking among them began to wonder if they were not dying unnecessarily because allied statesmen had bungled the peace.

They could not know that their commander-in-chief wished for an end to the killing just as fervently. Amid the daily cares of a siege that was costing more lives than he had

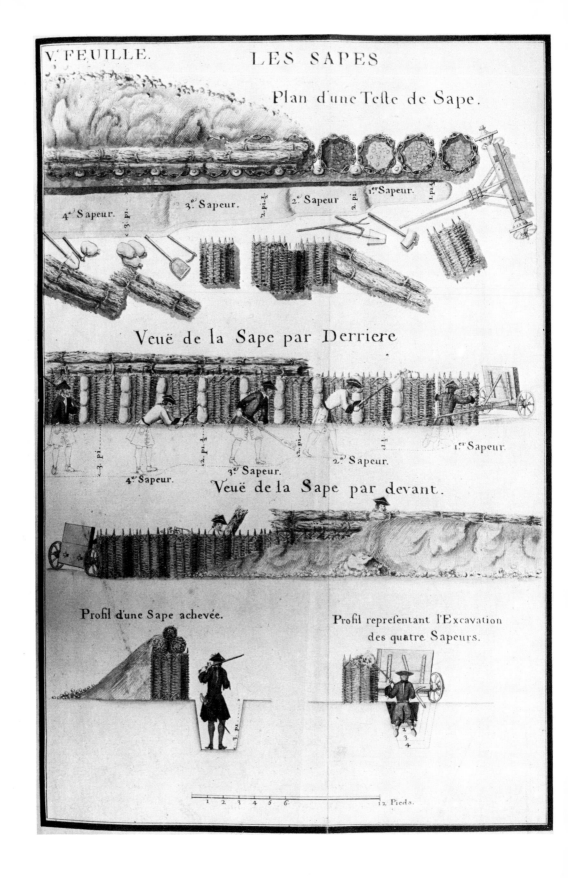

Ve FEUILLE.

LES SAPES

Plan d'une Teſte de Sape.

4.e Sapeur.   3.e Sapeur.   2.e Sapeur   1.er Sapeur.

Veuë de la Sape par Derriere

4.e Sapeur.   3.e Sapeur.   2.e Sapeur.   1.er Sapeur.

Veuë de la Sape par devant.

Profil d'une Sape achevée.

Profil repreſentant l'Excavation des quatre Sapeurs.

1 2 3 4 5 6.   12. Pieds.

hoped, and of feeding an army in a country where the barns were already empty, the Duke's mind kept returning to the peace exchanges still going on between The Hague and Versailles. For this was the period when he was most assiduously dispatching his 'private opinions' to Heinsius and Townshend about the merits of moderation and compromise. He still saw good reason to hope for an early peace, although it was a reason which, as he remarked in a letter to Sarah on 30 July, at the same time distressed his sense of humanity:

> . . . that which gives me the greatest prospect for the happiness of being with you is, that certainly the misery of France increases, which must bring us to a peace. The misery of all the poor people we see is such, that one must be a brute not to pity them. May you ever be happy, and I enjoy some few years of quiet with you, is what I daily pray for.[14]

In August, while the bombs were being rolled into the underground galleries of Tournai, came news of fresh trouble between Sarah and the Queen, although how much Sarah chose to tell her husband about it is not clear. The Queen had written to inform Sarah that at last she had had enough of being bullied and ranted at: 'It is impossible for you to recover my former kindness, but I shall behave myself to you as the Duke of Marlborough's wife and my Groom of the Stole.'[15] Sarah thereupon rushed to seize her quill, draw up and dispatch to the Queen

> . . . a long narrative of a series of faithful services for about twenty-six years past. And knowing how great a respect her Majesty had for the writings of certain eminent divines, I added to my narrative for the directions given by the author of *The Whole Duty of Man* with relation to friendship.[16]

How the Duke must have groaned to hear of this latest quarrel between the two women who dominated his life, with all it implied for his own influence; how he must have despaired at this further evidence that his wife was totally deaf to all his patient advice to show tact and restraint for both their sakes.

Despite all his cares, he still remained outwardly serene-tempered as ever. One day, for example, when he was out riding with one of his commissaries, Marriott, and it began to rain, the Duke

> called his servant for his cloak. The servant not bringing the cloak immediately, he called for it again. The servant, being embarrassed with the straps and buckles, did not come up to him. At last, it raining very hard, the Duke called to him again, and asked him what was he about that he did not bring his cloak. 'You must stay, Sir,' grumbled the fellow, 'if it rains cats and dogs, till I can get at it.' The Duke turned round to Marriott, and said very coolly, 'Now I would not be of that fellow's temper for all the world.'[17]

Instructions from a manual for use by French sappers, Traité de l'Ataque des Places

Immediately Tournai fell, the Duke set off to besiege Mons to the south-east, a nine-day march without a single day's halt for rest, and all in the squelching mud and relent-less rain of that unspeakable summer. Once again, Villars, outwitted by Marlborough's sheer speed and unexpectedness of direction, moved too late to save Mons or reinforce the garrison. But this time Villars, although late, was, with Louis XIV's blessing, game for a fight. On 7 September he advanced towards Mons from the west: a feint. Two days later he sidestepped to the south, drove back a force of allied cavalry, and then, a mile to the north-east of a tiny village called Malplaquet, camped with the last army of France to offer battle to the Duke of Marlborough and Prince Eugène. Villars had chosen his ground well: in his own words, the position was 'narrow enough to give the enemy a formidable task in forcing it but sufficiently well protected by woods on the flanks to prevent our being overlapped on the flank by superior numbers.'[18]

The news of Villars's advance to Malplaquet was brought to the Duke at a moment when his mind was full of domestic anxiety; in the middle of writing a heartfelt letter to Sarah, who had reproached him for his 'unkind refusal' of her requests to chide the Queen for her conduct towards her.

The battle of Malplaquet,
11 September 1709

... I can take pleasure in nothing as long as you continue so uneasy as to think me unkind. I do assure you, upon my honour and salvation, that the only reason why I did not write

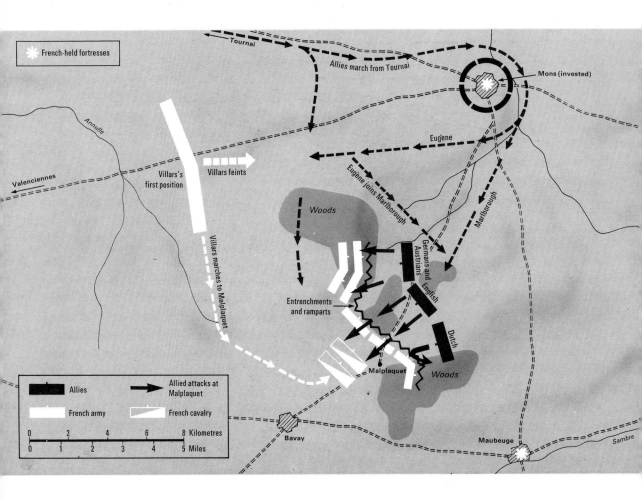

was, that I am very sure it would have had no other effect than that of being shown to Mrs Masham . . . I beg you to be assured, that if I ever see the queen, I shall speak to her just as you would have me; and all the actions of my life shall make the queen, as well as all the world, sensible that you are dearer to me than my own life. . . . [19]

It was at this point that he had to break off and switch his mind from his unhappy wife to the problem of Villars and the French army. A considerable part of the allied forces and all their artillery had not yet arrived. At first, therefore, the Duke feared that Villars might be intending to attack before the whole allied army was concentrated. When during the morning the Duke and Eugène rode out with a strong escort to reconnoitre towards the French, they were not encouraged by what they saw: no sweeping open horizons as at Blenheim and Ramillies, but close and folded countryside broken up by brimming ditches and ponds, and lanes afloat with mud. Dense woods sprawled across the south-western skyline as far as the eye could see to right and left through the misty, saturated atmosphere. There was only one gap through these woods; a little more than a mile across, and filled with French troops.

Despite some cannonading, the French made no attempt to advance further: by nightfall it was clear that they were beginning to dig in where they were. Next day, 10 September, the allied guns came up, together with the rest of the army, except for twenty battalions under General Withers which were still a day's march away. Though the French could be heard in the woods felling trees to make defences, and be seen digging earth ramparts across the open ground in their centre, the Duke and Eugène decided not to attack that day, but wait until the morrow, when the twenty missing battalions would have arrived. At Blenheim in 1704 they had cheerfully sent the Margrave of Baden off to Ingolstadt with 20,000 men on the eve of the battle, so confident were they of beating Tallard with inferior numbers. Now it was five years later, five years of cumulative stress and overwork, and they chose to wait for their twenty extra battalions even if it meant that the French were given another twenty-four hours to strengthen an already formidable position.

The final decision to take up the opportunity of a battle offered by Villars was reached in a council of war on the evening of 10 September. Whereas the allied commanders had seen no reason to seek a battle earlier in the campaign, when peace still seemed in the offing, the situation was different now. For it was clear that the French would never accept the allied terms, unless forced to do so by another great victory.

In the early morning of 11 September 1709 the allied army began to advance through the mists breathed out by the sodden fields. About half-past seven the mist began to lift in the warmth of the sun – a Blenheim or a Ramillies morning. 'Really it was a noble sight,' recollected General Lord Orkney, 'to see so many different bodies of men marching over the plain to attack a thick wood where you could see no men.'[20]

But in that thick wood there were in fact forty battalions of French infantry deployed in depth; there were lines of trenches; dense entanglements of branches stripped of leaves and their ends sharpened. The gap between the woods in the centre of the French position

Part of Marlborough's letter to Lord Townshend describing the battle of Malplaquet

was blocked by ramparts of earth and chained logs, angled to allow flanking fire, and with gaps to permit counter-attacking cavalry to pass through. Thirty-seven battalions of infantry and most of Villars's eighty guns defended these ramparts and the edges of the wood lying to the south side of the gap. Behind the ramparts, the infantry and the guns Villars had posted all his cavalry.

The battle of Malplaquet showing French defences of logs chained together. Oil sketch by Louis Laguerre

The Duke's and Eugène's orders for the battle took strangely little account of the enormous strength of Villars's position. It is likely that they were not even aware of it – a failure of reconnaissance – because the day after the battle the Duke commented, as if making a belated discovery, that, 'Upon viewing the field . . . I find the enemy were very strongly posted, besides their entrenchments. . . .'[21] Rather than attempting to manœuvre Villars out of his defences by a wide march to the north or south round his protective woodlands, the allied commanders chose to launch their army in a frontal assault. As at Ramillies and Blenheim, the initial weight of the attack was to fall on the French flanks

in order to induce the enemy to drain troops from his centre, where eventually the decisive blow was to be struck. It was a stale conception; perhaps all that a tired man with nagging personal worries could think of. The only novelty, or subtlety, lay in that General Withers's detached force of twenty battalions was to advance from the north behind the woods guarding Villars's left flank, and attack straight off the march.

All through the day the allied assaults smashed against the French defences and recoiled, smashed and recoiled, like storm waves against a sea wall. Between 16,000 and 18,000 allied soldiers fell – a fifth of those engaged – before the French centre was at last broken, and the enemy forced into retreat. Even then it was a retreat in good order. The oldest veterans present had never seen such carnage. Eugène himself was wounded; Villars too.

> I can liken this battle [wrote General Lord Orkney to a friend] to nothing so much as an attack on a counterscarp from right to left, and I am sure you would have thought so, if you had seen the field as I did the day after. In many places they lie as thick as ever did a flock of sheep. I really think I never saw the like; particularly where the Dutch Guards attacked it is a miracle. I hope in God it may be the last battle I may ever see. A very few of such would make both parties end the war very soon. . . . None alive ever saw such a battle. God send us a good peace.[22]

Colonel Blackader, who took command of the Cameronians after his commanding officer was killed, was similarly appalled:

> . . . in all my life I have not seen the dead bodies lie so thick as they were in some places about the retrenchments particularly at the battery where the Dutch Guards attacked. . . . The Dutch have suffered most in the battle of any. Their infantry is quite shattered. . . .[23]

Only the British, being reserved for the final onslaught on the French centre, got off relatively lightly, with fewer than six hundred killed and 1,300 wounded out of 14,000 engaged.

The Duke himself ran a high fever after the battle, with aching limbs and burning lips; sleepless, tormented by one of his worst headaches. The postscript he now scribbled on his unposted letter to Sarah betrays his own revulsion from the violence of the day:

> I am so tired that I have but strength enough to tell you that we had this day a very bloody battle; the first part of the day we beat their foot, and afterwards their horse. God Almighty be praised, it is now our power to have what peace we please, and I may be pretty well assured of never being in another battle; but that nor nothing in this world can make me happy if you are not kind.[24]

To Godolphin he spoke of it as 'a very murdering battle'. Even three weeks later, in replying to a letter from Godolphin lamenting the casualties, he was hardly less affected:

> . . . in so great an action it is impossible to get the advantage, but by exposing men's lives; but the lamentable sight and thoughts of it have given me so much disquietude, that I

believe it is the chief cause of my illness; for it is melancholy to see so many brave men killed with whom I have lived these eight years, when we thought ourselves sure of a peace.[25]

Yet, with the battle over, he did all he could to relieve the sufferings of the wounded, allied and French alike. As he reported to the Secretary of State on 16 September:

Upon viewing the field of battle . . . and finding great numbers of French officers and soldiers who had crept into the neighbouring houses and in the woods, wounded in a miserable condition for want of assistance, I wrote to both the Marshals to acquaint them with it that they might send a number of waggons to fetch them away. . . .[26]

In his letter to Villars the Duke began by saying that he was much upset to learn that Villars had been wounded in the battle, but that he hoped his wound would have no lasting ill-effects. It was a characteristic gesture of kindness and courtesy towards a beaten opponent. A badly wounded Irish émigré officer in the French service, Peter Drake, who saw the Duke on the field after the battle, recorded another such gesture. When Drake appealed to the Duke to send him back under his parole of honour to the French army so that his wounds might be dressed, the Duke

immediately called for Cardonnel who was his secretary and then at hand, and asked him how came all these poor gentlemen (meaning the prisoners) were not sent away, he having sent orders for the purpose, and desired carriages to be got ready for those that were not able to walk. . . .[27]

Despite the carnage the Duke believed that Malplaquet had achieved its object: 'we have so beaten them,' he wrote to Heinsius on the evening after the battle, 'that you may have what peace you please.'[28] He judged wrongly. For such were the effects of the battle in France, England and The Netherlands that the possibility of peace on present allied terms had become more remote, not less. As the Duke himself freely acknowledged, the French had never in the entire conflict fought better. They had lost 11,000 men to the allies' 18,000. Malplaquet served to fire, not douse, French morale. From the gilt and glass of Versailles to the wood and rushes of village taverns the French people toasted the two heroes who had saved the honour of France – Villars, who refused to leave the field though badly wounded and in agony, and Boufflers, who led the unavailing charges of the Maison du Roi sword in hand, and then brought the army off in good order at the end of the day.

In England and The Netherlands on the other hand the appalling allied losses and the indecisiveness of the victory greatly strengthened all those who were in favour of an early compromise peace. Malplaquet was a godsend to the Tories and their pamphleteers, and to Robert Harley in particular, in his patient, secret instruction of the Queen, who was herself sick of war and the death of men. The slow mysterious tide of English opinion, which in 1708 had supported the Whigs in their policy of war until a hard peace was won, was now ebbing away from them. The Whig cabinet itself was riven by intrigues and quarrels.

There was in all this a personal tragedy for Marlborough. His own feelings about war and peace during 1709 had been far more in tune with the nation's than had been those of his Whig colleagues. Had he therefore elected to make a stand in the spring and summer against the Whig peace terms, he would have caught the tide of national opinion; the tide of the future. He had elected not to make such a stand because of the Whig Junto's apparent power. Yet in the event the Whig Junto's power had already become hardly more than a shell. Moreover, the Duke's inglorious efforts to avoid being blamed personally for the policy of the Whigs by reducing himself to a mere instrument had hopelessly failed. In Godolphin's words, the two of them were 'railed at every day, for haveing a mind, as they call it, to perpetuate the warr, and wee are told wee shall bee worry'd next winter, for refusing a good peace, and insisting on terms which it was impossible for France to perform.'[29]

Politically too, therefore, the Duke's request to the Queen in the month after Malplaquet to be made Captain-General for life could not have been more ill-timed or ill-judged. It was a prodigal gift of ammunition to the growing army of his critics. The Tories believed – or professed to believe – that like Cromwell he was aiming to use his position at the head of the army to become 'perpetual dictator'.

In November, with only the fortress of Mons as a further trophy of military success, the Duke sailed for England. On the 18th he stepped on to the shingle at the Suffolk fishing village of Aldeburgh, a huddle of cottages, a church and a half-timbered moot hall marooned amid marshes, heath and wind. For Marlborough it was a landfall uneasy with forebodings; and he was to find these forebodings more than fulfilled in the course of the winter to come.

CHAPTER FOURTEEN

THE MALICE OF
A BEDCHAMBER WOMAN

As 1710 came in, the ninth year of the war, the country was beginning to feel that much as it enjoyed victories while the bells were ringing, they were no longer enough. The gentry flinched at the taxes necessary to keep ever larger armies in the field; the poor were growing tired of furnishing recruits and going hungry because of high food prices. And the Whig government, the men of war, were ever more split by internal differences and animosities. Robert Harley, observing the scene with a sage professional eye, judged that the time had now come to open his campaign to topple the Whigs from power, and revenge himself on Marlborough and Godolphin for the humiliating defeat they had inflicted on him two years earlier. Yet Harley was not solely inspired by revenge. Because of the Duke's and Godolphin's apparent concord with Whig policy, he saw them as obstacles to the compromise peace which he and his closest associate, Henry St John, believed that England needed.

The Queen served as Harley's willing ally. She was nevertheless far from being his tame creature, as one day he was to find out. She had no wish to exchange her tutelage under the Marlboroughs for another; she meant to be a real queen at last. Indeed Anne's memories of 'Mrs Morley's' long years of deference to 'Mr and Mrs Freeman' provided her with her own motive for wanting to see the Marlboroughs' power broken. But Harley and the Queen recognized that this process must be accomplished by stealth, by undermining rather than frontal assault; otherwise the Duke, with his immense prestige in the country, might defeat them, as he had defeated them at the end of 1708.

At the beginning of January 1710 chance opened the way for them to begin their mining operations. The death of Lord Essex left vacant the governorship of the Tower of London and the colonelcy of his regiment of dragoons. Soon the Duke learned that the Queen, without consulting him as Captain-General, had appointed Earl Rivers as Governor of the Tower and promised the colonelcy of dragoons to Abigail Masham's incompetent soldier brother Jack Hill. The Duke, who had his own candidates for both vacancies, at once saw that here, under the guise of the Queen's prerogative right to make military appointments, he faced a challenge to his authority over the army itself. He was the more disquieted because he was very well aware that he had his enemies in the army; jealous cliques ready to croak and criticize. If once he ceased to be the sole channel of advancement, he would lose the whip that kept the restless pulling with the remainder of the team.

The Duke did not find his audiences with the Queen on the topic agreeable experiences. It was hard to believe that this woman, as aloof and cold as her profile on a coin, had once been an intimate friend, fond and trusting. The Duke for his part was at his most loftily dignified. Of Jack Hill's promised colonelcy he observed: 'It is, Madam, to set up a standard of disaffection to rally all the malcontent officers in the army.'[1] But the Queen had all too evidently made up her mind not to hearken to anything he said. Dismissed at the end of a galling interview with the words, 'You do well to consult with your friends,' he strode from the royal closet in a rare state of open anger.

'. . . as aloof and cold as her profile on the coin . . .' A coin, with Queen Anne's profile, struck to commemorate Malplaquet

As his choler subsided, he considered what he should do. Realizing how much really lay at stake in the superficially trivial enough matter of these appointments, the Duke made up his mind to force the Queen to choose finally between himself and Abigail. If the Queen would not give way, then this was the moment to resign and enjoy that 'quiet' he longed for. He therefore looked to his Whig colleagues to rally in his support. After all, it was their fight too; a victory for the Queen and Harley over the two appointments, together with the survival of Abigail as an essential go-between, threatened the Junto no less than himself. At first the Junto – his 'friends' in the Queen's word – backed his decision to resign. Then they wavered; the divisions among them opened up afresh. The moderates looked for escape in a compromise. Lord Somers saw the Queen in private and pointed out to her that the Duke was 'not to be considered merely as a private object, because all the eyes of Europe are fixed upon him'; and that to weaken his authority would have dire effects throughout the army and beyond.

The Queen remained adamant; Marlborough remained determined to resign. By way of giving public expression of his state of mind, he left the court and went down to join Sarah at Windsor Lodge. But when he was absent from the next privy council meeting, the Queen did not even bother to inquire where he was – which enraged the Duke more. He dispatched a draft letter of resignation for Godolphin to show to their Whig colleagues before it was sent to the Queen. But anxious conclaves at the Duke of Devonshire's house found the Junto more split and irresolute than ever. Marlborough now learned that the men to whom last year he had committed his career, to whom he had shown such submissive loyalty, would not after all stand with him. Even his old friend Godolphin, a man now crumbling under his anxieties and responsibilities, counselled moderation. The Duke found himself alone. And once again, at a turning point in his life, he could not bring himself to take, and act on, his own solitary decision. Once again he demonstrated that 'he did not love to be singular', allowing himself to be persuaded by Godolphin to delete from his letter the crucial last sentence telling the Queen that she must dismiss Abigail or accept his resignation. The letter the Duke actually dispatched was therefore no more than an impotent, if heartfelt, expression of anger:

I beg your Majesty will be so just to me, as not to think I can be so unreasonable as to be mortified to the degree I am, if it proceed'd only from this one thing. . . . But this is only one of a great many mortifications I have met with, and as I may not have many opertunitys of writting to you, let me beg of your majesty to reflect what your own people, and the rest of the world must think, who have been witnesses of the love, zeal and duty, with which I have serv'd you, when thay shall see that after all I have done, it has not been able to protect me against the mallice of a bedchamber woman. . . .[2]

While this letter was still on its way to the Queen, however, she and her private advisers, noting the Duke's ominous retirement to the country, had thought better of provoking him too far at this stage. She summoned Godolphin and informed him that of the two appointments in dispute she would not after all insist on Jack Hill's colonelcy. At this the Duke's professional instinct scented an enemy poised on the brink of running, and with the offensive spirit he always showed in the field but so rarely off it, he now wanted to press on and expel Abigail from the royal bedchamber into the street. For his instinct also told him that this was the moment to 'venture', and smash the threat from Abigail and Harley once and for all.

But again Godolphin and the Junto counselled against a drastic course; if the Duke would not accept the compromise the Queen had graciously offered, he would, they argued, lay himself open to the charge of tyrannizing over her. And again the Duke yielded to the consensus of his colleagues.

For the Duke, for Godolphin and for the Whig Junto the affair of Lord Rivers's and Jack Hill's appointments marked that first fatal act of appeasement which opens the way to step-by-step defeat.

Marlborough himself was back in the Low Countries organizing the coming campaign when in March the Queen and Harley scored their next victory; one which they had not even sought, but which instead had been served up to them by a calamitous blunder on the part of the Whig Junto. The Junto – with Godolphin's concurrence – impeached and put on trial before the House of Lords a High Tory cleric, one Dr Sacheverell, who the previous November had delivered a sermon denouncing certain fundamental Whig doctrines. It was the Junto's calculation that by convicting and heavily punishing Sacheverell in a show trial before the nation they would paste the label 'Jacobite' on him and thereafter on the Tories in general. By this means the Tories would be confounded and the Whigs' own supporters rallied. Instead the Whigs provided an opportunity for all the simmering popular hostility towards them to erupt in public. Each day Sacheverell was escorted to Westminster like a hero by his fellow citizens. The Queen was present throughout the trial. So too were the ladies of nobility. The 'mobile' – the mob – got drunk in Sacheverell's support, and rioted in true English style. As the trial went on, it was observed that moderate peers like Somerset and Shrewsbury were ominously drifting away from support of the government towards Harley's middle-of-the-road Tories. And in the outcome, as Godolphin reported to the Duke, 'all this bustle and fatigue' resulted in the conviction of Sacheverell by only sixty-nine votes to fifty-two. A motion to block his preferment in the Church was lost by one vote. His sole punishment was to be barred from preaching for three years. The

The trial of Dr Sacheverell. A contemporary cartoon. Engraving

bull the Whig matadors had hoped ceremonially to kill in the arena of national opinion lumbered off in triumph, leaving them gruesomely gored amid the jeers of their enemies.

Marlborough nevertheless remained 'resolved never to part from the interests of the Whigs'. He confessed himself 'amazed' that Lord Shrewsbury, who had voted for Sacheverell's acquittal, 'could think it possible for the Tories to be strong enough to ruin the Whigs, in conjunction with the Lord Treasurer and me'.[3] But it was Shrewsbury, not the Duke, who read the political future aright. In clinging on to the Whigs Marlborough was like a shipwrecked sailor mistaking a waterlogged spar for sound and buoyant timber. It was a perhaps understandable mistake; he was out of England, out of touch; his knowledge of the trial derived only from Sarah's and Godolphin's letters. Moreover, having spent some ten months of every year for the last nine years abroad, he had lost touch generally with the subtle shifts and movements of British politics and opinion.

The Whig Junto too failed to read the right lessons from the Sacheverell trial, and there was no similar excuse for them. They completely failed to comprehend the nation's desire for an end to the war. In March 1710 fresh peace talks opened between the allies and France, this time at Geertruidenberg. Although Louis XIV was prepared to make further concessions – give up Alsace, pay a subsidy to the allies in aid of their efforts to evict his grandson from Spain – the Whig government's instructions to Lord Townshend allowed for no compromise over the terms demanded in 1709. The Dutch, well bribed by the Barrier Treaty, supported the Whig demands; the Habsburg Empire, never behind in greed, likewise. Lord Cowper, the Lord Chancellor and perhaps the wisest member of the Junto, wrote of the allied peace terms: 'For my part, nothing but seeing so great men believe it could ever include me to think France reduced so low as to accept such terms.'[4]

Marlborough for his part was even more careful than in the previous year to take no responsibility at all for the negotiations, styling himself 'white paper' on which the cabinet could write its instructions. It was a sad role for the man who had once led the alliance; and sadder still that the Duke should have largely chosen it for himself. For, as his troubles mounted and his spirit flagged, he was gradually yielding to a mood of fatalistic acceptance. 'I am so weary,' he wrote to Sarah after his arrival in the Netherlands, 'and care so little for the management of any body but yourself, that I am very indifferent how anything goes, but what leads me to a quiet life.'[5] He entertained scant hope that the Geertruidenberg negotiations would succeed; taking it that he would have to do his best once more to seek peace at the head of his army. Nevertheless, as he confessed to Sarah on 14 April, he was so discouraged by everything he saw that

> I have never, during this war, gone into the field with so heavy a heart as I do at this time. I own to you that the present humours in England give me a good deal of trouble; for I cannot see how it is possible they should mend, till every thing is yet worse.[6]

In all the circumstances it was hardly surprising that he did not feel emboldened to undertake some brilliant but risky stroke. Instead, on 23 April, he laid siege to the fortress of Douai, as the first move in a methodical offensive aimed at clearing a way right through the French triple chain of frontier fortresses, and then advancing on the town of Arras.

While the Duke and Eugène were besieging Douai and manœuvring against Villars – still weak and in pain from his wound at Malplaquet but no less able – news came from Sarah of more trouble at home. She and the Queen had had another tremendous quarrel.

After the Queen the year before had pronounced their friendship over, she and Sarah remained at least on speaking terms over official business. Such a purely formal relation⁄ship did not prevent Sarah, in her obsession with her wrongs, from tirelessly writing indictments and remonstrances to the Queen. Moreover, Sarah's notion of the speaking terms appropriate between Groom of the Stole and Queen had hardly served to minimize friction. According to Lord Dartmouth,

> The last free conference she had with her was at Windsor, where Mrs Danvers, who was then in waiting, told me, the duchess reproached her for above an hour with her own and her family's services, in so loud and shrill a voice, that the footmen at the bottom of the back⁄stairs could hear her: and all this storm was raised for the queen's having ordered a bottle of wine a day to be allowed for her laundress, without her acquainting her grace with it. The queen, seeing her so outrageous, got up, to have gone out of the room: the duchess clapped

her back against the door, and told her that she should hear her out, for that was the least favour she could do her, in return for having set and kept the crown upon her head. As soon as she had done raging, she flounced out of the room, and said, she did not care if she never saw her more: to which the queen replied very calmly, that she thought the seldomer the better.[7]

Although Dartmouth was no friend to the Marlboroughs, there is in all this circumstantial detail the ring of an authentic eye-witness account.

In April Sarah came to hear that tales had been carried to the Queen that she, Sarah, was in the habit of passing rude comments about her sovereign. Carried away once more by her mania for self-vindication, Sarah sought an interview with the Queen. The Queen manœuvred in retreat: this or that day would be inconvenient; Sarah might put it in writing. She put it in writing, assuring the Queen that she merely wanted an opportunity to state her case, and would expect no reply. Finally Sarah went to Kensington Palace and there and then asked the page-in-waiting for an immediate audience with the Queen. While the page departed on this errand, the Duchess of Marlborough, once the most powerful woman in the country after Anne herself, waited in a windowseat in the gallery like, in her own words, 'a Scotch lady with a petition, instead of a trusted and lifelong confidante'.

The Queen would see her. But when the two women stood face to face, Anne adopted the same tactics that had maddened even Marlborough into a rage during their interview about Jack Hill's colonelcy. She refused to respond to anything Sarah had to say. Instead at intervals throughout Sarah's implorings she simply delivered variations on the same catch phrase: 'I will give you no answer'; 'You desired no answer, and you shall have none'; 'You said you desired no answer, and I shall give you none'; 'I shall make no answer to anything you say'; 'You desired no answer, and you shall have none.'

By such means the Queen reduced Sarah to streaming tears of chagrin and despair – a triumph of the dull over the clever; of the always homely over the still handsome. Mrs Morley had evened the score at last. Finally Sarah, utterly beside herself, told the Queen: 'I am confident you will suffer in this world or the next for so much inhumanity.' The Queen was still not to be drawn. 'That will be to myself,' she answered and left the room. These were the last words they were ever to exchange.[8] Then Sarah was back in a windowseat, drying her red and puffy eyes before she swept through the malicious gaze of the court and home to Windsor Lodge.

To Sarah's letter about these gloomy events, the Duke could only reply offering sympathy and good advice: the Queen's treatment of her was 'so harsh, that I think you should be persuaded not to expose yourself any more in speaking to her majesty'.[9] In fact the two women were never to see each other again. But Sarah's letter was not the only depressing item to arrive on Marlborough's table in that same batch of post. It also brought him news that the Queen, evidently at Harley's prompting and without prior consultation with Godolphin or other ministers, had sacked the Whig Lord Chamberlain and replaced him with the Earl of Shrewsbury. It was an ominous demonstration both of her independence and her intent.

In May the political atmosphere grew murkier with intrigue and menace; Marlborough's own son-in-law, Lord Sunderland, was tipped as the Whig minister next in line for dismissal. Unease gnawed at the Duke's peace of mind.

> I hear of so many disagreeable things [he wrote to Sarah on the 19th] that make it very reasonable both for myself and you to take no steps but what may lead to a quiet life. This being the case, am I not to be pitied, that am every day in danger of exposing my life for the good of those who are seeking my ruin?'[10]

At least he was in better health now. 'I am this day three-score,' he informed Godolphin on 26 May, 'but I thank God, I find myself in so good health, that I hope to end this campaign without being sensible of the inconveniences of old age.'[11]

Three days later a letter from Robert Walpole, the Secretary-at-War, informed him that the Queen was once more seeking to erode his authority over the army. The Duke had submitted the names of colonels to be promoted to brigadier, limiting the fortunate officers to a certain date of seniority, in order not to upset the delicate balance of precedence throughout the national contingents which made up the army in British pay. However, by a remarkable but genuine coincidence, Colonel Masham, Abigail's husband, and Colonel Hill, her brother, were one place too low on the colonels' list to qualify. The Queen believed, with some reason, that the world would think that they had been deliberately left out. She ordered Walpole to include their names without telling the Duke. Walpole, loyal to his chief, refused and insisted on letting the Duke know. So the Duke again faced a challenge in which broad principle and the explosively personal were messily entwined.

He decided that he must stand firm on the principle. But as before his Whig colleagues looked the other way. Finding himself once more without support, the Duke therefore had no alternative but to accept another defeat. Colonels Masham and Hill both became brigadiers.

By June the Queen was expressing her intention of dismissing Lord Sunderland. For she and Harley had now measured the Junto's spinelessness and disarray. It was time to bring down one of their big men – and who better than Sunderland, hated by the Queen, occupying one of the principal offices of state, and having as a victim the added advantage of being the Marlboroughs' son-in-law?

The Duke recognized that the moment had come to fight a decisive battle. As he pointed out to Sarah, 'if the Whigs suffer Lord Sunderland to be removed, I think in a very short time everything will be in confusion.'[12] He realized that the Queen and Harley were looking beyond Sunderland to the complete destruction of the Whigs. Yet he had little faith in the Whigs' willingness to stand together and fight. He had now come to see what a disastrous misjudgment he had made in committing his own future to the Whigs.

Would not you have some time ago thought anybody mad [he asked Sarah] that should have believed it would ever have been in the power of Mr Harley and Mrs Masham to make the Whigs to remain tamely quiet?[13]

John, 2nd Duke of Argyll (1678–1743). Painting by William Aikman (1682–1731)

Nor was the campaign going as well as he had hoped. The siege of Douai still dragged on owing to the pedantic slowness of the allied engineers. The army itself was now split by faction: a clique of officers round the ambitious and jealous Duke of Argyll croaked away diligently that 'The mighty Prince of Blenheim', as Argyll termed Marlborough, was prolonging the war for his personal benefit.

Robert Walpole, Earl of Orford (1676–1745). Painting by Sir Godfrey Kneller

Under all the pressures Marlborough's military nerve itself was beginning to weaken now. 'My wishes and duty are the same,' Marlborough confessed to Godolphin on 12 June, 'but I can't say that I have the same sanguine prophetic spirit I did use to have; for in all the former actions I did never doubt of success, we having had the great blessing of being of one mind. . . .'[14] The sniping of Argyll and his Tory friends over in England particularly embittered him:

> . . . I must every summer venture my life in a battle, and be found fault with in the winter for not bringing home a peace, though I wish for it with all my heart and soul.[15]

On 29 June, the same day that the French garrison of Douai marched out in surrender, the Duke received a letter from Godolphin with the news that the Queen had finally dismissed Sunderland. Not a single one of Sunderland's Whig colleagues resigned with him. The news plunged the Duke even deeper into a despondency which the taking of Douai did nothing to relieve:

> God knows [he replied to Godolphin] what we shall be able to do more in this country. As it is like to be my last campaign I hope He will bless us with some farther success, and that things may be made easier for those that shall succeed me; for, as it now is, my head is perpe-tually hot. This, joined with the disagreeable things I received from England, makes me every minute wish to be a hermit. When you have this letter pray burn it; for my desire is, that nobody should know my complaints, but that the world may continue in their error of thinking me a happy man; for I think it better to be envied than pitied, for there is no such thing as good nature left in this world.[16]

In London and in the capitals of Europe it was feared that the dismissal of the Duke's son-in-law would provoke him into resigning, and Godolphin with him. The Queen therefore wrote to the Lord Treasurer in order to allay their all too justified apprehensions about the future, and dissuade them from giving up their posts before she and Harley were ready to sack them.

> I have no thoughts of taking the Duke of Marlborough from the heade of the army, nor I dare say nobody els(e); if he & you should do soe wrong a thing at any time . . . as to desert my service, what confusion might happen would lye at your doors, & you alone would be answerable & nobody els(e). . . .[17]

This deftly turned piece of hypocrisy was not the only appeal the Duke was to receive. Godolphin and all the Whig ministers implored him to remain at the head of the army. Heinsius and the Habsburg Emperor added their own entreaties. All were agreed that he must stay for the sake of the Grand Alliance and of Europe. Torn and troubled as he was, Marlborough decided that they were right; he must go on. But he was resolved henceforward to be nothing more than a soldier at the head of the army. In the summer of 1710, having long shed his higher responsibilities for allied policy, the Duke even sought to limit his diplomatic contacts to mere routine matters.

So acute had become his sense of insecurity that he might have been back among the plottings and beheadings of his early court life under Charles II and James II. He told Sarah that he could say little in his letters because he was sure they were being opened. In his anxiety for her, he warned: 'For God's sake let me beg of you to be careful of your behaviour, for you are in a country amongst tigers and wolves.'[18] Give nothing away, keep out of trouble, offer no target, smile – the old habitual responses of the 1680s and 1690s were triggered again.

At the same time his fatalism deepened. Perhaps it was all God's punishment for having too much pride and ambition. After the thanksgiving service for the taking of Douai, he confided to Sarah: 'We must look upon this correction of His as a favour, if it atones for our past actions.'[19]

At the beginning of July the Duke and Eugène with 120,000 men faced Villars with a larger army west of Arras, the main objective of the allied offensive. Villars once again had chosen his position well. Should they attack him? The Duke had already taken the trouble when Douai fell to ask Heinsius whether or not it was politically necessary to risk a battle. Heinsius, possibly surprised by this unwonted deference to his strategic wisdom after so many years of being told by Marlborough what the allies ought to do, answered that he left the decision to the generals, but added his layman's opinion that a battle was not called for. The generals considered Villars's strong position and his superior numbers, and went off to besiege Béthune instead. The Duke had by now abandoned a project for landing a force at Calais or Boulogne in conjunction with the advance of the main army. His reasons were not military, but political and personal, as he explained to Godolphin at the beginning of August: '. . . as everything is now, I dare attempt nothing, but what I am almost sure must succeed; nor am I sure that those now in power would keep my secret.' And he added two days later: 'Besides I now feel, though I mean never so well, should I not have success, I should find too many ready to blame me; so that if I am more cautious than heretofore, I hope the queen will approve of it. . . .'[20]

Meanwhile Louis XIV had broken off the peace negotiations at Geertruidenberg.

In the last week of August the same post brought Marlborough a cold and brief note from the Queen and a letter from Godolphin, both of them bearing the worst tidings of the year, and, to the Duke, the least expected. Godolphin had been dismissed as Lord Treasurer. Moreover, the Treasury had been put in commission and Harley appointed Chancellor of the Exchequer.

The Queen did not even reward Godolphin with a final audience for his years of devoted overwork in her service. Instead of returning his white staff, symbol of his office, to her personally, he was ordered simply to break it – just as Anne had broken and discarded him.

Godolphin's dismissal offered the Duke his last pretext and opportunity for giving battle to the Queen and Harley. He was still a national hero and a figure of immense European prestige. Indeed in not sacking the Duke along with Godolphin, the Queen and Harley acknowledged that he was still indispensable, even to them. If the Duke were to resign, it would explode a crisis of the first magnitude, both in England and abroad; and Harley's stealthy task would be rendered impossible.

Personal feelings and personal loyalty might also have been expected to impel the Duke into resignation, even though Godolphin himself implored the Duke to stay at his post for the public good, for Godolphin's fall, in the Duke's own words, occasioned in him 'very melancholy thoughts'. 'It is impossible for me to express', he wrote to his old friend on 30 August, 'the very uneasy and extravagant thoughts I have had since the news of your being out.'[21]

Nevertheless, this time Marlborough does not seem even to have considered resigning. It was as if after having been dissuaded from resigning on earlier occasions he had reached a final decision to soldier on come what may.

Whatever happens [he told Godolphin on 28 August], whilst I have life, I shall be faithfully yours. I have taken my resolution of troubling my head as little as is possible with
politics, but apply my thoughts wholly how to finish this campaign to the best advantage. . . .[22]

The Duke and Sarah were to make good his promise; Godolphin, a relatively poor
man, was to live with them and be looked after by them until his death in 1712.

Despite this personal fidelity, Marlborough's reaction to the fall of his closest friend
was curiously passive, and yet at the same time in keeping with all the personal and
political dealings of his life; a further manifestation of that lack of toughness of will, of
readiness to risk, of sheer pugnacity even, which contrasts so strangely with his behaviour
in the face of a French army. Nevertheless, there was a fresh element now. After nine years
of crushing work and responsibility he was spiritually an exhausted man; and in the
face of the Queen's hurtful malice and his enemies' remorseless attacks he had yielded
to a fatalism always latent in his character. It was a fatalism which lay perilously close, in
a personal sense, to defeatism; and defeatism is the prelude to defeat, the ultimate of
humiliations.

In the field, however, he still slogged on with his old pertinacity. Béthune surrendered
on 28 August 1710, and the allied forces moved on to besiege the fortresses of Aire and
St Venant simultaneously.

Meanwhile Harley was consummating his protracted and cunning political campaign
with final victory. By the middle of September the last of the Whig Junto had been
prised from the great offices of state. The way was clear for a general election, which in
that age followed rather than preceded a change of government. In October Tories of
every colour from moderates like Harley himself to near-Jacobites swept the polls; and
in the new Parliament there were some three hundred and twenty Tories to one hundred
and fifty Whigs.

Harley's power was now unassailable; the Duke had missed his last chance of beating
him off. Nevertheless, the advent of Tory supremacy presented the Duke yet again with
that harsh and familiar choice: should he go or should he stay? He pondered the problem
all through a bleak and rainy autumn while Aire and St Venant were falling. He was
still pondering it in December, back in the Mauritshuis at The Hague, where he
lingered in his reluctance to return to England and thereby shrink from a great European
figure into a butt of party venom and insult.

He could of course simply resign – no longer as a political counterstroke, but in order
to escape from bondage to his political foes into the quiet of retirement. If he went now,
he would go at his own time and of his own volition, and not when his enemies should
please. On the other hand, he could seek to make a deal with the new ministry. After all,
St John, the new Secretary of State, had once been his close and admiring colleague as
Secretary-at-War; it was a friendship he could play on.

Harley and St John wished to conclude such a deal. They needed Marlborough in
order to hold the alliance together until they had completed secret peace negotiations
with Louis XIV, and could therefore force the allies into agreeing to a peace. They

*Marlborough's sword. The
inscription on the blade reads:
'This was the Sword of John
Duke of Marlborough & worn
by him in all his Victories from
y^e Year 1701 to y^e Year 1712'.*

discreetly sounded the Duke out through an intermediary, John Drummond, a Scots merchant living in Amsterdam. Drummond reported to Harley on 9 December that Marlborough was 'resolved to live with you if you will make it practicable or possible for him; he will not enter into the heats of party debates. . . .'[23] He added that Marl- borough 'pretty passionately' asked: 'do they imagine I must make the first advances after all the insults and affronts they have put on me?' This was not enough for the Tory leaders. St John replied to Drummond that an arrangement was only possible if the Duke 'comes home and disengages himself from the Whigs; if he puts a stop to the rage and fury of his wife. . . .'[24] Moreover, since the Queen wanted Sarah out of her court offices, the Duke must also press her into resigning them.

At base, therefore, the Duke was being asked to choose between the Queen's new ministry on the one hand, and Sarah on the other.

The Tory ministers had picked on the one issue in the Duke's life over which he could never appease, never compromise, never manœuvre. Already at the beginning of October, he had assured Sarah that

> My greatest concern is, if possible, to avoid the harsh usage which is most certainly resolved to be put in practice against you, for whom I must ever be more concerned than for all the other things in the world.[25]

So there could be no question of his going over to the Tories. Should he then after all resign, in the face of all their provocations – officers known to be close adherents of his cashiered on trumped-up charges; those hostile to him promoted? Yet he was equally determined not to join the Whigs in opposition; he meant henceforth to steer clear of party, which he had always detested, and which he now had all the better reason for despising. The course of action which would have been most to his own liking was to retire completely to the country. Three considerations stopped him. In the first place, the allies, especially his colleague Eugène, pleaded with him to remain in command. Secondly, the Queen, sickly hulk that she was, might die at any time; and with crypto- Jacobites thronging the Tory benches in the House of Commons, the Protestant Hanoverian succession stood in danger of being overturned in favour of the Pretender James III. Marlborough therefore wished to retain command of the army as a safeguard against its falling into Jacobite hands. And thirdly there was the simple matter of duty. As he was to tell the Hanoverian envoy to The Netherlands in spring 1711, 'I call God to witness that I love my Queen and my country, and it is for this motive that I have made so much effort to keep my post.'[26]

Marlborough studying a plan of Bouchain with General Armstrong. Painting by Enoch Seeman (1694–1744). Sarah said of it, 'I really think that picture of your grandfather with Mr Armstrong as like him as I ever saw.'

The Tory triumph presented another problem which touched him near; his huge and still unfinished palace of Blenheim, near Woodstock. It was being built out of crown funds: a gift from the Queen and the nation. There was a danger that under the new ministry these funds would dry up; that the Duke would find himself paying the work- men out of his own pocket. He and his Duchess – who never liked Blenheim, and thought it 'the greatest weakness' the Duke ever had – were at one over this question.

They would take care to give no orders whatsoever to the architect or workmen; all instructions must come from the Treasury. If no such instructions were forthcoming, the building would have to moulder away unfinished in the rains and frosts. Yet this characteristic hardheaded shrewdness overlay yet more bitter disillusion, for to the Duke Blenheim Palace had always meant much as the symbol of his victories. 'Whilst Lord Godolphin was in,' he wrote to Sarah in October, 'and I had the Queen's favour, I was very earnest to have had it finished; but, as it is, I am grown very indifferent.'[27]

In January 1711 he at last returned to England to make his humiliating peace with his enemies. The common people cheered him home; but the Queen was cold, expressing with brief formality her desire that he should continue to serve. His interview later with St John showed him how far he had fallen. Henceforward, he was brusquely told, he was to be nothing more than the unquestioningly obedient military instrument of the Queen's new ministers, Messrs Harley and St John. Only on that condition could he hope to retain his command. He was also told that 'his true interest consisted in getting rid of his wife [from her court offices] . . . as soon as he could. . . .'[28]

London society looked on the returned Duke and wondered to see him 'much thinner and greatly altered'[29]; the youthful face decayed into a haggard and ageing visage. 'Marlborough has suffered so much', wrote the Imperial Ambassador, 'that he no longer looks like himself.'[30]

On 27 January 1711 the Duke saw the Queen in a last attempt to save Sarah from dismissal. He brought with him a letter from Sarah to the Queen in which she contritely, abjectly, apologized for all or anything she might have done to offend her, and begged for forgiveness. The Queen refused to look at the letter. The Duke implored her to do so; and with reluctance she broke the seal and read it:

> Though I never thought of troubling your Majesty in this manner again, yet the circumstances I see my Lord Marlborough in, and the apprehension I have that he cannot live six months, if there is not some end put to his sufferings on my account, makes it impossible for me to resist doing everything in my power to ease him. . . .[31]

And so on. The Queen, however, was not in the mood to forgive, but to enjoy the pleasures of cruelty and power. 'I cannot change my resolution,' she told the Duke. He went on, nevertheless, to entreat her not to dismiss Sarah until the end of the war; he sought to convince her of the sincerity of Sarah's contrition and regret. His reward for this grovelling was the Queen's demand for the Gold Key, symbol of Sarah's office, within three days. At this the Duke fell on his knees before her and begged that at least it might be ten days. The Queen, gazing down on this man who had made herself and her reign all they were, changed her mind. She now demanded that the Key be delivered up in two days instead of three.

In the first week of March 1711 Marlborough arrived at The Hague to make ready for what was to prove his last campaign. He plunged – no doubt with relief – into the

Sarah Marlborough with the
Gold Key at her waist. Painting
by Sir Godfrey Kneller

familiar business of organizing and concentrating an international army and getting it into the field. Ageing and crumbling in health though he now was, he seemed to have lost little of his capacity for work. Day after day the letters poured forth from his writing table in the Mauritshuis: to kings and princes about the sizes of their contingents and the times and places of rendezvous; to bread contractors; to various city fathers about billets and forage; letters about the stocking of forward magazines; letters about recruits and remounts and the hiring of wagons.

Yet he was not allowed to forget his tribulations in England. Sarah still remained too much of a fighter, too certain she was right, to heed his warnings to go to the country and shut up. Instead she attacked the Tory ministers by all possible means, including that favourite device of the age, the broadside or lampoon. Quite apart from the embarrassment caused to her husband, who was striving to maintain at least outwardly cordial relations with Harley and St John for the sake of the campaign, the productions of her hack writers naturally invited replies of a highly personal nature from those employed by the ministry. Marlborough, a sensitive man, and never more so than now, did not take the Tory lampoons with the robust contempt which the Duke of Wellington was to reserve for print. He repeatedly implored Sarah to be discreet for his sake:

> ... whilst I am in the service I am in their power, especially by the villainous way of printing which stabs me to the heart; so that I beg of you, as for the quiet of my life, that you will be careful never to write anything that may anger them ... I must beg you will, for my sake, be careful in your discourse, as well as in your letters.[32]

This year the Duke had hoped to bring greatly superior numbers against Villars. Fate and the Tory ministry trampled on these hopes. The ministry withdrew five of his British battalions for an expedition against Quebec to be commanded by Abigail's brother Jack Hill; an enterprise which ended unsurprisingly in disaster. In April the Habsburg Emperor Joseph died of smallpox, and was succeeded by Charles VI (Charles III, the allied candidate for the Spanish throne). This blew out the foundations of allied policy, for they had no new candidate in mind, and it was as unthinkable that the Spanish Empire should be united to the Habsburg crown as to the French. The Emperor's death directly affected Marlborough's plans, moreover, because the Imperial government in Vienna recalled Prince Eugène and his troops from the Low Countries to Germany as a precaution against unrest and foreign interference.

On 13 June, a day of stunning heat, Eugène rode away for the Rhine, and the Duke led the allied army into the field for the last time.

He was inferior to the French in numbers now; and Villars, always good at digging, had spent the winter constructing a powerful line of field fortifications all the way from the Channel coast at Montreuil to Valenciennes, protected along its whole length by rivers, canals, or diverted watercourses. Villars dubbed them, with characteristic braggadocio, the Ne Plus Ultra Lines. Nevertheless, the Duke still intended to break through them and take the fortress of Bouchain, guarding the junction of the rivers

Sensée and Scheldt, which would open the way for an advance yet deeper into Louis XIV's kingdom.

He planned to deceive Villars into thinking that his offensive was to fall on the western sector of the Lines, near Arras; then to countermarch eastward and break through the Lines in the east round Arleux on the River Sensée and only some seven miles from Bouchain. Here he knew from intelligence reports that causeways had been left across the defensive inundations for the use of local peasants. But first the Duke had to neutralize the fortifications of Arleux, which barred access to the causeways – and do so without alerting Villars that this was where the allied attack was to fall.

There followed a brilliant exercise in psychological deception; perhaps the most subtly cunning manœuvres of his whole career. On 6 July he took Arleux in a night attack, garrisoned it and left orders to strengthen its fortifications. On 20 July he transferred the main body of the army to the western sector of the French defences, near Arras – duly followed by Villars. Villars, however, an active, enterprising commander, detached a force to retake Arleux – just as the Duke hoped and intended. Moreover, having retaken it, Villars ordered that the fortifications of Arleux be demolished so that, as he saw it, they could no longer be of use to the Duke. This was equally as the Duke had wished. For Villars had been tricked into himself demolishing the defences at the point where the Duke proposed eventually to launch his decisive attack. Nevertheless, in public the Duke professed to be deeply chagrined at Villars's 'success'. For the benefit of French spies he angrily proclaimed his intention of 'being even with Villars'. The Duke's own soldiers and the French command alike became convinced that the Duke was meditating an attack against the Ne Plus Ultra Lines on the sector west of Arras from his present position near Vimy Ridge. In view of the strength of the Lines in this sector there was consternation among Marlborough's ranks – the more so when he unaccountably sent the guns and baggage off under strong escort to Douai. The conviction in both armies that the Duke was about to launch a grand assault grew even stronger when he ostentatiously reconnoitred the French defences with his staff. According to an officer who rode in his escort:

> . . . with an air of assurance, and as if he was confident of success, he pointed out to the army general officers the manner in which the army was to be drawn up, the places that were to be attacked. . . . In short, he talked more than his friends about him thought was discreet. . . .[33]

Late on 4 August 1711 the Duke ordered the army to prepare itself for battle in the morning. Villars, absolutely certain that he was about to be attacked and having therefore drawn in all his garrison troops (including those from Arleux), waited behind his powerful defences with keen anticipation of success.

But that night, just after the discharge of a cannon had signalled tap-to, the Duke issued the order to strike tents. Within an hour the whole allied army, with the Duke riding at its head, was swinging eastwards through a silent countryside splashed black

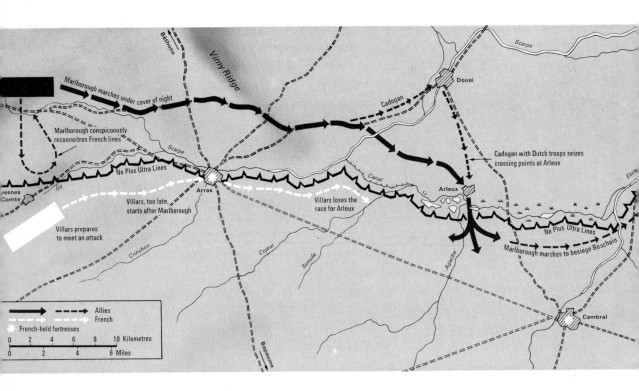

*'. . . a brilliant exercise in
psychological deception . . .'
Breaking the Ne Plus Ultra
lines, 6 July–5 August 1711*

and silver by the brilliance of a full moon. Meanwhile Cadogan had ridden ahead to
Douai to take command of the troops and guns sent off so unaccountably by the Duke
the day before; his task was to seize the causeway at Arleux. Next morning the Duke
received word from Cadogan that he had safely occupied Arleux, now deserted and
demolished by the French, passed over the causeways and established a bridgehead
beyond the inundations.

Daylight found the tricked and furious Villars striving desperately to catch up. His
cavalry and the allied infantry were marching parallel on opposite sides of the Lines,
and in close sight of each other. But the French commander was hours too late. Marlborough's troops covered forty miles in eighteen hours, each foot soldier carrying fifty
pounds of kit on his back, and despite a fierce sun striking down on to his red- or blue-
coated shoulders. When Villars at last arrived opposite Arleux, the Duke was already
through the allegedly impregnable Ne Plus Ultra Lines, and without losing a man.
As a British officer wrote, 'never did a player on the stage act a part to greater perfection,
than did his Grace through the whole course of this complicated scheme.'[34] Eugène
sent the Duke his enthusiastic congratulations; even St John was warmed for a moment
into his old admiration. Yet some criticized the Duke for failing now to force on a battle.
This was not for want of desire on his part, for in July he had told Godolphin that he
believed a battle 'to be in the interest of the common cause, as well as for mine own
honour',[35] but because the allied army was simply no longer strong enough. In any case

the Duke, now a man of sixty-one, was for the time being so exhausted by mental and physical exertion that he had to take to his bed for a few days: '. . . the last six weeks', he admitted, 'have given me frequent and sensible remembrances of my growing old.'[36]

Nevertheless, on 9 August he opened the siege of Bouchain. To undertake the siege of a first-class fortress in the presence of a considerably larger French army was itself as hazardous and delicate an operation as the Duke had ever undertaken. He brought to it undimmed qualities of leadership, untarnished skills in handling men, which still gave him a complete personal ascendancy over all nationalities and all ranks in his polyglot army.

The Prince of Anhalt-Dessau, one of the heroes of Prussian military legend, recalled how on one occasion during the 1711 campaign, he took deep affront at some order or instruction of the Duke's and went off in a furious rage to protest to him about it. As he entered the Duke's room ready to do battle, the Duke came forward, embraced him and said:

> My dear Prince . . . I was just sending to beg the favour of your company in order to have your opinion upon a design I have formed for attacking the enemy, which I cannot undertake without your approval and assistance in the execution, for there are no troops I depend on like those under your command, nor any general in the army but yourself whose head and heart I can trust so in the conduct of an enterprise of such importance. If your Highness will be pleased to sit down, I will inform you of the particulars of my scheme. . . .

When Anhalt-Dessau returned to his friends, he confessed that 'the ascendancy of that man is inconceivable. I was unable to utter an angry word; he totally disarmed me in an instant.'[37]

During the siege of Bouchain, Captain Parker of the Royal Regiment of Ireland was waiting to attack some forward defences thrown up by Villars's army. So strong were these defences, so crammed with troops and guns, that he 'wished much that the Duke might take a nearer view of the thing', but guessed that the Duke must be fully occupied on some other part of the front.

> But while I was musing, the Duke of Marlborough . . . rode up quite unattended and alone, and posted himself a little in the right of my company of grenadiers, from whence he had a fair view of the . . . enemy works. It is quite impossible for me to express the joy, which the sight of this man gave me at this very critical moment. I was now well satisfied that he would not push the thing unless he saw a strong probability of success; nor was this my notion alone; it was the sense of the whole army, both officer and soldier, British and foreigner. . . . He stayed only three or four minutes, and then rode back. We were in pain for him while he stayed, lest the enemy might have discovered him, and fired at him; in which case they could not well have missed him. He had not been longer from us than he stayed, when orders came for us to retire.[38]

On 14 September, with Villars helpless to intervene, Bouchain surrendered and for the last time the Duke gazed upon a defeated enemy.

The passing of the Ne Plus Ultra Lines and the taking of Bouchain were Marl-borough's answers to his critics and his enemies. Each achievement was to merit a tapestry to itself in the sequence woven in Brussels under the Duke's own supervision to depict his campaigns, as against only one for the year of Blenheim. It was a mark of the Duke's special pride in achievements won in the face of personal adversity, and against superior numbers and France's ablest soldier.

While the Duke had been fighting, Harley (now Lord Treasurer and Earl of Oxford and Mortimer) and his colleagues had been secretly negotiating with Louis XIV. When Parliament met on 17 December 1711 the Queen was able to announce, with a passing sneer at the Duke, who was present, that 'notwithstanding the arts of those who delight in war, both time and place are appointed for opening the treaty of a general peace'. It was time for the Tories to discard the Duke, and not merely discard him, but discredit him. On 1 January 1712 the Commissioners of Public Accounts laid a report before the Commons accusing the Duke of turning public funds to his own profit. On 11 January the Queen announced to the Privy Council that she had decided to dismiss him from all his employments 'that the matter might have impartial examination'. To the Duke himself the Queen graciously sent a letter 'so very offensive that the Duke flung it in the fire, though he was not a man of passion'.[39]

Now at last he could enjoy his quiet with Sarah.

Was Marlborough, as some have contended, the 'greatest' of British soldiers? Was he, as some have sought to decide, more or less able than Wellington? Their circumstances were so different as to make it impossible to answer such questions. Marlborough from the very beginning commanded the principal army of the anti-French coalition, and in the principal theatre; Wellington did not carry similar responsibilities until the Waterloo campaign. While Marlborough was throughout the war the dominant personality on the allied side, carrying immense diplomatic and political responsibilities, Wellington only achieved equivalent station, if he ever did, in 1814–15. And while Marlborough throughout was the principal director of allied grand strategy in all theatres of war, Wellington never was.

Marlborough was not an innovator, an inventor of completely new tactical systems, like Gustavus Adolphus of Sweden. He was, like Wellington and Napoleon, content to take over and bring to perfection in the field existing tactics and equipment. As a practical soldier he was concerned with what he knew would work amid all the hard-ships and confusions of war. Strategically too he was by no means revolutionary; he stood in the tradition of the great French commanders of his youth, Condé, Turenne, Luxembourg. Nevertheless, it would be unfair, for example, to criticize the Duke for failing to march straight on Paris à la Napoleon. For the scope and intensity of war is determined by its political and social frame. Napoleonic warfare demands a French Revolution first. Marlborough commanded in an age of monarchy and aristocracy, not of

'... as hazardous and delicate an operation as the Duke had ever taken.' The siege of Bouchain; detail from a tapestry woven by De Vos after L. de Hondt

the sovereign people; of cool calculation, not of mass hatred. His war was fought for limited political objectives, not for some romantic ideal. It never occurred to him, therefore, to step outside those universally accepted rules and conventions of his time which limited war's destructiveness.

Moreover, the Duke, unlike Napoleon or Wellington (except in the Talavera campaign), was an allied commander, and an allied commander without the unquestioned authority that, for example, Eisenhower was to enjoy. Time and again the defaultings or timorous counsels of his allies held the Duke back, or brought his plans to nothing.

It is with William III that he can most fairly be compared, for they fought the same enemy under similar political and strategic conditions, including obstructive allies (in William's case the English!). Yet whereas William was King of England and Stadtholder of the Dutch Republic, and Marlborough was only a subject without even the title of allied generalissimo, Marlborough's success was vastly beyond William's.

The Duke's particular genius – though not genius in the conventional romantic style – lay in that he was able by tact, perseverance and sheer talent for management to create out of a ramshackle coalition an instrument of war formidable enough to bring the greatest monarchy in Europe to its knees. Without the Duke it is inconceivable that the alliance could have lasted ten years and conducted an ultimately successful war.

It is the very range of his abilities – so much greater than those of a mere able general like Turenne or Luxembourg or Eugène – that makes Marlborough outstanding. He comprehended the interaction between the operations of one army and another; one theatre and another; between operations on land and sea. His mind was a complete map of the war, in which every detail was present and yet ordered in relation to the whole. He understood too – as few generals or politicians ever have – the relationship of strategy to high policy. His battles were always fought in a political context and to promote political objectives. The aim of all his efforts was not the purely military one of 'victory' but the political one of 'a good peace'. His judgment, moreover, was cool, far-sighted, sagacious; there could be no greater contrast to the hot-blooded and hasty opportunism of his descendant Winston Churchill.

As an administrator he performed continuous miracles, for, in an age when inefficiency and muddle were the rule, he actually made things work. His troops always had bread, shoes, clothing, tents or billets. His horses always had oats. When he marched, he arrived at his destination with his army intact and in a fit state to fight. These were achievements often beyond the French monarchy despite all its vaunted and elaborate administrative machinery.

Yet all these talents would have meant little without the Duke's immense reserves of energy and stamina; without the willpower and self-discipline which enabled him to triumph over difficulties, discouragement and despondency. For no other British soldier has ever carried so great a weight and variety of responsibility; and this is Marlborough's real title to a unique place in British history.

CHAPTER FIFTEEN

THE GREATEST CAPTAIN
OF THE AGE

The Queen and the Tory ministry might dismiss him from his post of Captain-General; they could not dismiss him from the regard of his fellow countrymen. Beyond London and its smart political spites, in the countryside where most Englishmen lived, Tories as well as Whigs drank his health. His receptions at Marlborough House, the town mansion built for Sarah by Sir Christopher Wren next door to St James's Palace, were crammed with people come to gaze upon the man who had won such victories. Eugène too was in

Marlborough House, next door to St James's Palace and built for Sarah by Sir Christopher Wren – the south front in 1720. Engraving by J. Harris (active 1680–1740) after J. Lightbody

The Saloon at Marlborough House, with Laguerre's oil paintings of the Duke's victories

London that January; another hero for the people in the street to cheer, invited by the Whigs and allied envoys in London in order to embarrass the new ministry. But the Tories deftly retorted this gambit on their foes by using Eugène's presence to disparage Marlborough as a soldier. Eugène showed himself staunchly loyal to his fallen comrade. When Lord Oxford (Harley) observed while entertaining him to dinner, 'I consider this day as the happiest of my life, since I have the honour to see in my house the greatest captain of the age,' Eugène replied in an allusion to Marlborough's dismissal, 'If it be so, I owe it to your Lordship.'[1]

Marlborough was able totally to refute the charges brought against him of misappropriating public funds. He showed that he had taken from the army bread contracts and the payments for hire of mercenaries no more than the percentages allowed by established precedent or by the Queen's express authority. In any case, the money had been spent on his superb intelligence service; and items such as spies high up in the French court, privy to Louis XIV's strategic decisions, were not cheap. Nevertheless, the House of Commons, with its Tory majority, divided on party lines over the Commissioners' Report, and voted that the payments made to the Duke were illegal. St John tacitly acknowledged the flimsiness of the government case, however, by not proceeding to impeach the Duke.

So the Duke and Sarah enjoyed their first year together for ten years: quiet days at Holywell House or Windsor Lodge; visits to Woodstock to see how Blenheim Palace was progressing; grandchildren to see. It cannot have been pleasant for him, nevertheless, merely to read about the course of the year's campaign – especially as it was one peculiarly shameful to England. The Duke's successor, the Duke of Ormonde, was under instructions from the government to engage in neither battle nor siege; instructions which, while Villars, the French commander, had been informed of them, Ormonde was to keep secret from Eugène and the Dutch. For the Tory ministry was now acting in collusion with Louis XIV over the making of a peace. At the end of January 1712 the peace conference opened at Utrecht, although hostilities still continued. In July, however, the Tory government concluded a separate armistice with the French, and the British contingent was withdrawn from the allied army. It marched out of camp to the jeers of its Dutch and German comrades; its ranks seething with shame and chagrin. And Eugène, without the Duke and without the redcoats, was beaten at Denain by Villars. The war was sputtering out in sad anti-climax.

Nevertheless, the final Treaty of Utrecht in 1713 gave the allies all they had originally gone to war to secure, even if far less than they might have had in 1709. Although Louis XIV's grandson was accepted as Philip V of Spain, Louis undertook in return that the crowns of Spain and France should never be united. The Spanish Empire was split up: Spain and the Indies to Philip V, and the Spanish Netherlands and lands in northern Italy to the Habsburg Emperor. The Dutch got their barrier of fortresses, though it was not so grand as once they had hoped for.

For France the Treaty of Utrecht marked an end for eighty years of her ambition to

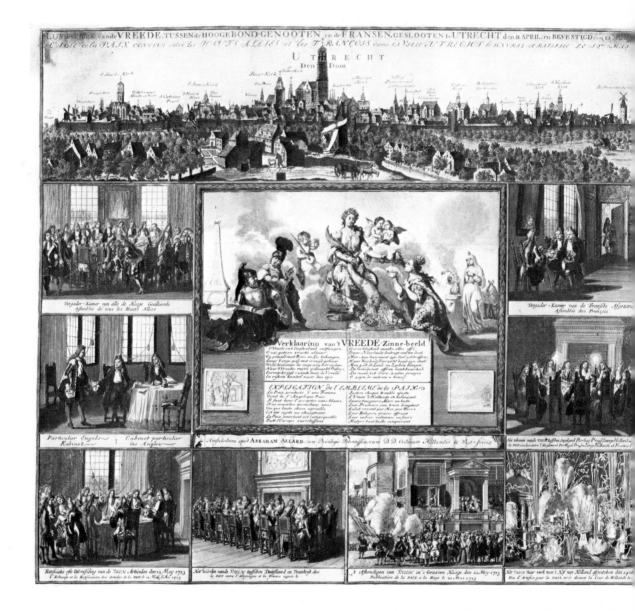

A broadsheet celebrating the Treaty of Utrecht, 1713

dominate Europe. This was the measure of the crippling damage sustained by the French state and French society in the course of the Duke's ten campaigns; damage the lasting effects of which were to contribute to the eventual collapse of the French monarchy in 1789.

And England – England emerged from Marlborough's war a major European power, the world's greatest seapower and the world's most buoyant commercial nation. Her Protestant succession was formally recognized by Louis XIV; she gained Nova Scotia and Newfoundland from France; Gibraltar and Minorca from Spain; she was enriched by an exclusive trading concession with the vast Spanish overseas empire. On the fields of Blenheim, Ramillies and Oudenarde, England had been launched on that rise to greatness which one day was to make English the lingua franca of the planet.

In September 1712, after Godolphin died, the Duke went to live abroad, soon to be joined by Sarah. It was in the nature of a triumphal progress from court to court: ceremonial honours from the rulers, and cheering from the people. In the course of their travels the Duke made his only visit to his principality in Bavaria; and the Prince of Mindelheim was received with due pomp by his loyal subjects. Unfortunately the Duke was to lose Mindelheim, though not his princely title, under the peace treaty.

But while the Marlboroughs were travelling, Queen Anne was failing. In 1713–14 all political calculations, all hopes for England's future, turned on her approaching death. Although Louis XIV had accepted the Protestant or Hanoverian succession, the Tory party in England cherished sentimental feelings towards James II's son, the Pretender James III. Lord Oxford – and even more so Bolingbroke – leaned ominously towards Jacobitism, well knowing that Hanover favoured the Whigs. It might have been the Exclusion Crisis or the year 1688 come again – couriers going to and fro; secret conclaves; each man looking to his loyalty and his future.

The Whig leaders plotted and prepared, and kept in constant touch with Hanover. Marlborough, who had just fought a long war to preserve the Protestant succession and deliver England from being a French satellite, was hardly likely to relish the advent of another Roman Catholic monarch under Louis XIV's thumb. He too was in constant touch with Hanover. At the same time, by way of typically prudent re-insurance, he was also in touch with the Jacobite court in France – just as he had kept up contacts with James II's exiled court after 1688. After all, his lifetime had seen a Lord Protector in England instead of a king; a king restored; a king deposed; and a king invited to take his place, to say nothing of Monmouth's rebellion and innumerable plots. A wise man did his best to ensure that the right side prevailed, but nevertheless kept his options open. In the 1690s Marlborough had taken this as far as feeding James II's gullible ministers with 'secret' but in fact out-of-date and useless information about English military operations. Now, in 1714, he wrote to his nephew the Duke of Berwick asking him to solicit a pardon from 'James III' for his part in deposing his father. Berwick recommended that his uncle should have his pardon, shrewdly observing, 'One may as well give these people as good as they bring, for I see nothing else in all Marlborough says and indeed he has never behaved himself otherwise.'[2] Words and nothing else – Berwick had exactly summed up the nature of Marlborough's Jacobite contacts since 1688.

To Hanover the Duke offered rather more: his sword. It was arranged that he should take command of the English troops remaining in the Low Countries in the event of a disputed succession. Yet he did not take a leading part in the preparations for the Elector George's succession, which lay in the hands of a younger generation of Whig politicians; possibly a sign of fast-declining health and vigour, that frequent but unlooked-for consequence of retirement and the sudden cessation of terrible pressures.

In the event his sword was not needed. On her deathbed in July 1714 Queen Anne appointed the Duke of Shrewsbury, a moderate Whig and an elder statesman, as Lord Treasurer and chief minister. The spectre of a Jacobite restoration vanished in the bright morning sun of Hanover. And the first state paper signed by the Elector as King George I was a commission re-appointing the Duke of Marlborough to the post of Captain-General.

It was another era, and he was already a curiously old-fashioned figure – a man who had risen from obscurity to greatness through the court and by royal favour; the last to do so in English history. For with the death of Queen Anne power passed from the royal palaces to the grand, calm country houses of the Whig aristocracy.

LEFT '. . . he paused before his portrait by Kneller, gazed at it for a space, and remarked with sad wonder: "That was once a man."' This is the portrait in question.

In 1716 the Duke's favourite daughter, Anne Sunderland, gentle and loving, died of fever. It hit him almost as hard as the death of his son Jack in 1703; and just as on that occasion, he and Sarah went to Holywell House to be alone with each other in their bereavement. Within three weeks of her death and while they were still at Holywell, the Duke was disabled by a stroke. Although he partially recovered he was now like a great tree blasted by lightning. Once when faltering round the vast enfilades of state rooms at Blenheim he paused before his portrait by Kneller, gazed at it for a space, and remarked with sad wonder: 'That was once a man.'[3] Now his dependence on Sarah, always so remarkable, became total; he was never at ease, in Sarah's words, 'if I was not within call. . . .'

. . . though he had often returns of his illness, he went many journeys, and was in all appear-
ances well, excepting that he could not pronounce all words, which is common in that
distemper, but his understanding was as good as ever. But he did not speak much to strangers,
because when he was stopt, by not being able to pronounce some words, it made him uneasy.
But to his friends that he was used he would talk freely, and since his death . . . many . . .
of my friends have remarked to me with pleasure, the things they heard him say, and the just
observations he made upon what others had said to him; and he gave many instances of
remembering in conversation what others had forgot.[4]

RIGHT 'Marlborough has suffered so much that he no longer looks himself.' Marlborough in 1712, after his dismissal. Painting by Sir Godfrey Kneller

He still enjoyed a game of cards and a visit to Bath; he still acted as peacemaker between Sarah and their surviving daughters, Henrietta Godolphin and Mary Montagu, in their continual quarrels. Most of all he took pleasure in seeing Blenheim Palace gradually rise to completion. This was his own chosen monument; massive and masculine, it looms across the English countryside like the charge of a victorious army.

Yet he took a simpler and more domestic pleasure in the mansion too: choosing the furniture, the looking glasses and the pictures; superintending the planting of the park, and inspecting the ice house built for the ice creams of summers he would never see. And in 1719 he and Sarah were able to go and live there, even though the building was still not finished, and would not be until long after his death. Now he was able to stroll slowly on Sarah's supporting arm through the new parterres and plantations laid out by Mr Wise, the landscape gardener; to taste the fruit from his new trees; and at last realize the dream which had solaced him long ago amid the worst of the war.

But he only had three years to enjoy it. In June 1722, while he was staying at Windsor Lodge, he suffered yet another stroke; and this time there was no hope of recovery, although he lingered on day by day, conscious and lucid still. On 26 June (15 June old style) his two daughters arrived at the Lodge; for Sarah an unexpected and unwelcome visitation. She had always felt the children to be an intrusion between herself and her husband; she had had duty to spare for them, but little love, for all her love belonged to him. Now, with 'my soul . . . tearing from my body' at the knowledge that in a very few hours he would be gone, Sarah had to share the last of him with them. She begged that they would not stay long in his room. In agony of suspense and distress, she waited for them to come out again so that she could return to him. But

> They staid a great while (as I thought) and not being able to be out of the room longer from him I went in though they were still there, and kneel'd down by him. They rose up when I came in and made curtsys but did not speak to me and after some time I call'd for prayers: when they were over, I ask'd the Duke of Marlb. if he heard them well and he answer'd yes and he had join'd in them.[5]

As it grew dark Sarah asked him if he would like to be moved from his narrow couch into his bed. He felt himself carried on the couch to the bedroom, lifted and laid against the pillows. Candles were brought in. The room, not large, was as overcrowded as his levées once had been; there were members of the family, doctors, apothecaries, surgeons and servants, all the impotent panoply of human care. And still Sarah could not get rid of her daughters and have him to herself. At last she requested them and other kinsfolk to leave the room. Since it was their mother's request, Henrietta and Mary could not possibly yield to it, even over their father's deathbed. Instead they argued about it. Only when Sarah made her request for the third time did they go with reluctance and ill-grace. Then the room grew quiet at last round the dying man.

In the night hours, as if it were time to strike tents and march, he began to slip away; and by dawn he was gone.

MORT ET CONVOI
DE L'INVINCIBLE MALBOROUGH.

TOMBEAU.

MALBOROUGH
s'en va-t-en
guerre ; Mironton
mironton mirontai-
ne : Malborough
s'en va-t-en guerre,
ne sait quand revien-
dra.

Ne sait quand re-
viendra , ne sait
quand reviendra : il
reviendra à Pâques ,
mironton mironton
mirontaine : il re-
viendra à Pâques ou
à la Trinité.

La Trinité se pas-
se , mironton etc.
Malborough ne re-
vient pas.

. Madame à sa tour
monte mironton etc.
si haut qu'elle peut
monter.

Elle voit venir son
Page, mironton etc.
de noir tout habillé.

Beau page , ah !
mon beau page, mi-
ronton etc. quelle

nouvelle apportez.

Aux nouvelles que
j'apporte , mironton
etc. vos beaux yeux
vont pleurer.

Quittez vos habits
roses, mironton etc .
et vos satins brochés.

Monsieur d'Mal-
borough est mort ,
mironton , etc. est
mort et enterré.

J'ai vu porter en

terre, mironton etc.
par quatre officiers.

L'un portait sa
Cuirasse , mironton
etc. et l'autre son
Bouclier.

L'un portait son
grand Sabre, miron-
ton etc. et l'autre
rien ne porta.

A l'entour de sa
tombe mironton etc.
Romarins l'ou plan-
ta.

Sur la plus haute
branche , mironton
etc. le Rossignol
chanta.

On vit voler son
ame , mironton etc.
au travers des lau-
riers.

Chacun mit ven-
tre à terre , miron-
ton etc. et puis se
releva.

Pour chanter les
victoires, mironton

etc. que Malborough
remporta.

La cérémonie fai-
te , mironton etc.
chacun s'en fut cou-
cher.

Les unsavec leurs
femmes, miron. etc.
et les autres tous
seuls.

Ce n'est pas qu'il
en manque, miron.
etc. car j'en connais
beaucoup.

Des blondes et
puis des brunes, mi-
ronton etc. et des
chataignes aussi.

J'en dis pas da-
vantage , miron-
ton etc. car en voilà
assez.

FIN.

MONTBÉLIARD ,
de l'imprimerie de Deckherr.

A French broadsheet announcing the death of Marlborough

The Marlborough family tomb in the chapel at Blenheim Palace. Designed by William Kent (1685–1748) and executed by John Michael Rysbrack (1664–1770). Notice at the foot Tallard's surrender to Marlborough at Blenheim.

BIBLIOGRAPHICAL REFERENCES

Chapter One

1 SICCO VAN GOSLINGA. *Mémoires relatifs a la Guerre de succession de 1706–1709 et 1711 etc.* 1857, pp. 42–4
2 Ibid.
3 4th EARL OF CHESTERFIELD. *Letters to His Son.* Ed. Lord Mahon. London 1845–53, I p. 221.
4 Lord Hervey to Sir R. Cocks, July 1704, quoted in: G. M. TREVELYAN. *England Under Queen Anne,* II *Ramillies and the Union with Scotland.* Longmans Green, London 1932, p.5 Footnote.
5 W. COXE. *Memoirs of John, Duke of Marlborough,* new ed. Henry G. Bohn, London 1847, I pp. 83–4
6 Chesterfield I pp. 221–2
7 Copy letter in the Blenheim Papers, GI 7
8 C. T. ATKINSON. *Marlborough and the Rise of the British Army.* G. P. Putnam's Sons, London 1921, p. 120
9 W. S. CHURCHILL. *Marlborough: His Life and Times.* Sphere Books, London 1967, II p. 32
10 Loc. cit.
11 ABEL BOYER. *The History of the Reign of Queen Anne, digested into Annals.* London 1703, I p. 12

Chapter Two

1 SIR G. MURRAY, ed. *The Letters and Dispatches of John Churchill, First Duke of Marlborough from 1702 to 1712.* John Murray, London 1845, I p. 4 Footnote.
2 For a full discussion of this question of Marlborough's powers and status, see Introduction to: B. VAN 'T HOFF, ed. *The Correspondence 1701–1711 of John Churchill, First Duke of Marlborough, and Anthonie Heinsius, Grand Pensionary if Holland.* Werken van het Historisch Genootschap te Utrecht, 4de serie, no 1. Utrecht; The Hague 1951

It appears certain that Churchill (op. cit. II p. 102) is in error in arguing that Marlborough was given a patent as Deputy-Captain-General and pay of £10,000 per annum, or that he was in formal terms appointed commander of all the allied forces.
3 Letter of 13 July 1702, Coxe I p. 90
4 C. VON UND ZU DOHNA. *Mémoires originaux sur le règne et la cour de Frédéric I, Roi de Prusse.* Berlin 1833, pp. 151–2

5 Van 't Hoff, No 39
6 Blenheim Papers, E 2
7 To Heinsius, 1 August 1702, in: C. VON NOORDEN. *Europäische Geschichte im achtzehnten Jahrhundert.* Düsseldorf 1870, I p. 261 Footnote 2
8 D. CHANDLER, ed. *The Marlborough Wars: Robert Parker and Comte de Mérode-Westerloo.* Longmans, London 1968, p. 20
9 Blenheim Papers, E 2

Chapter Three

1 *Dispatches,* IV p. 119
2 Calendar of State Papers (Treasury Books) 1672–5, p. 830
3 Letter of 26 November 1676. *Correspondance Politique, Angleterre,* Archives de la Ministère des Affaires Etrangères, T. 120ᶜ, 1676, Folio 206
4 Op. cit. Folio 221
5 Op. cit. Folio 231
6 Blenheim Papers, E 2
7 G. J. WOLSELEY. *Life of Marlborough.* London 1894, I p. 307
8 THOMAS BRUCE, EARL OF AILESBURY. *Memoirs.* Ed. W. E. Buckley. Roxburghe Society, London 1890, I p. 245
9 Calendar of State Papers Domestic: King William's Chest v No 96
10 Blenheim Papers, AI 11
11 Van 't Hoff, No 46
12 Op. cit. No 47
13 Blenheim Papers, E 2
14 G. M. TREVELYAN. *England Under Queen Anne,* I *Blenheim.* Longmans Green, London 1930, p. 180
15 Ailesbury, II p. 535
16 Blenheim Papers, AI 14
17 Coxe, I p. 182
18 Van 't Hoff, No 51
19 4 September 1702, in Blenheim Papers, AI 14
20 2 October 1702; Van 't Hoff, No 59
21 14 October 1702; von Noorden, I p. 264 Footnote 3
22 *Dispatches,* I p. 48
23 Blenheim Papers, AI 14
24 Coxe, I p. 99 Footnote.
25 Blenheim Papers, AI 14
26 Blenheim Papers, GI 9
27 Ibid.

Chapter Four

1 Coxe, I p. 102
2 Blenheim Papers, GI 10: *A Vindication of the Conduct of the Duchess of Marlborough*
3 W. BRAY, ed. *Diary and Correspondence of John Evelyn* FRS. George Routledge, London 1906, p. 529
4 Evelyn Mss. quoted in: SIR TRESHAM LEVER. *Godolphin: His Life and Times.* John Murray, London 1952, p. 113
5 Op. cit. p. 129
6 Blenheim Papers, E 20
7 Loc. cit.
8 Blenheim Papers, E 6
9 Coxe, I 107
10 Loc. cit.
11 Blenheim Papers, AI 14
12 Loc. cit.
13 Letter to Godolphin, 2 July 1703, Coxe I p. 123
14 Loc. cit.
15 Van 't Hoff, No 133
16 Coxe, I p. 128
17 Van 't Hoff, No 141
18 Blenheim Papers, AI 14
19 Van 't Hoff, No 142
20 Loc. cit.
21 Coxe, I p. 138
22 Op. cit. p. 110
23 Op. cit. pp. 110–11
24 Loc. cit.

Chapter Five

1 Van 't Hoff, No 124
2 T. LEDIARD. *The Life of John, Duke of Marlborough.* London 1736, I pp. 285–7
3 Churchill, II p. 250
4 Lady Pye to Abigail Harley, April 1703, in: HMC 15th Report, Portland Papers, IV p. 59
5 Churchill, II pp. 243–4
6 Loc. cit.
7 Blenheim Papers, E 1
8 Loc. cit.
9 Loc. cit.
10 Loc. cit.
11 Loc. cit.
12 Quoted in: IRIS BUTLER. *The Rule of Three: Sarah, Duchess of Marlborough, and Her Companions in Power.* Hodder and Stoughton, London 1967, p. 84
13 *Correspondance Politique, Angleterre,* T. 120ᶜ, 1676, Folio 248

14 All from Blenheim Papers, E 1
15 Loc. cit.
16 Loc. cit.
17 Loc. cit.
18 Blenheim Papers, E 2
19 Loc. cit.
20 Loc. cit.
21 *Dispatches*, I p. 250
22 *Feldzüge des Prinzen Eugen*. Vienna, Imperial General Staff, 1876–81, Series I, VI p. 737

Chapter Six

1 Blenheim Papers, E 1 (1)
2 Blenheim Papers, A I 14
3 *Dispatches*, I p. 271
4 Van 't Hoff, No 172
5 Blenheim Papers, AI 14
6 Chandler, p. 31
7 Blenheim Papers, AI 14
8 Van 't Hoff, No 177
9 Blenheim Papers, E 2
10 Loc. cit.
11 *Dispatches*, I p. 296
12 Op. cit. p. 293
13 Op. cit. p. 299
14 Loc. cit.
15 *Feldzüge*, VI Supp. p. 131
16 Blenheim Papers, E 2
17 B. M. Add. Mss. 9114 *Hare's Journal* (An Account of his Grace the Duke of Marlborough's Expedition into Germany)
18 Loc. cit.
19 Blenheim Papers, E 2
20 Loc. cit.
21 Loc. cit.
22 Loc. cit.
23 Trevelyan *Blenheim*, p. 371
24 Churchill, II p. 325
25 *Feldzüge*, VI Supp. p. 131
26 Blenheim Papers, E 2
27 Churchill, II pp. 349–50

Chapter Seven

1 *Dispatches*, I p. 399
2 Chandler, p. 166
3 Op. cit. pp. 166–7
4 Op. cit. p. 167
5 J. J. G. PELET & F. E. DE VAULT. *Mémoires militaires relatifs à la succession d'Espagne sous Louis XIV*. Imprimerie Royale, Paris 1836–42, IV p. 576
6 *Hare's Journal*
7 Chandler, p. 162
8 Op. cit. p. 169
9 Op. cit. p. 173
10 Lediard, I p. 248
11 Loc. cit.
12 Pelet, IV p. 568
13 ANON. *The Lives of the Two Illustrious Generals*. London 1713, p. 72
14 GEORGE HAMILTON, EARL OF ORKNEY. 'Letters of the First Lord Orkney during Marlborough's Campaigns', ed. H. H. E. Cra'ster, *English Historical Review*, April 1904

15 Lediard, I p. 429
16 Op. cit. I p. 393
17 Original at Blenheim Palace

Chapter Eight

1 *Hare's Journal*
2 Op. cit.
3 Op. cit.
4 DUC DE SAINT-SIMON. *Mémoires*. Ed. A. de Boislisle. Librairie Hachette, Paris 1896, XII p. 185
5 Blenheim Papers, AI 14
6 Blenheim Papers, E 2
7 Blenheim Papers, AI 14
8 Loc. cit.
9 Trevelyan *Blenheim*, p. 395
10 Op. cit. p. 396
11 Coxe, I p. 231
12 Trevelyan *Blenheim*, p. 397
13 Saint-Simon, XII p. 199
14 Op. cit. XII pp. 201–2
15 Blenheim Papers, E 2
16 Loc. cit.
17 Loc. cit.
18 Blenheim Papers, AI 14
19 Blenheim Papers, E 2
20 Coxe, I p. 246
21 Churchill, II p. 413
22 Lediard, I p. 470
23 Loc. cit.
24 Evelyn
25 Blenheim Papers, E 2
26 Lever, p. 152
27 Coxe, I p. 16
28 Letter to Bishop Burnet quoted in Butler p. 57
29 Churchill, I p. 204
30 Loc. cit.
31 Coxe, I p. 19
32 SARAH, DUCHESS OF MARLBOROUGH (& NATHANIEL HOOKE). *An Account of the Conduct of the Dowager Duchess of Marlborough, from her First Coming to Court, to the Year 1710*. London 1742, pp. 17–18.
33 Op. cit. p. 67
34 Op. cit. pp. 75–6
35 Blenheim Papers, E 18
36 GILBERT BURNET *History of My Own Time*, 2nd ed. Oxford 1833, V p. 1
37 Op. cit. p. 2 Footnote
38 Churchill, II p. 58
39 *Conduct*, p. 126

Chapter Nine

1 Blenheim Papers, E 3
2 Coxe, I pp. 266–7
3 Op. cit. p. 267
4 Op. cit. p. 274
5 Op. cit. pp. 274–5
6 *Dispatches*, II p. 78
7 Op. cit. p. 74
8 Churchill, II p. 438
9 *Dispatches*, II. p. 87
10 Coxe, I pp. 281–2

11 Op. cit. p. 282
12 Loc. cit.
13 EHR April 1904
14 Coxe, I p. 296
15 Op. cit. p. 297
16 Van 't Hoff, No 316
17 Op. cit. No 318
18 Coxe, I pp. 303–4
19 Letter of 20 August 1705, in: Pelet, V p. 602
20 Loc. cit.
21 Loc. cit.
22 *Hare's Journal*
23 Van 't Hoff, No 324
24 Coxe, I p. 312
25 Trevelyan *Ramillies*, p. 56
26 Coxe, I p. 318
27 *Dispatches*, II p. 249
28 Van 't Hoff, No 324
29 Churchill, II p. 30
30 *Dispatches*, II p. 518
31 Coxe, I p. 362
32 Op. cit. p. 404
33 Pelet, VI p. 20
34 Coxe, I p. 405
35 Blenheim Papers, E 3
36 Loc. cit.
37 Coxe, I p. 407
38 *Dispatches*, II p. 518

Chapter Ten

1 J. M. DE LA COLONIE. *The Chronicles of an Old Campaigner 1692–1717*. Trans. W. C. Horsley. John Murray, London 1904, p. 305
2 Coxe, I p. 418
3 Pelet, VI p. 19
4 EHR April 1904
5 Loc. cit.
6 Colonel Cranstoun, HMC Portland Papers, IV p. 309
7 Loc. cit.
8 La Colonie pp. 312–13
9 Trevelyan *Ramillies*, p. 115
10 Burnet, V p. 269
11 Loc. cit.
12 Coxe, I p. 418
13 Op. cit. p. 424
14 Loc. cit.
15 Op. cit. p. 426
16 Loc. cit.
17 Loc. cit.
18 Blenheim Papers, BII 32
19 Pelet, VI p. 94
20 Goslinga, pp. 42–4
21 *Dispatches*, II p. 17
22 Anecdote in: Ailesbury, II pp. 584–7
23 Goslinga pp. 42–4
24 *Dispatches*, III pp. 212–13
25 Coxe, I p. 473
26 Chesterfield, p. 202
27 Burnet, V p. 149 Footnote by Lord Dartmouth
28 W. SEWARD. *Anecdotes of Some Distinguished Persons*. London 1795, II p. 299
29 Loc. cit.

30 Trevelyan *Ramillies*, p. 9
31 Loc. cit.
32 Ailesbury, II p. 541
33 Coxe, I p. 345
34 Op. cit. p. 452
35 Op. cit. p. 460
36 Van 't Hoff, No 452
37 *Dispatches*, I p. 594
38 Coxe, I pp. 263–4
39 Op. cit. p. 279
40 Trevelyan *Ramillies*, p. 8
41 Blenheim Papers, E 2
42 Coxe, I p. 168
43 Op. cit. p. 215
44 Op. cit. pp. 263–4
45 Blenheim Papers, E 3
46 Coxe, II p. 107

Chapter Eleven
1 Coxe, I p. 481
2 Van 't Hoff, No 429
3 Lediard, II p. 166
4 Blenheim Papers, E 3
5 Loc. cit.
6 Loc. cit.
7 Cranstoun, Portland Papers, IV pp. 439–41
8 Atkinson, p. 325
9 Van 't Hoff, No 401, 3 July 1706
10 Lever, p. 159
11 Sir John Clerk of Pennikuik, quoted in: J. FLEMING. *Robert Adam and His Circle in Edinburgh and Rome*. John Murray, London 1962, p. 19
12 Blenheim Papers, AI 37
13 Lever, p. 163
14 Coxe, II p. 9
15 Lever, p. 164
16 *Conduct*, pp. 185–6
17 AGNES STRICKLAND. *Lives of the Queens of England*, XII. London 1848
18 Blenheim Papers, E 3
19 Lever, p. 154
20 Blenheim Papers, AI 37
21 Blenheim Papers, BII 32
22 Blenheim Papers, E 3
23 HMC Bath Papers, I p. I
24 *Conduct*, pp. 205–6
25 Letter of 8 November 1707, Blenheim Papers, E 3
26 Coxe, II pp. 191–2
27 Op. cit. p. 192
28 Lever, p. 197

Chapter Twelve
1 Van 't Hoff, No 584
2 Loc. cit.
3 Op. cit. No 593
4 Op. cit. No 609
5 Op. cit. p. 389 Footnote
6 Coxe, II p. 235
7 Op. cit. pp. 238–9
8 Op. cit. p. 240
9 Op. cit. p. 241
10 Op. cit. p. 243
11 Churchill, III p. 326

12 Op. cit. p. 327
13 Loc. cit.
14 Loc. cit.
15 Coxe, II p. 252
16 Op. cit. pp. 252–3
17 *Dispatches*, IV p. 101
18 Op. cit. p. 102
19 Goslinga, p. 54
20 Coxe, II p. 265
21 Loc. cit.
22 *Dispatches*, IV p. 115
23 Churchill, III p. 361
24 Atkinson, p. 340
25 Op. cit. p. 342
26 Coxe, II p. 267
27 Op. cit. p. 265
28 Saint-Simon, XVI p. 201
29 Coxe, II p. 265
30 Butler, p. 206
31 *Conduct*, p. 258
32 Lever, p. 204
33 Coxe, II p. 277
34 Op. cit. p. 290
35 Blenheim Papers, BII 32
36 Letter to Sarah, 9 August 1708, Blenheim Papers, E 4
37 Coxe, II p. 373
38 *Dispatches*, IV p. 109
39 Coxe, II p. 273
40 Op. cit. p. 267
41 *Dispatches*, IV p. 129
42 Coxe, II p. 273
43 Loc. cit.
44 Churchill, III p. 212
45 Coxe, II p. 303
46 Op. cit. p. 290
47 Op. cit. p. 312
48 Op. cit. p. 320
49 Op. cit. p. 336
50 Op. cit. p. 321
51 Op. cit. p. 307

Chapter Thirteen
1 A. LEGRELLE. *La Diplomatie française et la succession d'Espagne*, 2nd ed. Braine-le-Comte 1892, V pp. 385–6
3 Coxe, II p. 403
4 Op. cit. p. 402
5 Op. cit. p. 402
6 Op. cit. pp. 409–10*
7 Wolseley, p. 307
8 10 July 1709, Van 't Hoff, No 754
9 Letter to Heinsius, 10 August, Van 't Hoff, No 771
10 Blenheim Papers, BI 23
11 Blenheim Papers, BII 32
12 Loc. cit.
13 *Dispatches*, IV p. 393
14 Coxe, II p. 424
15 *Conduct*, pp. 224–6
16 Loc. cit.
17 Seward, II pp. 301–2
18 Atkinson, p. 395
19 Coxe, II pp. 461–2

20 EHR April 1904
21 *Dispatches*, IV p. 599
22 EHR April 1904
23 A. CRICHTON. *The Life and Diary of Lt- Colonel Blackader*. Edinburgh 1824, p. 352
24 Coxe, II p. 462
25 Op. cit. p. 464
26 *Dispatches*, IV p. 599
27 G. M. TREVELYAN. *England Under Queen Anne*, III *Peace and the Protestant Succession*. Longmans Green, London 1934, p. 17
28 Van 't Hoff, No 789
29 Lever, p. 218

Chapter Fourteen
1 Coxe, III p. 7
2 Blenheim Papers, BII 32
3 Coxe, III p. 27
4 Op. cit. p. 35
5 Op. cit. p. 27
6 Op. cit. p. 39
7 Burnet, V p. 454 Footnote
8 *Conduct*, pp. 238–44
9 Coxe, III p. 56 .
10 Op. cit. p. 47
11 Op. cit. p. 48
12 Op. cit. p. 81
13 Op. cit. p. 87
14 Op. cit. p. 50
15 Loc. cit.
16 Op. cit. p. 92
17 Blenheim Papers, BII 32
18 Coxe, III p. 93
19 Op. cit. p. 92
20 Op. cit. p. 136
21 Op. cit. pp. 127–8
22 Loc. cit.
23 HMC Portland Papers, IV pp. 634–5
24 Op. cit. p. 634
25 Coxe, III p. 93
26 Churchill, IV p. 312
27 Coxe, III p. 141
28 G. PARKE, ed. *Henry St John Viscount Bolingbroke: Letters and Correspondence*. London 1798, I p. 77
29 Churchill, IV p. 298
30 Op. cit. p. 310
31 Coxe, III pp. 175–6
32 Letter of 16 April 1710, op. cit. pp. 194–5
33 Chandler, pp. 100–1
34 Op. cit. pp. 103–4
35 Coxe, III p. 224
36 Atkinson, p. 448
37 Churchill, IV p. 343
38 Chandler, p. 108
39 HMC 8th Report, Marlborough Papers p. 16

Chapter Fifteen
1 Coxe, III p. 288
2 Atkinson p. 481
3 S. J. REID. *John and Sarah Marlborough*. London 1914, p. 413
4 Coxe, III p. 422
5 Sarah's 'Green Book', Blenheim Papers, GI 9

BIBLIOGRAPHY

UNPUBLISHED DOCUMENTS

The Blenheim Papers, Blenheim Palace, Oxfordshire

Correspondance Politique, Angleterre, Archives de la Ministère des Affaires Etrangères, Quai d'Orsai, Paris

Hare's Journal (An Account of his Grace the Duke of Marlborough's Expedition into Germany), British Museum Additional Manuscripts 9114

PUBLISHED DOCUMENTATION

Bray, W., ed. Diary and Correspondence of John Evelyn FRS. London 1906

Calendar of State Papers (Domestic and Treasury Books)

Feldzüge des Prinzen Eugen, Series 1, 7 vols, VI. Vienna, Imperial General Staff, 1876–81

Historical Manuscripts Commission:
Portland Papers IV
Bath Papers I and II
Marlborough Papers (Eighth Report)
Hare Papers (Fourteenth Report, Appendix Par II)

Hoff, B. van 't, ed. The Correspondence 1701–1711 of John Churchill, First Duke of Marlborough, and Anthonie Heinsius, Grand Pensionary of Holland (Werken van het Historisch Genootschap te Utrecht, 4de serie, no 1). Utrecht; The Hague 1951

Marlborough, Sarah, Duchess of (and Nathaniel Hooke). An Account of the Conduct of the Dowager Duchess of Marlborough, from her First Coming to Court, to the Year 1710. London 1742

Murray, Sir George, ed. The Letters and Dispatches of John Churchill, First Duke of Marlborough from 1702 to 1712, 5 vols. London 1845

Orkney, George Hamilton, Earl of. 'Letters of the First Lord Orkney during Marlborough's Campaigns', ed. H. H. E. Cra'ster, English Historical Review, April 1904

Parke, G., ed. Henry St John Viscount Bolingbroke: Letters and Correspondence, 4 vols. London 1798

Pelet, J. J. G., and Vault, F. E. de. Mémoires militaires relatifs à la succession d'Espagne sous Louis XIV, IV–VI. Paris 1836–42

BIOGRAPHIES OF JOHN AND SARAH CHURCHILL

Anon. The Lives of the Two Illustrious Generals. London 1713

Atkinson, C. T. Marlborough and the Rise of the British Army. London 1921

Burton, I. F. The Captain-General: The Career of John Churchill, Duke of Marlborough 1702–1711. London 1968

Butler, Iris. The Rule of Three: Sarah, Duchess of Marlborough and Her Companions in Power. London 1967

Churchill, W. S. Marlborough: His Life and Times, 4 vols. London 1967

Coxe, W. Memoirs of John, Duke of Marlborough, 3 vols., new ed. London 1847

Lediard, T. The Life of John, Duke of Marlborough, 3 vols. London 1736

Reid, S. J. John and Sarah Marlborough. London 1914

Wolseley, G. J. Life of Marlborough, 2 vols. London 1894

MEMOIRS

Ailesbury, Thomas Bruce, Earl of. Memoirs, 2 vols. Ed. W. E. Buckley. London 1890

Burnet, G. History of My Own Time, 2nd ed. Oxford 1833

Chandler, D., ed. The Marlborough Wars: Robert Parker and Comte de Mérode-Westerloo. London 1968

Chesterfield, 4th Earl of. Letters to His Son. Ed. Lord Mahon. London 1845–53

Crichton, A. The Life and Diary of Lt-Colonel Blackader. Edinburgh 1824

Dohna, C. von und zu. Mémoires originaux sur le règne et la cour de Frédéric I, Roi de Prusse. Berlin 1833

Goslinga, S. van. Mémoires relatifs à la Guerre de succession de 1706–1709 et 1711 etc. 1857

La Colonie, J. M. de. The Chronicles of an Old Campaigner, 1692–1717. Trans. W. C. Horsley. London 1904

Saint-Simon, Duc de. Mémoires, ed. A. de Boislisle, XII. Paris 1896

GENERAL WORKS

André, L. Michel le Tellier et Louvois, 2nd ed. Paris 1943

Barnett, Correlli. Britain and Her Army 1509–1970. London 1970

Boyer, Abel. The History of the Reign of Queen Anne, digested into Annals, I. London 1703

Coombs, D. The Conduct of the Dutch: British Opinion and the Dutch Alliance During the War of the Spanish Succession. The Hague 1958

Fleming, J. Robert Adam and His Circle in Edinburgh and Rome. London 1962

Hill, C. The Century of Revolution 1603–1714. Edinburgh 1961

Johnston, S. H. F., ed. 'Letters of Samuel Noyes, Chaplain of the Royal Scots 1703–4', Journal of the Society for Army Historical Research, 1959

Legrelle, A. La Diplomatie française et la succession d'Espagne, 2nd ed. V. Braine-le-Comte 1892

Lever, Sir Tresham. Godolphin: His Life and Times. London 1952

Noorden, C. von. Europäische Geschichte im achtzehnten Jahrhundert, I. Düsseldorf 1870

Ogg, D. England in the Reigns of James II and William III. Oxford 1957

Plumb, J. H. The Growth of Political Stability in England 1675–1725. London 1967

Scouller, R. E. The Armies of Queen Anne. Oxford 1966

Seward, W. Anecdotes of Some Distinguished Persons, II. London 1795

Stacke, H. Fitzmaurice. 'Cavalry in Marlborough's Day', The Cavalry Journal, October 1934

Strickland, Agnes. Lives of the Queens of England, XII. London 1848

Sturgill, C. C. Marshal Villars and the War of the Spanish Succession. Lexington 1965

Trevelyan, G. M. England Under Queen Anne, 3 vols. London 1930–4

Walton, C. History of the British Standing Army AD 1660 to 1700. London 1894

Whistler, L. Sir John Vanbrugh: Architect and Dramatist 1664–1726. London 1938

ILLUSTRATION ACKNOWLEDGMENTS

249 LEFT Scottish National Portrait Gallery, Edinburgh. Photo: Annan, Glasgow
RIGHT National Portrait Gallery, London

253 Duke of Buccleuch. Photo: Churchill Centenary Trust

254 Duke of Marlborough, Blenheim Palace. Photo: Jeremy Whitaker

257 Petworth House. Photo: Courtauld Institute of Art, London

260 Tom Stalker-Miller

263 Duke of Marlborough, Blenheim Palace. Photo: Jeremy Whitaker

265 Photo: Department of the Environment

266 Photo: Department of the Environment

268 Bibliothèque Nationale, Paris

270 Duke of Marlborough, Blenheim Palace. Photo: Jeremy Whitaker

271 The Rt Hon. the Earl Spencer TD, Althorp. Photo: Derrick Witty

272 Duke of Marlborough, Blenheim Palace. Photo: Jeremy Whitaker

274 Bibliothèque Nationale, Paris. Photo: Giraudon

275 Duke of Marlborough, Blenheim Palace. Photo: Jeremy Whitaker

INDEX

QUEEN ♣

ANNE *by y.* Grace *of* God *of* Great Britain France and *Irel.* Queen Defender *of y. Fa*

IV ♣

The Magistrates of Oudenard wait upon the D. of Marlboro desire his protection & swear fidelity to K.C. y. *III* June the 3. 1706.

VIII ♣

The D. of Marlboro obliges Limburg to surrender at dis= cretion. Sept. 28. 1705.

II

Sept. y. *5* renders Grace y. Brot...

II ♦

Aeth Taken by y. Lord Overkerk octo. 4. 1705.

I ♣

Liberte

Joseph Emperour of Germany born July 16. 16...

KING ♥

His Royal Highness George Prince of Denmark

Born. 1653.

III

The P... at the...

KING ♣

Charles III. King of Spain born October 1.st 1685.

III ♥

y. 128 Ensigns & 34 Standards, Taken at Blenheime Carried through y. City of Lon= don set up in Westmin.r Hall. Jan 3.d 1705.

VIII ♦

The Burgomasters & Magistrates of Brussells present the D. of Marlborough with y. keys of y. City in a Gold Bason Oct. 27. 1706.

IV

The 26... at Ramill... City of Lon...